SOCIALIST REGISTER 2021

THE SOCIALIST REGISTER

Founded in 1964

To get online access to all Register volumes visit our website
http://www.socialistregister.com

SOCIALIST REGISTER 2021

BEYOND DIGITAL CAPITALISM

NEW WAYS OF LIVING

Edited by LEO PANITCH and GREG ALBO

THE MERLIN PRESS
MONTHLY REVIEW PRESS
FERNWOOD PUBLISHING

First published in 2020
by The Merlin Press Ltd
Central Books Building
Freshwater Road
London
RM8 1RX

www.merlinpress.co.uk

British Library Cataloguing in Publication Data is available from the British Library

ISSN. 0081-0606

Published in the UK by The Merlin Press
ISBN. 978-0-85036-761-4 Paperback
ISBN. 978-0-85036-762-1 Hardback

Published in the USA by Monthly Review Press
ISBN. 978-1-58367-883-1 Paperback

Published in Canada by Fernwood Publishing
ISBN. 978-1-77363-297-1 Paperback

Printed and bound in the UK on behalf of Stanton Book Services

CONTENTS

CONTRIBUTORS

Greg Albo teaches in the Department of Politics at York University.

Hugh Armstrong is Emeritus Professor of Social Work at Carleton University.

Pat Armstrong is Distinguished Research Professor of Sociology at York University.

Grace Blakeley is a staff writer at *Tribune* and author of *Stolen: How to Save the World from Financialisation.*

Jerónimo Montero Bressán is a researcher with the National Scientific and Technical Research Council (CONICET) in Argentina.

Pratyush Chandra is a political activist and writer based in New Delhi.

Pritha Chandra is Professor of Linguistics, Department of Humanities and Social Sciences, Indian Institute of Technology, New Delhi, India.

Matthew Cole is a PhD researcher in the Work and Employment Relations Division at the University of Leeds Business School.

Robin Hahnel is Professor of Economics at Portland State University.

Christoph Hermann is a Lecturer in the Department of History at University of California, Berkeley.

Derek Hrynyshyn teaches in the Department of Communication Studies at York University in Toronto, Canada.

Ursula Huws is Professor of Labour and Globalisation at the University of Hertfordshire, and founder of Analytica Social and Economic Research.

Larry Lohmann works with The Corner House, a UK-based solidarity and research organization.

Tanner Mirrlees is Associate Professor of Communication and Digital Media Studies at Ontario Tech University.

Mao Mollona is a Senior Lecturer in Anthropology at Goldsmiths, University of London.

Bryan Palmer is Emeritus Professor of History at Trent University, Ontario, Canada.

Hugo Radice is Head of the School of Politics and International Studies at the University of Leeds.

Joan Sangster is Emeritus Professor of History at Trent University, Ontario, Canada.

Benjamin Selwyn is Senior Lecturer in International Relations and International Development at the University of Sussex.

Sean Sweeney is Director of the International Program for Labor, Climate, and Environment at the CUNY School of Labor and Urban Studies.

John Treat is a writer, researcher, and organizer with Trade Unions for Energy Democracy.

Charles Umney is Associate Professor in the Work and Employment Relations Division at the University of Leeds Business School.

PREFACE

Preparing the 2021 *Socialist Register* amidst the accelerating Coronavirus pandemic has been a considerable challenge. Our earlier decision that the time was ripe to explore 'new ways of living' in the twenty-first century through two successive volumes of the *Register* – under the rubric of 'Beyond Market Dystopia' for the 56th annual volume, and 'Beyond Digital Capitalism' for this 57th volume – was taken long before the greatest health crisis by far in over a century exploded, quite literally on a global scale, through the course of the first half of 2020. This crisis fully exposed for all to see the severe consequences of longstanding neoliberal state practices beholden to the blinkered competitive individualism of the proponents of pro-market ideology. And it drove them – however belatedly, confusedly and temporarily – to undertake the types of massive social expenditures they had derided only months before. ('There *is* such a thing as society', Boris Johnson solemnly admonished the ghost of Margaret Thatcher in 10 Downing Street). But the pandemic also posed a new challenge for socialists, including for us as the editors as well as for all the contributors to this volume who we invited to analyze the nature of digital capitalism and its contradictions. Could we now do this in ways that also captured the significance of the pandemic and what it spoke to in terms of imagining, struggling for, and planning for, new ways of living?

In addressing how far digital technology has become integral to the capitalist market dystopia of the first decades the twenty-first century we were deliberately seeking to counter so much facile futurist 'cyber-utopian' thinking that has proliferated through these decades. The proof of capitalism's continued dynamism, even in the face of severe global economic crisis, lay in the most successful and most celebrated high-tech corporations of the new information sector which really were restructuring and refashioning not only our ways of communicating but of working and consuming, indeed ways of living. Yet precisely because this was taking place within the logics of capitalist accumulation and exploitation, and through the reproduction of capitalist social relations, this produced new contradictions and irrationalities. Perhaps none of these was greater than those revealed by the contrast between the investment, planning, and preparation that went into the interminable competitive race for 'more speed' by way of reducing latency in digital communications by so many milliseconds, on the one hand, and on the other the lack of investment, planning, and preparation that underlay the scandalous slowness of the responses to the spreading Covid-19 pandemic around the world.

It is now over two decades since that the *Register* published in the 1999 volume Ursula Huws' foundational essay, 'Material world: the myth of the weightless economy', whose purpose was to 're-embody cyberspace' by making visible 'the material components of this virtual world'; and it is exactly twenty years ago that her famous 'The making of a cybertariat?' was the lead essay of the 2001 volume, *Working Classes, Global Realities.* It is thus highly appropriate that her new essay, 'Reaping the whirlwind: Digitalization, restructuring, and mobilization in the Covid crisis' should also open the current volume. In addressing the changes sweeping through global labour markets during the pandemic, sharply accelerating existing trends while exposing new contradictions, Huws explores the clear polarizations between those working isolated in their homes via their computers under lockdown conditions, and those 'who deliver the physical goods and services the home-bound need to survive and care for their bodily needs when they become sick, at great personal risk'. And 'in the vacuum left by government incompetence', she explores how far 'the near-universal access to digital technologies that is a prerequisite for the management of both sets of workers also provides them with new ways to communicate and organize'.

Locating today's digital capitalism within the history of technological change is the remit of the three essays that follow, all carrying forward the *Register*'s long-standing commitment to rejecting techno-determinist explanations of economic and political developments and focusing instead on the social relations in which new technologies develop and are deployed. Bryan Palmer, beginning with how 'the conventional divisions of day and night, labour and leisure, private and public' have collapsed in on one another during the pandemic lockdowns, traces the contested meaning of working time in a sweeping historical survey of centuries of class struggles amidst the massive technological changes unleashed by industrial capitalism. Larry Lohmann's strikingly original essay reveals that 'it makes more strategic sense for the left to approach the striking innovations in automation advanced over the past decade by the likes of Facebook, Google, Amazon, Baidu, Tencent, Alibaba, Microsoft and Apple as a new level of the *mechanization of interpretive work* than to acquiesce in mystifying labels such as *artificial intelligence* (AI).' Matthew Cole, Hugo Radice, and Charles Umney confirm the emergence of what they call 'a new digital Taylorism' through an analysis of the impact of computerization, datafication, platformization as well as AI in terms of the economic and social consequences of technological change in capitalist societies, and not least through the changes in the *vertical division of labour* that has always accompanied the increasingly detailed technical division of labour in production in the modern corporation. All three of these essays revalidate the centrality of working class struggles as socialists try to 'look beyond techno-determinist and capitalist futures, and seize the virtual as well as the physical means of production.'

Grace Blakeley's essay begins by noting that during the course of the pandemic the share value of Microsoft, Apple, Amazon, and Facebook reached 20 per cent of that of the 500 largest US corporations ('an unparalleled level of market concentration'), which enriched their chief executives by tens of billions of dollars even as the rest of economy collapsed. She then goes on to analyze how such high-tech capital monopolistic, and monopsonistic, power developed over recent decades via the concentration and centralization of high-tech corporate capital in close conjunction with finance capital as well as the American state. For his part, Tanner Mirrlees focuses on the great significance of these corporate giants being cultural and political as well as economic powerhouses, 'interwoven with daily ways of life in myriad forms', thereby intensifying the mass media industries' long engagement in the commodification of life under consumer-capitalism. Yet Mirrlees argues that while this is where the analysis of 'digital', 'communicative', or 'platform' capitalism today 'needs to *begin*, this is not where it should end. For something else is happening that was inconceivable for most of the second half of the 20th century, when socialists in the West were largely kept out of the mass media's one-to-many communications regime. Digital technologies and social media platforms are today being used by socialists for communicating within and against digital capitalism, and for socialism on a remarkably large scale.' Derek Hrynyshyn takes this further by soberly analyzing the severe limits of regulatory reforms against these corporate media giants and then thinking through how socialized platform media, unlike today's highly centralized public broadcasters, could be decentralized so as to help realize a fully democratic socialism.

Mao Mollona surveys the representation of workers in cinema in the course of the transition from film to the digital video medium, ranging broadly from Steve McQueen's *Western Deep* in South Africa to Wang Bing's *West of the Tracks* in China, to Mollona's own *Steel Lives* in Sheffield in contrast with Ken Loach's latest film, *Sorry We Missed You*. He concludes that 'revolutionary cinema is not about specific technologies, aesthetics, or social processes, but emerges from the encounter between specific conditions of production, circulation, and consumption, contingent working class struggles and forms of radical imagination'. Joan Sangster's essay reminds us that the experience of an invasive 'surveillance capitalism' – which Loach depicts through the construction worker who signs a Faustian pact to become an 'owner driver franchisee' parcel delivery driver, (and the consequent 'slow descent to hell' for his family) – is in fact nothing new, but has long been the experience of women workers, especially in capitalism's service sectors. As she puts it, a 'feminist eye for highly asymmetrical power relations of gender and race and a materialist concern with the "kernel of human relations" at the heart of capitalism, namely the lived experience of exploitation, should guide our exploration of the surveillance of working women's bodies'. But far from reifying these workers as dehumanized ciphers of capital (which is what Mollona insists Loach's film leaves us with), Sangster also uncovers their various modes of resistance, focusing specifically on today's ever more intensified surveillance of the 'aesthetic labour' of flight attendants and retail workers.

This volume then turns to a series of essays, by Jerónimo Montero Bressán, Sean Sweeney and John Treat, Ben Selwyn, Pat and Hugh Armstrong, and Pritha and Pratyush Chandra respectively, which examine today's proof of market dystopia amidst the pandemic in such facets of everyday life as clothing, transit, food, eldercare, and health. These remarkable essays go on to propose how to organize alternative ways of living in each of these areas, not least, as Sweeney and Treat conclude, by 'adapting technological change in ways consistent with achieving our socialist goals'. This is followed by Christoph Hermann's visionary essay on 'Life after the Pandemic': insofar as 'the global pandemic caused by the Covid-19 virus, more than any previous crisis, has demonstrated the difference between production for profit and provision for need', the case is powerfully made here for a general strategy aimed at the full decommodification of society. And in light of what the economic planning to realize such a 'needs-based economy' would entail, the essay that follows by Robin Hahnel – the most consistent advocate of planning versus markets for the last four decades – elaborates further on the participatory structures that will be so crucial for democratic socialist economic planning. Finally, the volume concludes with Greg Albo's comprehensive examination of the extensive literature on 'postcapitalism', demonstrating in these writings the persistent tendencies of technological determinism and conventional notions of a mixed economy of private and public goods. While revealing as well in this literature a proliferation of political hedges and qualifications around the need for class struggles, explicitly oriented to finding an exit from capitalist value production, the essay shows how important it is for socialists to offer signposts rather than detours to a democratic socialist future.

We are very grateful to all of our contributors for the effort and creativity they put into their essays, especially under the difficult conditions created by the pandemic. So are we grateful to our assistant editors, Steve Maher and Alan Zuege, and to Adrian Howe and Tony Zurbrugg of Merlin Press, for all their help in preparing this volume for publication in such conditions. And great thanks are once again due to Louis Mackay, the *Register*'s cover designer for so many years, for yet another brilliant cover for this volume.

LP
GA
August 2020

REAPING THE WHIRLWIND: DIGITALIZATION, RESTRUCTURING, AND MOBILIZATION IN THE COVID CRISIS

URSULA HUWS

This essay addresses the changes sweeping through global labour markets during the coronavirus pandemic, looking in particular at the concentration of capital and expansion of market share by global corporations, bringing with it the digital management of supply chains and an exponential growth in algorithmic control and surveillance of workers. Pandemic lockdown conditions have exposed very clearly the polarisations in the workforce between 'fixed' workers, physically isolated in their homes but closely monitored via their computers, working virtually, and the precariously employed mobile ('footloose') workers, disproportionately made up of black and migrant workers, equally closely monitored, who deliver the physical goods and services the home-bound need to survive and care for their bodily needs when they become sick, at great personal risk.

This represents a sharp acceleration of existing trends but also brings new contradictions. The near-universal access to digital technologies that is a prerequisite for the management of workers also provides them with new ways to communicate and organise. In the vacuum left by government incompetence, communities have come together locally to develop their own solutions to support the vulnerable, discuss ideas about what reforms to campaign for, mobilize against employers and organize demonstrations to express their outrage against racism and state violence in an upsurge of initiatives many of which rely crucially on digital, online forms of organisation. In the process new social models are being developed that prefigure what a more inclusive post-Covid society might look like.

2008-2019: A DECADE OF RADICAL RESTRUCTURING

The world economy in which the coronavirus arrived in 2019 was one that was already in upheaval. In the preceding decade, the restructuring of capital after the 2008 crisis sent convulsions throughout the global economy and its labour markets. The desperate search for new sources of profit led to increasingly cut-throat competition among manufacturing companies, intensifying the need to get their goods to market as quickly as possible. This drove investment in infrastructure, including China's Belt and Road Initiative, and exerted extreme pressure on production and logistics workers all along the value chain, from mine to assembly plant to port to ship to road to warehouse and, in the 'last mile', to the home of the consumer, without whose purchase no profit could be realised. Helped by ever more sophisticated digital technologies and the willing connivance of neoliberal governments, other companies found new sources of profit in the artificially created markets for outsourced government services, in the process rendering much public sector work precarious, casualized and low paid. Yet other companies transformed themselves into twenty-first century *rentiers,* collecting tithes from the public for their (increasingly essential) use of such virtual products as software licenses, maintenance contracts, insurance policies, phone contracts, or wi-fi networks. In other cases, labour itself became a commodity from which rent was levied, with a company taking a cut each time its online platform was used for ordering a taxi or a domestic task in a system that externalises all risk to the workers.

In the course of these upheavals, vast areas of life that were previously outside the direct scope of capitalism were brought within its orbit, generating new kinds of commodities ranging from bio products to ready meals, from cosmetic surgery to streamed entertainment.[1] And working conditions were transformed for tens of thousands of workers, now subjugated to the depersonalised, algorithmically managed discipline of global capitalism.

The scale of these changes is hard to overestimate. Here are just a few facts. In 2018 seven of the ten most valuable companies in the world (Apple, Google, Microsoft, Amazon, Facebook, Tencent, and Alibaba) were using platform business models, and it was estimated by McKinsey that 30 per cent of global economic activity would soon be mediated by digital platforms.[2] The global value of online retail sales (the main driver of growth in parcel delivery volumes) tripled from $1,196 billion in 2013 to $3,306 billion in 2019.[3] In the UK, by 2017 more than a third of all public spending was spent on procuring goods, works, and services from external suppliers.[4]

My own research,[5] carried out between 2016 and 2019 in thirteen European countries, revealed large numbers of people using online platforms to find work. Platform work is usually carried out as a top-up to other earnings, representing less than 10 per cent of their income for most, with only a small minority saying that it constitutes all their income. It forms part of a spectrum of casual, on-call work providing a subsistence income for the working poor. Some of this work is carried out in real time and space, often in public spaces. Those doing driving or delivery work range from 1.4 per cent (in the Netherlands and Sweden) to 12.3 per cent (in Czechia) of the adult population, but in the UK (the only country for which we have trend data) this proportion increased from 1.5 per cent to 5.1 per cent between 2016 and 2019, showing how rapidly it is growing. In every country the proportion doing this type of highly visible platform work in public spaces is exceeded by those doing more hidden types of work providing household services in other people's homes, ranging from 2.4 per cent in Sweden to 11.8 per cent in Czechia. But this too is exceeded by an even more common type of platform work – work that is carried out virtually, using online means. Independent of spatial location, as it is, online platform labour is carried out in direct competition with workers in other parts of the world – so, unsurprisingly, the highest levels are found where average earnings are lowest compared with international competitors.

It seems clear that at a time when earnings were falling in real terms or at best stagnating, and austerity policies had been biting hard, people were looking for any source of income they could find to make ends meet. One of the most important mechanisms for doing this before the financial crisis – credit – was much less readily available after the crisis, making the online economy an increasingly important resource to tap into.

In the UK (where we did surveys in 2016 and 2019) we can see the exponential growth of platform work. Over this three year period, the number of working age adults who said they did work obtained via an online platform at least once a week doubled from an estimated 2.8 million people to an estimated 5.8 million (from 4.7 per cent to 9.6 per cent of the adult population). People were turning to the internet to make money in other ways too: over the same period the proportion of people renting out rooms via online platforms such as Airbnb soared from 8.2 per cent to 18.7 per cent, while those selling self-made products via platforms like Etsy rose from 10 per cent to 20.2 per cent. A high proportion of the UK population (60.7 per cent) were users of platform services by 2019. Although wealthier households were more likely to do so, more than half (50.9 per cent) of those earning less than £20,000 per year were platform customers, including many who were themselves platform workers. Three quarters (76 per cent) of people who said that they provided driving or delivery services via platforms at least weekly were also users of such platforms at least monthly (rising to 92.8 per cent who did so at least yearly), while two thirds (67.2 per cent) of those who provided services in other people's homes at least weekly were also customers for such services at least monthly (89.6 per cent at least yearly).[6] There was thus effectively a doubling of both supply and demand for platform-based service labour during this short three-year period.

In the labour market, work for formally designated online platforms represented the visible tip of a much larger iceberg. Even more important than the growth of platform work was the phenomenally fast spread of digital management practices across the general workforce. In the UK in 2016 one person in ten reported using an app or website to be informed of new tasks but by 2019 this had more than doubled to 21 per cent of the adult working-age population. Barely half of these workers were platform workers. The use of apps or websites to record what work had been done rose over the same period from 14.2 per cent to 24.6 per cent. Again, most people reporting these practices were *not* platform workers. Nearly a quarter (24 per cent) of UK adults surveyed in 2019 – of whom nearly half (11.7 per cent) were *not* platform workers – also reported having their work rated by customers. By 2019, therefore, the upheavals caused by the restructuring of capital over the previous decade were already reflected in titanic labour market turbulence, with an erosion of standard employment contracts and dramatic growth in the digital management and surveillance of the workforce.

2020: ECONOMIC AND SOCIAL IMPACTS OF THE COVID-19 PANDEMIC

The great lockdown imposed on most populations in early 2020 thus arrived in highly dynamic circumstances, as in a rapidly moving vehicle. In some sectors its impact was like the slamming of brakes, with activity coming to an abrupt, screeching halt. In others, it was more like an equally abrupt stamp on the accelerator sending existing trends careening forward at breakneck speed.

Stop and go in the labour market

Transport industries came to a standstill, with airline workers laid off and hundreds of thousands of seafarers marooned on their ships for months.[7] Companies in the travel and tourism sector, as well as Airbnb hosts, faced financial ruin.[8] Many production industries, as well as brick-and-mortar retail and other service industries, were shut down. As images of stranded oil tankers, boarded up high streets, and closed factories filled our screens, the environmental impacts became evident in clear skies and suddenly visible views of distant horizons, and audible in the sound of birds whose songs were no longer drowned out by traffic noise.

The braking effects on the labour market are likely to leave lasting traces as temporary layoffs are transformed into permanent job losses. Not only are many employees of small and medium-sized enterprises made redundant when their employers go out of business but it also seems likely that larger organisations will seize on the pandemic as an excuse to casualize or downsize.

Though the braking effects are dramatic, the acceleratory effects of these activities are likely to be even more far-reaching in their implications. These include huge increases in the numbers of people working from home, in the use of online ordering of goods and services, and in labour linked to their delivery. The coronavirus crisis has made visible and accentuated an increasing polarisation across the labour market between 'fixed' and 'footloose' work and workers,[9] whereby the needs of those who are immobilized, whether through job constraints, incapacity, old age or the risk of contamination, are increasingly met through the hyper-mobility of other travelling workers who must deliver them the goods and services they cannot fetch for themselves, provide them with physical care, or transport them to and from the locations where they need to be treated in person. This has swelled the ranks of the precariously employed workers, disproportionately made up of migrants and people from black and ethnic minorities (BAME), whose lives have been put physically at risk and, for this and other reasons, make up a shockingly high proportion of deaths from the Covid virus.[10] Though their personal safety is sacrificed, they are among the least likely to be protected by employment rights such as sick pay, job protection, or minimum wages.

The growth in this mobile workforce, expanded by the addition of many made redundant from other industries, obliged to work in 'real' time and space, has been mirrored by an enormous growth in 'virtual' working among white-collar workers (who are also more likely to be white-skinned[11]) obliged by office closures and demands for social distancing to work from their homes and connected digitally to their employers, clients or customers. A third of Europeans reported taking up teleworking as a result of the pandemic.[12] While working under very different conditions from the mobile workers who serve their needs, and better protected physically, these home-based workers do have one feature in common with them: they are ever more likely to be working under the digital gaze of a global corporation, something to which I will return later in this essay.

Concentration and expansion of capital

Meanwhile, these new conditions enabled an astonishing expansion of some sectors of capital and concentration of wealth. Research by the US Institute for Policy Studies and Americans for Tax Fairness reported in June 2020 that the wealth of the top five billionaires (Jeff Bezos, Bill Gates, Mark Zuckerberg, Warren Buffett, and Larry Ellison) had seen their combined net worth grow by $584 billion during the first three months of 2020, in a period when $56.5 trillion was wiped off the value of household wealth. That Bezos, CEO of Amazon, was the greatest winner in absolute terms, with a growth of $43.8 billion over the three-month period, comes as little surprise given the enormous growth in online shopping. In percentage terms, his 38.7 per cent increase was exceeded by a phenomenal 58.6 per cent expansion in the fortune of Zuckerberg (CEO of Facebook) over the same period, benefitting from the turn to online communication among a locked-down, isolated population. Two others of the big five, Gates and Ellison, also make their money from the digital economy (Microsoft and Oracle).[13] The fifth, Buffet is a more classic capitalist with fingers in many pies, including a significant shareholding in Apple as well as banks and food companies. Berkshire Hathaway, the company of which he is CEO, cannily sold off all its airline holdings early in 2020.

These billionaires are emblematic of a much larger trend whereby large corporations are expanding their grip. Sometimes this is achieved by extracting various forms of rent, for example from software licenses, which rises in proportion to the growing use of digital technologies. Under lockdown conditions, needless to say, the demand for such technologies has grown exponentially. For example the videoconferencing service Zoom reported that by April 2020 its usage had grown to 300 million meeting participants a day, up from just 10 million in December 2019 (bringing in $328 million in revenue during its February–April quarter).[14] In other cases, global corporations (such as supermarkets, fast food chains and online platforms providing household services) are colonizing huge areas of the economy formerly dominated by small firms and individual traders, helped by their ability to organise just-in-time delivery to isolated consumers using a dispersed, digitally controlled workforce.

Further beneficiaries from the crisis include the companies whose profits are based on the outsourcing of public services. After an early dip in demand when the pandemic first emerged, before government policies had been formulated to address it, it became clear that the outsourcing companies saw the Covid crisis as a promising new source of contracts. In June, 2020 there was a 40 per cent increase in invitations to tender for public contracts, with the publication of £4.3 billion worth of Covid-19 contracts in the UK, including a £326 million contract relating to the creation of temporary hospitals for the treatment of Covid-19, and a £750 million contract for an infection survey, as well as several contracts to supply videoconferencing for remote consultations with patients. Demonstrating graphically how the poverty of the general population becomes an opportunity for further corporate aggrandizement, two large contracts were awarded by the Department for

Education to support students from disadvantaged backgrounds, one for the provision of free school meals and one for laptops and educational devices.[15] The size of this sector can be illustrated by the fact that since 2012, the UK government has awarded private contracts to the tune of £3.5 trillion.[16]

The growth of 'logged' labour

We thus have a situation in 2020 where there is, on the one hand, a growing dominance of the labour market by very large global corporations relying heavily on digital technologies to organise workflow and manage their workforce and, on the other, a growing reliance by the general population on digital technologies not just to acquire the goods and services they need for survival but also to access paid work and carry it out – whether this is from the physical isolation of their homes, travelling to deliver goods or provide services, or in the risky settings of hospitals, care homes, schools, warehouses, fields, food processing plants, and other spaces deemed sufficiently essential for workers to be obliged to work there in face-to-face contact with others, despite the risk of infection.

This is expanding the amount of labour that falls into the category I have elsewhere described as 'logged'[17]– a form of work characterised by three features, each of which can be described as 'logged' using a different meaning of the term. First, the component labour processes are broken down into separate tasks, much as a felled tree is broken down into separate logs, which (although these tasks may in practice require considerable tacit skills to deliver) are treated as standardized and interchangeable from the point of view of execution and reward. Second, the management and control processes are mediated by online platforms, with the worker or service user required to be online (or 'logged on') in order to be notified of what work is available and report the progress of its delivery. Third, the very fact that every aspect of the work is managed online means that each interaction leaves a digital trace, generating data that can be used not only to record and track current activities but also to build ever more sophisticated algorithms to enhance the efficiency of future ones. Both workers and users are therefore subjected to close surveillance, meaning that their activities are also 'logged' in the sense that was historically used to describe the tracking of movements in ships' logs.

The surveillance of workers is achieved by a variety of means including GPS, facial recognition, audio recording of customer service calls and shopping and social media browsing history and covers the minutiae of labour processes in extraordinary detail. For example, the system used by UPS to monitor its 450,000 drivers uses over 200 sensors in each delivery van to collect information that is combined in a continuous stream with GPS data and information from customers and hand-held scanners. This is analyzed to prescribe precise protocols for driver behaviour right down to details such as how to start the truck with one hand while buckling with the other and where to put your pen.[18] Cogito, a system used in call centres to analyze recordings of calls, claims to 'measure and interpret data about speakers' energy, empathy, participation, tone, and pace in real time'. Another, CallMiner, 'sends three to five notifications a minute to an agent on a typical call, ranging from … "messages of congratulation and cute animal photos when software suggests a customer is satisfied" to "a suggestion to 'calm down' and a list of soothing talking points" when caller frustration is detected'.[19] Another AI-based system, Isaak, already in use in the UK in several law firms, a training company and an estate agent, gathers data on a range of actions which it then uses to gain 'real-time insights into each employee and their position within the organisational network', showing managers 'how collaborative workers are and whether they are "influencers" or "change-makers"'.[20]

Such examples could be multiplied many times over. Suffice it to say that there has been a mounting use of such surveillance tools since the arrival of the pandemic. One example, Sneek, which 'stays on throughout the workday and features constantly-updating photos of workers taken through their laptop camera every one to five minutes', reported a tenfold increase in signups in March 2020, and boasted over 10,000 users.[21]

The logging of labour does not just contribute to its standardization and intensification, putting workers under continuous pressure while increasing their inter-changeability. It also removes – or renders very difficult – the possibility of direct dialogue between workers and their managers. When the only means of communication is an anonymous digital interface, there is no possibility of identifying the source of power or negotiating with it. Even if the system malfunctions and there is a valid cause for complaint, the best that can normally be achieved by a determined worker is to get through, via an automated contact centre or chatbot, to another equally alienated worker with little or no power to over-rule the system, in a Kafkaesque world in which responsibility is endlessly deflected and there is no answering back to authority. The normative model of industrial relations laid down in developed economies in the twentieth century is thereby bypassed as conclusively as the normative standard employment contracts that were negotiated within this model.

THE COUNTER-MOVEMENTS

History tells us that to every movement there is a counter-movement and, moreover, the greater and faster the change, the larger and more vehement the backlash is likely to be. The unprecedented scope and scale of the pandemic crisis seems capable of provoking a veritable tsunami of reaction among the victims of this latest capitalist upheaval.

The end of 'there is no alternative'

One of the most striking impacts of the crisis has been the unmasking of the neoliberal notion that 'there is no alternative' that was part of the political common sense for so long that there can be few workers under the age of 55 who even remember a time when other views prevailed. Its dominance spanned the mass unemployment resulting from the deindustrialisation of the 1980s and the austerity policies introduced after the financial crisis of 2008, insisting that the sufferings of millions were inevitable and unchallengeable. In the long run, it claimed, only the market can win. Allowing the state to intervene is a distortion of that market and will ultimately only prolong the pain. But if we let that market rip, look what goodies it can bring us: cheap products, new technologies to support a lazy lifestyle, an endless stream of entertainment, personal fulfilment, freedom of choice, and flexibility!

The arrival of the pandemic exposed this myth for all to see, making it abundantly clear that the market cannot cope in a real crisis and the state has an important role to play and is, indeed, essential for many other purposes than the maintenance of law and order. Governments that claimed for decades that there was no cash to provide basic health and social services suddenly found the resources to spend billions on subsidies to employers to furlough workers and bail out ailing institutions. The sense of having been hoodwinked is accompanied by a dawning realization that political choices were possible in the past – and still are. As this realization has sunk in, a great wave of anger has been released that all that sacrifice was for nothing – an anger that has meshed with other forms of rage against the neoliberal state, for example the way that its policing and incarceration policies (always curiously exempt from the cuts that affected other public spending) are used murderously against BAME people.

This critique has not come from nowhere, of course. It was already evident, for example, in the growing support for the alternative visions promoted by Jeremy Corbyn and Bernie Sanders in the late 2010s, in particular among the generation that entered the labour market (or tried to) in the period following the 2008 crisis, whose life experiences had taught them that however 'self-reliant' or 'creative' they might be, the market did not offer them the opportunities it promised. Those that did not fall into depression or anomie were already actively campaigning for change before the virus struck, including exploring new political and social options. It was also fed by responses to the climate change crisis, which also peaked in 2019, as fires blazed across Australia and global icecaps melted. By mid-2020, it appeared that some kind of tipping point had been passed during the pandemic in which disbelief in 'there is no alternative' had been suspended among a critical mass of the population, suggesting a new openness to alternative ideas.

Mobilization

The late 2010s did not just see a change in attitudes among the young, it also witnessed a growth in new forms of social mobilization, of which the Black Lives Matter movement is perhaps the most celebrated example. There was also a mushrooming of new forms of organization among precarious workers, such as the National Domestic Workers Alliance in the USA and the App Drivers and Couriers Union (ADCU) in the UK, both of which have expanded their membership and activities during the pandemic period. Both organizations have developed an analysis that lays particular emphasis on the fact that the majority of their members are BAME, and are building on this politically. Along with many other such bottom-up mobilizations, they have developed a shrewd analysis of labour market trends, illustrated recently in the observation by James Farrar, General Secretary of the ADCU, that after the Pandemic 'the apps are going to come roaring back. We're going to see a world dominated by apps'.[22] These organizations have also fostered international solidarity, for instance in the setting up of the International Domestic Workers Federation (IDWF) in 2014 and the International Alliance of App-Based Transport Workers (IAATW) in 2019.

As well as the development of new organisations to represent precarious workers, further evidence of this new mobilization comes from a rise in the membership of traditional trade unions. In 2019, for example, the UK Trades Union Congress (TUC) reported a 100,000 increase in membership in a single year.[23] A year later, after the pandemic had hit, traffic on the TUC's Join a Union website page in May 2020 was six times higher than in May 2019 and most new members are from non-union backgrounds. Female union membership in the UK is at a record high, at 3.69 million. The influx of care workers into the public sector union Unison is up 202 per cent.[24] The late 2010s also experienced a wave of strikes and other forms of industrial action among low-paid workers in companies ranging from Amazon to McDonalds, a wave which swelled further during the pandemic crisis. For example, over 800 strikes, walkouts, sickouts and other disruptions were recorded in the US between March and June 2020, many of them in hitherto non-union workplaces.[25]

While most of these actions took a very physical form, their organization could scarcely have been possible without the widespread use of electronic communications. And the success of these actions, in terms of engendering publicity and, very often, drawing attention to the outrageously hostile responses to them on the part of employers and police, can also be attributed to the distribution of live evidence captured on smartphones and broadcast via social media. Social media, too, have provide forums for serious discussion of alternative social models to be campaigned for when the world emerges from lock-down, ranging from worker co-operatives to universal basic income schemes, from alternatives to prison to the creation of green jobs.

Indeed, during the coronavirus crisis there has been an unprecedented flowering of collaborative, local, bottom-up community-based initiatives, often organized by digital means, for example to distribute food to the hungry, supply social support to the isolated elderly, arrange housing for the homeless, or provide refuges for victims of domestic abuse or alternative schooling for locked-down children.[26] Shocked by the failure of the state to provide them with the means of survival and personal protection, appalled by the irresponsibility and selfishness of employers, and enraged by the behaviour of the police, many people, equipped with their new technologies and the ability to use them creatively and, in some cases, with more time on their hands than usual, are emerging from the torpor of the neoliberal years with fresh energy and motivation. In doing so, they are developing prefigurative models of what an alternative post-Covid society might look like, and, by giving them concrete form, stimulating an awareness that such alternatives are possible and thus helping to bring such a society into being.

CONCLUSION

The history of capitalism is a double one in which each development contains within itself the seeds of its own destruction. Once the technical division of labour reached a point where it was necessary to have a workforce that was literate and numerate, that literate, numerate workforce used these new skills to organize itself and demand democratic representation. Once the spatial division of labour reached a point where it required fast international communications to coordinate it, workers were able to use the telegram and the telephone, and later the email, fax, and text message, to connect with each other and share their experiences. Now that we have a digitally managed global workforce that requires a smartphone or laptop with an app on it to be summoned to work, then these new tools too can be used for organizing resistance. And while the further development of capitalism requires innovation, then the workers who experiment with new ways of doing things, generate new ideas and imagine new applications and organizational solutions can turn their skill, intelligence and creativity to inventing alternative ways of living and organizing the economy and society. Sow the wind and reap the whirlwind.

NOTES

1 I have written at greater length about these developments in *Labour in Contemporary Capitalism: What Next?* London, Palgrave Macmillan, 2019.

2 Jennifer L. Schenker, 'The Platform Economy', *The Innovator,* January 2019, available at: innovator.news.

3 Apex Insight, *Global Parcel Delivery Market Insight Report,* 2020, available at: apex-insight.com.

4 Tom Sasse, Benoit Guerin, Sarah Nickson, Mark O'Brien, Thomas Pope, and Nick Davies, *Government Outsourcing: What has worked and what needs reform?* London: Institute for Government, 2019. Available at: www.instituteforgovernment.org.uk.

5 Ursula Huws, Neil H. Spencer, Matt Coates, and Kaire Holts, 'The Platformisation of Work in Europe: results from research in 13 European countries', Brussels: Foundation for European Progressive Studies, 2019.

6 Ursula Huws, Neil H. Spencer, and Matt Coates, *Platform Work in the UK 2016-2019,* Brussels and London: Foundation for European Progressive studies and the Trades Union Congress, 2019.

7 Tim Bowler, 'Seafarers in limbo as coronavirus hits shipping', *BBC News,* 16 April 2020.

8 Joan Faus, 'This is how coronavirus could affect the travel and tourism industry', *World Economic Forum with Reuters*, 17 March 2020, available at: www.weforum.org. Tripp Mickle and Preetika Rana, '"A Bargain With the Devil" – Bill Comes Due for Overextended Airbnb Hosts,' *Wall Street Journal,* 29 April 2020.

9 I made this distinction in Ursula Huws, 'Fixed, footloose, or fractured: Work, identity, and the spatial division of labor in the twenty-first century city', *Monthly Review* 57(10), 2006, pp. 34-44.

10 Haroon Siddique, 'Key findings from Public Health England's report on Covid-19 deaths' *The Guardian,* 2 June 2020.

11 Office of National Statistics, *Coronavirus and homeworking in the UK labour market: 2019,* available at: www.ons.gov.uk.

12 Oscar Vargas Llave, 'COVID-19 unleashed the potential for telework – How are workers coping?' *Eurofound*, 9 June 2020, available at www.eurofound.europa.eu,

13 Chuck Collins, Institute for Policy Studies, 18 June 2020, available at: ips-dc.org.

14 Jacob Kastrenakes, 'Zoom saw a huge increase in subscribers – and revenue – thanks to the pandemic', *The Verge,* 2 June 2020.

15 Tussell, *Factsheet #2: Covid-19 & UK Public Procurement,* May 2020; Tussell *Factsheet #4: Covid-19 & UK Public Procurement,* July 2020, available at: www.tussell.com

16 Tussell, *2019 Update on Strategic Suppliers*, March 2020, available at: www.tussell.com.

17 Ursula Huws, 'Logged labour: a new paradigm of work organisation?', *Work Organisation, Labour and Globalisation* 10(1), 2016, pp. 7-26.

18 Moritz Altenried, 'On the Last Mile: Logistical Urbanism and the Transformation of Labour', *Work Organisation, Labour & Globalisation* 13(1), 2019, pp. 114-29.

19 Camilla Cannon, 'Recorded for Quality Assurance: The datafication of affect in the call-center industry', *Real Life,* 19 September 2019.

20 Robert Booth, 'UK businesses using artificial intelligence to monitor staff activity', *The Guardian*, 7 April 2019.

21 Aaron Holmes, 'Employees at home are being photographed every 5 minutes by an always-on video service to ensure they're actually working – and the service is seeing a rapid expansion since the coronavirus outbreak', *Business Insider,* 23 March 2020.

22 Accessed on June 29, 2020 from: www.facebook.com/ADCUnion

23 Carl Roper, 'Trade union membership rises by 100,000 in a single year – but challenges remain', TUC, 30 May 2019, available at: www.tuc.org.uk.

24 Lesley Riddoch, 'Unions thriving amid national crisis', *The Scotsman,* 22 June 2020.

25 Jason Koslowski, 'A Historic Wave of Workers' Struggle is Sweeping the U.S. – and It's Speeding Up' *Left Voice*, 22 June 2020. On the actual number of strikes, see Chris Brooks, 'Fact Check: Have there been 500 wildcat strikesin June?', *organizing work*, 23 June 2020, available at www.organizing.work.

26 There is no space to detail here the many examples. Those who are interested can find some listed in the Facebook group 'Prefiguring a positive post-COVID society'.

THE TIME OF OUR LIVES: REFLECTIONS ON WORK AND CAPITALIST TEMPORALITY

BRYAN D. PALMER

There are times in history when time itself is considered differently, even seized in ways that break decisively with past practice. Revolutions are such moments: the rigidity of established calendars is often overturned. 'Time was not only the formal framework within which the Revolution took place,' notes Mona Ozouf in her study, *Festivals and the French Revolution*, 'it was also the raw material on which it obstinately worked.'[1]

Crisis, like revolution, can lead to reconfigurations of time and how it is conceived. The Covid-19 pandemic of 2020, the time of the writing of this essay, is just such a moment, a catalyst that has accelerated and intensified developments in the making over the recent past. Time and how it factors into the restructuring of work are central to these changes; reconsiderations of capitalist temporality seem especially relevant.

The crisis unleashed by the coronavirus prohibited millions of people throughout the world going from their homes to their work, the conventional divisions of day and night, labour and leisure, private and public, collapsing in on one another, fracturing distinctions, such as working week/weekend, that seemed etched into the bedrock of daily routine. Governments were forced to ante-up immense sums, far outstripping anything comparable in the long history of Keynesian restitution and relief, just to keep large and small capital afloat and sustain countless workers whose capacity to contribute 'a fair day's work for a fair day's wage' within established conventions was suddenly terminated. Many of these furloughed workers will undoubtedly lose their jobs permanently. For others the expectation has become that they will work from home, obliterating long-recognized differentiations of their waged lives of labour and their domestic spheres of down-time and reproduction. In many ways, huge swaths of capitalist economies have been 'gigified'. Other sectors, labelled 'essential', have been situated at the crossroads of unrealistic and unrealizable expectations of 'service' and the draconian demands of arbitrary authority. Hospital and long-term care facility workers, on the one hand, have been called upon to give of their time and their lives in ways that are unconscionable, while labour in food provisioning, on the other, has experienced pressures not faced outside of wartime, evident in the insistence that certain production facilities, such as meatpacking plants, remain functional, whatever the dysfunctionality of their working environments.

The costs of all of this and so much more are currently incalculable, but what will be exacted over the course of the next years, possibly decades, is undoubtedly going to be great. Understandings of what constitutes working time has evaporated for many, who must now do their jobs, day and night, squeezing waged working time into spaces among competing minutes and hours where childcare, shopping for necessities, and doing the boss's bidding congeal. Limitations on working time, secured through centuries of struggle, as well as widely recognized entitlements to health and safety in the workplace, largely won in the post-1965 era, have been thrown out the pandemic-shattered window. Will capital and the states that serve its interests readily retreat from the Pandora's Box that the Covid-19 pandemic has not only pried open, with respect to time and the working day, but detonated?

For socialists time and its meaning and organization have always been a central concern, if only because capitalism has placed such a premium on controlling time and subordinating it to its imperatives. At the current conjuncture, time has become *the* challenge for socialists to address, not only because it defines what does and does not constitute the working day, but because it is increasingly obvious that time and its organization defines life itself. Will time continue to be compressed into capital's needs, or will it be reimagined as liberation, struggled through and over in ways that enhance the project of human emancipation?

What follows presents an argument about time that: 1) outlines how class struggles over time have been essential to the rise of the workers' movement; 2) explores the complexity of Marx's understandings of these conflicts and their tendency to be incorporated into capital's project, resulting in the intensification of exploitation; 3) locates E.P. Thompson's writing on time and work discipline within the particular concerns and context of the 1960s New Left, offering a suggestion of how this treatment of time extended orthodox Marxist understandings of primitive accumulation; and 4) closes by discussing how time and its meanings in twenty-first century capitalism demand a rethinking of positions, espoused by Andre Gorz and others in the 1980s, that associated the need for new policies around time with dismissals of the role of the working class in social transformation. Time, always a frontier of class struggle, has been pushed today to the forefront of contentious labour-capital relations.

TIME REDUCED TO A STANDARD

Lucy Larcom, a Lowell 'mill girl' who wrote poems titled stoically 'The Early Doomed' and 'The Complaint of a Nobody,'had little liking for the clattering machinery of early nineteenth century Massachusetts textile factories. When she finally decided to quit her disquieting workplace, the paymaster inquired: 'Going where you can earn more money?' Larcom responded quickly, 'No, I am going where I can have more time.'[2] Karl Marx, separated from Larcom by an ocean and a world of difference, nonetheless understood well this female mill operative's aspiration. 'Time,' he wrote in an 1865 address to the First International Workingmen's Association, 'is the room of human development.'[3]

Capitalism, which time has served well for so long, has little concern with human development. Its idea of progress narrows economic interests to what benefits its hegemonic component, capital. This capital has become, in Stavros Tombazos's words, 'the logic of history and the concrete history of a logic: the economic time of capitalism.' As Jonathan Martineau notes, 'Measured and organized time therefore goes hand in hand with its alienation in our modern temporal order, for the simple reason that time is measured and organized not by us, but by capital, not for us, but for capital.'[4]

Max Weber recognized how Benjamin Franklin captured the spirit of nascent capitalism:

> Since our Time is reduced to a Standard, and the Bullion of the Day minted out into Hours, the Industrious know how to employ every Piece of Time to a real Advantage in their different Professions: and he that is prodigal of his Hours, is, in effect, a Squanderer of Money. I remember a notable Woman, who was fully sensible of the intrinsic Value of *Time.* Her husband was a Shoemaker, and an excellent Craftsman, but never minded how the Minutes passed. In vain did she inculcate to him, *That Time is Money.*[5]

What for Franklin was posed as a question of morality and the individual is for socialists posed as the remaking of a human nature conducive to capitalist development. In rethinking time, socialists reimagine an alternative order and the ways in which men, women, and children will reinvent themselves through an entirely different understanding of and orientation to temporality, refusing to accept that it is only there for humanity as a measurement of utility for commerce, commodification, and capital.

Lewis Mumford, who like Weber (and R.H. Tawney to a lesser degree) recognized the intimate relationship of religion, capitalism, and the new regime of time, added an appreciation of technology's importance. He noted that, 'during the first seven centuries of the machine's existence the categories of time and space underwent an extraordinary change, and no aspect of life was left untouched by this transformation.' The clock, not the steam engine, was for Mumford 'the key machine of the modern industrial age,' which could have done without coal or iron easier than it would have been able to dispense with calculations of time.[6]

Marx appreciated the contradiction at the heart of capital's insatiable, vampire-like need to simultaneously create disposable labour time for the few at the same time as it converts this free time for the many into surplus labour time appropriated for accumulation. Capital's subjugation of labour was extended and sustained by withdrawing wealth from immediate mass consumption so that 'the output of the time employed in direct production must be larger, relatively, than is directly required for the reproduction of the capital employed in these branches of industry.'[7]

On the one hand, the costs of reproducing labour – the infrastructure of human development such as housing, treatment of children, literacy, and the horizons of culture – are constrained to the point that working people have been forced, in different ways, different places, and throughout different historical epochs, into worsening material circumstances. Their prospects, in all spheres of life, are lived as *limitation*.[8]

On the other hand, the resources expended in reproducing capital have historically been vast, including costs that registered not in bullion but in bodies. Beginning with the commercial revolution of the sixteenth and seventeenth centuries this included the formidable freight – and benefits to the select few – of empire's expansion (so often driven by war), the ravages of colonialism with the attendant subjugation of indigenous populations from the Americas to the Antipodes, and the slave trade. With the eighteenth and nineteenth century revolutions in transportation and communication looming large in the Industrial Revolution, an epoch of transformation was marked by the global expansion of railways, canals, aqueducts, and telegraph systems.[9] Not unrelated to this vast expenditure was the establishment of mechanisms of monitoring and regulation, from archives to asylums, and including prisons, police forces, and public education systems, generally under the auspices of national states servile to capital's needs.[10]

For Marx this imbalance in the ledger of human development vs. capitalist appropriation was the antithesis of the socialized expansion of real wealth, in which 'the development of the power of social production … [grows] so rapidly that … production is now calculated for the wealth of all [and] *disposable time* will grow for all. For real wealth is the developed production of all individuals. The measure of wealth is then not any longer, in any way, labour time, but rather disposable time.' Instead, what happens under the regime of acquisitive individualism is the reduction of a segment of the labouring people to *surplus population,* condemned to poverty as 'the constant under-and-over-production of modern industry' necessarily leads to 'fluctuations and convulsions …'[11] Time and its appropriation by capital thus culminates in a political economy of commonplace dispossession, ordered by instability, want, and recurring crises. Redress comes only through revolutionary reversal.[12]

Marx saw the way out of this subordination and its destructive consequences in struggles of a transitional kind, in which time figured prominently. Socialized humanity had to reconfigure time, 'rationally regulating' how it interacted 'with Nature, bringing it under [its] common control, instead of being ruled by it …' That this could only be accomplished in conjunction with engagement with the material realm of necessity was fundamental to Marx's understanding of the dialectics of development, both human and economic. '[T]he true realm of freedom,' he insisted, would only 'blossom forth' as time, the archetypal natural phenomenon, served the 'associated producers,' rather than feeding capital's voracious appetites.[13] This class struggle for shorter hours was, in Marx's words, 'protection' for the working class 'against the serpent of their agonies'. Capital's insatiable need to consolidate labour time produced lethal consequences, 'shortening the extent of the labourer's life, as a greedy farmer snatches increased production from the soil by robbing it of its fertility'. With time reduced to money, to be *spent* in its interests, capital 'extends the labourer's time of production during a given period by shortening his actual life time'.[14] It was thus necessary for the proletariat to erect an 'all-powerful social barrier', in the form of legislation limiting the length of the working day, that would prevent labourers from voluntarily selling themselves and their families 'into slavery and death'. As the bourgeoisie proclaimed itself humanity's saviour with its 'pompous catalogue of the "inalienable rights of man"', workers offered on their part 'the modest Magna Carta of a legally limited working day', making clear 'when the time which the worker sells is ended, and when his own begins'.[15] As mandatory as this struggle to reduce working time was, however, Marx understood that it could only be an intermediate action. '[T]he shortening of the working day,' he wrote, 'finds at last a limit in the generalization of labour. In capitalist society spare time is acquired for one class by converting the whole life-time of the masses into labour-time.' The ultimate futility of reducing the hours of formal, waged labour under capitalism, as absolutely crucial as this was in escalating class struggles, was that, 'The working day is thus not a constant, but a variable quantity. ... The working-day is ... determinable, but is, *per se,* indeterminate. ... To appropriate labour during all the 24 hours of the day is ... the inherent tendency of capitalist production.'[16]

This call to limit the length of the working day, against which much of the self-activity of the nineteenth-century working class could be measured, was thus both necessary and insufficient as a basis of proletarian emancipation. For in redefining time itself, the working class necessarily confronted recognition that its struggles were not simply for a 'fair day's wage for a fair day's work', but rather, instead, for the 'Abolition of the wages system'.[17]

Short Time Committees and Ten-, Nine-, and then Eight-Hour Leagues became synonymous with uprisings of workers, who proclaimed themselves 'Merchants of Their Time', doing so in ways that stretched the demand for reducing the hours of labour into wider spheres of social transformation: 'Onward in column! Mass your powers! For justice, and EIGHT HOURS!'[18] In Lucy Larcom's Lowell, a Ladies Short Time Committee mobilized throughout February-March 1867, reversing traditional patterns of seating in workers' meetings, banishing men to the balcony, and inspiring local politicians to advocate women's suffrage.[19] Pioneer Canadian socialist and member of the Knights of Labor, Phillips Thompson, championed the eight-hour day in the 1880s, claiming that shorter hours would 'annihilate at one blow the gaunt, ragged, hungry, horde of unemployed ready to work for anything they can get, whose idleness is the result of the overwork of their more fortunate fellows – the "reserve" force which capital always has at its command in the event of a strike or lockout'.[20] The reclamation of hours came to be regarded as simply part of the routine relations of capital and labour. Alain Corbin calls this part of 'the daily arithmetic of the nineteenth century'.[21]

Blood was spilled in these short hours campaigns, with the battle for the eight-hour day in Chicago culminating in a 4 May 1886 confrontation on the Haymarket. In the wake of a bomb throwing that left workers and police injured or dead, the first 'Red Scare' in American history was unleashed. Five anarcho-communists were railroaded to the gallows.[22] Small wonder Marx insisted that, 'The creation of a normal working day is, therefore, the product of a protracted civil war, more or less dissembled, between the capitalist class and the working class'.[23]

These battles over time, so fundamental to working-class interests, came to be fought out through workers *adapting* to the logic of capital's reduction of time to an input in the production of profitable commodities. Nothing was dearer to the accumulative heart of the capitalist than to intensify work at the same time as the period of employment was curtailed. This imperative was sustained by capital's hegemonic status within a civil society premised on property, shored up by a state dedicated to the rights of ownership. *Acceptance* of this *order* was a cornerstone of the legal regime on which trade union recognition and the realization of its potential entitlements, including collective bargaining, would eventually balance.

Marx wrote before much of this came to pass. But he certainly appreciated the dualism at the heart of the struggle over the hours of labour, recognizing how 'Legal limitation of the working day' could put an end to some of the egregious 'amenities' of capitalist exploitation, at the same time that 'the shortening of the working-day' provided 'an immense impetus to the development of productivity'. He wrote: 'There cannot be the slightest doubt that the tendency that urges capital, so soon as a prolongation of the hours of labour is once for all forbidden, to compensate itself, by a systematic heightening of the intensity of labour, and to convert every improvement in machinery into a more perfect means of exhausting the workman, must soon lead to a state of things in which a reduction of the hours of labour will again be inevitable.'[24]

In the radical arsenal of what is needed to bring capitalism's human toll to a halt, an entirely new sensibility about time has long figured prominently. Marxists such as Paul Lafargue did their best to cultivate this assault on received wisdoms and conventional assumptions. Lafargue's 1880 refutation of 'The Right to Work', first published in the French weekly *Egalité*, insisted on 'The Right to Be Lazy'. It implored revolutionary socialists to counter capitalist ethics. One component of this was a conception of time that 'kills us second by second', and 'strikes with its anathema the flesh of the laborer; its ideal is to reduce the producer to the smallest number of needs, to suppress his joys and his passions and to condemn him to play the part of a machine turning out work without respite and without thanks'. Only when the working class returned to its 'natural instincts,' claimed Lafargue, could it accustom itself to toiling minimally and 'reserving the rest of the day and night for leisure and feasting'. In the freedom from working time, Lafargue suggested, lay the possibility of a 'new universe'.[25]

TIME FOR YOU AND TIME FOR ME

As the twentieth century progressed, revolution and counter-revolution contended for the affections and aspirations of the masses. Capital could count on war and militarism, imperialism and varied other higher stages of domination, as well as a multitude of ways in which workers were divided from one another (racism, labour market segmentation, the gendered differences of the productive and reproductive spheres, etc.) to shore up its project of accumulation.

One aspect of capitalist hegemony was its systematic capacity, like Prufrock, to measure out life's time in coffee spoons:

> … time for all the works and days of hands
> That lift and drop a question on your plate;
> Time for you and time for me,
> And time yet for a hundred indecisions,
> And for a hundred visions and revisions,
> Before the taking of toast and tea.[26]

The resistance of workers to time as a commodity/property right of the employing class played out in various ways. These could be both an expression of relentless class struggle *and* a reinforcement of the logic of capital's ultimate authority.

As a massive 1913 textile workers' struggle in Paterson, New Jersey shut down the United States silk capital for four months, the Eight-Hour League, led by the Industrial Workers of the World, championed 'Americanism from below' among the 25,000 strikers, most of whom were immigrant women and children. Saddled with both housework and millwork, the women were ardent champions of reducing the hours of labour. They reacted with glum silence, however, when the anarchist agitator Carlos Tresca suggested at one mass rally that with the desired shorter hours, working men and women would be less tired and have more time to spend with one another. Expecting to get a laugh, Tresca joked, 'More babies'. Women were not amused. Noting their glum response, Wobbly leader Big Bill Haywood, interrupted Tresca's address to correct him, 'No, Carlos, we believe in birth control – a few babies, well cared for'. The largely female crowd reacted with laughter and loud applause.[27]

Thus while capitalism weathered many a storm, its hegemonic hold over recalcitrant labour and other potential opponents was challenged in countless ways, including, in 1917, by the world's first proletarian revolution. In *Ten Days That Shook the World*, John Reed's classic account of the Russian

Revolution of 1917, he recognized the emergence of a 'newer, swifter life'. A whole nation in ferment and disintegration ushered in 'the Pageant of the Rising of the Russian Masses', time's normal restraints cast aside to make way for 'the Talk'. Lectures and debates took place everywhere, as workers poured out of massive factories to hear Social Democrats, Socialist Revolutionaries, and Anarchists hold forth. 'For months in Petrograd, and all over Russia, every street-corner was a public tribune. … At every meeting, attempts to limit the time of speakers voted down, and every man free to express the thought that was in him.'[28]

When the Soviet Union introduced the seven-hour day in some industrial employments, this initially contrasted with the situation in the US where the five-day, 40-hour work week proved elusive. Most often it was the preserve of solidly organized crafts in the building trades, associated with the conservative American Federation of Labor unions. On the eve of the Great Depression, manufacturing workers in the United States still tended to work long hours, barely 20 per cent having work weeks of less than 48 hours, with a staggering 54 per cent burdened with weekly hours exceeding 49 and climbing to over 60. It was not until the World War II years of the 1940s that American unions cracked the 40-hour work week, when this had largely already been attained in Europe and Australia much earlier.[29]

After a century and more in which workers and their rising trade unions, in Eric Hobsbawm's words, 'learned the rules of the game,' the labour movement and its shorter hours campaigns had, at least for a significant layer of reasonably well-paid and securely organized (mostly male) workers, pressured capital into concessions around the length of the working day.[30] Workers fought, 'not against time,' as some interpreters felt they would have in earlier, ostensibly task-oriented modes of production, 'but about it'.[31] In Prufrock's sad refrain, time could indeed be measured out in coffee spoons, its purchase registering in needed tea and toast, but in the you and me of decisions and indecisions, visions and revisions, time's possibilities were choked back by overwhelming inequities.

Time turned decidedly against workers, the stopwatch becoming, by 1915, a hated symbol of capital's penchant for rationalizing labour's every move. As David Montgomery has noted, with the introduction of Frederick Winslow Taylor's system of 'scientific management' into American machine shops and other industries, the components of the labour process constituting workplace life were subject to subdivision, minutely broken down by time-study men whose contempt for workers was so palpable as to be brazen. For the Taylorite managers, time's measurement was the progress of science in the service of capital. 'We use the stopwatch,' pontificated

Carl Barth, a mathematician and engineer who took Taylor's teachings into the Watertown Arsenal in Massachusetts, precipitating a walkout of the government-employed moulders that led to a ban on time studies in state-run weapons depots and navy yards from 1915-1949, 'because the sun dial will not do.'[32] If Taylor, Barth, and other like-minded stopwatch wielding time-and-motion study 'experts' were not as effective in their reconstruction of working time as they often claimed, far-seeing capitalists like Henry Ford envisioned new ways of remaking a combative working class.[33]

In a climate of ongoing change, intensification of labour, and repetitious clashes over punching the workplace clock, time was eventually incorporated into the customary pace and tone of recognized capital-labour conflict. It was largely at the margins of the workers' movement where time was radically rethought, reconfigured as a decisive component of potentially transformative class struggles. Georges Sorel, in his *Reflections on Violence* (1906), attempted to transcend the limitations of present-mindedness, not unlike Lafargue, prodding the trade union movement to reach beyond convention to envision a future '*in some indeterminate time*' where residual relations and constrained conceptions could be left behind.[34] Understandings such as these intersected – consciously at times, unconsciously more routinely – with the kinds of counter-planning on the shop floor that took place informally in many workplaces, unorganized as well as organized.[35] But such rupturing and repudiation of capitalist time was quite distant from the legally constituted regimes of collective bargaining that increasingly structured understandings of how time should be fought over by trade unions.

The battle over time thus never really died, it just ran out of hours. Time's centrality passed as it became monetized. Union-led mobilizations for shorter hours quieted, the formal struggle over the length of the working day stalemated in the epoch of relative capitalist prosperity, Keynesianism, the stabilization of an industrial relations regime acknowledging limited trade union power, and the consolidation of the welfare state. If there were signs that, by the 1950s, trade unionism's forward march in the advanced capitalist economies of the west was faltering, the gains registered by organized labour were considerable and continued into the 1960s and early 1970s. Time was not so much off the table, as integrated into collective bargaining in ways that reinforced a militant economism, where conflict's prime consideration was the wage.[36] 'Time nowadays must be pursued,' noted Sebastian de Grazia in 1962, but as it was chased, 'it hides out,' defeating the very notion of leisured, *free* time.[37]

Assembly-line labourers pushed the United Automobile Workers (UAW) to strike over shorter hours in 1958, but Walter Reuther was having none of it, backing away from curtailing hours and proclaiming the need for a 'non-inflationary' (i.e., monetarily concessionary) settlement. Twelve years later, in 1970, stuck on the necessity of the 40-hour workweek, UAW head Leonard Woodcock toyed with the idea of bargaining for a four-day week that bumped the hours of daily labour to ten, an intensification of exploitation that many workers balked at accepting.[38]

Detroit's Black Workers' Congress, successor to the League of Revolutionary Black Workers, led a series of summer 1973 unauthorized work stoppages at a number of Detroit-area Chrysler plants, angered in part by an enforced seven-day week imposed on 60 per cent of the automobile labour force. Disgusted by the UAW's acceptance of compulsory overtime in 1973 contract negotiations, African-American militants branded the new collective agreement nothing more than a '54-hour week pact'. They countered with the audacious demand to reduce the work week to 20 hours.[39] Others, often left-wing critics of trade union officialdoms, struggled to keep the 1930s rallying cry of 30 hours work for 40 hours pay alive. Such radical stands on the hours of labour found little favour within the mainstream leadership of organized workers.[40] The fight for shorter hours had become, by the mid-to-late twentieth century, largely confined to a codicil of collective agreements protecting a minority of workers shielded by trade union entitlements, a shrinking percentage of the labour force. This was an emphatic point in André Gorz's 1980 declaratory *Farewell to the Working Class,* a book we will return to at the end of this essay.[41]

AN INTERREGNUM: TIME AND THE 1960s

The 1960s proved the last gasp of the post-war economic boom. A seeming settling of the long struggle over the hours of labour prodded historians and social scientists to consider the 'problem' of leisure, a topic that quietly morphed into a revival of interest, often posed quite mechanically, in Edward A. Ross's sociological concern with social control.[42] The Twentieth Century Fund, its Board of Trustees a Who's Who of liberal social scientists and progressive mandarins such as Adolf A. Berle, J. Kenneth Galbraith, Robert S. Lynd, and Arthur Schlesinger, Jr., commissioned a wide-ranging study of time, work, and leisure published in 1962.[43] Sociologists and historians developed a keen interest in popular recreations and the work/leisure divide, especially as this related to understandings of modernization in mainstream political science and anthropology.[44] Sidney Pollard provided a pioneering statement on how factory discipline was inculcated during the Industrial Revolution. This was a process of economizing time. In the words of Sidney and Beatrice Webb, an 'enforced asceticism' assailed the leisure activities of the plebeian masses as 'examples of immoral idleness'.[45]

Marx's *Economic and Philosophical Manuscripts of 1844,* largely unknown before the 1930s, and widely available in English only in the 1960s, had a profound impact.[46] In materializing Hegelian understandings of alienation, Marx's 1844 reflections resonated with the contradictions of an ostensibly affluent society, which had not managed to overcome human estrangement through the establishment of the welfare state.[47] Marx extended Hegel's claim that 'Time is the negative element in the sensuous world' by insisting on the differentiated and conflictual relation of specific classes to time, in which the working day was lived as '*loss of realization,*' as '*bondage'* to the commodity, by which capital's appropriation could only be experienced as '*estrangement,* as *alienation*'. Labour time was conceived as *external* to the worker, and in a language entirely congruent with the sensibilities of youth radicalization, a New Left penchant for human liberation, and the post-war accent on the affluent society and leisure, Marx's words resounded in varied chambers of oppositional thought. With labour 'not voluntary, but coerced,' it was conceived as '*forced*', merely a *means* to satisfy needs external to it, the bedrock of these needs being time itself. Tom Bottomore quoted these 1844 philosophical manuscripts of Marx in 1965 when he stressed that workers under capitalism, especially young workers not weighted down with the residue of the constraining experience of the past, grasped intuitively the discrepancy between their conditions at work and their time off the job. The worker, Marx insisted, 'feels himself at home only in his leisure time,' a view reflected in *An Essay on Liberation* by Herbert Marcuse.[48]

Reconsiderations of time, its meanings and its possibilities, were central to this confluence. In the workplaces of advanced capitalism young workers battled bosses, states, and union bureaucrats, influenced at times by developing New Left thought.[49] Marcuse's *One-Dimensional Man* envisioned the end of capitalist scientific rationality in 'the possibility of an essentially new human reality – namely existence in free time on the basis of fulfilled vital needs'.[50] If this seemed, in the words of the 1962 founding document of the Students for a Democratic Society, 'The Port Huron Statement', 'to seek the unattainable,' it was the only way to 'avoid the unimaginable'.[51]

E.P. THOMPSON: TIME IN THE AGE OF AFFLUENCE, APATHY, AND ALIENATION

This was not all that far removed from the thought of E.P. Thompson as he charted his way into the 1960s as part of the first British New Left. His concerns included the need to explore historical subjects of oppression, dispossession, and rebellion in ways that might indicate a 'correlation with Marx's notion of alienation'. How people change and are changed, Thompson argued in a highly critical review of Raymond Williams' *The Long Revolution* (1961), was exactly where 'in 1844 … Marx began'.[52] Thompson's opening essay in the first New Left Books collection of position papers, *Out of Apathy*, declared, against a kind of Fabian gradualism, a new urgency to mobilize opposition against capitalist atrophy and popular disengagement. Apathy and alienation, Thompson argued, could only be countered by breaking from the 'conventions within which our life is confined'.[53] Time was just such a constraint.

Thompson's monumentally influential *The Making of the English Working Class*, first published in 1963, followed these early New Left publications, and prompted him to move his research orientation back in time, addressing the eighteenth-century context in which predecessors of the insurgent workers he had written about in the 1790-1832 years were prepared for proletarianization. This led him into the nether world of customary rights and non-acquisitive sensibilities that figured prominently in pre-industrial socio-economic relations, culminating in the 1991 collection of essays, *Customs in Common: Studies in Traditional Popular Culture*. The first of the essays comprising this new approach to the preconditions of class formation to be published was 'Time, Work-Discipline and Industrial Capitalism', a wide-ranging investigation into capitalism's moulding of human nature to the disciplines of the regimental clock and the dictates of property/accumulation.[54]

Lauded as among its author's finest historical writings, 'Time, Work-Discipline and Industrial Capitalism' has seldom been scrutinized theoretically, situated within the socio-cultural and political context in which it was written, or assessed in terms of its ongoing relevance.[55] When 'Time, Work-Discipline and Industrial Capitalism' was being written, Thompson was adamantly opposed to the academic fashion of modernization theory, which inundated conventional social science departments in English-speaking universities in the 1960s, exercising an impact on social and economic history well into the 1970s. Modernization became nothing less, in the words of the *May Day Manifestos* of 1967 and 1968, on which Thompson worked with Raymond Williams, Stuart Hall, and others, than the 'theology' of a new capitalism. Positivistic, utilitarian, and quantitative, modernization seemed to Thompson to smooth the transition to industrial capitalism, compressing it into a model of the path travelled from 'primitive' social formations to 'advanced' ones, reifying routes supposedly taken in Western Europe and North America and simplistically and categorically dichotomizing the 'traditional' and the 'modern'. This foreclosed the possibility of intervening in the politics of a

1960s crisis-ridden British society, doing so in a suppression of history and its complexities: 'Modernization is the ideology of the never-ending present,' declared the *May Day Manifesto, 1968,* 'a technical means for breaking with the past without creating a future … human society diminished to a passing technique. No confrontation of power, values, or interests, no choice between competing priorities, is envisaged or encouraged.' Modernization theory was perfectly adapted to power's global penchant for continuing the ideological project of shaping a 'disciplined workforce'.[56]

In countering modernization theory as a barrier to be broken down in transcending apathy, alienation, and the failures of a reformist social democracy, so evident in the Labour Party in power, Thompson as an author of the *May Day Manifestoes* undoubtedly looked to the first transition to industrial capitalism in Britain. Socialism's meaning was being perverted in the propaganda push of a corporate partnership of 'the Government and industry and the banks and the unions.' In the twinned concerns of how a socialist opposition might struggle in the 1960s and how an appreciation of the costs entailed in the transition to industrial capitalism in the eighteenth century might be revealed, Thompson turned to time. The *May Day Manifesto 1968* called attention to the,

> remarkable fact that in both Britain and the U.S.A. there was practically no reduction in working hours in the twenty-five years between 1940 and 1965, although during this time output per man hour was much more than doubled in real terms. Only a few unions have fought for a shorter working week and often this is in effect a way of obtaining overtime rates. The hours worked stay the same, and this suits the giant corporation thrice over: the corporation pays less for its labour; the worker buys another car or television set instead of taking part of his extra wage in leisure; and a pool of unemployed or underemployed workers remains outside the corporation to pull down the price of labour.[57]

If, today, this passage would necessarily have to be rewritten to address the gendered reality of technology, consumption, and *reproductive, domestic labour*, in which a part of the wage is expended on household technologies that either extend the working day of wives or intensify their toil, the point about time and its utility to capital was well made.[58]

Thompson's excursion into the problem time posed for industrial capitalism at the point of its origins constituted an empirical and conceptual investigation into how a labour force was recruited, not physically to this factory or mill or mine, but to the sensibilities that structured how wage labour was to be conducted, whatever the setting. His operative assumption was that time subordinated to capital's needs stood in stark contrast to the traditional approach of peasants tilling the soil, artisans working in handicraft production, or women tending to the myriad tasks of domestic life. An essential aspect of this historic process was the creation of a disciplined wage labouring class, a prerequisite if capital was to achieve a hegemonic hold over a society increasingly forged in its image, *capitalism*. This foundational process of establishing capitalism's preconditions has conventionally been discussed in terms of what Marx designated the original or primary accumulation, often referred to as primitive accumulation, in which the expropriation of the peasantry and colonization loomed large.[59] These historical undertakings, in Marx's words, were 'written in the annals of mankind in letters of blood and fire.'[60]

What Thompson did was take the process of dispossession, and read into it an appreciation of the cultural dimensions of habituating workers-in-the-making to an entirely different mindset, one in which time was not associated with natural cycles, but structured by capital's imperatives. He asked the question: 'If the transition to mature industrial capitalism entailed a severe restructuring of working habits – new disciplines, new incentives, and a new human nature upon which these incentives could bite effectively – how far is this related to changes in the inward notion of time?'[61] This was to situate a Thompsonian maxim – that class formation 'owes as much to agency as to conditioning' and that the working class 'was present at its own making' – in a somewhat different light than is generally associated with the author of *The Making of the English Working Class*.[62] It construed agency very much within the determination of capital and, as such, was a conceptualization expressing Thompson's attempt to bring to bear Gramscian understandings of hegemony on his research into time and class formation.[63]

As the clock tick-tocked in ways that structured labouring people into new relationships with work and its disciplines, an entire culture changed. In the making of plebeian producers into capitalist workers, the internalization of time discipline featured decisively. 'The stress of the transition,' Thompson wrote, 'falls upon the whole culture: resistance to change and assent to change arise from the whole culture.' He concluded that, 'What we are examining here are not only changes in manufacturing technique which demand greater synchronization of labour and a greater exactitude in time routine in *any* society; but also these changes as they were lived through in the society of nascent industrial capitalism.'[64]

There is in this passage, and in the 'Time, Work-Discipline and Industrial Capitalism' essay as a whole, much to appreciate, including the sharp insistence that analysis demands assessment, not of a vague, declawed industrialism, a terminology congruent with modernization theory, but of a capitalism driven by power and property. Written with brio and animated by Thompson's increasing attraction to anthropological concerns, addressed in ways congruent with historical materialism, the discussion of time and its disciplining function in developing capitalism ranged broadly, not just over historical periods from the medieval to the modern, but across spatial differentiation as well. He alluded to E.E. Evans-Pritchard's study of the Nuer of the Nile Valley; Pierre Bourdieu's commentary on Algerian peasants; and writings on Latin America, exposing Thompson to the criticism of generalizing indiscriminately.[65]

Thompson's instinctual animosity to the disciplinary logic of capitalism led to his bewilderment that sociologists in the 1960s were discussing 'the "problem" of leisure'. 'How did it come to be a problem,' he asked? Swept up in the ideology of affluence's moment, Thompson wondered what had contributed to 'the industrialized world' breaking out 'of the poverty-stricken economies of the past', asking if the relaxation of immiseration would result in the Puritan-driven valuation of time decomposing. 'Will people begin to lose that restless urgency, that desire to consume time purposively, which most people carry just as they carry a watch on their wrists?'[66] Viewed retrospectively, after the passage of more than half a century, what stands out in a reading of 'Time, Work-Discipline and Industrial Capitalism' is how much the argument about time was situated at the apex of capitalism's post-World War II boom.

Biting, perhaps rather too deeply, into the apple of capital's self-promotional claims of having delivered 'enlarged leisure', Thompson looked to the past for answers about how time might be passed, rather than consumed and spent. '[I]f the purposive notation of time-use becomes less compulsive, then people might have to re-learn some of the arts of living lost in the industrial revolution,' he suggested, elaborating: 'how to fill the interstices of their day with enriched, more leisurely, personal and social relations; how to break down once more the barriers between work and life. And hence would stem a novel dialectic in which some of the old aggressive energies and disciplines migrate to the newly industrialized nations, while the old industrialized nations seek to rediscover modes of experience forgotten before written history.' A few years later, addressing his differences with Leszek Kolakowski, Thompson alluded to his essay on time when speculating how, 'The energies and anxieties of producing and consuming man may give way before more relaxed modes of existing and experiencing man, for whose goals we must look to Athenian and even "Indian" precedents'. In all of this Thompson was insisting that the task-orientations of peasant, village, and domestic economies were 'more humanly comprehensible than timed labour', that the 'community' of tasked work showed the 'least demarcations' between 'work' and 'life', and that 'social intercourse and labour' were 'intermingled' in historical epochs not 'accustomed to labour timed by the clock'.[67]

So pressing was the need to address the alienations of the 1960s present, in which the disciplines of time seemed overbearing, with resistance arising from so many quarters, that Thompson underestimated the rigours, oppressions, and differentiations of diverse task-oriented work developed through centuries in political economies predating the arrival of industrial capitalism and its time-managed workplaces. He certainly never questioned a fundamental assumption: that the more life and work converged, the better. This was a premise that failed to confront how decisively capital had, by the 1960s, penetrated all aspects of human experience, a process of subjugation not as evident in earlier, often pre-capitalist, times. Equally salient, Thompson's presuppositions understated the oppressions of women's lives, constrained as they were by the symmetries of reproductive work and waged employment, gendered timetables structured by a domesticity that was itself often a harsh taskmaster.[68]

Nature, as Emmanuel Le Roy Ladurie shows in his study, *The Peasants of Languedoc*, could be a brutal disciplinarian, especially when working in tandem with seigniorial overlords whose penchant to tithe and tax was unrestrained.[69] And as both Le Roy Ladurie for France and Rodney Hilton for England have noted, in estates-ordered landed societies, the clergy played a pivotal role in justifying the transfer of peasant surplus to the nobility. As powerful voices of 'ideological mystification', churches and their spokesmen occupied a privileged place in the hierarchies of a social order that, in Montaillou, Le Roy Ladurie likened to an 'island in time'. If time was not money, and the work day was not unduly fixed in a regularized timetable, time was indeed alienated by authorities outside of the natural cycles of pre-clock society. The cleric was 'the guardian of time', which is perhaps why heresy was so often the engine of rebellion in peasant societies and Inquisition a favoured vehicle of restraint and reasserting order.[70] To be sure, fishing and seafaring folk integrated their lives with the tides rather than timepieces, but the unpredictability of storms and other natural calamities, not to mention the arbitrary disciplines most seamen endured at the hands of officers and captains, places working life in occupations that Thompson saw as ordered by environmental compulsions in a slightly different light.[71]

Henri DeMan, in an early discussion of the possibility of joy in work, appreciated the extent to which even the relatively unsupervised and unregimented labours of peasants and craftsmen could never escape the elements of necessity that involved a 'renunciation of the freedoms and enjoyments of the present for the sake of future advantage'.[72] As Adriano Tilgher long ago noted, the idea that work was drudgery, an unpleasant burden not far removed from punishment, was commonplace until at least the Renaissance.[73] None of this diminishes the basic point of Thompson's essay about how capitalism reconfigured working time, subjecting it to new disciplines, but it necessarily tempers his attractions to labouring in the task-oriented economies of earlier societies.

These societies, as Thompson himself demonstrated so well in accompanying essays in *Customs in Common*, were never an undifferentiated 'community'. His suggestion that capitalist change fell upon 'the whole culture' with 'resistance to change and assent to change aris[ing] from the whole culture', begs the question of what a whole culture might be, how it is constituted, and whether or not it congeals too much that necessitates interrogation and differentiation. Thompson had been, a few years before the publication of 'Time, Work-Discipline and Industrial Capitalism', rightly critical of Raymond Williams' distillation of culture as a 'whole way of life' demanding that it be rethought as a 'whole way of *conflict* … a way of *struggle*'. This way of conflict/struggle could never entirely be understood as a 'whole'. Williams later, in 1977, accepted the validity of this critique, pointing out that it had not entirely been resolved in either Thompson's writings or his own.[74]

Thompson certainly recognized that the plebeian and working-class people on whom time discipline was imposed over the centuries fought and clawed back against this relentless orchestration of time. Their resistance, however, comes to something of an accommodated end. In this Thompson perhaps truncated treatment of the problem of time, understating the ways in which 'the whole culture' was criss-crossed with fragmentations that manifested themselves in the dialectics of recalcitrance, undercutting a sense of 'wholeness'. To be sure, capital appropriated time and redefined it according to the logic of its political economy. Yet throughout society, in immigrant families or among the marginalized, capitalist time-sense was incompletely inculcated. Among indigenous peoples whose colonization was never, ultimately, complete, time was worked through in ways that defied the ultimate subordination of the dispossessed.[75] Moreover, so crisis-ridden was capitalism, over the *longue durée*, that its recurrent downturns and cycles of boom and bust threw time's work-disciplinary authority off kilter with depressing regularity. If this reality-check was obscured in the seeming largesse of the ostensibly leisured 1960s, it was about to be brought home with a vengeance in the post-1973 years of economic stagnation and crisis-induced instability.[76]

'Time, Work-Discipline and Industrial Capitalism' rewrote the history of primitive accumulation, but it did so apparently unaware of how much it contributed to and expanded Marx's discussion of this history of establishing and extending the preconditions on which capital could build, ensuring exploitation's endurance. By incorporating the materiality of the cultural, Thompson remained true to his refusal of the base-superstructure metaphor, expanding understandings of dispossession to include the appropriation of time and the pivotal turn to reconstructing human nature.[77] His essay took the discussion of capital's power and its needs in new and important directions.

Yet it also fell into the common trap, evident since Marx, of stopping the process of capitalism's ongoing necessity of always creating anew the climate in which acquisitive individualism thrives. Primitive accumulation has generally been seen as the initial, but time specific, project of establishing the preconditions of capitalist accumulation. As such it is located *at* a particular time *in* history, a precursor to capitalism proper. It is less commonly seen as an historical process necessary *throughout* time, securing and preserving capital's continuity. As indigenous scholar Glen Sean Coulthard has recently noted, primitive accumulation is an ongoing phenomenon.[78] This persistent, continuous nature of primitive (or original/primary) accumulation was first posited by Peter Kropotkin in *Modern Science and Anarchism* (1901) and has been commented on by others subsequently.[79] Because capitalism necessarily ruins at the same time that it creates, its destructiveness demands the making of new conditions. These sustain fresh means of accumulation, even as capital's subordination of time, and how this aligns with changes in the labour process and the reconstitution of exploitation, necessarily changes.

After a 1960s interregnum, in which time seemed to be sustaining a particular relation of labour and leisure, alienation the price paid for affluence, the recurring cyclical nature of capitalist crisis did not so much reconstitute what was acceptable as 'a fair day's work' as violently circumscribe the very consideration of this notion within everyday understandings of class relations. Concern, academic or otherwise, with the 'problems' of leisure society did not last, for the need to address this condition of a privileged sector of humanity soon waned. Leisure, in the sense that Thompson himself had envisioned the possibilities growing out of the 1960s, itself became chimeric. Alienation remained, but it was now pummelled by the mailed fist of industrial capitalism's shrinking, insecure, or 'flexible' employment opportunities. These came to the fore in the reconstructed class relations of the advanced capitalist countries, but similar processes were evident as well in the intensifying exploitation of enterprises of the global South, not to mention in the relations of labour-capital-state throughout what remained of the 'actually-existing' socialist planned economies. Capital melded the new with the old, but kept its stranglehold over time well within its tightened grip. *Plus ça change, plus c'est la même chose.*

OUR TIMES: THE VAMPIRE SUCKS BACK

In 1930 John Maynard Keynes wrote a speculative essay, 'Economic Possibilities for Our Grandchildren'. He prophesied what the world would be like in 2030. Even if Keynes has ten years to go on his prediction, we can be fairly certain, barring a cataclysmic revolutionary transformation, that one of his suggestions of how generations living into the twenty-first century would fare will prove about as far off base as it is possible to imagine. For Keynes predicted that the work day would be a three-hour shift, five days of toil amounting to a mere fifteen hours.[80]

Keynes believed in capitalism's rational capacity to utilize technology and various kinds of income redistribution to lessen the gap separating rich and poor. Everyone would gain. The leisure society would have arrived. It was not to be. Capitalism devoured components of itself; unleashing war, it produced the terror of weapons of mass destruction; traversing and trampling the globe, its imperialist quest for profit knew few bounds; and it ravaged the ecology. Periodic crises – depressions and downturns – were endemic to its always-changing political economy, 'cleansing' the capitalist body of the Darwinian failures of a species as brutal in its natural selection as any known to the evolutionary process. It was the dispossessed who bore the brunt of capitalism's pernicious consequences: the indigenous populations of the new world long alienated from the lands and resources that sustained their subsistence economies; the have-nots in town and country of the west's 'advanced', old-world, economies; the peoples of colour who constituted, within these privileged countries and as the mass of population in those areas of the world subordinated to them, a reserve army of labour to be drawn on as capital required. Capital was not, *pace* the hopes of Keynes, rational. It left the many out of both its calculus and conditioning of development. Time's consideration rarely extended to appreciations of how 'a fair day's work' might be envisioned, focusing instead on how that working day – whatever is length or reconfiguration – might serve capital's needs. This was in the best of times.

The worst of times were coming. What looked like the stabilization of the eight-hour day and the possibility of new ways in which time could be taken back by the working class in a post-World War II era of seeming affluence, trade union power, and welfare state provisioning collapsed as global capitalism entered into a new period of extensive and extending crises in the post-1973 years. A fiscal crisis of the state curbed the capacity of governments to alleviate human distress and wrote *finis* to the 'fair-weather' concern with legitimation that had sustained working-class entitlements and widened welfare's safety-net.[81] We have lived in the shadow of this demise for decades.

One of the many casualties has been a retaking of time, as Marx indeed suggested would happen with his recognition that 'the working-day is not a fixed, but a fluid quantity', an elastic bond that capital seeks constantly to stretch, imposing 'no limit to the working day, no limit to surplus labor'. Marx insisted that the capitalist would always struggle 'to make the working day as long as possible,' making 'two working days out of one' could that be done.[82] This is a particular case of the more general process of class formation which, in Nick Dyer-Witheford's words, 'is a vampire relationship … a transfer of energy, time, and consciousness – *aka* the extraction of surplus value – from one section of a species to another'.[83]

OECD Employment Outlook statistics tell one part of the aggregate story. Between 1970 and 2005 the hours worked per employed adult in the United States went up 12 per cent. In 2004, more than 10 million American workers estimated that they worked, on average, 6.8 unpaid hours a week at home, in addition to the regular remunerated work week they put in at a formal workplace.[84] Unions were part of the backtracking. Germany's powerful IG Metal Union, once in the global vanguard of reducing the length of the working day through collective bargaining, faced a 2006 demand from Volkswagen that it back off an established 29-hour work week. In order to avoid lay-offs and the possibility of plant closures, the union conceded, upping the hours of work per week to 34, with no additional pay.[85]

The leading economies of the European Union developed robust social safety nets, which have been stretched to their limits by the 2008-2009 financial meltdown and the Covid-19 pandemic. A 'short working time policy' in Germany, known as *Kurzarbeit,* provides up to 67 per cent of wages lost for employees whose working time has been constricted or terminated due to companies forced to reduce activity or close. Even as roughly one-quarter of Germany's workforce drew on the *Kurzarbeit* subsidy in March-April 2020, the pressures to extend the length of the working day and increase productivity have been longstanding.[86] Recent estimates are that the average work week in Canada and the United States approaches

47 hours, with the comparable figure in the technology and finance sectors topping out around 60.[87] In the former's auto industry, productivity has been climbing since the 1990s, rising as much as 22.5 per cent in the half-decade after the 2008-2009 downturn, encompassing increases of 45.5 per cent in output and 18.8 per cent in hours worked. Workers nevertheless find themselves thrown on the capitalist scrapheap as plants are closed to further rationalize production.[88]

To traverse the globe is to witness a truly primitive accumulation in action. China's factories provide a glimpse into how rapid proletarianization fast tracks a workforce into the structures of time on terms that, if not an articulation of pristine capitalism, are indeed dictated by markets beholden to capital.[89] In the Fordist Chinese auto sector, a privileged industrial employment governed by the kind of two-tier labour dualism demanded by auto makers in the United States and Canada (and acceded to by the unions), 'temporary' and 'formal contract' workers staff the same assembly lines. Recently recruited from peasant fields, younger temporary labourers lack any kind of job security and earn roughly one-half to two-thirds of what their more permanent counterparts are paid. Dispatched to factories by labour agencies or bureaus, the numbers of these second-tier workers soared to over sixty million by 2010, comprising 20 per cent of the entire actively employed population of China. When class struggle regularly erupts, one of the most galvanizing issues is overtime, which is excessive at the same time as it is virtually the only way of offsetting the shortfalls in wage payments received by temporary workers, who are routinely subject to labour theft. In other jobs, more sweated than auto, employment conditions harken back to those of the first Industrial Revolution, with hours of work approaching eighty a week. Yet even this compares favourably to child workers in Bangladesh, known to toil twenty-hour days, sleeping on the factory floor.[90]

Time is central to virtually all of the tendencies in late capitalism to automate, digitize, and restructure work. Working time, at a global level, has been contracting for some time. By the end of the 1990s, unemployment and underemployment topped one billion persons, or roughly 30 per cent of the entire working population of the world.[91] As labour intensifies in some sectors and the working day extends into the night, an assault on working time is ongoing in other employments, labouring people's means of subsistence cut back with abandon. Over the course of the next three decades, automation and digitalization are projected to eliminate anywhere from 40 to 60 per cent of jobs in countries like the United States and less competitive Euro economies, such as Portugal and Greece. In the sweated garment, textile, and footwear shops of Vietnam and Cambodia, fully 85 per cent of jobs are threatened by automation.[92] Leisure is not an option for these displaced workers. For those left standing on assembly lines, at work benches, or in super-exploited industries, however, the working day has often either been lengthened, or spread over multiple jobs, where more hours are required to achieve earnings sufficient to replenish the bare necessities of life.

In the Walmart-ization of retailing, working time in the megastores is closely monitored. Among the 'associates' servicing the floors, time has been shifted downward by capital to less than 30 hours a week, allowing oligopolistic companies to opt out of the costs of health care, pensions, paid holidays, and other legally-mandated responsibilities. An atomized sales, stocking, and cash register workforce is poorly paid, likely to move on to other jobs when opportunities present themselves, and sufficiently fragmented and isolated to be unlikely to sustain a unionization drive. Time's coerced limitation secures capital's needs, a Walmart internal management memo of 2006 noting that, 'the cost of an Associate with 7 years of tenure is almost 55 percent more than the cost of an Associate with 1 year of tenure, yet there is no difference in his or her productivity'. Walmart gained notoriety in a series of class-action suits filed between 2000-2010 that targeted company practices of forcing people to work off-the-clock, denying overtime, and refusing employees mandated lunch and rest breaks. During the Covid-19 pandemic, this arbitrary and authoritarian managerial practice roused ire among Walmart 'associates' affiliated with United for Respect: they insisted that in failing to provide workplace protections, the retail giant put its employees and customers at risk: thousands of workers were infected with the coronavirus and more than twenty died as a consequence.[93]

Among the warehouse workers at Walmart, how time is used to discipline and demean resembles the 'drive system' of the early twentieth century, as foremen cajole workers constantly, accelerating the pace of work. Hours do not so much need to be cut back in order to curtail the legal responsibilities of complementing the formal hourly wage with the counterpart of a benefit package of social provisions, because this component of the Walmart workforce is often contracted out from labour suppliers. A labour process similar to that of the World War I era combines Taylorism's monitoring of work motions and pace with a more traditional penchant to push the worker to exhaustion. One warehouse worker told Arun Gupta: 'You'd be working a 14-hour day and they would come by your trailer and say, "You're 8 minutes off pace".'[94]

Capital has managed, as it has throughout its history, to subordinate time in ways that are new at the same time as it revives older patterns of coercion.

But the logic of its appropriation of time remains unwavering, a constant in the shifting class relations and changing nature of class struggle. In the current moment, with capital very much in the ascendant and labour relatively beaten back, the stick of time has been bent in particularly retaliatory directions. Precarious employment, lacking both job security and access to 'a fair day's work' on a regular basis, is summed up in the old joke from the 1990s. Told that the administration of President Bill Clinton created ten million jobs in its first four-year term, a worker responded, 'Yeah, and I have three of them'.[95]

The fusion of new and old is perhaps most evident in the so-called gig economy, where artificial intelligence, digital platforms, mobile communications, and other technologies intersect with globalization and revamped labour processes to transform the nature of work and, most emphatically, of working time.[96] Employment in this economy of ostensible knowledge production is less likely to be tied to a traditional, factory-like workplace, or even structured into a specific company. Hiring is done on demand, often at a distance; flexibility is the watchword, casualization the consequence. Boosters of the gig economy like to claim that upwards of 40 per cent of the United States workforce is now employed in this sector.[97] Dispersed throughout the world, this kind of work is *informalized* the better to make the regulation of hours and wages/salaries as well as the enforcement of social security provisions subject to any national jurisdiction impossible.[98]

All of this fits with 'new' and 'innovative' technologies as well as the ideological onslaught of neoliberalism, but it is also quite 'old' inasmuch as it breaks down conventional post-Industrial Revolution divisions between work and life. Labour in the gig economy can be done from anywhere: at the park, in a café, reclining on a bed. Promoted as a positive, this symbiosis of work/life torpedoes any notion of free time, with employers utilizing platforms to develop twenty-four hour surveillance of their workforce, monitoring whether someone goes off gig to check their email, cuddle the cat, prepare a casserole, or tiptoe to the bathroom. Much of this toil is in fact mind-numbingly routinized. Its myriad alienations are compounded by its below-the-poverty-line remuneration. Mere pennies per piece of information are paid to construct compilations of data that are then marketed by monopolies like Amazon. In the case of work-on-demand employment orchestrated by centralized corporate platforms (such as what is done by Uber or Lyft), ownership of the 'means of production' (a vehicle) is the responsibility of the worker. Illusions of independence thus fuel the gig economy. But the work is actually a throwback to the 'putting out system' of early capitalism, and downloads many costs, not only of essential tools but significant components of social reproduction (health and dental care, savings for retirement, provisions for holidays) on to workers paid, not by the hour, but the task, often minutely delineated. The result is, as Marx long ago noted, 'the forcible prolongation of the working day beyond its natural limits'.[99] The promised dream of self-employment heaven quickly dissipates; insecurity and intensifying exploitation turn into a gigged nightmare. For many the light at the end of the gig economy's carpal tunnel is simply not visible.[100]

Stanley Aronowitz captures something of the scissors-like separations of late capitalism's political economy of time, looking back longingly on the workers' movement's commitment to the shorter-hours movement and all that this led to:

> This is a time of work without end for many Americans and work-shortage for many others: youth, blacks and other 'minorities' and women whose jobless rate is higher by a third than men's. Behind the statistics lie a political and cultural transformation that has already wiped out the gains of three generations. A hundred years ago the dream of the eight-hour day animated the labor movement to a new level of organization and militancy.[101]

Yet we have reached a new point in the history of the struggle over time and what constitutes the hours of working labour. The rallying cry of 'eight hours' will no longer, in each and every instance, suffice, just as 'a fair day's work for a fair day's wage' demands reconsideration.

TIME: FAREWELL TO WHAT AND TO WHOM?

Aronowitz and others have suggested the need to place the accent in current discussions on less work, a stand resonating with the 1980s calls of André Gorz and Rudolf Bahro for 'a policy of time' and a 'new economy of time' as ways of changing 'the social order and the quality of life under capitalism'.[102] And yet these suggestions may not be enough. As long as time is subject to capital's control, as it invariably has been, is, and will be under capitalism, the vampire will suck back more than it ever allows those subordinate to its needs to take for themselves.

Gorz, for instance, is instructive with respect to the limitations of an analytic framework that demands less work, more leisure, and a new approach to consumption. All of this is supposedly achievable under a capitalism sufficiently reformed so as to sustain a post-industrial socialism in which the traditional working-class has been exorcized, replaced by the agency of 'non-producers' who now occupy the front lines of change. Like Keynes, Gorz presumed that automation, job-sharing, part-time work, and flexible employment were all possible under capitalism in ways that could result in a revolutionary transformation of labour time, reducing the working day dramatically.

'Free time,' for Gorz, assumes 'the abolition of work.' Work is presented *only* as debasement, a process of individualized estrangement stripped of collective possibility. '[P]roletarians have internalized their dispossession in order to affirm their complete dependence and their need to be taken charge of completely. … Since their work is of use to society but not to themselves, society should meet all of their needs and pay a wage for every kind of work.' In a passage that, read against the global experience of Covid-19, reveals starkly Gorz's transmutation of an understandable dislike of how work is organized under capitalism into an unwarranted denigration of those who do it: 'any worker, employee or civil servant can take a malicious pleasure in rigidly adhering to the hierarchical rules and turning their work against the goals it is supposed to serve. … [It] is the attitude of all the public employees who avenge themselves on the public for the hierarchic oppression they endure by refusing to do or say or know anything outside of their specific duties.' Even acknowledging that Gorz, author of the famous, *Strategy for Labor: A Radical Proposal,* which reflected the imaginative spirit of the New Left 1960s, was capable of so much more in his extended discussions of the working class than this subsequent declaration at the beginning of the depressing 1980s, it was nonetheless a sad statement of displacement.[103] It spirals downward from a misreading of Marx's insistence on the dialectical relations of the 'the sphere of necessity' and 'sphere of autonomy', with Gorz asserting their categorical separation: 'they cannot be merged'. Yet the realization of autonomy will never be won, as Marx fully recognized, outside of a recognition of and engagement with necessity. *Farewell to the Working Class,* for all of its insights in demanding a recalibration of time in the project of human emancipation, did so via a false utopianism, in which work and the working class were understood one-dimensionally as negation, and class struggle, consequently, regarded as an atavism.[104]

Gorz failed to grasp two fundamental tenets of the 'Saint Marx' that, in his 'post' analytics, he was intent on deprecating: first, that class formation, as tortuous a historical process as it may be, is necessarily a *collective* as opposed to *individualized* undertaking; and second, that time's meaning, under capitalism and proceeding beyond it into socialist reconstruction, will always be a class *struggle.* As Marx wrote decisively, 'in the history of capitalist production, the determination of what is a working day, presents itself as the result of a struggle, a struggle between collective capital, i.e., the class of capitalists, and collective labour, i.e., the working class'.[105]

Assuming, against Marx, that capital's capacity to expand production was infinite, Gorz paid no attention to imperialism and its role in sustaining the economic well being of empires and their metropolitan centres. His concerns around time were very much those of a 'first world' problem, and were thus profoundly racialized. Parisian time was what needed addressing; time in Algiers, not so much. He premised his predictions on the historical trajectory of the advanced capitalist economies of the west continuing their forward march, with annual productivity increases of 5 per cent supposedly easily achievable. This, Gorz postulated, would see the length of the working week falling to 20 hours by 2001. From the womb of this birth mother of new values, cultures, and human relationships would spring an entirely new species nature, one liberated from the shackles of an ethic of speed, punctuality, and the inhibiting sensibility, inculcated since childhood, that 'we're not here for fun'. Authority itself would mellow, forced to treat wage earners as 'autonomous individuals, seeking their cooperation rather than demanding their obedience'. In this elevation of humanity, wage labour would 'progressively cease to form the centre of people's lives', the working class finally bid *adieu*. Time's liberation could come from power's pronouncements: 'the freeing of time through a free choice of working hours is the best and most rapid way of "changing the quality of life" and, at the same time, of creating jobs. In the social and postal services, in local government, the hospitals and health-care centres, all that is needed is a simple ministerial directive to ensure that work in one's own freely chosen time become a reality.'[106]

How distant this suggestion of easing into freely chosen time is from what has developed over the four decades since the publication of Gorz's manifesto. Rather the reverse has happened, an understandable development given Marx's prescient commentaries. 'Saint Marx', as it turns out, is a better guide to time and how it has been put to use under late capitalism than the Gorz of *Farewell to the Working Class*.

Marx, after all, appreciated that progress, innovation, and enhancement of productivity aside, under capitalism advance will not shorten labour time, but prolong it, abbreviating the hours necessary for a generalized social reproduction, but 'not the labour necessary for the capitalist'. Human development, rather than the betterment of one privileged societal segment, can only happen when time itself is sprung from the vampire's clutches, so that 'the power to shift the natural burden of labour from its own shoulders to those of another layer of society' is taken away from an elite minority.[107]

Such a view presumes, of course, that there is *such a thing as society*. This kind of outlandish notion actually rests on a quite old, long overdue, and equally outlandish premise: that society only truly exists when the very discussion of 'a fair day's work' has been rendered obsolete by the abolition of classes and the wage system that sustains their inequalities.

This was perhaps why Thompson ended his discussion of 'Time, Work-Discipline, and Industrial Capitalism' with a passage from William Wordsworth's *The Prelude* (1805). Wordsworth, discontented with the 'unreasoning progress of the world', feared that the 'mighty workmen of our later age', struggling with 'the chaos of futurity', would fall prey to 'the keepers of time'. These 'guides and wardens of our faculties', wrote Wordsworth, were 'Sages who in their prescience would control/All accidents, and to the very road/Which they have fashioned would confine us down/Like engines ...'[108]

Our roads out of *The Prelude's* presentation of confinement will be paved with entirely new understandings of time, realized in refusals of the meanings of minutes, hours, and days concocted by those segments of capital once powerful enough to control it. Time freed is an imperative of ongoing class struggles, grasped by rejecting the inclination to subordinate all considerations of temporality to the grid on which paychecks are calculated and the hours of work recorded. The commitment to 'a fair day's work for a fair day's pay', so rightly and righteously beloved by past generations of workers' activists, was also dear to capital's accumulative heart. Our times demand a new dedication: to the abolition of the wage system, the transcendence of which will be premised on a repudiation of the fairness of any wage. For wages designate that work itself should be the responsibility and required activity of one social stratum, forced to produce for a much smaller privileged layer of people who control the hours of an alienated working day. As graffiti adorning the walls bordering the besieged Parisian streets in May 1968, declared, 'Beneath the paving stones – the beach!'[109] For at the beach, time is not so much ordered, compensated, and then spent, as it is enjoyed.

My thanks to Rick Gruneau, Russell Jacoby, Gavin Smith, Joan Sangster and the editors of the *Socialist Registser* for their comments on earlier drafts of this essay.

NOTES

1 Mona Ozouf, *Festivals and the French Revolution*, Cambridge and London: Harvard University Press, 1988, p. 158.
2 Lucy Larcom, *A New England Girlhood* [1869], quoted in Herbert G. Gutman, 'Work, Culture, and Society in Industrializing America, 1815-1919,' in Herbert Gutman, ed., *Work, Culture, and Society in Industrializing America,* New York: Knopf, 1976, pp. 27-8.
3 Karl Marx, *Value, Price and Profit*, New York: New York Labor News, 1943, p. 62.
4 Jonathan Martineau, *Time, Capitalism and Alienation: A Socio-Historical Inquiry into the Making of Modern Time*, Chicago: Haymarket, 2016, p. 168. See also Stavros Tombazos, *Time in Marx: The Categories of Time in Marx's Capital,* Chicago: Haymarket, 2014, pp. 219, 300, 305; and for a useful discussion of Marxist perspectives on working time, Christoph Hermann, *Capitalism and the Political Economy of Work Time,* New York: Routledge, 2015, pp. 24-31.
5 *Poor Richard's Almanac,* January 1751, in L.W. Labaree and W.J. Bell, eds, *The Papers of Benjamin Franklin,* Volume IV, New Haven, Connecticut: Yale University Press, 1961, pp. 86-7; Max Weber, *The Protestant Ethic and the Spirit of Capitalism,* London: George Allen & Unwin, 1930, esp. pp. 48-50. See as well R.H. Tawney, *Religion and the Rise of Capitalism*, Harmondsworth: Penguin, 1966.
6 Lewis Mumford, *Technics and Civilization,* London: Routledge & Kegan Paul, 1934, pp. 12-18, addresses 'The Monastery and the Clock.' See, as well, Carlo M. Cipolla, *Clocks and Culture,* New York: Walker, 1967; David Landes, *Revolution in Time: Clocks and the Making of the Modern World,* Cambridge, Massachusetts: Harvard University Press, 1983.
7 Karl Marx, *Grundrisse: Foundations of the Critique of Political Economy (Rough Draft),* Harmondsworth: Penguin, 1973, p. 707.
8 See, among possible sources, Frederick Engels, *Condition of the Working Class in England in 1844*, London: George Allen & Unwin, 1943; Engels, *The Housing Question*, London: Lawrence & Wishart, 1943. One strength of E.P. Thompson's *The Making of the English Working Class* (Harmondsworth: Penguin, 1968) was to address this limitation forcefully in its discussion of 'Standards and Experiences' (pp. 347-84).
9 Maurice Dobb, *Studies in the Development of Capitalism,* New York: International Publishers, 1973; E.J. Hobsbawm, *The Age of Capital, 1848-1875,* New York: Charles Scribner's Sons, 1975.
10 See especially Michel Foucault, *History of Madness,* London and New York: Routledge, 2006; Foucault, *Discipline and Punish: The Birth of the Prison,* New York: Pantheon, 1977. On the meaning of archives in this context, see Thomas Richards, *The Imperial Archive: Knowledge and the Fantasy of Empire,* London and New York: Verso, 1993.
11 Karl Marx, *Grundrisse,* p. 708; Tombazos, *Time in Marx,* p. 309.
12 Karl Marx, *Capital,* Volume III, New York: International Publishers, 1970, pp. 263-4.
13 Marx, *Capital,* Volume III, p. 820.
14 Karl Marx, *Capital,* Volume I, New York: International Publishers, 1970, pp. 302, 265.
15 Marx, *Capital,* Volume I, p. 302.

16 Marx, *Capital*, Volume I, pp. 232, 256-7, 530.

17 Marx, *Value, Price and Profit*, p. 74.

18 George E. McNeil, ed., *The Labor Movement: The Problem of To-Day,* Boston: A.M. Bridgman, 1887, pp. 470-82; Edward R. Place, 'Eight Hours,' *The Socialist,* 8 July 1876; Hermann, *Capitalism and the Political Economy of Work Time,* pp. 109-16.

19 David Montgomery, *Beyond Equality: Labor and the Radical Republicans, 1862-1872,* New York: Knopf, 1981, p. 286.

20 Phillips Thompson [Enjolras], *Palladium of Labor,* 21 February 1885.

21 Alain Corbin, *Time, Desire and Horror: Towards a History of the Senses,* Cambridge: Polity Press, 1995, p. 5.

22 Paul Avrich, *The Haymarket Tragedy,* Princeton, NJ: Princeton University Press, 1984; James Green, *Death on the Haymarket: The Story of Chicago, the First Labor Movement and the Bombing That Divided America,* New York: Pantheon, 2006.

23 Marx, *Capital,* Volume I, p. 299. Marx seemed to have 'borrowed' these words – in their exact presentation – from Theophilus Fisk, 'Capital Against Labor,' An Address Delivered at Julian Hall Before the Mechanics of Boston, 5 May 1835, quoted in Steve Fraser, *The Age of Acquiescence: The Life and Death of American Resistance to Organized Wealth and Power,* New York: Little Brown, 2015, p. 81.

24 Marx, *Capital,* Volume I, pp. 409-10, 417, 547

25 Paul Lafargue, *The Right to Be Lazy and Other Stories,* Chicago: Charles H. Kerr, 1907, pp. 4, 53, 56. See also Peter Kropotkin, *The Conquest of Bread,* New York: Putnam's, 1906.

26 T.S. Eliot, 'The Love Song of J. Alfred Prufrock,' *Poetry: A Magazine of Verse,* 6, June 1915.

27 David R. Roediger and Philip S. Foner, *Our Own Time: A History of American Labor and the Working Day,* New York: Greenwood, 1989, pp. 182-3.

28 John Reed, *Ten Days That Shook the World,* New York: Boni and Liverlight, 1919, pp. 10, 14, 16.

29 Roediger and Foner, *Our Own Time,* p. 243; Hermann, *Capitalism and the Political Economy of Work Time,* pp. 116-25.

30 E.J. Hobsbawm, 'Custom, Wages and Work-Load in Nineteenth-Century Industry,' in Hobsbawm, *Labouring Men: Studies in the History of Labour,* London: Weidenfeld and Nicolson, 1968, p. 362.

31 E.P. Thompson, 'Time, Work-Discipline and Industrial Capitalism,' in E.P. Thompson, *Customs in Common: Studies in Traditional Popular Culture,* New York: New Press, 1991, p. 388.

32 David Montgomery, *Workers' Control in America: Studies in the History of Work, Technology, and Labor Struggles,* New York: Cambridge University Press, 1979; Montgomery, *The Fall of the House of Labor: The Workplace, the State, and American Labor Activism, 1865-1925,* New York: Cambridge University Press, 1987, p. 221; Hugh G. J. Aitken, *Scientific Management in Action: Taylorism at Watertown Arsenal, 1908-1915,* Princeton: Princeton, NJ: Princeton University Press, 1985.

33 Joshua Murray and Michel Schwartz, 'Collateral Damage: How Capital's War on Labor Killed Detroit,' *Catalyst,* 1, Spring 2017, p. 126; Hermann, *Capitalism and the Political Economy of Work Time,* pp. 59-64.

34 Georges Sorel, *Reflections on Violence,* New York: Collier, 1961, pp. 124-5; Stephen Kern, *The Culture of Time and Space, 1880-1918,* Cambridge, Massachusetts: Harvard

University Press, 1983, pp. 103-4.

35 Stanley B. Mathewson, *Restriction of Output Among Unorganized Workers,* New York: Viking Press, 1931; Jack Kramer [Marty Glaberman], *Punching Out,* Detroit: Our Times, 1952; Bill Watson, *Counter-Planning on the Shop Floor,* Boston: New England Free Press, 1971; Montgomery, *Workers' Control in America;* Ben Hamper, *Rivethead: Tales from the Assembly Line,* New York: Warner Books, 1991.

36 On the 1950s and trade unions showing signs of stasis, see Eric Hobsbawm, *The Forward March of Labour Halted?* London: Verso and *Marxism Today,* 1981; Michael Goldfield, *The Decline of Organized Labor in the United States,* Chicago and London: University of Chicago Press, 1987.

37 Sebastian De Grazia, *Of Time, Work, and Leisure,* Garden City, NY: Doubleday, 1962, p. 312.

38 William Serrin, *The Company and the Union: The 'Civilized Relationship' of the General Motors Corporation and the United Automobile Workers,* New York: Knopf, 1973, pp. 175, 292-4, 301-3.

39 Roediger and Foner, *Our Own Time,* p. 272; James Geschwender, *Class, Race, and Worker Insurgency: The League of Revolutionary Black Workers,* Cambridge: Cambridge University Press, 1977, p. 193; Jeremy Milloy, *Blood Sweat and Fear: Violence at Work in the North American Auto Industry, 1960-1980,* Vancouver and Toronto: UBC Press, 2017, p. 31.

40 The demand of 30 for 40 remains current, justified in Hermann, *Capitalism and the Political Economy of Work Time,* pp. 198-9.

41 André Gorz, *Farewell to the Working Class: An Essay on Post-Industrial Socialism,* London: Pluto, 1982.

42 Edward A. Ross, *Social Control: A Survey of the Foundations of Order,* New York: Macmillan, 1901.

43 De Grazia, *Of Time, Work, and Leisure.*

44 Harold Wilensky, 'The Uneven Distribution of Leisure: The Impact of Economic Growth on 'Free Time',' *Social Problems,* 9, Summer 1961, pp. 32-56; Keith Thomas, 'Work and Leisure in Pre-Industrial Society,' *Past & Present,* 29, December 1964, pp. 50-62; Richard D. Brown, 'Modernization and Modern Personality in Early America: A Sketch of a Synthesis,' *Journal of Interdisciplinary History,* 2, 1972, pp. 201-28.

45 Sidney Pollard, *The Genesis of Modern Management: A Study of the Industrial Revolution in Great Britain,* Harmondsworth: Penguin, 1968, reprint of original 1965, pp. 215, 228;

46 Henri Lefebvre, *Critique of Everyday Life: Foundations for a Sociology of the Everyday,* Volume II, New York and London: Verso, 2002, pp. 206-7; Marshall Berman, *Adventures in Marxism,* London and New York: Verso, 1999, pp. 7-21.

47 Richard Titmuss, *The Irresponsible Society,* London: Fabian Society, 1960 and E.P. Thompson, ed., *Out of Apathy,* London: New Left Books/Stevens & Sons, 1960.

48 Herbert Marcuse, *Reason and Revolution: Hegel and the Rise of Social Theory,* London: Oxford Press, 1941, p. 240; Karl Marx, *The Economic and Philosophical Manuscripts of 1844,* New York: International. 1964, pp. 108-11; T.B. Bottomore, *Classes in Modern Society,* London: George Allen & Unwin, 1965, pp. 74-5; Marcuse, *An Essay on Liberation,* Boston: Beacon Press, 1969, p. 20.

49 See Peter B. Levy, *The New Left and Labor in the 1960s,* Urbana and Chicago: University of Illinois Press, 1994; Ian Milligan, *Rebel Youth: 1960s Labour Unrest, Young Workers, and New Leftists in English Canada,* Vancouver: UBC Press, 2014; Sean Mills, *The Empire*

Within: Postcolonial Thought and Political Activism in Sixties Montreal, Kingston: McGill-Queen's University Press, 2010.

50 Herbert Marcuse, *One-Dimensional Man,* Boston: Beacon Press, 1964, p. 231.

51 Tom Hayden, *The Port Huron Statement: The Visionary Call of the 1960s Revolution,* New York: Public Affairs Press, 2005.

52 E.P. Thompson, 'The Long Revolution,' in Cal Winslow, ed., *E.P. Thompson and the Making of the New Left: Essays & Polemics,* New York: Monthly Review, 2014, pp. 198, 200. See also, E.P. Thompson, 'The rising cost of righteousness,' *Views,* 7, Spring 1965, pp. 76-9, a short story addressing *gendered alienation* that is discussed at length in Carolyn Steedman, 'A Weekend with Elektra,' *Literature and History,* 6, Spring 1997, pp. 17-42.

53 E.P. Thompson, 'At the Point of Decay,' and 'Revolution,' in Thompson, ed., *Out of Apathy,* esp. pp. 14, 287.

54 E.P. Thompson, 'Time, Work-Discipline and Industrial Capitalism,' *Past & Present,* 38, February 1967, pp. 56-97, was reprinted in Thompson, *Customs in Common,* pp. 352-403, and I will cite the article in this later 1991 printing.

55 Thompson's essay on time receives brief descriptive mention in standard accounts, but seldom in ways that engage with its arguments critically. The article is essentially by-passed in most of the recent scholarship addressing Thompson, including Tim Rogan, *The Moral Economist: R.H. Tawney, Karl Polanyi, E.P. Thompson, and the Critique of Capitalism,* Princeton and Oxford: Princeton University Press, 2017.Commentaries appearing in the late 1980s introduced concerns congruent with criticisms below, but lacked the contextualization or commentary on Marxism that are central to my engagement with Thompson's text. See Richard Whipp, 'A time to every purpose: an essay on time and work,' in Patrick Joyce, ed., *The historical meaning of work,* Cambridge: Cambridge University Press, 1987, pp. 210-36; Thomas C. Smith, 'Peasant Time and Factory Time in Japan,' *Past & Present,* 111, May 1986, pp. 165-87.

56 Raymond Williams, ed., *May Day Manifesto, 1968,* Harmondsworth: Penguin, 1968, p. 45; Stuart Hall, Raymond Williams, Edward Thompson, *1967 New Left May Day Manifesto,* London: No publisher, 1967, pp. 5-7.

57 Williams, ed.,*May Day Manifesto, 1968,* p. 49.

58 For insightful discussions of domestic labour's extension amid prolifering technologies see Ann Oakley, *Woman's Work: The Housewife, Past and Present,* New York: Vintage, 1976; Ruth Schwartz Cowan, *More Work for Mother: The Ironies of Household Technologies from the Open Hearth to the Microwave,* New York: Basic Books, 1983. Hermann, *Capitalism and the Political Economy of Work Time,* pp. 96-104 offers a voice of nuanced dissent.

59 On 'Time, Work-Discipline and Industrial Capitalism' and primitive accumulation see Bryan D. Palmer, *The Making of E.P. Thompson: Marxism, Humanism, and History,* Toronto: Hogtown, 1981, pp. 92-3. Richard Johnson may be alluding to this when he suggests that Thompson's essay addresses 'a history of the construction of some of the conditions' which Althusser, in has accent on the logic of capital, 'takes for granted and eternalizes'. See Richard Johnson, 'Three problematics: Elements of a Theory of Working-Class Culture,' in John Clarke, Chas Critcher, and Richard Johnson, eds, *Working-Class Culture: Studies in History and Theory,* London: Hutchinson, 1979, p. 280.

60 Orthodox statements on primitive accumulation include Marx, *Capital,* I, pp. 713-74; Rosa Luxemburg, *The Accumulation of Capital,* London: Routledge and Kegan Paul, 1951; Dobb, *Studies in the Development of Capitalism,* 177-254; John Saville, 'Primitive

Accumulation and Early Industrialization in Britain,' *Socialist Register, 1969,* London: Merlin, 1969, pp. 246-71. See also Michael Perelman, *The Invention of Capitalism: Classical Political Economy and the Secret History of Primitive Accumulation,* Durham North Carolina: Duke University Press, 2000.

61 Thompson, 'Time, Work-Discipline and Industrial Capitalism,' in Thompson, *Customs in Common,* p. 354.

62 Thompson, *The Making of the English Working Class,* p. 9.

63 See Theodore Koditschek, 'The Possibilities of Theory: Thompson's Marxist History,' in Roger Fieldhouse and Richard Taylor, eds, *E.P. Thompson and English Radicalism,* Manchester and New York: Manchester University Press, 2013, p. 76; Thompson, *Customs in Common,* pp. 10-11. Thompson had worked through, in a preliminary way, Gramsci's notion of hegemony in his response to Anderson and Nairn in the mid-1960s, and much of his comment there is pertinent to how he approached time and work-discipline. See E.P. Thompson, 'The Peculiarities of the English,' in Thompson, *The Poverty of Theory and Other Essays,* London: Merlin, 1978, p. 73: 'Class power might now be seen, not merely as scarcely disguised dictatorship but in far more subtle, pervasive, and therefore compulsive forms.' This was how he saw the imposition of time work-discipline.

64 Thompson, 'Time, Work-Discipline and Industrial Capitalism,' in Thompson, *Customs in Common,* p. 382.

65 On anthropological sensibilities see E.P.Thompson, 'History and Anthropology' in Thompson, *Persons and Polemics: Historical Essays,* London: Merlin, 1994, pp. 201-27; Thompson, 'Anthropology and the Discipline of Historical Context,' *Midland History,* 1, Spring 1972, pp. 41-55. On task economies and the problem in Thompson's essay with universalizing generalizations see Marcel van der Linden, 'Studying Attitudes to Work Worldwide, 1500-1650: Concepts, Sources, and Problems of Interpretation,' *International Review of Social History,* 56, 2011, p. 38.

66 Thompson, 'Time, Work-Discipline and Industrial Capitalism,' in Thompson, *Customs in Common,* pp. 400-401, 358.

67 Thompson, 'Time, Work-Discipline and Industrial Capitalism,' in Thompson, *Customs in Common,* p. 401; 'An Open Letter to Leszek Kolakowski,' in Thompson, *The Poverty of Theory and Other Essays,* p. 380. See also, Thompson, *Customs in Common,* 14-15.

68 Bringing the domestic sphere and social reproduction into the picture of peasant economies complicates matters further Gavin Smith suggests the necessity of situating what is commonly referred to as social reproduction in closer proximity to conventional economic production and waged work. See Gavin Smith, *Livelihood and Resistance: Peasants and the Politics of Land in Peru,* Berkeley and Los Angeles: University of California Press, 1989. See as well, Meg Luxton, *More than a Labour of Love: Three Generations of Women's Work in the Home,* Toronto: Women's Press, 1980; Wally Seccombe, "Marxism and Demography," *New Left Review,* 137, January-February 1983, pp. 22-47.

69 Emmanuel Le Roy Ladurie, *The Peasants of Languedoc,* Urbana, Chicago, and London: University of Illinois Press, 1980.

70 Emmanuel Le Roy Ladurie, *Montaillou: The Promised Land of Error,* New York: Vintage, 1979, esp. the discussion of 'Concepts of Time and Space,' pp. 275-87; Rodney Hilton, *Class Conflict and the Crisis of Feudalism: Essays in Medieval Social History,* London: Hambledon Press, 1985, p. 119. On heresy, rebellion, and inquisition see Carlo Ginzburg, *The Cheese and the Worms: The Cosmos of a Sixteenth-Century Miller,* New

York: Penguin, 1982; R. Hilton, ed., *Peasants, Knights, and Heretics: Studies in Medieval English Social History,* Cambridge: Cambridge University Press, 1976; Bryan D. Palmer, *Cultures of Darkness: Night Travels in the Histories of Transgression – From Medieval to Modern,* New York: Monthly Review Press, 2000, 23-48.

71 Marcus Rediker, *Between the Devil and the Deep Blue Sea: Merchant Seamen, Pirates, and the Anglo-American Maritime World, 1700-1750,* Cambridge: Cambridge University Press, 1987.

72 Henri DeMan, *Joy in Work,* London: George Allen & Unwin, 1929, p. 67.

73 Adriano Tilgher, *Work: What It Has Meant to Men Through the Ages,* New York: Harcourt, Brace & Company, 1930.

74 See Thompson, 'The Long Revolution,' in Winslow, ed., *E.P. Thompson and the Making of the New Left,* pp. 187-213; Raymond Williams, *Politics & Letters: Interviews with New Left Review,* London: New Left Books, 1979, p. 135.

75 See, for instance, Gutman, 'Work, Culture, and Society in Industrializing America,' pp. 3-78; Tamara Harven, *Family Time and Industrial Time: The Relation Between Family and Work in a New England Industrial Community,* London and New York: Cambridge University Press, 1982; and for a fascinating discussion of time and work in the slave South, Mark M. Smith, *Mastered by the Clock: Time, Slavery, and Freedom in the American South,* Chapel Hill and London: University of North Carolina Press, 1997. A revealing indication of how indigenous peoples, in spite of the violence, dispossession, and pressures of colonization, retain a sense of time attuned to hunting, fishing, and harvesting, is evident in Hugh Brody, *Maps and Dreams: Indians and the British Columbia Frontier,* Vancouver & Toronto: Douglas & McIntyre, 1982.

76 See Bryan D. Palmer and Gaétan Héroux, *Toronto's Poor: A Rebellious History,* Toronto: Between the Lines, 2016.

77 Ellen Meiksins Wood, 'Falling Through the Cracks: E.P. Thompson and the Debate on Base and Superstructure,' in Harvey J. Kaye and Keith McClelland, eds, *E.P Thompson: Critical Perspectives,* Philadelphia: Temple University Press, 1990, 125-52; Thompson, 'History and Anthropology,' pp. 218-24.

78 Glen Sean Coulthard, *Red Skin, White Masks: Rejecting the Colonial Politics of Recognition,* Minneapolis: University of Minnesota Press, 2014, pp. 8-13.

79 Peter Kropotkin, *Modern Science and Anarchism,* London: Freedom Press, 1912, p. 83.

80 John Maynard Keynes, *Essays in Persuasion,* New York: Norton, 1963, pp. 38-73.

81 James O'Connor, *The Fiscal Crisis of the State,* New York: Palgrave Macmillan, 1973.

82 Marx, *Capital,* I, pp. 352-5.

83 Nick Dyer-Witheford, *Cyber-Proletariat: Global Labour in the Digital Vortex,* Toronto: Between the Lines, 2015, p. 8.

84 US. Bureau of Labor Statistics, 'Work at Home in 2004,' 27 September 2005, http:www.bls/gov/news; Siri Hedréen, 'Where is That Fifteen-Hour Work Week We were Promised,' *Business News Daily,* 18 July 2019.

85 Hedréen,' 'Where is That Fifteen-Hour Work Week?'; Hermann, *Capitalism and the Political Economy of Work Time,* esp. pp. 133-43.

86 See P. Cahuc and S. Carcillo, 'Is short-time work a good method to keep unemployment down?' *Nordic Economic Policy Review,* 1, 1990, pp. 133-; Carolyn Look, 'Explaining Kurzarbeit, or Saving Jobs the German Way,' *Bloomberg News,* 7 April 2020.

87 Hedréen, 'Where is that 15-Hour Work Week We Were Promised?'

88 André Bedard, 'Recent Trends in Canadian Automotive Industries,' *Statistics Canada,*

June 2013, www150statcan.gc.ca; Sam Gindin, 'Stopping the GM Shutdowns,' *Jacobin,* https://jacobinmag.com/2019/01/gm-oshawa-democraticplanning-nfta, 14 January 2019.

89 See the discussion in Giovanni Arrighi, *Adam Smith in Beijing: Lineages of the Twenty-First Century,* London: Verso, 2007.

90 Lu Zhang, 'Whose Hard Times? Explaining Auto Workers Strike Waves in Recent-Day China,' in Leon Fink, Joseph McCartin, and Joan Sangster, eds, *Workers in Hard Times: A Long View of Economic Crises,* Urbana, Chicago, and Springfield: University of Illinois Press, 2014, 213-42; Yu Chunsen, "All Workers Are Precarious: The 'Dangerous Class' in China's Labour Regime,' in Leo Panitch and Greg Albo, eds, *Socialist Register, 2020: Beyond Market Dystopia – New Ways of Living,* London: Merlin, 2019, esp. pp. 146-7; Ching Kwan Lee, *Against the Law: Labor Protests in China's Rustbelt and Sunbelt.* Berkeley: University of California Press, 2007; Ju Li, 'From 'Master' to 'Loser': Changing Working-Class Cultural Identity in Contemporary China,' *International Labor and Working-Class History,* 88, Fall 2015, pp. 190-208; Annelise Orleck, *'We Are All Fast-Food Workers Now': The Global Uprising Against Poverty Wages,* Boston: Beacon Press, 2018, p. 134.

91 Michael Denning, 'Wageless Life,' *New Left Review,* 66, November-December 2010, pp. 79-97; Stanley Aronowitz, 'The Last Good Job in America,' in Stanley Aronowitz and Jonathan Cutler, *Post-Work: The Wages of Cybernation,* New York: Routledge, 1998, p. 213.

92 Birgit Mahnkopf, 'The Future of Work in the Era of 'Digital Capitalism',' in Panitch and Albo, eds., *Socialist Register, 2020,* pp. 111-12.

93 Mary Pat Tifft, "Workers know and run Walmart but are denied a voice," *Financial Times,* 3 June 2020.

94 The above paragraphs draw on Arun Gupta, 'The Walmart Working Class,' in Leo Panitch, Greg Albo, and Vivek Chibber, eds, *Registering Class: 50 Years, 1964-2014 – The Socialist Register, 2014,* London: Merlin, 2013, pp. 1-39. See also Orleck, *We Are All Fast Food Workers,* pp. 29-32; and Hermann, *Capitalism and the Political Economy of Work Time,* pp. 79-86.

95 Aronowitz, 'The Last Good Job in America,' p. 213. See also, Barbara Ehrenreich, *Nickle and Dimed: On (Not) Getting By in America,* New York: Henry Holt, 2001; Hermann, *Capitalism and the Political Economy of Work Time,* pp. 143-5. Precarity is not the basis of a new class formation, but rather the intensification of the insecurity that has always been foundational to labouring life. See Bryan D. Palmer, 'Reconsiderations of Class: Precariousness as Proletarianization,' in Panitch, Albo, and Chibber, eds, *Socialist Register, 2014,* pp. 40-62.

96 Note the general discussion in Hermann, *Capitalism and the Political Economy of Work Time,* pp. 86-92.

97 Diane Mulcahy, 'Universities Should Be Preparing Students for the Gig Economy,' *Harvard Business Review,* 3 October 2019; Mulcahy, *The Gig Economy: The Complete Guide to Getting Better Work, Taking More Time Off, and Financing the Life You Want,* New York: Amacom, 2017; Thomas Oppong, *Working in the Gig Economy: How to Thrive and Succeed When You Choose to Work for Yourself,* London: Kogan Page, 2018.

98 Birgit Mahnopf, 'The Future of Work in the Era of 'Digital Capitalism',' and Michelle Chan, 'A New World of Workers: Confronting the Gig Economy,' both in Panitch and Albo, eds, *Socialist Register, 2020,* pp. 104-42; Ursula Huws, 'The Underpinings of

Class in the Digital Age: Living, Labour, and Value,' in Panitch, Albo, and Chibber, eds, *Socialist Register, 2014,* pp. 80-107; Huws, *The Making of a Cybertariat: Virtual Work in a Real World,* London: Merlin, 2003.

99 Marx, *Grundrisse,* p. 399.

100 See Nikil Saval, *Cubed: A Secret History of the Workplace,* New York: Doubleday, 2014, pp. 298-303; Sarah Kessler, *Gigged: The End of the Job and the Future of Work,* New York: St. Martin's Press, 2018.

101 Aronowitz, 'The Last Good Job in America,' p. 213.

102 Jonathan Culter and Stanley Aronowitz, 'Quitting Time: An Introduction,' in *Post-Work,* p. 20; Gorz, *Farewell to the Working Class,* pp. 126-44; Gorz quoted in Roediger and Foner, *Our Own Time,* p. 277; Rudolf Bahro, *The Alternative in Eastern Europe,* London: Verso, 1981, p. 407.

103 Gorz's discussions of class and time extended over a number of works, as is evident in the discussion in Hermann, *Capitalism and the Political Economy of Work,* pp. 31-3. I address only *Farewell to the Working Class,* arguably Gorz's most influential text.

104 Gorz, *Farwell to the Working Class,* pp. 39-40, 125; André Gorz, *Strategy for Labor: A Radical Proposal,* Boston: Beacon Press, 1967. For critiques of *Farewell* see Richard Hyman, "André Gorz and His Disappearing Proletariat," in Ralph Miliband and John Saville, eds., *Socialist Register, 1983,* London: Merlin, 1983, pp. 272-95; Leo Panitch and Sam Gindin, "Transcending Pessimism: Rekindling Socialist Imagination," in Leo Panitch and Colin Leys, eds, *Socialist Register, 2000: Necessary and Unnecessary Utopias,* London: Merlin, 2000, pp. 13-17.

105 Marx, *Capital,* I, p. 235.

106 Gorz, *Farewell to the Working Class,* pp. 134-5, 144.

107 Marx, *Grundrisse,* p. 825; Marx, *Capital,* I, p. 530.

108 William Wordsworth, *The Prelude; or, Growth of a Poet's Mind; an Autobiographical Poem,* No Place: DjVu Editions/Global Language Resources, 2001, p. 73; Thompson, *Customs in Common,* p. 403.

109 Dark Star Collective, *Beneath the Paving Stones: Situationists and the Beach, May 1968,* Oakland, California: AK Press, 2008.

INTERPRETATION MACHINES: CONTRADICTIONS OF 'ARTIFICIAL INTELLIGENCE' IN 21ST-CENTURY CAPITALISM

LARRY LOHMANN

Political struggles since the nineteenth century have repeatedly pushed left movements to seek footholds among the spiralling, ever-renewing contradictions of capitalist industrial mechanization and its relation to work and energy. Barely even begun by Karl Marx, one of their great pioneers, these investigations and experiments remain fragmentary and contested.[1] Yet the crises now being thrown up and exacerbated by twenty-first century digital mechanization, even as they confront the left with fresh puzzles, may offer opportunities for shedding new light on this longer history of automation.

This essay sets out three lines of argument in response to these challenges. The first is that it may be more useful to movement organizing to stress continuities between industrial-era and digital-era value-creation than to focus only on differences. The second is that the contradiction between living and dead labour that Marx identified in the nineteenth century not only persists in the most intimate reaches of today's digital economy, but also remains fundamental both to understanding crisis and to identifying possibilities for radical political change. The third is that it may make more strategic sense for the left to approach the striking innovations in automation advanced over the past decade by the likes of Facebook, Google, Amazon, Baidu, Tencent, Alibaba, Microsoft, and Apple as a new level of the *mechanization of interpretive work* than to acquiesce in mystifying labels such as *artificial intelligence* (AI).

Pace some theorists of 'cognitive capitalism', the contradiction between the 'dead knowledge of capital' represented in algorithms and computers and the 'living knowledge of labour' is not a '*new* form of antagonism' superseding the 'traditional opposition between dead labour and living labour inherent to industrial capitalism'.[2] It is, in essence, the same antagonism. In the nineteenth century, it would have been self-defeating for labour movements to have consented to the emerging fantasy that the process of division of labour combined with fossil fuel-powered mechanization represented the early stages of an asymptotic approach toward some hypothetical final state of capitalism in which all workers could be completely and forever 'deskilled', all human labour 'replaced', made 'redundant' and valueless and allowed to relax under benign machine supervision, and all knowledge 'transferred' into self-provisioning machines that might or might not remain under the control of the capitalists out of whose drive, ingenuity and self-discipline they had supposedly sprung. It would be equally self-defeating today for labour movements to go along with what Aaron Benanav dubs the 'new automation discourse, propounded by liberal, right-wing and left analysts alike', according to which 'we are on the verge of achieving a largely automated society, in which nearly all work will be performed by self-moving machines and intelligent computers' and humans can be put out to pasture while capitalism (or fully automated communism) rolls on.[3]

This is why it may be helpful from a left perspective to avoid the jargon of *artificial intelligence* in favour of the term *interpretation machine*.[4] Since Charles Babbage's time, the main jobs of the word 'intelligence' have been to conceal proletarian work, reinforce class, racial, and gender divides, and to justify social surveillance. Already in the nineteenth century, as historian Simon Schaffer makes clear, elite efforts 'to make machines look intelligent' were proceeding hand-in-hand with attempts to degrade and render invisible the 'human skills which accompany them' – the 'labour force which surrounded and ran them' and constituted the 'sources of their power' – as well as with projects to build out the ideological edifice of orthodox economics.[5] The word 'artificial', meanwhile, carries much the same reactionary baggage as its antonym 'natural'. As logician Charles Sanders Peirce was already pointing out well over a century ago, it's never been possible to locate a 'faculty of discussion' or cognition in any 'natural' structures (brains, tongues, lips, lungs) that exclude 'artificial' ones (inkstands, pencils, alembics, typewriters, books, hand calculators, iPhones, neural nets) – or vice versa.[6] Insofar as there can be said to be such a thing, 'intelligence' has always been 'artificial'; conversely, any 'intelligence' *called* 'artificial' is likely in fact to be as 'natural' as it comes, insofar as it is useful at all. Encouraging a critical approach to twenty-first century digital developments, the term 'interpretation machine' implicitly acknowledges these political and historical realities, whereas the phrase 'artificial intelligence' tends to hide them.

MECHANIZING INTERPRETATION

Capitalist labour, like any other kind of work, has always involved interpretation. It cannot but be thoroughly 'cognitive', 'symbolic', and 'affective', right down to the swing of the hammer of the most brutalized or 'deskilled' assembly-line drudge. Particular ability sets connoted by phrases like 'skilled labour,' 'mental work', 'knowledge work', 'symbolic analysis', or 'immaterial labour' – whether the specialized, acquired fine judgement of machine tool operators or photocopy machine repairers or the creative theorizing of postdoc physicists and advertising executives – are never much more than a thin layer of icing on top of the vast multi-coloured cake of everyday interpretive capacities brought into play in the actions not only of every so-called 'unskilled' worker doing the most 'manual' labour but also of nearly every human being over the age of five.[7]

Even more than any particular tasty icing, it's this larger cake, consisting of some of the 'deepest, most hard-won human capabilities',[8] that capital is now increasingly striving, in obedience to its contradictory imperatives, both to have and to eat. The following are a few interlinked examples of the generic interpretive skills in question:

- *Recognizing* new instances of old categories or exemplars: optical characters, images, faces, places, voices, retinas, sentences, intentions, emotions, preferences, paths, vistas, flows, diseases, sexual orientations, patterns of biological growth and so forth. This quotidian, skilled 'labour of perception'[9] is performed mostly unconsciously by every human being nearly every second of every day, whether for pay or not, requiring minimal training examples and minimal energy expenditure.
- *Translating*, a historically-constrained relationship-building skill whose power-laden, collective exercise gives rise to what come to be recognized at various moments as crystallized meanings and beliefs[10] (and ultimately, in the computer age, to the even more reified, specifically twentieth-century artefacts of 'signals', 'information', 'instructions', 'commands', and 'communication').[11] While most colourfully displayed by multilingual individuals, this improvisatory work is also constantly done – typically without much thought being given to the matter – by anyone trying to understand others speaking the *same* language.[12]
- *Wayfinding*, another everyday 'reproductive' socio-natural skill of orienting oneself and adjusting one's movements as one feels one's way

along a path – a type of work essential to daily life, the acquisition of knowledge, commodity circulation, and capital accumulation alike.[13]

- *Sensing, searching for, and retrieving knowledge* as part of *learning* processes whose goals are mobile.
- *Remembering* as a skilled social activity undertaken in challenging times in order to 'articulate the past historically'[14] in ways that make it possible to find ways forward through uncertainty.
- *Calculating*, including the ability to recognize and interpret mathematical symbols, carry out mathematical procedures differently in different or unanticipated contexts, and decide appropriate levels of precision.[15]
- *Knowing how to follow a rule flexibly*, for example, knowing the difference between 'following a rule' in ways prescribed by capital and 'working to rule', the familiar form of labour protest.
- *Understanding what questions to ask* in order to extend conversations, smooth relationships, clarify context, move past misunderstandings or fruitfully probe various unknowns. One example is the ability to find questions making it possible to decide whether it is appropriate in given circumstances to interpret unexpected utterances as reflecting strange beliefs and normal understandings of word-meanings or shared beliefs but unusual understandings of word-meanings.[16]
- *Anticipating* the likes, dislikes, and decisions of others.
- *Intending* others with whom one is interacting to *recognize* one's intentions to produce responses, and for this recognition to be part of the reasons for the responses.[17]
- *Learning, building and exercising trust or respect* toward persons, institutions, nonhuman organisms and experimental apparatuses in the course of everyday practices of negotiating, caring, conducting financial transactions, hunting, or doing science.[18]
- *Playing, teasing, joking, messing around, formulating metaphors or analogies*, and so on.[19]

None of these seemingly mundane activities in itself constitutes a 'trade' or 'occupation' in the usual senses used during the past 500 years (weaver, papermaker, midwife, bricklayer, scrivener, fitter, nurse, construction worker, cook, lorry driver, homemaker, musician, strawberry picker, computer programmer, chemist, logger, market analyst, office cleaner, lawyer). But they do form, in varying combinations, a necessary part of each of them. Indeed, it's the exercise of these abilities that, when assimilated into capital, arguably constitutes the core of the 'living labour' that Marx contrasted to the 'dead labour' crystallized in machines and repetitive mechanical procedures. Encapsulated by Ludwig Wittgenstein in a single gnomic phrase, 'knowing how to go on',[20] they've always been essential across the board in making capital's rule sets, divisions of labour, machines, and algorithms function as required to accumulate surplus.[21]

Since the industrial revolution, it has been a commonplace that one trade after another can be expected to be automated away over time (scrivener, longshoreman), while others can be expected to come into being (sewer cleaner, software engineer). Similarly, jobs may be mechanized out of existence in the US, say, only to be reincarnated in Indonesia or Vietnam. Or women in Europe may leave the kitchen to take charge of expensive machines circulating shipping containers while cheap live-in nannies from the Philippines move in to help raise the children.[22] As Marx argued in volume three of *Capital*, however obvious it may seem to an individual capitalist that displacing or weakening one set of workers using mechanization is the 'immediate source of increasing profit', somewhere in the system injections of new living labour, whether in the form of old or new trades, will ultimately have to compensate if declines in the rate of profit are to be forestalled.[23] So relentless is this process of the 'reorganization of the organic composition of capital'[24] – the churning redistributions and augmentations of living labour across the world that allow surplus value to be drained from less mechanized to more mechanized sectors – that the state has had to make it its business to help smooth over the disruptions that inevitably result for capital itself.

Perhaps the only thing new about this dynamic in the twenty-first century is the degree to which not only individual 'occupations' but also various aspects of the core of living labour itself are undergoing mechanization – inevitably paired, again, with surges in the recruitment of living human labour power at numerous points in the system. During the last decade in particular, almost every skill on the above list has, to a certain extent, been successfully automated:

- *Recognizing and classifying* (mechanized by, for example, facial, voice, and character recognition software, 'sentiment detection' and 'opinion mining' devices[25] and automated medical diagnosis technologies).
- *Translating* (mechanized by Google Translate programmes that can simultaneously correlate, at blinding speeds, thousands of long strings of symbols in one language to 'equivalent' strings in another).
- *Wayfinding* (mechanized by Google Maps, GPS systems, driverless car technology and predictive analytics software that can shift the task

of optimizing deliveries 'to algorithms rather than tribal employee knowledge').[26]

- *Searching for and retrieving knowledge* (mechanized by Google, Baidu, or Bing digital string search engines, book digitization technologies and so forth).[27]
- *Remembering* (mechanized by software recognizing and sorting huge stores of digitized information from the past).
- *Calculating* (mechanized via speedy floating-point processors).
- *Following a rule flexibly* (mechanized through statistically-based machine learning programmes – for example spam filters – that progressively 'learn' from masses of human-labelled data rather than being programmed to match abstractions written out by experts).
- *Extending and fulfilling conversations by choosing the right questions to ask* (mechanized in, for example, automated personal assistants such as Alexa and Siri as well as the therapeutic programme ELIZA as early as the 1970s).[28]
- *Intending* others with whom one is interacting to *recognize* one's intentions to produce responses, and for this recognition to be part of the reasons for the responses (ditto).
- *Anticipating* the likes, dislikes and decisions of others (mechanized through predictive algorithms that identify what books, movies or political propaganda various populations are likely to appreciate).
- *Building trust relations among humans in bulk and at high speeds* in order to cut transaction costs associated with traditional 'trusted intermediaries' such as lawyers, bankers, state guarantors and so forth (mechanized using computer-intensive cryptographic and 'distributed ledger' technologies including blockchain, Bitcoin, and 'smart contracts' automating the human interpretive work traditionally necessary for contracts, private property, and commercial transactions and collapsing contract drafting, execution, payment, settlement, and enforcement into a single activity).[29]
- *Interpreting and enforcing welfare, labour and credit law* (mechanized using computer systems such as India's Aadhaar system, which automatically determines citizens' entitlements using stores of biometric and demographic data, or China's reputation-scoring system).
- *Building and exercising trust among scientists and their apparatuses* (mechanized via scientific discovery machines such as BACON).[30]
- *Building and practicing respect between human and nonhuman beings* (mechanized through artificial intelligences grafted onto agricultural fields, forests and animals to monitor and care for them, a la 'precision' or 'digital' agriculture and 'self-owning forests').[31]

- *Playing, teasing, messing around, formulating metaphors* and so forth (mechanized via, for example, care-home or therapeutic robots such as Pepper, Chapit, or Zora; prospective sex robots; champion chess or Go programmes such as AlphaZero; or software for producing art works).[32]

This new wave of automation has been facilitated by an unprecedented 'perfect storm' bringing together three technical advances into a powerful synergistic package. One is 'deep learning' software that can continuously teach itself what algorithms or recipes are best at predicting whatever it wants to predict, assuming it is fed enough data (a newfangled instance of 'machines making machines'). Another is computerized public surveillance, Application Programming Interfaces, CAPTCHAs (Completely Automated Public Turing Tests to Tell Computers and Humans Apart), online quizzes, and other labour capture mechanisms for the construction and continuous augmentation of the requisite enormous libraries or stocks of digitized bits of information out of un-digitized flows of human culture – for example, labeled and encoded JPEG images or sentence and sentence-pairs coded as series of ones and zeros. Included are devices through which image-recognition software or Google Translate parasitize the voluntary, almost unconscious linguistic work of hundreds of millions of smartphone owners exchanging gossip or snapshots on Facebook or other platforms. A third ingredient is the big increases in computer processing speed and capacity that make it possible to use deep learning algorithms to convert these growing mountains of 'big data' into cheap, accurate, micro-targeted predictions in breathtakingly short times, as well as carry out the advanced cryptographic operations necessary for automated-trust electronic currencies like Bitcoin.

This trifecta of innovations has helped reawaken ambitions to automate not just this or that particular occupation, and not just this or that specialized interpretive skill, but living labour as such, to the extent that computer science prophets like Andrew Ng of Baidu and Stanford refer to AI as 'the new electricity', while *The Economist* sees digitized data as 'the new oil'.[33] Interpretation machines are being groomed both as a new 'infrastructure' that will eventually become a taken-for-granted background of enhanced capitalist activity across the globe and as a separate economic sector that can be hived off from others, much as an 'energy sector' was hived off in the twentieth century. Transcending garden-variety automation that takes place piecemeal in specific industries, interpretation machines are seen as capable of making ineluctable inroads into white-collar, pink-collar, blue-collar and no-collar employment across the board.[34] Trust machines, for example, in the eyes of libertarian techno-visionaries like Nick Szabo and the shadowy blockchain inventor known as Satoshi Nakamoto, could drastically reduce capital's need not only for bankers and lawyers but also for courts, regulators, notaries public, auditors, registrars, portfolio managers, real estate agents, shipping clerks, credit scorers, insurers, police, and whole layers of the accounting and nature conservation professions and much of the state itself, slashing transaction costs everywhere.[35] Combined with search engines, they could eliminate whole layers of human-infested back-office operations and make it economical to register, privatize, monetize and make globally visible and exchangeable the tiniest and most exotic bits of property, ranging from the natural germicide produced by a species of Amazon frog to the informally-held rights to half a hectare of a slum settlement in Kenya or the individual debt of a street seller in Mumbai. Through automated verification and settlement, it could also speed up the transfer of goods through global trade corridors spanning numerous frontiers. At the same time, machines recognizing changes in risk information worldwide could feed data into millions of automatically self-adjusting individual smart insurance contracts in real time, supposedly 'rationalizing' and reducing underwriting firms' exposure to high-risk customers. Wayfinding machines, in addition, could automate away the labour of lorry and delivery drivers as well as a range of logistics and transport workers of other kinds.

Intensified mechanization of recognition, search, anticipation and wayfinding also opens up possibilities of further automating what Ursula Huws and others have identified as 'consumption labour'.[36] Once shoppers' constituent skills of recognizing needs, browsing, interpreting and responding to advertisements, evaluating products for their suitability, ordering, paying, and finding their way homeward are broken down and the divided labour duly farmed out to interpretation devices, consumers can be mechanized into tens of millions of 'virtual yous'[37] that are sold to corporations. Machines capable of simultaneously forecasting the reactions to specific commodities of that many separate individuals accurately and cheaply enough would be able not just to suggest items for a customer's consideration – as already happens – but also to ship them to her before she has ordered them without much risk of their being angrily returned. That would uncover and eliminate one more impediment to high-velocity circulation. Interpretation machines can also partially automate 'prosumption' labour – the unpaid, informal work of consumers or voters who volunteer feedback, personal data, design ideas, reviews, and geographical knowledge to corporations in ways that benefit their production, sales and circulation strategies.

THE OLD IN THE NEW

It's easy to be dazzled by the scale and scope of such efforts to mechanize the most generic forms of living labour into dead labour crystallized into amalgams of giant data centres, neural network software, global fibre and satellite links, and smartphones and other worldwide sensors by the billions. But as capital leans into its 'informational' turn, powered by massive state involvement, it's crucial to be clear that it isn't leaving any of its fundamental contradictions behind. As Dan Schiller observes, the 'specificity of digital capitalism' needs to be set '*within* abiding structural trends and historical crisis tendencies rather than in a putative break with them or an evolution out of them'.[38]

First, it should be noted in passing that there's nothing new about the mechanization of interpretation as such, but only about the extent, speed and stealth of its advances over the past ten years or so. For centuries, capital has been isolating and automating one or another of the smaller interpretive skills embedded in labour and the physical tools and devices attached to it, partly to reduce its vulnerability to small groups of workers in command of big or dangerous machines. From the mid-eighteenth century, mechanical steam engine 'governors' were devised to 'recognize' and regulate the speed of steam flow as no human mediator could, helping to inaugurate an era of the machine as an 'infomechanical relay between flows of energy and information'.[39] Steam power in turn made it possible for other devices such as textile machines to 'categorize', 'measure', and respond to variations in their own inputs with superhuman rapidity. Thermostats (or what the nineteenth century prophet of labour control Andrew Ure, one of their developers, called 'heat governors')[40] could 'sense' more accurately than any human how hot something was, and 'communicate' their findings more quickly to furnaces or boilers schooled in how to 'read' them. Nineteenth century Jacquard looms using punched cards to mechanize the craft of human silk weavers rapidly 'translated' symbol types into one another, speeding up production of luxury cloth 24 times and undercutting workers' bargaining power.[41] Similar interpretation skills were later automated in census machines, artillery targeting systems, 'numerical control' for machine tools, and word processors and DVD players. Twentieth century autopilots were meanwhile 'taught' to 'observe' and modify aircraft responses faster than any human pilot could.

Second, today's interpretation machines follow closely the pattern of older industrial machines in that they make little pretence of doing just what their human 'models' do. Strictly speaking, they don't duplicate skills. Instead, they identify, isolate, and activate facsimiles of particular *fragments* of human action, amplifying and reproducing them repetitively at high speeds in order to produce uniform outputs in bulk, using an omnibus 'energy' organized by thermodynamics. The golem or witch's apprentice thus created then in turn has to be treated to constant, meticulous oversight by humans employing other skills – including care and cleaning skills – in order to produce, preserve, or circulate surplus value. Capacities to perform this new work also tend to be devalued and degraded as further frontiers of capitalist renewal are sought.

For example, the nineteenth century spinning machine was never designed to do everything that a human spinner did when she was spinning – improvise on certain learned routines of eye, finger, thread, wood, and arm; keep in mind the needs of the market or the home; be sociable; sustain a family or community; and so on. It did something much more limited and rigidly repetitive. What it did was also physically more dangerous, insofar as it was driven by quantities of force that the individual artisan wouldn't have known what to do with, and that required the thoroughgoing reorganization of landscapes to extract and transport machine-ready energy before transforming it, via manufacturing, into unusable waste forms. The spinning machine's human tenders, in turn, had to alter the use of their own interpretive abilities in order to adapt to the simple, accelerated rhythms of the whole assemblage and keep the high-powered contraption running, drawing on reserves of resilience that were often quickly worn out.

By the same token, what a twenty-first century interpretation machine such as Google Translate does results in an output of sentences, but is not the 'same thing' that human interpreters do. Instead, via the internet, Google Translate gloms onto billions of digitized data strings representing sentences – products of oceans of the living work of past and present generations of humans and nonhumans. It then subjects this 'big data' to computer operations that are even more endlessly repetitive than the spinning machine's in order to mass-produce cheap predictions – probabilistically rather than linguistically[42] – about which sentence-to-sentence equivalences would likely be most acceptable to human translators, especially those working in international business. And it constantly corrects its own procedures on the basis of new digitizations provided free of charge by users of electronic devices around the world. Facebook's own 'prediction engine', meanwhile, 'ingests trillions of data points every day, trains thousands of models – either offline or in real time – and then deploys them to the server fleet for live predictions'. In 2018, Facebook's assembly line manufactured more than six million of these 'prediction products' per second, or over 189 trillion saleable commodities per fiscal year.[43] Again, such interpretation machines do not do

– and are not intended to do – what, say, human planners do when trying to foresee the future. For one thing, they produce a much greater number of predictions. They transform past living labour into a frozen or 'dead' form much more quickly, extensively and accurately than any division of labour using manual rule sets. Their predictions are also generally better than any human's prediction of his or her own behaviour. In addition, they are capable of surprising observers with leaps that look 'unprogrammed', as both Charles Babbage and Alan Turing had already demonstrated in their day.[44] But they also do not exercise the Wittgensteinian skill of 'going on' that is one distinguishing feature of living labour – a difference that becomes painfully obvious when they go into a 'tailspin' owing to unexpected events such as the Covid-19 pandemic.[45]

Google Translate's relationship to thermodynamic energy is also similar to that of the spinning machine. With its giant, publicly-subsidized server centres, transmission networks and big data-trained natural language processing models, Google Translate too needs quantities of electricity that human interpreters wouldn't know what to do with, again demanding professional management of humans and nature in fossil-fuel extraction zones.[46] Overall, digital energy consumption is growing by about nine per cent annually worldwide, with the carbon emissions of blockchain 'trust machines' alone already on the order of those of a medium-sized country;[47] the energy cost of a single blockchain transaction mediated by the leading firm Ethereum was reported in April 2019 to be 35,000 watt-hours, compared to the less-mechanized Visa figure of 1.69 watt-hours.[48] Partly as a result, interpretation machines' proliferating wastes, like the wastes of nineteenth century industry, call for further armies of compensated and uncompensated human and nonhuman clean-up workers that were simply not required for the work of human spinners or translators.[49] Over time, these workers too can be expected to 'wear out', in the sense that, for whatever reason, they can no longer deliver the services capital requires cheaply enough.[50] As with the spinning machine, there is no activity that stays constant through the process of 'being mechanized'; indeed, the whole world is changed.

These parallels need some sharpening. The capitalist process of splitting up human activity and energizing stereotyped repetitions of the fragments – visible in both the spinning machine and in Google Translate – did not emerge out of nowhere. For Charles Babbage, the inventor of the Analytical Engine and one of artificial intelligence's nineteenth-century grandparents, industrial machines were just a way of carrying forward the earlier mission of divisions of labour. This was to decompose the integral ability sets embodied in craftspeople, particularly those with what Babbage called 'higher' or 'mental' skills, into 'simpler', dumber, more quantifiable, surveillable, and supervisable components. The advantages were multiple. Measurable quantities of purchasable task could be precipitated out of the amorphous labour power confronting the capitalist. Bosses could more easily avoid paying for anything in excess of the 'precise quantity' of 'skill or force' that they deemed necessary for any manufacturing process that it was their prerogative to identify, describe, and subdivide. The costs and lost time of apprenticeship could be reduced. The supply of workers competing for the less 'skilled' jobs that resulted could be increased, making them cheaper and more replaceable and dispensable. Opaque webs of relationships and duties among the workforce could be transformed, simplified and redistributed along the lines of a hub-spoke structure, with 'master manufacturers' at the disciplinary centre – a profit-panopticon linkage that was later developed in a very different way in 'dataveillance' or what Shoshana Zuboff calls 'surveillance capitalism'.[51] As far as possible, 'intelligence' and its ownership could be centralized in the same way, as Taylorism and managerialism continued to attempt to do in the twentieth century. Each fragment of the split-up activities could then supposedly be replaced by machine motions, moderating the possible increase in demand for the augmented supply of 'unskilled' labour and further sharpening the distinction between bosses at the centre and workers around the periphery.[52] The machine would become, in the words of Babbage's brilliant colleague Ada Lovelace, 'the being which executes the conceptions of intelligence'[53] possessed by the master. It would 'consign class struggle on the shop floor to the rank of an unscientific superstition', as Caffentzis paraphrases Andrew Ure.[54] Surplus value could be conceptualized as flowing from machines that were the product of capital's own digitized intelligence combined with steam power, rather than from the uncompensated exercise of workers' biologically- and socially-evolved ability to 'go on' in a non-mechanical fashion on the basis of just a few examples.

Marx, Babbage's 'most penetrating London reader',[55] understood that this fantasy about how surplus was produced had already restructured much of Victorian reality. Accordingly, he put in a lot of effort to 'traverse' it, to borrow the Lacanian term.[56] Marx acknowledged that the productive move from combinations of *trades* (along with various trades' tools) to combinations of centralizable *processes* (along with industrial machines) increased the 'number of workers who [could] be exploited simultaneously using the same capital' and reduced the labour time necessary for the reproduction of labour power, in effect again cutting the wage bill, undermining workers' bargaining power and independence, and freeing up capital for other uses. But he also took care to emphasize that the new mechanized hub-spoke structure was not static but dynamic, and was irremediably rent by contradiction. The 'surplus population' of living labour generated by machinery did not simply increase linearly and without limit in proportion to the spread of machinery. Machinery itself was dynamic – if it 'continually casts out adult workers', he said, it also 'needs to expand continuously ... in order merely to "re-absorb" them, to draw them back in'.[57] The mechanized 'transformation of guild masters and their journeymen into capitalists and wage labourers', Marx added, should not be confused with a universal, long-term 'displacement of the wage labourers themselves by the application of capital and scientific knowledge'.[58] More machines and the associated tendency of the rate of profit to fall intermittently pushed capital toward renewed demands for masses of living (including reproductive) labour in one or another zone of the system, via the transformation of value into price,[59] regardless of how capital construed labour's 'skill' and 'intelligence'.

It's here that the non-incidental role of thermodynamics in the capitalist projects of both the nineteenth and the twenty-first centuries needs to be re-emphasized. As Marx noted, it was the growth of the division of labour that invited a 'mightier moving power than that of man', not the other way around. That 'moving power' – a generic, superhuman force making possible the widespread and extremely regular repetition, at extremely high speeds, of the stereotyped, 'dumb' subroutines of human action that divisions of labour had already split apart and made more measurable, predictable and disciplinable – took the form of the new, commensurated 'energy' that emerged in the late eighteenth and nineteenth centuries. This new 'energy' – organized by thermodynamics and virtually synonymous with a systematic, productive reorganization of landscapes around a logic of degradation[60] – was essential in turn in enabling capital to subject the skills of still more enclosure-dispossessed workers, whose labour-power could now be easily bought by property owners, to centralized disassembly, reorganization and control, facilitating 'combined labour' (or what Marx somewhat confusingly called 'simple cooperation') on ever more populous factory floors.[61] Just as a complete visualization of the spinning machine would have to take in not only children dodging in and out among its rapidly-rotating bobbins and cotton plantation slaves lifting hoes, but also coal miners crouching in countless stuffy underground chambers, so too a complete visualization of today's interpretation machine would need to encompass not only data centre staff replacing tensor processing units and DRC miners enduring abuse, but also interruptions to the flows of major rivers worldwide.[62]

One confirmation of the enduring nature of these features of capitalist mechanization is that the scare quotes around those intentional verbs that were used above to describe nineteenth century thermostats or steam engine governors ('recognize', 'translate', 'measure', 'know') evidently need to be kept firmly in place when describing what twenty-first century interpretation machines do. It may be true that early AI critics like Hubert Dreyfus and John Haugeland turned out to be completely wrong to suggest that a computer could never beat a world chess champion, make a transcendently original move in the game of Go, or deliver a beautifully balanced translation of a page of Proustian prose.[63] It is also true, conversely, that AI visionaries like Demis Hassabis of Google's DeepMind or Robert Mercer, the machine translation pioneer who became a billionaire hedge fund manager and financier of the Donald Trump and Brexit campaigns, turned out to be absolutely right in seeing the future of interpretation devices not in attempts to encode the experience of experts into machines,[64] nor in getting machines to work just like the human mind, but rather in letting artificial neural networks 'do it their way'[65] via incessant, energy-intensive crunching of gigantic masses of data that (the chess and Go examples perhaps excepted) are continually produced by labour-intensive processes carried out all over the world. But neither the incidental failures of vision of the likes of Dreyfus or Haugeland nor the triumphs of the likes of Hassabis or Mercer changes the reality that the prospect of 'replacing' living human labour in the process of capital accumulation – and thereby removing the contradiction that Marx identified between living and dead labour – remains so distant that it is virtually irrelevant to foreseeable strategies of anti-capitalist resistance. Successful machine simulations of various isolated fragments or manifestations of human interpretive skills – ranging from putting a name to a face to competing at Jeopardy at championship level – have only highlighted the fact that a working facsimile of what is called artificial *general* intelligence (AGI) – or even just a machine that could hold up its end of a wide-ranging conversation, convincingly reproduce the performance of a single neuron, sustain what David Graeber calls the 'baseline communism' that underpins worker coordination,[66] or participate in Marx's 'simple cooperation' – is still a very long way off. So far, the capabilities of interpretation machines are not all that much less 'bitty' than those of the old steam engine governors; the contrast isn't as marked as it may look between the nineteenth century spinning machine, which could only wastefully repeat one stereotyped shard of past human actions again and again, and the deep learning-trained Alexa robot.

INTERPRETIVE LABOUR TODAY

The upshot is that so-called artificial intelligence isn't any closer to making living labour obsolete than nineteenth century industrial machines were. Nor was that ever the point of either mechanization movement, no matter how loudly capitalist ideologists might occasionally assert the contrary. Capital doesn't really need, and probably couldn't afford, machinic labourers that perform the functions of well-rounded, versatile interpreters.[67] It can already get plenty of the human variety at bargain prices. Thus computer scientist Hamid R. Ekbia and anthropologist Bonnie Nardi compile evidence showing that recent artificial intelligence advances, instead of representing an incremental step toward full automation, exemplify a more complex strategy of *heteromation*, or 'extraction of economic value from low-cost or free labor in computer-mediated networks' so dispersed and anonymizing that workers can be 'treated as nonpersons' – one more wheeze devised by capital for coping with the tendency of the rate of profit to fall.[68] 'Automation vs. human labour is a false dichotomy', affirm Microsoft's Mary L. Gray and Siddharth Suri in a comparative study of how Silicon Valley's new, supposedly 'intelligent' devices require the incessant 'ghost work' of millions of human assistants that remain a good deal shrewder in most respects.[69] Sociologist Harry Collins, an acute long-time student of grassroots technical practice, reckons that a machine of 'human-like intelligence' is simply not on the cards 'unless it is fully embedded in normal human society' in a way that is unlikely to be the 'result of incremental progress based on current techniques'.[70] Even Geoffrey Hinton, the revered computer scientist known as the 'godfather of deep learning', who clings stubbornly to the idea that 'unsupervised' machine learning free of inputs from living human labour will someday become possible,[71] no longer believes that 'true' AI can be achieved by continuing to develop current energy- and data-intensive simulation techniques.[72]

In what ways, exactly, do twenty-first century interpretation machines, like nineteenth century industrial machines, function merely to redistribute, transform, and extend the exploitation of living labour rather than progressively eliminate it? It is not merely that incessant human interpretive work continues to be fundamental for Graeber's 'baseline communism' among workers – that cooperative, empathetic interaction without which no office or supply chain could operate.[73] It is not merely that it continues to be essential for the automation-resistant unpaid care and reproductive labour that has always propped up industrial capital;[74] or for the 'reading of the land' practiced by nearly all farmers; or for the thinking that 'solves new problems for which there are no routine solutions'; or for the type of communication that involves 'persuading, explaining, and in other ways conveying a particular interpretation of information'.[75] Nor is it only that the same type of activity is central to the performance of the satellite armies of pieceworkers, outworkers, or contract labourers that have historically finished by hand in their homes what machines and their human attendants within factory walls could not accomplish, or could not accomplish cheaply enough;[76] or indispensable in what Marx called the 'intermediary' or 'preliminary' work tending the colonial plantations or running the mines extracting the masses of raw materials that such factories have so voraciously consumed.[77]

It is also that creative, living interpretive labour continues to be fundamental to the minute-to-minute and week-to-week productive actions of specific machines themselves. Nineteenth century spinning jennies required 'both mental and physical finesse' from the child workers 'deftly moving from one heavily vibrating machine to the next' to reach their hands between moving spools to clear debris.[78] Locomotives demanded complex recognition, interaction, and wayfinding skills from every individual in the teams of labourers charged with cleaning them out and keeping them running. In order to be able to reorganize, dismantle, and mechanize trade skills with any success via divisions of labour and fossil-fuelled heat engines, capital has always needed, at the same time, to harness more and more of this *unmechanized* interpretive labour. Even at the level of their most minute motions, industrial machines would have simply broken down or gone feral, rendering them useless to capital, had they not constantly been supplied with large local and distant injections of fresh living labour to mind the controls, improvise interfaces, do repairs, deal with unpredictable events, manage updates, recognize and absorb wastes, undertake clean-ups, manage emergency shutdowns, cope with accidents, digitize and de-digitize, tend raw material flows, meet with bankers, enforce racial and gender divides, and so forth. The more machines capital enlisted, the more workers it needed that were *not* machines. The more dead labour it had on hand, the more living labour it required.

So, too, the twenty-first century artificial intelligence systems that make possible Facebook or Uber phone apps are dependent on an 'always-on labour pool' – accessible via the online Application Programming Interfaces of on-demand 'microwork' labour market platforms such as Amazon's Mechanical Turk – to provide human input to censor texts, update image databases, double-check photo IDs and so on.[79] The Clearview facial recognition machine couldn't work without the unsung, unpaid work of humans labeling billions of images on the internet in return for networking privileges.[80] Putatively fully-automated, blockchain-based 'smart contracts' turn out to require volumes of the creative human work of observation and legal interpretation if they are not to implode,[81] while the PARO robot (shaped like a cuddly baby harp seal), which cost $15 million to develop, requires constant help from humans, both staff and patients, if it is to have a chance of effectively doing its job mechanizing care of dementia sufferers in homes for the elderly.[82] Facebook's algorithms for manufacturing saleable predictions designed to cut circulation time by increasing click-through rates for targeted advertising – no matter how many tens of thousands of servers stacked in giant refrigerated data centres are enlisted to execute them – would meanwhile grind to a halt without the billions of hours of human interpretation work done by its users every day when they like, comment, scroll through status updates or merely find their way from one neighbourhood to another.[83] While Facebook currently has around 48,000 workers who have signed conventional labour contracts in exchange for wages, it can also tap the labour of more than 2.6 billion users who have consented to terms of service according to which their routine, living data-processing labour is swapped for platform interaction services. No surprise, then, that the market capitalization/workforce ratio at Facebook is $20.5 million per paid employee, compared to General Motors' figure of $231,000.[84] Whatever the century, interpretive skills continue to make up the common core of living labour under capitalism.

The main difference between the two centuries in this respect is that, thanks to those 'deep learning' algorithms, fast processors, and advanced surveillance technologies combined with cheap thermodynamic energy, capital can now collect directly, and on a daily basis, many more of the quintillions of tiny moments of the exercise of the integrated interpretive skills that the global human population acquired as babies and young children, and, by transforming them into big data, add them to the 'elements of profit' that Marx wrote of in the first volume of *Capital* more than 150 years ago. (Quite suddenly it has become possible for capitalists to view conventional trust-building work, say, as 'slow' and 'inefficient', a perceptible 'fetter' or 'bottleneck' in production, circulation and consumption.) Just as thermodynamically-energized industrial machines helped spread the wage labour relation across the world beginning in the nineteenth century,[85] so twenty-first century interpretation machines are enabling and necessitating recruitment not only of more wage work but also of the deeper regions of unpaid human labour. What the *Wall Street Journal* was already hailing in 2012 as 'largest unpaid workforce in history'[86] practices no single occupation, but must be on the job at all times if Jeff Bezos, Eric Schmidt, and Jack Ma are to continue to get richer. In a more thoroughgoing and fine-grained way than it could achieve merely via the continuing reorganization, exploitation, and degradation of thin layers of apprenticeship-inculcated trade skills, capital is now able to feed directly from the bigger cake of billions of 'lifetime[s] of being a human person from infancy on: of memories that begin in childhood, ... of the development of habits of observation, compassion, empathy and sympathy',[87] and much, much more. As clearly as in the nineteenth century, the 'preservation and thus also the reproduction of the value of products of past labour is *only* the result of their contact with living labour'.[88]

One often overlooked type of living human labour sustaining the twenty-first century wave of mechanization of interpretation is the labour of making this labour itself invisible. This 'invisibilization' work is not confined to the tasks that IT ideologues continue to perform in denigrating the skills of women, colonized peoples, the working class, or ordinary humans generally. What poses a special challenge to labour movements is that this invisibilization work is also done by those humans themselves as, minute by minute, they voluntarily attribute their ability to perform living labour to machines.[89] Already in the nineteenth century, Marx had noted that industrial capital required that workers be placed in a situation in which they ended up crediting industrial machines with the 'intellectual faculties' of the workers themselves. This business model is being greatly augmented today with the spread of advanced interpretation machines. Thus in the 1980s, as sociologist Harry Collins notes, when cheap pocket calculators 'multiplied' 7/11 by 11 and 'deduced' the answer to be 6.9999996, their human operators would reflexively reinterpret the result as 7 – yet still assume that the machine was doing all the work.[90] In 2017, users of automated Google directions across irregularly laid-out cities did the same when the machines confronted crossings where streets jog slightly before continuing along slightly different lines. Google tended to tell users to 'turn' on the cross street and continue for a couple of metres, and then 'turn' back to rejoin the street that they had in fact never left. Users had to put in a bit of impromptu but unacknowledged interpretation work to 'correct' what was then the machine's difficulty in simulating understanding of open-ended concepts like *turn* and *just go straight through the intersection.* (Any such 'bug' can in principle be eliminated with the application of more data, more algorithms and more energy, of course, but new bugs will then inevitably pop up to take their place.) By the same token, talk about 'driverless' cars typically ignores the fact that their development has been highly dependent on the labour-intensive 'reconstruction of Mountain View, California to be a safe place for these vehicles to navigate', to quote one artificial intelligence expert.[91] Similarly, an automated banking service reaching out to millions of poorer clients in Brazil turned out to rely on the street-corner merchants who mediated between them and the system's computer terminals, and whose low- or zero-cost everyday interpretive labour in collaboration with customers vanished into 'software' in the eyes of central managers.[92] In such examples, only the computation is visible as, to adapt Marx's words, 'the human steps to the side'.

As Collins observes, computer and cellphone interfaces are not there to get rid of this kind of living labour. They are there to hide it, by finding mechanical means for exploiting only the most everyday, unthinking interpretive skills that nearly everybody possesses. In helping to make users unaware of the growing unwaged living labour they're putting into their dealings with interpretation machines, well-engineered interfaces such as Windows, computer mice, internet browsers, and predictive text carry forward the capitalist mission of keeping uncompensated living work out of sight while burnishing the fetish of the self-running machine and the 'full automation' ideology that claims that machines are on an asymptotic approach toward 'replacing' humans in capital accumulation. Like the nineteenth century factory, artificial intelligence interfaces constitute an apparatus to keep workers 'ignorant of the secret springs which [regulate] the machine and to repress the general powers of their minds' so 'that the fruits of their own labors [are] by a hundred contrivances taken away from them'.[93] As Jason W. Moore has pithily put it, 'the condition that some work is valued is that most work is not'.[94]

Yet human workers, as George Caffentzis writes, 'can always kill capital in its most embodied and vulnerable form: the machine'.[95] Needing, seeking and often creating forces that it cannot quite control and commons that it encloses at its peril, capital can never keep the tools of its repeated un-doings entirely away from the hands of its resisters. That is as much a part of the politics of the new interpretation machines as it is of the politics of the old industrial ones. If risks of rapid depreciation are not recognized, IT firms' investment in the constant capital of (for example) server centres, big data storage, fibre lines, sensor processing units and deep learning architectures can become the 'source of an enormous dis-accumulation'.[96]

What are the specific contradictions afflicting interpretation mechanization and how might a historical perspective help popular movements work on them from the inside? Some contradictions are obvious and primary. One of them stems from the fact that capital's new interpretation machines inevitably reinforce its much longer-standing assaults on the life conditions of the world majority: their soils, their water, their relationships with plants and animals, their abilities to evade state surveillance and repression and regenerate commons. The poisonous symbiosis between interpretation mechanization and unsustainable energy and mineral development, for example, is coming up against growing revolts in 'sacrifice zones' of extraction and infrastructure development, whose inhabitants may well not be especially exercised about the specific exploitation of 'ghost workers' tending interpretation machines. So, too, the frontiers of 'iSlave' labour required to operate profitable IT hardware assembly zones can be expected to recede further, precipitating other crises. Then there are the repressed demands that occasionally burst out as the flip side of capital's efforts to invisibilize new stretches of living labour, as well as already-visible reactions against the increasingly-mechanized surveillance that forms a part of business, military, and bureaucratic plans alike – all evolving together with capital's obligatory displacement efforts.

Some contradictions may be more obscure, for example that between capital's perennial need for living Wittgensteinian skills of being able to 'go on' and its simultaneous assault on them via interpretation mechanization. As Shoshana Zuboff has documented, surveillance capital finds itself in a constant race to improve what she aptly calls its 'prediction products' – in her words, to make 'prediction approximate observation' more and more closely.[97] That entails widening and diversifying the digital architectures through which surplus from the worldwide exercise of Wittgensteinian abilities is extracted, unconsciously aiming at the contradictory 'ideal' of engineering that working public itself to the point of becoming so machine-like that the surplus dries up. The process is analogous to the one James C. Scott famously describes in *Seeing like a State*, in which a forestry science bent on extracting the maximum sedimented biological and social energies from trees moves from classifying and quantifying the diverse contents of existing forests more precisely and extensively to actively engineering them into predictable monoculture rows, with the result that the energies of the soil and the trees themselves become depleted and predictability blows up.[98] This type of contradictory dynamic, during which human actions and capacities are never stable, waiting around for machines to mimic them, but are constantly undergoing changes themselves, complicates political strategizing in the current moment. What happens to Mountain View as it is re-engineered to make its 'autonomous vehicles' look more autonomous? What happens to the law when, as Lauren Henry Scholz puts it, so many 'algorithms are introduced in institutional decision-making' that 'individuals outsource their valuation processes' to them?[99] When machines pump out millions of individually tailored Trump memes to audiences that – for a time – respond by becoming more uniform, isolated and predictable?

When programming skills themselves erode as, increasingly, software makes software? When capital's 'metric fixation' becomes turbocharged to the point that counterproductive tendencies become overwhelming?[100]

Which contradictions will bite, and when, how, and where, remains to some extent an open question. There are, moreover, some intrinsic counter-resistance characteristics almost baked into interpretation mechanization: the near-effortlessness of much of the interpretation work harvested by the big IT firms, which 'comes naturally' to almost all human adults; the resulting, almost 'built-in' invisibility of the work and the ease with which workers themselves attribute it to machines; as well as the extreme global dispersal of the workforce tending interpretation machines. Any serious evaluation of the future of resistance, however, is likely to need to take careful account of how today's interpretation machines fit into capital's longer history.

NOTES

I am grateful for comments from Hendro Sangkoyo, Soumitra Ghosh, Leo Panitch and Greg Albo.

1 For recent positive steps forward, see, for example, George Caffentzis, *In Letters of Blood and Fire: Work, Machines and the Crisis of Capitalism*, Oakland: PM Press, 2013; Andreas Malm, *Fossil Capital: The Rise of Steam Power and the Roots of Global Warming*, London: Verso, 2016; Matthew Huber, 'Energizing Historical Materialism: Fossil Fuels, Space and the Capitalist Mode of Production', *Geoforum*, 40(1), 2009, pp. 105-15; Cara New Daggett, *The Birth of Energy: Fossil Fuels, Thermodynamics and the Politics of Work*, Durham: Duke University Press, 2019; and Alf Hornborg, *The Power of the Machine: Global Inequalities of Economy, Technology and Environment*, Lanham, MD: AltaMira, 2001.

2 Carlo Vercellone, 'The Hypothesis of Cognitive Capitalism', paper presented at Historical Materialism Annual Conference, Birkbeck College and SOAS, London, 4-5 November 2005, p. 10, emphasis added.

3 Aaron Benanav, 'Automation and the Future of Work – 2', *New Left Review* 120(November/December), 2019, pp. 117-46, 117; 'Automation and the Future of Work – 1', *New Left Review* 119(September/October), 2019, pp. 5-38, 6. Among such theorists, whose genealogy stretches from characters in Dostoyevsky and Samuel Butler through 1950s and 1960s artificial intelligence pioneers such as John McCarthy, Herbert Simon, and Allen Newell, are Aaron Bastani, *Fully Automated Luxury Communism: A Manifesto*, Verso: London, 2019; Pedro Domingos, *The Master Algorithm*, New York: Basic, 2015; Martin Ford, *Rise of the Robots: Technology and the Threat of a Jobless Future*, New York: Basic Books, 2015; Nick Srnicek and Alex Williams, *Inventing the Future: Postcapitalism and a World Without Work*, London and New York 2015; Nick Dyer-Witheford et al., *Inhuman Power: Artificial Intelligence and the Future of Capitalism*, Pluto Books: London, 2019; Erik Brynjolfsson and Andrew McAfee, *The Second Machine Age: Work, Progress and Prosperity in a Time of Brilliant Technologies*, Norton: New York, 2014; Paul Mason, *Postcapitalism: A Guide to Our Future*, London: Penguin, 2015; Andrew

Yang, *The War on Normal People: The Truth About America's Disappearing Jobs and Why Universal Basic Income Is Our Future*, New York: Hachette, 2018; Nick Bostrom, *Superintelligence,* Oxford: Oxford University Press, 2014; Andy Stern, *Raising the Floor: How a Universal Basic Income Can Renew Our Economy and Rebuild the American Dream*, New York: Hachette, 2016; Peter Frase, *Four Futures: Life After Capitalism*, London: Verso, 2016; Ray Kurzweil, *The Singularity is Near*, New York: Viking, 2005; and Vitalik Buterin, 'DAOs, DACs, DAs and More: An Incomplete Terminology Guide', Ethereum blog, 6 May 2014, available at: blog.ethereum.org. For some of the likenesses between this 'automation discourse' and the recurring, contradictory capitalist fantasies of perpetual motion machines and 'circular economies', see Larry Lohmann, 'Blockchain Machines, Earth Beings and the Labour of Trust', Sturminster Newton: The Corner House, 2019, available at: www.thecornerhouse.org.uk.

4 This strategy has a long history, stretching from C. S. Peirce's use of the term *logical machine* in the nineteenth century to the computer scientist Mihai Nadin's insistence on *semiotic machine* in the twenty-first. See Peirce, 'Logical Machines', *American Journal of Psychology,* 1(1), 1887, pp. 165-70; Nadin, 'Semiotic Machine', *The Public Journal of Semiotics,* 1(1), 2007, pp. 57-75 and Winfried Nöth, 'Semiotic Machines', *Cybernetics and Human Knowing,* 9(1), 2002, pp. 5-21.

5 Simon Schaffer, 'Babbage's Intelligence', *Critical Inquiry,* 21(1), 1994, pp. 203-27; Schaffer, 'Babbage's Dancer and the Impresarios of Mechanism', in *Cultural Babbage: Technology, Time and Invention*, London: Faber, 1996, pp. 53-80.

6 Arthur W. Burks, ed., *The Collected Papers of Charles Sanders Peirce,* Vols. VII-VIII, Cambridge, MA: Harvard University Press, 1958, 7.362-366.

7 Matteo Pasquinelli recalls some of the longer history of left discussions around this point in 'On the Origins of Marx's General Intellect', *Radical Philosophy,* 2.06, Winter 2019, pp. 43-56. See also his 'Italian Operaismo and the Information Machine', *Theory, Culture and Society,* 32(3), 2015, pp. 49–68.

8 Hamid R. Ekbia and Bonnie Nardi, *Heteromation, and other Stories of Computers and Capitalism*, Cambridge, MA: MIT Press, 2017, p. 140.

9 Matteo Pasquinelli and Vladan Joler, 'The Nooscope Manifested: Artificial Intelligence as Instrument of Knowledge Extractivism', *Artificial Intelligence and Society*, forthcoming.

10 See, for example, Naoki Sakai, 'Translation', *Theory, Culture and Society,* 23(2-3), 2006., pp. 71-8; W.v.O. Quine, *Word and Object*, Cambridge: MIT Press, 1960; Donald Davidson, 'A Nice Derangement of Epitaphs', in Ernest Lepore, ed., *Truth and Interpretation: Perspectives on the Philosophy of Donald Davidson,* Oxford: Blackwell, 1989, pp. 433-46; Lydia He Liu, 'The Question of Meaning-Value in the Political Economy of the Sign', in Lydia H. Liu, ed., *Tokens of Exchange: The Problem of Translation in Global Circulations*, Durham: Duke University Press, 2000, pp. 13-41; Eduardo Viveiros de Castro, 'Perspectival Anthropology and the Method of Controlled Equivocation', *Tipití,* 2(1), 2004, pp. 3–22; Boaventura de Sousa Santos, 'The Future of the World Social Forum: The Work of Translation', *Development,* 48(2), 2005, pp. 15–22.

11 This second, specifically computational moment of reification or fetishization of meanings and beliefs was in fact pioneered in 1842 by Ada Lovelace in her editorial notes to her translation of L. F. Menabrea's *Sketch of the Analytical Engine Invented by Charles Babbage, Esq*., reprinted in B. V. Bowden, ed., *Faster than Thought: A Symposium on Digital Computing Machines*, London: Pitman and Sons, 1953, pp. 341-408. Lovelace,

together with Babbage, was inspired by the example of the dead labour (as Marx would have called it) frozen into the punched cards of the programmable Jacquard loom brought into service against Lyon silk-weavers in the early 1800s. (See James Essinger, *Jacquard's Web: How a Hand-Loom Led to the Birth of the Information Age*, Oxford: Oxford University Press, 2004.) Lovelace's reification was then built on in the 1930s and 1940s by Alan Turing in the UK, Claude Shannon in the US and many others. See Andrew Hodges, *Alan Turing: The Enigma*, Centenary Edition, Princeton: Princeton University Press, 2012; Claude Shannon and Warren Weaver, *The Mathematical Theory of Communication*, Urbana: University of Illinois Press, 1963.

12 Donald Davidson, *Inquiries into Truth and Interpretation*, Oxford University Press, Oxford, 2001; W.v.O. Quine, *Ontological Relativity and Other Essays*, New York: Columbia University Press, 1969; Daniel Dennett, *The Intentional Stance*, Cambridge, MA: MIT University Press, 1998; Hans-Johann Glock, 'On Safari with Wittgenstein, Quine and Davidson', in R. L. Arrington and H.J. Glock, eds., *Wittgenstein and Quine,* London: Routledge, 1996, pp. 144-72.

13 The classic explication of wayfinding (and its differences with navigating, mapping, and map-following) is Tim Ingold, 'To Journey Along a Way of Life: Maps, Wayfinding and Navigation', in Ingold, *The Perception of the Environment: Essays on Livelihood, Dwelling and Skill*, London: Routledge, 2000, pp. 219-42. 'One can no more know *in* places than travel in them,' Ingold writes (p. 229).

14 Walter Benjamin, 'Theses on the Philosophy of History', VI, 1940.

15 H. M. Collins, *Artificial Experts: Social Knowledge and Intelligent Machines*, Cambridge, MA: MIT Press, 1990; Hodges, *Alan Turing*; Jean Lave, *Cognition in Practice: Mind, Mathematics and Culture in Everyday Life*, Cambridge: Cambridge University Press, 1988.

16 Davidson, *Inquiries*; Lydia He Liu, *Clash of Empires: The Invention of China in Modern World-Making*, Cambridge, MA: Harvard University Press, 2006.

17 Paul Grice, *Studies in the Way of Words,* Cambridge, MA: Harvard University Press, 1991.

18 H. M. Collins, *Changing Order: Replication and Induction in Scientific Practice*, Chicago: University of Chicago Press, 1992; Steven Shapin, *A Social History of Truth: Civility and Science in Seventeenth-Century England*, Chicago: University of Chicago Press, 1994; Costas Lapavitsas, *Social Foundations of Markets, Money and Credit*, London: Routledge, 2003; Tim Ingold, 'From Trust to Domination: An Alternative History of Human–Animal Relations', in Ingold, *Perception*, pp. 61-76.

19 Johan Huizinga, *Homo Ludens: A Study of the Play Element in Culture*, London: Routledge, 1949.

20 Ludwig Wittgenstein, *Philosophical Investigations*, Translated by Elizabeth Anscombe, Oxford: Blackwell, 1953. See also Hannah Ginsborg, 'Wittgenstein on Going on', *Canadian Journal of Philosophy,* 50(1), 2020, pp. 1–17; Martin Kusch, *A Sceptical Guide to Meaning and Rules: Defending Kripke's Wittgenstein*, London: Routledge, 2006; and Harry M. Collins and Martin Kusch, *The Shape of Actions: What Humans and Machines Can Do*, Cambridge, MA: MIT Press, 1998.

21 The labour skills on this particular list heavily involve the use of human language. However, they sit on a longer spectrum of related abilities that does not suddenly come to an end at species boundaries, nor even organism or cellular boundaries. See, for example, Robert Rosen, *Anticipatory Systems. Philosophical, Mathematical, and Methodological Foundations*, New York: Springer, 2012; Mihai Nadin, 'Machine

Intelligence: A Chimera', *Artificial Intelligence and Society,* 34, 2019, pp. 215–42; Brian Massumi, *What Animals Teach Us about Politics,* Durham: Duke University Press, 2014; Robert W. Mitchell, ed. *Pretending and Imagination in Animals and Children,* Cambridge: Cambridge University Press, 2002; and Jason Hribal, *Fear of the Animal Planet: The Hidden History of Animal Resistance,* Oakland: AK Press, 2011. Nor are abilities to 'go on' centred exclusively on language even in humans, as witness the Soviet physiologist Nikolai Bernstein's work on 'repetition without repetition', which has been applied to the understanding of sports, music, medicine, and other activities; see Josef M. Feigenberg, *Nikolai Bernstein: From Reflex to the Model of the Future,* Translated by Julia Linkova, Zurich: LIT Verlag, 2014; and Mihai Nadin, ed., *Anticipation: Learning from the Past. The Russian/Soviet Contributions to the Science of Anticipation,* Cham: Springer, 2015. There's no space in this article to touch on the parallels between the contradictions that afflict the mid-twentieth century use of a fetishized notion of 'information' in interpretation machines and those that arise from its use in molecular biology and genetic engineering.

22 Arlie Hochschild, 'Love and Gold', in L. Ricciutelli, ed., *Women, Power and Justice: A Global Perspective,* London: Zed Books, 2005.

23 Karl Marx, *Capital,* Volume 3, Translated by D. Fernbach, London: Penguin Classics, 1991, pp. 270, 299.

24 Caffentzis, *In Letters of Blood and Fire,* p. 45.

25 Bing Liu, *Sentiment Analysis: Mining Opinions, Sentiments and Emotions,* Cambridge: Cambridge University Press, 2015; Shoshana Zuboff, *The Age of Surveillance Capitalism: The Fight for a Human Future at the New Frontier of Power,* New York: Public Affairs, 2019, p. 278.

26 'New Digital Supply Chains are Powered by Artificial Intelligence and Predictive Analytics', *Supply Chain, 24/7,* 17 December 2018, available at: 247customsbroker.com.

27 Kate Crawford and Trevor Paglen, 'Excavating AI: The Politics of Images in Machine Learning Training Sets', n.d., www.excavating.ai.

28 Joseph Weizenbaum, *Computer Power and Human Reason: From Judgement to Calculation,* New York: W. H. Freeman, 1976.

29 Lohmann, 'Blockchain Machines'.

30 Harry Collins, *Artifictional Intelligence,* Cambridge: Policy Press, 2018.

31 Lohmann, 'Blockchain Machines'; Catherine Tubb and Tony Seba, *Rethinking Food and Agriculture 2020-2030: The Second Domestication of Plants and Animals, the Disruption of the Cow, and the Collapse of Industrial Livestock Farming,* RethinkX, September 2019, www.rethinkx.com.

32 Leo Lewis, 'Can Robots Make up for Japan's Care Home Shortfall?', *Financial Times,* 17 October 2017.

33 Shana Lynch, 'Andrew Ng: Why AI Is the New Electricity', Insights by Stanford Business, 11 March 2017, available at: www.gsb.stanford.edu; Kiran Bhageshpur, 'Data is the New Oil – and that's a Good Thing', Forbes Technology Council, 15 November 2019, available at: www.forbes.com. See also David H. Autor, 'Why Are There Still So Many Jobs? The History and Future of Workplace Automation', *Journal of Economic Perspectives,* 29(3), 2015, pp. 3-30.

34 See, for example, the studies carried out by the Oxford Martin School Programme on the Future of Work, www.oxfordmartin.ox.ac.uk/future-of-work.

35 Lohmann, 'Blockchain Machines'.

36 Batya Weinbaum and Amy Bridges, 'The Other Side of the Paycheck: Monopoly Capital and the Structure of Consumption', *Monthly Review,* 28(3), 1976; Ursula Huws, 'The Underpinnings of Class in the Digital Age,' in Leo Panitch, Greg Albo, and Vivek Chibber, eds, *Socialist Register 2014*: *Registering Class*, London: Merlin Press, 2013, pp. 80-107.

37 Don Tapscott, 'Understand Blockchain in under 7 Minutes', Lloyds Bank, YouTube, 22 March 2018.

38 Dan Schiller, *Digital Depression: Information Technology and Economic Crisis*, Urbana: University of Illinois Press, 2014.

39 Pasquinelli, 'Italian Operaismo', p. 63, citing posthumously published work by Gilbert Simondon.

40 Andrew Ure, 'On the Thermostat or Heat Governor', *Philosophical Transactions of the Royal Society of London*, 1831.

41 Essinger, *Jacquard's Web*, p. 38.

42 Adam Geitgey, 'Text Classification is Your New Secret Weapon,' *Medium,* 15 August 2018.

43 Zuboff, *Surveillance Capitalism*, p. 254. See also 'Introducing FBLearner Flow: Facebook's AI Backbone', Facebook Code, 16 April 2018, available at: code.facebook.com/posts/1072626246134461/introducing-fblearnerflow-facebook-s-ai-backbone.

44 Simon Schaffer, 'Babbage's Dancer'. As early as the 1830s, Babbage was scoring public relations triumphs by demonstrating a machine that seemed to be able, as in one of Wittgenstein's imaginary rule-following games, to 'go on' in unexpected ways. Turing also stressed this phenomenon in his polemics of the 1940s and early 1950s.

45 Will Douglas Heaven, 'Our Weird Behavior during the Pandemic is Messing with AI Models', *MIT Technology Review*, 11 May 2020, available at: www.technologyreview.com. In the field of artificial intelligence, the disconnect between high-energy interpretation machine actions and low-energy Wittgensteinian 'going on' is continually being rediscovered and re-expressed in formulations that tend to differ only superficially: prediction is not observation (Zuboff, *Surveillance Capitalism*), decision is not choice (Weizenbaum, *Computer Power*), measurable, bit-string 'Shannon information' is not 'semantic information' (Daniel C. Dennett, *From Bacteria to Bach and Back: The Evolution of Minds,* London: Penguin, 2018), prediction is not anticipation (Nadin, 'Machine Intelligence'), computable games cannot satisfactorily model real-life situations (Espen Gaarder Haug and Nassim Nicholas Taleb, 'Why We Have Never Used the Black-Scholes-Merton Option Pricing Formula', 2007), and so forth.

46 For example, the CO2 emissions resulting just from the *training* (not the use) of a single deep-learning natural language processing model can run to 284 tonnes, five times that of a car driven for a lifetime (Emma Strubell, Ananya Ganesh and Andrew McCallum, 'Energy and Policy Considerations for Deep Learning in NLP', 57th Annual Meeting of the Association for Computational Linguistics, Florence, Italy, July 2019, available at: arxiv.org/abs/1906.02243). As with industrial mass production, machine translation is more efficient than human translation in high-bulk contexts. It has been estimated that it would take 100 megawatt-hours for properly trained humans to translate 500 million German sentences into English (half a million people working full time for nearly three weeks). By contrast, it took a typical neural machine translation system trained using data produced by the European Paracrawl project (paracrawl.eu) only seven megawatt-hours

over three days to do so (William Waites, 'Efficiency, Energy Use and Sustainability in Machine Translation', The Language Data Network, 20 December 2019, blog.taus.net/efficiency-energy-use-and-sustainability-in-machine-translation). If the only objective were to carry out a small job, however, as with conventional commodity production, it would be pointless to set up such an energy-hungry apparatus provided human translators were available.

47 Hugues Ferrebouf et al., 'Lean ICT: Towards Digital Sobriety', report for the Shift Project, Paris, March 2019, theshiftproject.org/en/article/lean-ict-our-new-report. Bitcoin's energy expenditures stem much more from cryptographic needs than do Google's or Facebook's, which are concentrated on computer processor workload and algorithm training together with the electronic surveillance of several billion data-processing volunteers.

48 Digiconomist, 'Ethereum Energy Consumption', n.d., digiconomist.net/ethereum-energy-consumption.

49 Nathan Ensmenger, 'The Environmental History of Computing', *Technology and Culture,* 59(4), 2018, pp. S7-S33; Mél Hogan, 'Data Flows and Water Woes: The Utah Data Center', *Big Data and Society*, July–December 2015, pp. 1–12; Camilo Mora, Randi Rollins, et al., 'Bitcoin Emissions Alone could Push Global Warming above 2°C', *Nature Climate Change,* 8, 2018, pp., 931-3; Jennifer Gabrys, *Digital Rubbish: A Natural History of Electronics*, Ann Arbor: University of Michigan Press, 2013. This is not to mention the waste of human beings and their talents described by Marx in the pages of *Capital* and now by, for example, Jack Linchuan Qiu in *Goodbye iSlave: A Manifesto for Digital Abolition,* Urbana: University of Illinois Press, 2016 and David N. Pellow and Lisa Sun-Hee Park in *The Silicon Valley of Dreams: Environmental Injustice, Immigrant Workers and the High-Tech Global* Economy, New York: New York University Press, 2002.

50 Jason W. Moore, *Capitalism in the Web of Life: Ecology and the Accumulation of Capital,* London: Verso, 2015.

51 Zuboff, *Surveillance Capitalism.*

52 Charles Babbage, *On the Economy of Machinery and Manufacture*, London: Charles Knight, 1832.

53 Quoted in Simon Schaffer, 'OK Computer', in M. Hagner, ed., *Ecce Cortex: Beitraege zur Geschichte des modernen Gehirns* Göttingen: Wallstein Verlag, 1999, pp. 254-85.

54 Caffentzis, *In Letters of Blood and Fire*, p. 153.

55 Schaffer, 'Babbage's Intelligence', p. 205.

56 Slavoj Zizek, *The Sublime Object of Ideology*, London: Verso, 1989.

57 Karl Marx, *Economic Manuscripts of 1861-63*, Part 3: Relative Surplus Value, available at: marxists.catbull.com.

58 Ibid.

59 Karl Marx, *Capital* Vol. 3, Translated by D. Fernbach, London: Penguin Classics, 1991, pp. 270 ff.

60 Larry Lohmann, 'Bioenergy, Thermodynamics and Inequalities', in M. Backhouse and F. Rodriguez, eds., *Bioeconomy and Global Inequalities: Knowledge, Land, Labor, Biomass, Energy, and Politics,* Palgrave Macmillan, forthcoming, www.thecornerhouse.org.uk; Larry Lohmann and Nicholas Hildyard, *Energy, Work and Finance*, Sturminster Newton: The Corner House, 2014, available at: www.thecornerhouse.org.uk.

61 Bruno Tinel, 'Why and How Do Capitalists Divide Labour? From Marglin and back again through Babbage and Marx', *Review of Political Economy,* 25(2), 2013, pp. 254-72. The new thermodynamic energy, of course, was also enlisted to accelerate the expansion of the very extractive frontier that helped make increased worker subjection possible. See Moore, *Capitalism in the Web of Life.*

62 Michelle Caruso-Cabrera and Ritika Shah, 'Why One Small Washington Town Has Seen so Many Bitcoin Miners Move in', *CNBC,* 11 January 2018; Mark Sounokonoko, 'China's Bitcoin Super Mines about to Power up for "Skyrocketing" Cryptocurrency', *Finance Nine,* 1 July 2019, available at: finance.nine.com.au.

63 Hubert L. Dreyfus, *What Computers Can't Do*, New York: Harper and Row, 1972; John Haugeland, *Artificial Intelligence: The Very Idea*, Cambridge, MA: MIT Press, 1985, pp. 173-6.

64 Jane Mayer, 'The Reclusive Hedge-Fund Tycoon Behind the Trump Presidency: How Robert Mercer Exploited America's Populist Insurgency', *The New Yorker,* 17 March 2017; David Silver, Thomas Hubert, Julian Schrittwieser et al., 'A General Reinforcement Learning Algorithm that Masters Chess, Shogi and Go through Self-Play', *Science,* 362(6419), 2018, pp. 1140-4.

65 David Runciman, 'AI', *London Review of Books,* 40(2), 25 January 2018.

66 David Graeber: *Debt: The First 5,000 Years*, Brooklyn: Melville House, 2011.

67 Peirce, 'Logical Machines'; Ted Chiang, *The Lifecycle of Software Objects*, Burton, MI: Subterranean Press, 2010; Ekbia and Nardi, *Heteromation,* p. 145.

68 Ekbia and Nardi, *Heteromation.*

69 Mary L. Gray and Siddharth Suri, *Ghost Work: How to Stop Silicon Valley from Building a New Global Underclass*, New York: Houghton Mifflin Harcourt, 2019.

70 Collins, *Artifictional Intelligence.*

71 Ibid. See also Anja Bechmann and Geoffrey C. Bowker, 'Unsupervised by Any Other Name: Hidden Layers of Knowledge Production in Artificial Intelligence on Social Media', *Big Data and Society,* January–June 2019: 1-11.

72 Axios, 'Artificial Intelligence Pioneer Says We Need to Start Over', *Communications of the Association for Computing Machinery*, 18 September 2018. Backpropagation, one key ingredient in current efforts to mechanize interpretation, simply 'does not capture the way the brain works', writes computer scientist Sridhar Mahadevan, one of Hinton's followers. See 'Why is Geoffrey Hinton Suspicious of Backpropagation and Wants AI to Start Over?', *Quora*, 21 September 2017, available at: www.quora.com.

73 Graeber, *Debt.*

74 Nancy Fraser, 'Behind Marx's Hidden Abode,' *New Left Review,* 86, 2014, pp. 55-72; Moore, *Capitalism in the Web of Life.*

75 Frank Levy and Richard Murnane, *The New Division of Labor: How Computers Are Creating the Next Job Market,* Princeton: Princeton University Press, 2004.

76 Gray and Suri, *Ghost Work*, pp. 38–63.

77 Marx, *Economic Manuscripts of 1861-63.*

78 Gray and Suri, *Ghost Work*, p. 43.

79 Ibid., pp. xxiii, 170.

80 'Clearview AI', Wikipedia; Clearview, 'Computer Vision for a Safer World', n.d., clearview.ai; Kashmir Hill, 'The Secretive Company That Might End Privacy as We Know It', *New York Times*, 18 January 2020.

81 Lohmann, 'Blockchain Machines'.

82 Ekbia and Nardi, *Heteromation*, pp. 131-40, 145. For an illuminating fictional account by a computer scientist of why the expense of hiring years of living human labour to train such 'companion machines' would discourage capitalist investment in them, see also Chiang, *Lifecycle*. 'Experience', concludes one of Chiang's characters, 'is algorithmically incompressible'.

83 The significance of machines that can tap this seemingly trivial form of work in bulk is exemplified in the finding of researchers at Microsoft's Bing search engine that 'even a 0.1 per cent accuracy improvement in our production [of predictions] would yield hundreds of millions of dollars in additional earnings' in delivering the most effective targeted ads to users (quoted in Zuboff, *The Age of Surveillance Capitalism*, p. 85). By 2015, 90 per cent of US smartphone owners used apps that required location data feeds (p. 221).

84 Scott Galloway, *The Four: The Hidden DNA of Amazon, Apple, Facebook and Google*, New York: Penguin, 2017, p. 6.

85 Huber, 'Energizing Historical Materialism', p. 110.

86 Doug Laney, 'To Facebook, You're Worth $80.95', *Wall Street Journal*, 3 May 2012.

87 Ekbia and Nardi, *Heteromation*, pp. 139-40.

88 Marx, *Capital,* Vol. 3, p. 524.

89 Collins and Kusch, *The Shape of Actions*; Hamid R. Ekbia, 'Heteronomous Humans and Autonomous Agents: Toward Artificial Relational Intelligence', in J. Fodor and I. Ruda, eds., *Beyond Artificial Intelligence: The Disappearing Human-Machine Divide. Topics in Intelligent Engineering and Infomatics*, vol. 9, Heidelberg: Springer, pp. 63-78.

90 Collins, *Artificial Experts*.

91 Nathan Ensmenger, presentation for Leverhulme Centre for the Future of Intelligence, 'The Future of Artificial Intelligence: Views from History', panel discussion at Cambridge University, 29 November 2018, available at: www.youtube.com.

92 Ekbia and Nardi, *Heteromation*, pp. 140-45.

93 William Thompson, *An Inquiry Into the Principles of the Distribution* of *Wealth Most Conducive to Humane Happiness Applied to the Newly Proposed System of Voluntary Equality of Wealth*, London: Longman, 1824, quoted in Pasquinelli, 'On the Origins', p. 50.

94 Jason W. Moore, ' Endless Accumulation, Endless (Unpaid) Work?', *Occupied Times,* 29 April 2015.

95 Caffentzis, *In Letters of Blood and Fire*, p. 46.

96 Ibid. Tensor processing units are an example of a hardware advance motivated by the needs of neural network machine learning. Other processor advances have been spurred by blockchain's trust-mechanization requirements.

97 Zuboff, *Surveillance Capitalism*.

98 James C. Scott, *Seeing Like a State: How Certain Schemes to Improve the Human Condition Have Failed*, New Haven: Yale University Press, 1999.

99 Lauren Henry Scholz, 'Algorithmic Contracts', *Stanford Technology Law Review,* 20, 2017, pp. 128-69.

100 Jerry Z. Muller, *The Tyranny of Metrics*, Princeton: Princeton University Press, 2018.

THE POLITICAL ECONOMY OF DATAFICATION AND WORK: A NEW DIGITAL TAYLORISM?

MATTHEW COLE, HUGO RADICE, AND CHARLES UMNEY

The economic and social consequences of technological change in capitalist societies have always been profound. For capitalists themselves, new technologies can have pervasive effects, rendering obsolete even the most profitable businesses, while simultaneously creating opportunities for early adopters. For workers reliant on the sale of their labour power, the effects are even more differentiated: new technologies create opportunities for those who can acquire necessary skills, but destitution for those whose capabilities are no longer required. Beyond the immediate economic outcomes for individuals and their communities, there are spatial, organizational, and cultural consequences that transform the fabric of society. These work their way through seemingly more distant domains such as education, science, and politics, and affect also the ideologies through which we understand the world. This applies especially to those 'broad-spectrum' innovations that eventually transform substantial parts of the social division of labour and its infrastructure: the steam engine, electric power, synthetic chemicals, the assembly line, the computer – and for present purposes, the new wave of information and communication technologies driven by mass datafication and artificial intelligence.

How such transformative technologies are understood is largely framed by the contesting ideologies of the day. In classical political economy, and later in neoclassical economics, the world of scientific knowledge functions naturally in tandem with that of entrepreneurship: 'science-push' meets 'demand-pull' in generating optimal trajectories of technological advance.[1] Heterodox critics contend that this alliance, far from being natural, is socially constructed within the institutions and practices of a particular time and place: technological change thus shapes the terrain on which capital and labour battle for control within the workplace. For employers, control depends upon being able to decide who is to carry out what tasks, and to enforce those decisions. Labour movements have therefore been obliged to make sense of such transformative technologies, and act in response to their effects. Today, especially in the developed capitalist world, long-established labour movements have been on the defensive for decades, while emerging forms of worker organization such as the 'platform economy' appear to be germinating everywhere.[2]

In his analysis of the workplaces of the first industrial revolution, Marx concludes that 'Large-scale industry possesses in the machine system an entirely objective organization of production, which confronts the worker as a pre-existing material condition of production',[3] and elsewhere he defines this condition as the *real subsumption of labour*.[4] A hundred years later, his analysis underpinned modern socialist studies of labour and the struggle for control in the workplace. Indeed, ever since the birth of industrial capitalism socialists have not only critically examined technology in its social context, but also looked forward to futures of work based on radically different principles. As Alfred Barratt Brown wrote in 1934, 'We need to look at the whole world of industry with fresh eyes, to ask ourselves again what we want to produce, and how we can best employ our powers in producing it, to the end that the work and its results may alike satisfy human capacities and human needs'.[5] This essay is concerned to look with fresh socialist eyes at the technologies that underpin our present world of work, and how they have been shaped and applied by capital to meet the needs of capital, oriented firmly towards the subsumption of wage labour in all its concrete forms. We cannot repurpose them towards our fundamental goal as socialists to build a world based upon equality and justice for all without directly challenging and contesting the existing social order. This requires, as always, both a broad vision of a sustainable, egalitarian and democratic society, and concrete proposals that can connect to existing struggles while also prefiguring radical change.

DATA, AI, PLATFORMS

In order to understand the present situation in the broader context of subsumption and the implications for the future of work, it is important to establish the key technological developments. While *Time Magazine* already named 'the Computer' as its man of the year in 1982, the present technological situation is defined by exponential increases in computer power, mass datafication, and advances in artificial intelligence (hereafter AI). These technologies are synergistic and combine as general-purpose tools through the model of the platform. The capacity of virtual machines (driven by AI) to capture and transform data allows companies to exponentially scale new forms of digital automation through network effects.[6] The rise in the mass use of smart phones, digitally mediated consumption, and machine-to-machine communications via the 'internet of things' in production has allowed for datafication on an unprecedented scale. Such technologies are leveraged through the platform model to exert greater control over not only labour as a whole, but our everyday lives. They offer the owners of such platforms the capacity to use AI to automatically monitor workers, operate machinery, process transactions, manipulate individual tastes, and even generate creative outputs.

Throughout the late 1990s and 2000s, there were massive amounts of public and private investment in information and communications technology (ICT) infrastructure. After the financial crisis of 2007-8, large-scale financial disruption pushed venture capital into new technologies, scaling up digital transformations and creating structural changes in the global ICT infrastructure to pave the way for the age of the intelligent machine. According to Internet World Stats,[7] internet connectivity has grown from 16 million (0.4 per cent) of the global population in 1995 to 4.57 billion (58.7 per cent) as of January 2020. As of 2018, 5.1 billion people (66 per cent) had mobile data connectivity. Growth in data normally follows what is known as Cooper's Law, in which traffic roughly doubles every 2.5 years, which means that 33 zettabytes (each a trillion gigabytes) of data captured and transmitted in 2018 will likely increase to 132 zettabytes in 2023 and 528 zettabytes by 2028.[8] Simultaneously, there have been significant advances in computing power. This has generally evolved in accordance with Moore's Law (1998), which states that the number of transistors in a dense integrated circuit doubles every two years.[9] Data on computer power since 2012 analysed by OpenAI shows that the largest AI training runs have been increasing their computer power exponentially, with a 3- to 4-month doubling time.[10] Today, the accuracy level of the top-performing machine intelligences, which nearly all rely on a form of AI called 'deep learning', generally exceeds the average accuracy level expected of human intelligence performing the same task.[11] These developments arguably mark a techno-scientific break with the computer age not only because they are transforming the socio-economic infrastructures of capital, but because they are facilitating the real subsumption of intellectual labour.

AI is diverse in its applications, ranging from the algorithm that tracks your activities on social media to recommend topics and products you might be interested in, to the highly advanced machine and 'deep' learning. According to the OECD's AI Experts Group (AIGO), an AI system is a 'machine-based system that can, for a given set of human-defined objectives, make predictions, recommendations or decisions influencing real or virtual environments. It uses machine and/or human-based inputs to perceive real and/or virtual environments'.[12] The tasks that machines can perform can be grouped into four broad categories: decision-support systems, organizer and knowledge management systems, natural language processing, and computer vision.[13] It is important to note that there is no artificial intelligence without data to train it and no capacity to process and analyse the colossal amount of data being generated without AI.

The rapid advance in the capacity of companies to capture and process data with AI has spurred investment, as companies have decided that it is the next digital frontier for value extraction.[14] A recent report by McKinsey Global Institute (MGI) placed the total annual value potential of AI across 19 industries and nine business functions in the global economy between $3.5 trillion and $5.8 trillion. According to the study, the greatest potential value impacts from using AI are in front-line service industries like marketing and sales, and in operational functions such as supply chain management and manufacturing. However, even among AI-aware companies, only roughly 20 per cent are actually using machine learning AI in a core business process or at scale.[15]

Linked to the development of these new technologies is the growth of investment in assets like intellectual property rights, branding, software, and data networks, which have different economic dynamics than traditional tangible assets.[16] The increasing importance of such assets to the regime of accumulation and business management has been referred to as the 'rise of the intangible economy'. In the United States, the United Kingdom and Sweden investment in intangible assets has outpaced that of tangible assets as a share of GDP.[17] In 2008, there were significant changes to the Systems of National Accounts (produced by the United Nations): R&D spending was reclassified as an asset investment, rather than production expenditure. This means that that the production of scientific knowledge is now in some cases fully subordinated into the production of assets (the majority of which are private). This has the consequence of creating an array of new valuation, governance and management dynamics of these assets as they are folded into the regime of accumulation.[18]

One of the most important intangible assets is data, which is now being treated as a form of capital in market-leading large firms.[19] Some of the largest companies in the world, like Facebook and Google, are essentially networks of virtual machines built on data capital. While not all data is valuable (much of it is simply streaming video from platforms like Netflix and YouTube), direct and triangulated data on worker and consumer behaviour is highly valuable. The data brokerage industry itself is already generating hundreds of billions of dollars annually. It has value because it can allow companies to anticipate shifts in markets, manipulate worker and consumer behaviour, and be used for mass surveillance by technology firms and states alike. Such data is also used for training the growing number of machine-learning algorithms that power AI applications across production and consumption.

The development of AI technologies has drastically reduced the marginal cost of the production of digital commodities.[20] The low marginal cost of intangibles facilitates exponential scaling through global connectivity and is driving the creative destruction at the core of our digital age.[21] Investors are more concerned with market domination and large short-term returns (venture capitalists aim for up to forty times their original investment) than any obligation to workers or society. Leaders of new technology platforms openly state that their aim is to create a monopoly and replace existing infrastructures.[22] This allows for accumulation through producing a surplus, but also accumulation through rent capture. The increasing centrality of digital innovation and automation to economies is multiplying the unequal distribution of innovation and monopoly rents, which overwhelmingly increase the income share of the wealthiest groups (executives, managers and shareholders) while benefiting the average worker very little.[23] This compounds the continual shift in income from labour to capital over the course of the past few decades.[24]

The data and AI-driven technologies of the current technological revolution have allowed for further decentralization of production with lower capital overheads in relation to their scalability.[25] Consequently, these technological shifts are one of the drivers of changing power dynamics in the workplace. The platform model of the firm is indicative of such shifts, as it appears to signify radical change towards a decentralized but pervasive form of class discipline over workers, and a return to less standardized and more precarious organizational form of work. While sweating work to private or home-based production is not new, task work platforms have been able to institute Taylorist management techniques despite the dislocation of the workplace through the use of GPS, apps, customer ratings and other forms of surveillance. When workers receive poor feedback and ratings from customers, the algorithm justifies their termination. This automates management mediation while hegemonizing the rating system. At the same time, there is growing evidence of systemic racial and gender biases in customer-driven ranking systems,[26] and such systems fail to provide a truthful assessment of platform workers regardless.[27]

However, we also need to be careful to not conflate the 'gig' or 'platform' economy with the specific platform model. The latter is a particular type of organisational technology reliant on piecework and algorithmic management,[28] while the former implies a much more diffuse sense of 'precarization' with many drivers beyond just technology.[29] Reflecting on these limits also reveals some of the limits to arguments rooted in technological determinism. Platforms purport to bring buyer and seller into expansive markets catalysed by network effects, but the gig model of labour discipline is not universally applicable and may conflict with conditions of exchange and production in many labour markets.[30] We know that the percentage of workers entering the gig economy remains a small minority, and work is concentrated in particular sectors.[31] However, the platform model more broadly refers to the new rent-seeking regime of accumulation that companies from Rolls Royce to Facebook utilize. The platform model of the firm more generally encourages the development of monopolies in the platform economy and the 'X-as-a-service' subscription model of market rents. The increased reliance on digitally connected devices has allowed for a regime of accumulation based on data extraction and rent seeking.

While datafication and the rise of AI have facilitated a 'platformization' of the regime of accumulation, gig platforms should not be reified as a unique or determinate driver of a new labour regime. They are part of a wider shift towards class discipline and the precarization of labour,[32] and need to be set in this context. Platforms may defy existing institutions for labour regulation and worker representation, but as we have noted, this is one contributing factor in a broader trend. Ironically, despite assumptions about the atomization of gig-based platform work, we are starting to see rapid growth in collective worker protest in the sector,[33] suggesting that the demise of collective contact at work through remote technologies is greatly over-stated (consider, for instance, food delivery platform drivers congregating at restaurants to pick up orders). On an ideological level, the conservative-cultural notion of the 'traditional working class' is entirely ill-equipped to get to grips with these shifts, since the individuals forming the backbone of these protests are often migrant workers or young people clustered in metropolitan areas; groups often implicitly excluded from the way the concept of the working class is mobilized today by reactionary voices.[34]

Although we should guard against exaggeration or catastrophism when it comes to Uber, Deliveroo, and other gig-based platforms, it is also plain that in various respects this model of employment relations allows companies to shift capital costs to workers, and impose novel forms of technologically mediated labour discipline. While production might have required specialist-situated knowledge in the past (such as the famous test for London cab drivers), algorithm-driven applications automate the need for it. Such a model allows companies to avoid disbursing proprietary technical knowledge (of the best routes or of surge times, for example), while reorganizing the exchange process to intensify competitive discipline over workers. These technological transformations allow for the formal and real subsumption of gig-based labour processes via platforms. The datafication of everyday life and the use of AI for visual analysis, natural language processing, and other types of intellectual processes is becoming increasingly pervasive. The recent COVID crisis has only catalysed such tendencies. But before we discuss the possible futures of datafication, AI, and platforms, it is important to examine the social relations that underpin such technological changes, in particular the historical evolution of capitalist management that gave rise to the contemporary moment.

TECHNOLOGY AND WORK: A CENTURY OF CONTESTATION

In the decades following the publication of *Capital*, the second industrial revolution largely bore out Marx's expectation that competition would lead to the concentration and centralization of capital, with the emergence of much larger enterprises. These firms now produced and sold in integrated national and even international markets, which stimulated the parallel growth of large enterprises in transport, communications, commerce, and financial services. Science and technology were deployed in increasingly unified machinery-based production systems across many sectors of industry, and this was accompanied by a proportional growth in clerical, technical, and managerial activities within firms. The rise of giant enterprises saw the emergence across industry, commerce, and finance of business elites who became the voice of capital in politics and also culture. In the US, Veblen identified opposing wings within this elite, one advancing the cause of 'business' motivated by profit, and the other around 'industry' motivated by technical efficiency and social welfare; this divide has clear affinities with the Marxian analysis of relations between banking and industry pioneered by Hilferding.[35] In this section, we consider the uneven and contested processes of subsumption of labour that resulted from these technological and industrial shifts. This subsumption has to be seen in the context of the wider retrenchment (and later resurgence) of liberalism.

Within the firm, there emerged a complex stratification of pay, job security, and status, from senior management, to 'white collar' administrative and technical roles, to manual 'blue collar' roles, in turn divided into skilled, semi-skilled, and unskilled. What this brought about was a *vertical division of labour* that accompanied the increasingly detailed technical division of labour in production. This is often characterized as a distinction between intellectual and manual labour, but even the most menial manual task requires that its conception is mentally appropriated by the worker executing it, while the intellectual worker who has conceived the task necessarily performs a range of manual tasks in the course of their paid worktime. The vertical division of labour forms a continuum whose length and granularity is determined by the concrete character of the various labours performed within a workplace.

Mass production systems were now increasingly organized around assembly lines in the case of the vehicle and engineering sectors, or continuous-flow processing systems in the chemical and mineral materials sectors. In both cases, direct production workers perform tasks that have indeed been predetermined. Work within these contexts was studied by pioneers of 'scientific management' like F.W. Taylor and the Gilbreths, who sought ways of designing tasks for the maximization of productivity and thereby profit. Insofar as they could succeed, they removed any possibility of workers exercising their own skill or judgement; this provided the basis for Henry Ford's claim that at his River Rouge plant, a worker completely new to the industry could carry out any assembly task with a few hours' instruction.

Such developments would appear to provide clear evidence that both technological and organizational change were removing all initiative from workers. But despite the attention given to these forms of work by academic and popular studies alike, only a relatively small proportion of workers are actually faced with such direct subordination to the machinery that they operate.[36] Of the remainder, a significant number of both manual and clerical workers do undertake straightforward tasks that can readily be timed with the aim of setting production and pay rates; for such workers also, tasks were in principle predetermined. Across the board, it of course remained open to workers, individually or collectively, to challenge the pace of work or to demand compensation in pay or better working conditions through go-slows, sabotage, or stoppages. However, their capacity to undertake such actions would remain very limited without state regulation and the security provided by public welfare. We need therefore to put workplace struggles in the broader context of labour markets and their regulation.

While skilled trades retained apprentice systems, the recruitment of other workers remained highly ad hoc at the start of this period, often being undertaken by long-serving workers from within their families or local communities. In addition, the proportion of precarious work, by the day or indeed by the task, remained high for the unskilled (and especially young workers) in transport and the distributive trades. The collective organization of workers developed apace, well beyond the traditional domain of craft unionism, but where legal rights were weak and enforcement inadequate, unions were predominantly focused on national legislation.[37] In Britain, concerns over pay and social conditions, and the perceived threat from the left, led the 1906 Liberal government to introduce state-run labour exchanges in 1910, and the 1911 National Insurance Act introduced sickness and unemployment benefits, though only for a minority of workers.

The ensuing decades saw a substantial strike wave across many sectors, and although more enlightened employers responded by developing consultation mechanisms, the strikes initiated a radical shop steward movement that unions struggled to control.[38] Between 1914 and 1945, amid global wars, financial crises, mass unemployment, and the breakdown of global trade and finance, industrial systems and workplace relations not surprisingly faced massive challenges for both management and workers. Overall, however, the advance of labour continued: fear of communism after 1917 prompted a mix of initial violent repression, and later substantial concessions by capital, in the form of union recognition, welfare legislation, and increasing state economic management, whether under democratic or authoritarian regimes. Within the workplace, the rigid prescriptions of Taylorism were moderated by the human relations approach, as for example in Mayo's Hawthorne Experiments at Western Electric and the later work of the Tavistock Institute on socio-technical systems.[39] Trade union recognition and collective bargaining brought organized labour fully into the arena of politics, with legislation in many countries establishing a legal framework in which employers, unions and the state were expected to find consensus; this was facilitated by the post-1945 economic recovery, and the legacy of Keynes in national economic policy-making in the context of the Bretton Woods order.

In the 1920s, US big business refined its management systems with the development of multi-divisional structures that allowed the internal financial control of their increasingly diverse product lines.[40] The increasing numbers of intellectual workers and the complexity of management systems also fuelled the growth of business schools and management consultancies, as well as scholarly interest across the fields of economics, sociology, and law. In the early 1930s, Berle and Means, drawing on the earlier work of Veblen and Commons, explored the potential conflict between managers and owners, and identified the degree of concentration of ownership as a key determinant of the outcome of this struggle.[41] The wider the ownership and the smaller the stake of any individual or family, the easier it would be for managers to pursue their own objectives, which might include not only technical excellence and higher salaries, but also social concerns with working conditions.

A decade later, and on a broader canvas, the former Trotskyist James Burnham saw the deep crisis of market capitalism in Europe and the US during the Great Depression, alongside the new economic regimes of both Nazi Germany and Soviet Russia, as signalling a social revolution that would usher in a 'managerial society'.[42] This view would be echoed in the post-war era, in the context of debates on the convergence of East and West on forms of 'industrial society', as epitomized by Galbraith's argument that industry was now controlled by a technostructure that had supplanted the power of financial markets.[43] This perspective chimed also with the economic advances of West Germany's 'social market economy', with fully institutionalized sectoral collective bargaining, workers represented on the boards of large companies, and their participation in the design and management of welfare and training systems.[44] The liberal ideology that had underpinned capitalism up to 1914 had by the 1960s retreated to a few energetic but marginal think tanks and university departments, largely ignored by governments, social scientists, and the business world.

The retreat of liberalism was exemplified in the US in the early 1960s, when there was widespread concern that both Western competitors and the Soviet bloc were eroding US dominance in the world economy. As growth slowed, there were increasing concerns that accelerating the 'automation revolution' would lead to unemployment and threaten industrial peace and prosperity, and a National Commission on Technology, Automation, and Economic Progress was established in 1964. Its 1966 report argued that while new technologies would indeed boost productivity, living standards, and growth in the long run, the state could and should protect workers adversely affected by new technologies. This would entail both fiscal stimuli to maintain full employment, and the expansion of training programmes for the displaced workers.[~45] In short, decisions about deploying new technologies were seen not as the sole prerogative of capitalists responding to market forces, but as matters for public debate, consensual solutions, and active state policies.

The overall advance of labour in industrial capitalism between the 1920s and 1970s has resonances also in the experience of the Soviet Union, and in Eastern Europe after 1948. Lenin's New Economic Policy of 1921 returned much of the economy to market regulation, but also signalled an end to the autonomous factory committees and workers' assemblies that had played such an important role in the Russian revolution.[46] In a banned polemical response to the launching of the NEP, Preobrazhensky highlighted the gap between the cadres and the mass of workers, which the fledgling USSR had inherited from capitalism: communism would require a massive programme of workers' education, to make it possible for them to participate fully in the collective planning of the economy.[47]

With the Left Opposition defeated by 1928, Stalin reduced the trade unions to the role of 'transmission belt' for the Party in industry, and any trace of autonomous workers' power disappeared. But in the early 1960s, a sudden economic slowdown across the Soviet bloc was attributed to excessively centralized planning. In that context, the new Czechoslovak party leadership commissioned academic studies of the economy, politics, and science and technology to provide the basis for intended reforms. In the last of these studies, Richta and his colleagues argued that the complexity and skill requirements of modern science-based industries undermined the normal forms of incentive used throughout the state enterprise system, namely the moral incentive of working for communist ideals, and the material incentive of monetary reward. What was now required was firstly a much higher universal level of technical training, and secondly the full involvement of workers at all levels in enterprise decision-making.[48] Instead, the USSR invaded Czechoslovakia and imposed a neo-Stalinist normalization on the Soviet bloc. Life for the average industrial worker was well illustrated soon after by a vivid study of Hungarian-style Taylorism, which workers resisted in much the same ways as Taylor's subjects – petty sabotage, hoodwinking the time-and-motion man, and stealing time and materials.[49]

By this time in the advanced capitalist West, the post-war boom had slowed down through the 1960s, with lower productivity growth and rising inflation. Growing international competition through trade and foreign investment began to destabilize giant corporations, governments, and the consensus politics that had presided over improved workers' living standards and ensured relative peace on the shop floor. Where did this leave the subsumption of labour in industrial capitalism by the 1970s? To the extent that workers, especially in the lower strata of the vertical division of labour, experienced stricter Taylorist discipline in the workplace, they could take comfort in their greater economic security and higher living standards; but just as sociologists were celebrating the end of ideology and class struggle,[50] efforts by governments and business to suppress rising inflation, rein in state spending and boost productivity met considerable resistance on the shop floor. Many countries experienced widespread labour unrest for the first time since the war, and a burgeoning intellectual New Left united with the trade union left in proposing forms of workers' control, international solidarity against multinational employers, and the planning of industrial modernization.

As this history makes clear, the development of industrial technology and organization could not be explained simply by Marx's identification of the unified machine system as the ideal form of the capitalist labour process. Within the workplace, capital's drive for control over production was indeed universal, but the actual evolution of both technology and organization was always shaped by a much broader constellation of factors involving markets, finance, states, and the global order. To paraphrase David Noble, technologies alone do not determine changes in social relations, but rather tend to reflect such changes.[51]

THE NEOLIBERAL TURN: TOWARDS REAL SUBSUMPTION

As the negotiated evolution of technology and work organization gave way to neoliberal unilateralism, the opportunity for capital to encroach on areas of intellectual labour previously insulated from formal and real subsumption became increasingly available through new technologies. There were highly visible changes taking place in the international political and economic order, as well as more subtle changes in enterprise, institutions, and technology which point towards a deepening of real subsumption, and particularly its extension into forms of intellectual labour catalysed by technological progress. This section traces this evolution.

By the end of the 1970s, the widespread return of inflation and unemployment, and the breakdown of the gold-dollar exchange-rate system, signalled a deep crisis for Keynesian economic management. Especially in the US and the UK, elements of a free-market alternative were visible in the turn to fiscal and monetary stringency, along with growing pressure for the state to retreat from consensus-based systems of regulation. The neoliberal revolution under Reagan and Thatcher, centred on privatization, deregulation, financialization, and globalization, began to spread across the developed capitalist world. Gorbachev's drive for reform quickly brought the Soviet system crashing down, while almost as quickly, China abandoned the Maoist variant for the introduction of markets at home and an open door to global capitalism. The 1984 debt crisis brought to heel a Third World that had been seeking in the 1970s to establish a new international economic order that could overcome the legacies of colonialism. Against these dramatic changes, labour movements and parties of the left everywhere endured a long and demoralizing series of retreats. Industry-level collective bargaining gave way in most sectors to plant-level deals, or indeed to the de-recognition of unions, especially as the outsourcing of many non-core activities became the norm in both private and public sectors.

However, there were also less visible organizational and ideological changes taking place, first in business enterprises and later in public institutions as well.[52] The managerial theories of the firm outlined earlier argued that management, or even a managerial class, had taken advantage of the decline of concentrated family share ownership to displace the power of capital. But now with the revival, deregulation and expansion of the financial sector from the 1970s onwards, the idea of a conflict of *social* interests between owners and managers transformed into the simple conflict of *individual* interests between 'principals' and 'agents'. Within a hierarchy running from profit-seeking shareholders at the top, through the many layers of management down to the shop floor, how could principals ensure that they controlled the actions of their subordinate agents? The answer was to develop carefully calibrated systems of reward and punishment based on measured performance. In this approach, it is *assumed* that everyone in an organization, regardless of the concrete content of their work, is solely motivated by self-interest, and owes no intrinsic loyalty to the organization as a whole. Tasks now need to be specified in terms that allow outcomes to be attributed to individual agents, and performance rewarded or punished in predetermined ways – a carrot-and-stick model that bases both the content of management and the rewards to the individual firmly on measured results.

As Michael Power set out in 1997 in *The Audit Society*,[53] the starting point for the wider development of this new model of management was the system of financial auditing long deployed to reassure investors about the financial probity of businesses. Power sets out the many ways in which the client-auditor relationship itself is subject to exactly the same problems as the 'internal' relation between principals and agents, to be addressed by the state regulation of auditing firms. But this in turn raises the problem of 'auditing the auditors': at worst, the regulator must revisit every calculation and every conclusion made in a given audit. To this must be added the understandable tendency for 'regulatory capture', long recognized by mainstream economists, in which the regulator shares the training and the world view of the regulated, and is therefore inclined to accept their judgements.

The audit model has been transplanted not only into business functions other than finance, but also into the management and control of public sector and non-profit bodies of all kinds. As Power explains, almost all activities making use of resources of any kind are now subject to continuous reporting that takes the form of 'rituals of verification', aimed at legitimating the subordination of all to the directives of their leaders. In the UK public sector, this began in the 1980s, when the privatization of state enterprises was accompanied by the introduction of a 'value for money' regime aimed at increasing the cost-effectiveness of what public provision remained. In the 1990s, this developed into the New Public Management model, in which public administration, both national and local, across sectors such as health, education, policing, criminal justice, the prison service, defence, etc., were obliged to remodel their management systems in accordance with private sector practices.[54]

The adverse effects of this new coercive model for intellectual workers have been chronicled in a burgeoning literature that addresses the relentless focus on performance targets, the downgrading of the culture of professional trust, and the use of quantitative data.[55] This surveillance makes possible the formal and real subsumption of intellectual labour in a range of new industries. The scientific management of the early twentieth century has given way to a new digital Taylorism in the twenty-first century, with its own regimes of control affecting the creative capacity of video game designers,[56] the problem-solving capacity of IT support functions,[57] and a variety of other types of intellectual labour. Damage is equally inflicted on the effectiveness of organizations as a whole, since the single-minded pursuit of specified targets regardless of any damage to performance elements that have not been targeted. The emphasis on vertical chains of information and control devalues horizontal interactions between those chains which otherwise might allow staff to learn directly from their peers.[58] All these issues, it should be noted, were long ago documented as key weaknesses in the Soviet model of central planning.[59]

The problems that are endemic to capitalist management stem from the fact that the information available to top management is always incomplete, since the processes to be managed are complex and constantly subject to external uncertainties and the irreducible indeterminacy of labour-power. The imposition of decision rules from above in these circumstances requires that subordinates behave in ways that can only be described as mechanical – or as one commentator recently put it, 'Our most urgent problem is not that robots are supplanting humans, but that we are forcing humans to be more like robots'.[60] In contrast, the behavioural economist Herbert Simon made clear in the 1950s that the only intelligent response to incomplete information is to allow a degree of 'organizational slack', and to tolerate, indeed encourage, local initiatives that ignore the rulebook when necessary.[61]

The technological transformations outlined in the first section have also generated a datafication imperative in labour processes, and in society more generally. This imperative requires the surveillance of machines, workers, consumers, processes, and relationships among them by all means available (often circumventing legal constraints). At the same time, the techniques of data extraction and use are opaque or even unintelligible to workers and consumers. Virtual machines capture behavioural data that can reveal very sensitive information about individuals and groups of people. Such data is used to subordinate and automate intellectual labour, including communication, management, and even emotional engagement. Through datafication and the use of virtual machines, the intellectual labour that has previously resisted real subsumption and automation is now being transformed in ways similar to manual waged labour. According to a report on the impact of the digital transformation on EU labour markets, workers' and consumers' data contributes without remuneration to 'the stock of intangible capital that will at some point replace their manual or intellectual labour'.[62] There are very limited social protections in this digital space and even less enforcement. This makes it difficult to secure the informed consent of the employee based on data protection guidelines, and even more difficult to leverage data as part of collective bargaining, undermining both workers' power and consumer privacy. The datafication and virtual automation of everyday life allows capital to harness knowledge about humanity in ways that subordinate humanity to the logic of those who control the machine.

Developments in platform technology as a means of transforming and organizing labour have also contributed to the subsumption of intellectual labour, albeit in an uneven way. Yet, as Simon Joyce observes,[63] gig-based platforms do not necessarily imply the real subsumption of labour to capital. In many cases, they may function as a means of reconfiguring the exchange process, while leaving the labour process itself relatively unchanged. For instance, in live music, digitalized forms of labour market intermediation are increasing price competition between groups of workers, creating profitable opportunities for online businesses, while having little effect on the labour process itself.[64] For Joyce, this suggests hybridized forms of partial subsumption, where capital can extract profits through reorganizing exchange processes rather than revolutionizing the labour process. Change in the latter case may be more indirect, as independent workers adjust their practice to conform to incentives determined by the platform's data-sorting systems, as in Yao's study of the 'Uberisation' of the Chinese legal profession.[65]

TOWARDS A SOCIALIST ALTERNATIVE

We have seen that the post-war economic, social, and political order enabled further advances in economic and social conditions to be pursued on a collective basis; in this context labour was able to make gains in the workplace up to the 1970s, and even to contemplate the transcendence of capitalism. The neoliberal turn has sought to reverse those gains once and for all by reconstructing the project of a market society, in which states and citizens alike are subordinated to the pursuit of profit, and in the workplace, the new technologies of information and communication seem to presage the real subsumption of all forms of labour. Meanwhile, the COVID-19 pandemic is accelerating these tendencies.[66]

At present, we take for granted a distribution of work that has been shaped by two centuries of industrial capitalism. In our discussion of the historical evolution of technology and work, we noted how work is highly differentiated up and down a steep vertical division of labour, including the key divide between intellectual and manual labour. This pattern of inequality has been socially constructed, and is reproduced by education systems that entrench the advantages of those born to parents who have higher levels of education, status, and wealth. If socialism is at its heart a classless society of equals, this surely requires that the vertical division of labour is radically challenged and dismantled. We should be arguing in concrete terms for an educational system that aims to provide *everyone*, without exception, with the capacity to contribute both intellectual and manual labour.

Andrew Sayer has argued that the 'contributive injustice' of unequal work is just as important as the 'distributive injustice' of unequal incomes, citing a wide literature on the social, economic and psychological consequences of restricting imaginative intellectual work to a privileged elite. He concludes: 'An unequal division of labour limits what some people can do and hence the extent to which they can develop their own abilities and find fulfilment, respect and self-esteem. Insofar as it indirectly shapes the contexts in which the next generation is brought up, it also tends to produce inequalities in their aspirations and abilities which appear to legitimize the very same unequal division of labour that gives rise to contributive injustice.'[67]

If this provides us with an alternative vision, that vision needs to be embedded in practical proposals that address today's issues and concerns. As regards AI and datafication, the only way intelligent machines will have a liberating effect on humanity is if the infrastructures they rely on, and the underlying technologies, are brought into public ownership and developed along socialist principles of maximizing free time rather than profit. We need to go beyond the limited strategic perspective of looking for a new social contract between capital and labour, and embrace instead an explicitly socialist strategy, centred on the redistribution of physical and digital assets to the public realm, and the transformation of social infrastructure through collective governance. It must also take into account the rising importance of intangible assets that drive the global digital economy.[68] This socialist strategy would leverage data, AI and platforms for realizing a twenty-first century socialism. We suggest three concrete steps toward this future.

First, the ethics of AI technologies and data gathering are largely governed by the boards of major tech firms, who advise the EU, the OECD, and other international institutions on policy. These institutions are invested in the continuation of global capitalism for the benefit of elites, and the ethics they are developing reflect such values. At best they offer an ideological counterweight to the authoritarian ethics of Chinese tech capital. At worst they are simply a distracting ruse masking the realities of surveillance, control, and behavioural modification. Socialist artificial intelligence should, by contrast, have a corresponding set of principles informed by socialist ethics, that is, a humanist and ecological ethics. This includes adopting a 'human-in-command' principle in relation to artificial intelligence that 'ensures that the final decisions affecting work are taken by human beings'.[69] Such an ethics puts technology to work based on human need and facilitates creative flourishing rather than framing it in such a way as to ideologically subordinate it to the capitalist valorization process. Retaining control over technology is particularly important from an ethical standpoint as AI increasingly mediates or substitutes human decision-making.

Second, ICT and data infrastructures are natural monopolies, much like natural resources like water and transport infrastructures like roads and railways. These should all be brought into democratic public ownership, and states should share the resources. The backbone of the internet should not be privately owned. Furthermore, the ownership and control of data should be democratically governed and de-commodified. Data is a public resource as vital as international energy and communications infrastructure. The privatization of data and data infrastructures facilitates the real subsumption of intellectual labour, but also risks the subsumption of social life to the machine-based market. As a transitional policy, states could develop a data commons to help manage public, private, and other types of data flows.[70] This could begin at the regional level by introducing local digital data commons initiatives and strategies, in order to drive the development and adoption of regional digital services.[71] The state should establish policy measures that develop shared ownership schemes for workers in all sectors. Expanding and equalizing the ownership of technology will ensure that all will have equal power to determine its development and use.

Finally, the data and AI-driven technologies of the current technological revolution create the opportunity to redistribute work time more evenly across the workforce, allowing the unemployed and underemployed to gain the work they need, while reducing the negative impact of overwork on those who work long hours. While overall during the twentieth century working time has gradually reduced, it has stalled recently.[72] The stagnation of work time reduction since the 1970s has occurred in spite of increases in both labour and multifactor productivity.[73] This evidence suggests that under capitalist social relations intelligent machinery will not lead to less work. We should therefore immediately reduce the working week for all workers to thirty hours maximum, allowing greater free time for non-market mediated activities. But the fundamental goal must be to look beyond techno-determinist and capitalist futures, and seize the virtual as well as the physical means of production in order to realize a world in which workers will decide whether technology displaces or augments labour, and what new tasks they might want to perform to meet the needs of society.

NOTES

This paper arose from a workshop on 'The Frontier of Control: Workplace Regimes from the 19th Century to the Gig Economy', hosted by the Independent Working Class Education Network in Leeds, October 2018. Thanks to Dave Berry, Simon Joyce, Vera Trappmann, Keith Venables and Colin Waugh for comments and support.

1 See e.g. Christopher Freeman, *The Economics of Innovation*, Harmondsworth: Penguin Education, 1974.

2 Simon Joyce, Denis Neumann, Vera Trappmann, and Charles Umney, 'A Global Struggle: Worker Protest in the Platform Economy', *ETUI Policy Brief: European Economic Employment and Social Policy*, No.2, 2020.

3 Karl Marx, *Capital* Volume 1, London: Penguin Books, 1976, p. 508.

4 Marx, *Capital*, 'Results of the Immediate Process of Production', pp. 1023-5.

5 Alfred Barratt Brown, *The Machine and the Worker*, Nottingham: Spokesman Books, 2014 [1934].

6 Based on Metcalfe's Law: this states that the number of unique possible connections in a network of n nodes can be expressed mathematically as the triangular number n(n-1)/2, which is asymptotically proportional to n squared. See James Hendler and Jennifer Golbeck, 'Metcalfe's Law, Web 2.0, and the Semantic Web', *Journal of Web Semantics*, 6(1), 2008, pp.14–20.

7 See: www.internetworldstats.com/stats.htm

8 Emil Björnson and Erik Larsson, 'How Energy-Efficient Can a Wireless Communication System Become?', *2018 52nd Asilomar Conference on Signals, Systems, and Computers*, Pacific Grove: CA, 2018, pp. 1252-1256.

9 Gordon Moore, 'Cramming More Components onto Integrated Circuits', *Electronics* 38(8), 1965. Moore predicted that the number of components per integrated circuit would double every year for at least another decade. In 1975 he revised his prediction to say that the number of components would double every two years.

10 OpenAI Inc. conducts research in the field of AI with the stated aim 'to ensure that artificial general intelligence benefits all of humanity'. See: openai.com/about. OpenAI is a for-profit corporation, whose parent organization is the non-profit organization OpenAI Inc. See also: Deven Coldewey, 'OpenAI Shifts from Nonprofit to "Capped-Profit" to Attract Capital', *techcrunch*, 11 March 2019.

11 See: Michael Chui, et al., *Notes from the AI frontier: Applications and Value of Deep Learning*, McKinsey Global Institute, 2018, available at www.mckinsey.com.

12 OECD, *Artificial Intelligence in Society*, Paris: OECD Publishing, 2019, p.15.

13 Stephen Allott, et al., *London: The AI Growth Capital of Europe*, London: Mayor of London, 2018, at www.london.gov.uk. See also: Claire Craig, et al., *Machine Learning: The Power and Promise of Computers that Learn by Example*, London: Royal Society, 2017, available at royalsociety.org.

14 See Jacques Bughin, *Skill Shift: Automation and the Future of the Workforce*, McKinsey Global Institute, 2018, available at www.mckinsey.com.

15 Chui, 'Notes from the AI Frontier'.

16 Jonathan Haskel and Sian Westlake, *Capitalism Without Capital: The Rise of the Intangible Economy*, Princeton: Princeton University Press, 2018.

17 Haskel and Westlake, 'Capitalism Without Capital', pp. 26-7.

18 Kean Birch, 'Technoscience Rent: Toward a Theory of *Rentiership* for Technoscientific Capitalism', *Science, Technology, & Human Values,* 45(1) 2020, pp. 3-33.

19 Jathan Sadowski, 'When Data is Capital: Datafication, Accumulation, and Extraction', *Big Data & Society,* 6(1) 2019, pp. 1-13.

20 Dominique Guellec and Caroline Paunov, *Digital Innovation and the Distribution of Income*, Cambridge, MA: National Bureau of Economic Research, Working Paper no. 23987, 2017.

21 Luc Soete, 'Destructive Creation: Explaining the Productivity Paradox in the Digital Age', in Max Neufeind, et al., *Work in the Digital Age: Challenges of the Fourth Industrial Revolution*, London: Rowman & Littlefield International, 2018, pp. 29–46.

22 See Peter Theil, *Zero to One: Notes on Startups, or How to Build the Future*, New York: Penguin Random House, 2014 (Theil is the co-founder of Paypal).

23 Soete, 'Destructive Creation'.

24 Loukas Karabarbounis and Brent Neiman, 'The Global Decline of the Labour Share' *Quarterly Journal of Economics,* 129, 2014, pp. 61–103. See also ILO/OECD, *The Labour Share in G20 Economies*, report to the G20 Employment Working Group, Antalya, Turkey, 2015, available at www.oecd.org.

25 Haskel and Westlake, 'Capitalism Without Capital'.

26 Joshua Brustien, 'Uber Says Tips Are Bad for Black People. But What About Ratings Bias?', *Bloomberg*, April 2016. See also Safiya Noble, *Algorithms of Oppression: How Search Engines Reinforce Racism*, New York: New York University Press, 2018.

27 Tom Slee, *What's Yours is Mine: Against the Sharing Economy*, 2nd edition, New York: OR Books, 2017.

28 Nick Srnicek, *Platform Capitalism*, Cambridge: Polity Press, 2017.

29 Gabriella Alberti, Ioulia Bessa, Kate Hardy, Vera Trappmann, and Charles Umney, 'In, Against and Beyond Precarity: Work in Insecure Times', *Work, Employment and Society,* 32(3), 2018, pp. 447–57.

30 Dario Azzellini, Ian Greer, and Charles Umney, *Limits of the Platform Economy: Digitalization and Marketisation in Live Music*, Hans Boecker Stiftung Working Paper 154, 2019.

31 Chris Forde, Mark Stuart, Simon Joyce, Liz Oliver, Danat Valizade, Gabriella Alberti and Calum Carson, 'The Social Protection of Workers in the Collaborative Economy', Brussels: European Parliament, November, 2017.

32 Alberti et al, 'In, Against and Beyond Precarity'.

33 Simon Joyce, Denis Neumann, Vera Trappmann, & Charles Umney, *A Global Struggle: Worker Protest in the Platform Economy*, Brussels: European Trade Union Institute, 2020.

34 Charles Umney, *Class Matters*, London: Pluto, 2018.

35 Thorstein Veblen, *The Theory of Business Enterprise,* New York: Charles Scribner's Sons, 1904; Rudolf Hilferding, *Finance Capital*, London: Routledge & Kegan Paul, 1981 [1910].

36 Even in 1972, D. T. N. Williamson found that only 30 per cent of UK engineering workers on the shop floor worked on assembly lines: see his 'The Anachronistic Factory', *Proceedings of the Royal Society of London,* A/331(1585), 1972, pp. 131–60.

37 By 1914, there existed also an international network of experts exchanging information on working conditions and labour legislation, preparing the ground for the creation of the International Labour Organization in 1919.

38 See G. D. H. Cole, *Workshop Organisation*, Oxford: Clarendon Press, 1922.

39 See Michael Rose, *Industrial Behaviour: Theoretical Development Since Taylor,* Harmondsworth: Penguin Books, 1975; D.S. Pugh, *Organisation Theory: Selected Readings*, Harmondsworth: Penguin Books, 3rd edition 1990.

40 Alfred D. Chandler, *Strategy and Structure: Chapters in the History of Business Enterprise,* Cambridge, Mass: MIT Press, 1962.

41 Adolf A. Berle and Gardiner C. Means, *The Modern Corporation and Private Property,* New York: Macmillan, 1932; Thorstein Veblen, *The Economic Theory of the Leisure Class*, New York: Macmillan, 1899; John R. Commons, *Economic Institutions*, New York: Macmillan, 1934.

42 James Burnham, *The Managerial Revolution, or What is Happening in the World Now,* New York: John Day, 1941. For Burnham, the underlying forces behind this were rooted not only in the technological and organizational demands of modern industry, but also in the natural reversion of politics to the single issue of power. For a thorough critique see George Orwell, 'Second Thoughts on James Burnham', *Polemic*, Summer 1946, pp. 13–33 (available at www.orwell.ru).

43 John Kenneth Galbraith, *The New Industrial State*, Boston: Houghton Mifflin, 1967.

44 See Oliver Nachtwey, *Germany's Hidden Crisis: Social Decline in the Heart of Europe,* London: Verso, 2018, Ch. 2.

45 The Report and selected submissions to the Commission are summarized in Howard Bowen and Garth Morgan, *Automation and Economic Progress*, Englewood Cliffs, NJ: Prentice-Hall, 1966. Significantly the 14 members of the Commission included three union leaders, alongside four businessmen, four academics, two public officials and the chair of the Urban League.

46 Simon Pirani, *The Russian Revolution in Retreat, 1920-24: Soviet Workers and the New Communist Elite*, Abingdon: Routledge, 2008.
47 Evgeny Preobrazhensky, *From the New Economic Policy to Socialism: a Glance into the Future of Russia and Europe*, London: New Park, 1963 [1922].
48 Radovan Richta, et al., *Civilization at the Crossroads: Social and Human Implications of the Scientific and Technological Revolution*, White Plains, NY: IASP, 1968.
49 Miklós Haraszti, *A Worker in a Workers' State*, Harmondsworth: Penguin, 1977.
50 Ralf Dahrendorf, *Class and Class Conflict in Industrial Society*, Stanford, CA: Stanford University Press, 1959; Daniel Bell, *The End of Ideology*, New York: Free Press, 1960.
51 David Noble, *Forces of Production*, New Brunswick: Transaction Publishers, 2011.
52 For a comprehensive account of these changes and their causes and consequences see Pierre Dardot and Christian Laval, *The New Way of the World: On Neoliberal Society*, London: Verso, 2015.
53 Michael Power, *The Audit Society: Rituals of Verification*, Oxford: OUP 1997.
54 Power, *The Audit Society*, Ch. 5.
55 Recent examples include David Graeber, *The Utopia of Rules*, Brooklyn, NY: Melville Publishing, 2015, and David Boyle, *Tickbox*, London: Little Brown, 2020.
56 Paul Thompson, Rachel Parker, and Stephen Cox, 'Interrogating Creative Theory and Creative Work: Inside the Games Studio,' *Sociology*, 50(2), 2016, pp. 316-32.
57 Clive Trusson, Donald Hislop, and Neil Doherty, 'The Role of ICTs in the Servitisation and Degradation of IT Professional Work,' *New Technology, Work and Employment, 33*(2) 2018, pp. 149-70.
58 Gillian Tett, *The Silo Effect*, New York: Simon & Schuster, 2015.
59 See Ronald Amann, 'A Sovietological View of Modern Britain', *The Political Quarterly*, 74, 2003, pp. 468–80.
60 See Ian Leslie, 'What the Struggle to Automate Housework Tells us About the Limits of the Robot Revolution', *New Statesman*, 30 November 2018, p. 38.
61 Herbert Simon, 'Theories of Decision-Making in Economics and Behavioural Science', *American Economic Review*, 49(3), June 1959, pp. 253-83. See also Richard M. Cyert and James G. March, *A Behavioral Theory of the Firm*, Englewood Cliffs, NJ: Prentice-Hall, 1963.
62 High Level Expert Group, *The Impact of the Digital Transformation on EU Labour Markets*, Brussels: European Commission, April 2019.
63 Simon Joyce, 'Rediscovering the Cash Nexus, Again: Subsumption and the Labour–Capital Relation in Platform Work,' *Capital & Class*, forthcoming 2020.
64 Azzellini, et al., *Limits of the Platform Economy*.
65 Yao Yao, 'Uberizing the Legal Profession? Lawyer Autonomy and Status in the Digital Legal Market,' *British Journal of Industrial Relations*, forthcoming 2020.
66 Preliminary research shows we have moved five years forward in consumer and business digitalization in a matter of around eight weeks. See: McKinsey & Company, *Consumer Sentiment Evolves as the Next "Normal" Approaches*, 12 May 2020, available at www.mckinsey.com.
67 Andrew Sayer, 'The Injustice of Unequal Work,' *Soundings*, 43, 2009, pp. 102-13, at p. 113. See also his 'Contributive Justice and Meaningful Work', *Res Publica*, 15(1), 2009, pp. 1-16
68 Haskel and Westlake, 'Capitalism Without Capital'.

69 ILO Global Commission on the Future of Work, *Work for a Brighter Future*, Geneva: International Labour Office, 2019.

70 Organization for Economic Cooperation and Development, *AI: Intelligent Machines, Smart Policies*, Paris: OECD, 2018.

71 Matthew Lawrence and Laurie Laybourn-Langton, *The Digital Commonwealth: From Private Enclosure to Collective Benefit*, London: Institute for Public Policy Research, 2018, p. 4.

72 Stan de Spiegelaere and Agnieszka Piasna, *The Why and How of Working Time Reduction*, Brussels: European Trade Union Institute, 2017.

73 See Organisation for Economic Cooperation and Development, 'Multifactor productivity', available at data.oecd.org.

THE BIG TECH MONOPOLIES AND THE STATE

GRACE BLAKELEY

As the effects of the coronavirus pandemic swept through the global economy, the average observer could have been forgiven for missing a critical piece of news: by May 2020, the combined market capitalization of the four largest US tech companies reached one fifth of the entire S&P 500.[1] Four companies – Microsoft, Apple, Amazon and Facebook – now account for 20 per cent of the combined value of the 500 largest US corporations – an unparalleled level of market concentration. Firms that, just a few decades ago, were plucky start-ups aiming to disrupt the fast-growing tech sector are now some of the most powerful monopolies on the planet. And the trends towards monopoly are not limited to the tech sector. In 1975, the largest 100 US companies accounted for nearly half of the earnings of all publicly listed companies; by 2015, their share reached 84 per cent.[2]

Such trends should not come as a surprise to Marxists. Over several pages at the end of Volume 1 of *Capital*, Karl Marx explains capitalism's inherent tendency towards centralization, which ultimately overpowers the centrifugal forces of competition.[3] While informing the reader that a full explanation of the laws of centralization 'cannot be developed here', he hints towards the mechanisms that underpin this process. First, the productivity of labour increases with the scale of production, allowing larger firms to outcompete their rivals – a variant of the argument of 'economies of scale' found in neoclassical economics. Second, 'with the development of the capitalist mode of production, there is an increase in the minimum amount of individual capital necessary to carry on a business under its normal conditions'.[4] Smaller capitalists without large pools of previous earnings crowd into more competitive sectors as they are unable to compete with incumbents in more developed sectors, leaving larger, more established firms with even more market power. As these established firms increase their earnings, they are able to undertake greater levels of investment than their rivals, further boosting their relative productivity and consolidating their monopoly positions.

Marx goes on to point out that the emergence of stock markets and the development of the credit system deepen the processes of the concentration and centralization of capital. Large companies able to float their shares on the stock market gain an advantage over their private rivals when it comes to access to investment. And financial institutions, themselves monopolistic entities that centralize lending and investment, are more likely to lend to larger, more established firms. These two factors are closely intertwined given the role played by large financial institutions in managing the relationships between corporations and stock markets.

It is, however, important to keep in mind that capitalism cannot exist without competition – though competition can, of course, take on many different forms. Far from bringing about stability in world markets and the relations between states, the centralization of capitalism leads, Marx argues, to quite ruthless levels of competition and an increase in the 'the mass of misery, oppression, slavery, degradation, exploitation'.[5] The factors driving this immiseration stem from the complex relationship between monopolies, markets, and capitalist states.

While neoclassical economists might not refer to the big tech companies as 'monopolies' (because they do not appear to charge a mark-up on their goods and services), these firms do resemble both rentiers and monopsonists. These are not ordinary monopolies as they provide many useful services for free or at very low prices. It would be very difficult for these companies to generate high profits from selling a service that can be produced at zero marginal cost: if Google started to charge customers for searching the web, users would simply migrate to another search engine, which could easily expand to accommodate the new demand. As a result, the prices of many digital services are low, or zero – because prices converge on the costs of production.

But while the dynamics of production at zero marginal cost lead to lower prices, they also generate tendencies towards monopoly and rent-seeking. This is because the business models of the big tech giants do not rest on the provision of free digital services – a strategy from which no profit could be generated. Instead, they collect an extremely valuable commodity produced by their users – data – and sell it, using their control of access to users, to advertisers, researchers, or states to generate profits.[6] The extraction and commodification of this data by the big tech giants is a new method for the generation of economic rents.[7] Business models based on the monopolization of a particular online 'space' use network effects to establish near total market dominance. Monopsony power is then used to exploit workers, gouge suppliers and avoid taxes on the one hand, and monopoly power used to acquire users' data for free, often without sufficient privacy safeguards, on the other. Prices do not seem to exceed the costs of production, so neoclassical economists cannot detect the existence of a monopoly – yet workers, suppliers, taxpayers, and even consumers still suffer as a result.

THE TECH CORPORATIONS AND FINANCE

Capitalist corporations can only become monopolies if they are able to access the investment needed to gain total market dominance – and as the twenty-first century has progressed, this has proven easier than ever, especially in big tech. The tech companies emerged in a world of falling profits and associated rising volatility in financial markets – both of which facilitated their access to investment. Many of these companies were initially either unprofitable or loss making, as they had not yet developed to a sufficient size to exploit the network effects that would provide the foundation for their monopoly power. As a result, they required significant amounts of upfront investment to maintain their operations and to scale up to reach a position of market dominance that would allow them to turn a profit.

The most propitious time for these firms to access such investment was in the wake of a crisis that had depressed returns and when investors were desperately seeking out the next big thing. For the tech companies, this meant either the tech crisis of the early 2000s, after which Google launched its IPO, or the financial crisis of 2008, after which many companies went public, including Facebook and Twitter.[8] The cheap capital – in part a result of unorthodox monetary policy – swashing around the global economy in the wake of a financial crisis that had depressed returns everywhere provided the perfect conditions for these plucky tech companies to become the behemoths that we know today.

Firms as large as Alphabet or Amazon require specialist financial institutions to manage their relationships with their investors. These relationships are often marked by tension – the strategies used by investment banks to price IPOs in the tech sector have irritated firms like Alphabet, which has consistently attempted to work around the investment banks that operate as middlemen between corporations and financial markets.[9] The most notable recent example of such issues came with the failed attempt to launch an IPO for WeWork, which the corporate executives put down to incompetence and greed among the investment banks and the investment banks ascribe to incompetence and dishonesty at WeWork. Both explanations have some merit.[10]

But while these tensions are often the ones to make headlines, they conceal the otherwise very close relationship between companies like Alphabet, Facebook, and Microsoft and investment banks like Goldman Sachs, JP

Morgan, and Morgan Stanley (the grip of these three firms on advising the tech giants has been described as 'vicelike').[11] In fact, part of the reason that these tensions over public listings are now becoming more prominent is that the appeal of going public is lessened in an economy where it has never been easier for large firms to access capital: the benefits of going public have to be large for many firms to give up the advantages of operating as private companies. And the relationships between large companies and private investors create, if anything, a more significant role for financial institutions.

Today, the mass of capital that would be required to compete with companies like Alphabet or Facebook is unimaginably large. Their sheer scale is now what allows these companies to maintain their monopoly positions, even as many consumers express dissatisfaction with the services they are providing. These firms simply have too much money to be challenged, with market capitalizations larger than the GDP of the average state. After years of generating supernormal profits even in a period of slow economic growth, many of these firms are sitting on huge piles of cash that they are unable – or unwilling – to invest in innovation or production. The resultant 'corporate savings glut' poses a significant theoretical challenge to economists and is a source of concern for policymakers.[12]

In fact, the corporate savings glut is accelerating the financialization of the average monopoly firm by inverting the usual relationship between financial institutions and corporations. Rather than simply supporting companies to access capital from sceptical investors, many financial institutions are now helping large firms to invest their 'savings' in financial markets. Far from hoarding cash, the big tech giants, and many other large monopolies, have used their savings to buy up corporate and government bonds.[13] In doing so, they often were taking advantage of their close relationships with existing investment banks to take on new debt and invest it in riskier, higher-yielding corporate bonds elsewhere in the world. As a consequence, tensions have emerged in the relationships between the big banks and big tech: the tech companies, less regulated and vastly less unpopular than the investment banks, are increasingly the leading partners in a relationship where they were once mere clients.

The investment strategies pursued by the tech giants are not neutral: they both derive from and reinforce the imperialistic relationships that govern the world economy. The value chains used by many large monopolies engaged in commodities production span the globe – low value-added activities take place in the periphery, where profits are often generated, while high value-added activities take place in the core, where profits are repatriated.[14] For 'tech' firms like Apple, which derive most of their profits from ordinary commodity production, these relationships are obvious: hyper-exploited Foxconn workers in China manufacture iPhones using rare earth metals extracted by desperately impoverished workers in sub-Saharan Africa, while largely unproductive workers in 'head office' located in the US benefit from inflated wages.

The profits of firms like Google and Facebook are predominantly derived from the wealthier economies where advertising revenues are higher, but their accounting and investment strategies reinforce the hierarchies of the world market. Most of their revenues are derived from advertising commodities that are produced according to the logic of imperialism. Many succeed in generating huge profits by avoiding tax and shifting their profits to a few key low-tax jurisdictions in the North and to tax havens dotted around the global South, which warp the economies of the latter and keep these states dependent on foreign investment flows.[15] These firms may then use these profits to buy up higher-yielding assets from 'riskier' parts of the global economy, allowing them to extract value from the periphery of the world system by adopting new modes of imperialism in much the same way as multinationals that actively undertake production in these locations.

MONOPOLIZATION AS AN EFFECT OF STATE POLICY

The centralization of capital can exacerbate many of the pre-existing tendencies towards crisis that exist within capitalist economies. In repressing wages, dodging taxes and gouging suppliers in a ceaseless drive towards higher profits, monopolistic firms tend to increase wealth and income inequality.[16] At the same time, monopolistic corporations often prefer to invest their returns into speculation over existing assets than to invest productively where returns are constrained by the impact of inequality on demand. In this way, centralization can increase the mass of profits – and therefore the pool of capital available for investment – while simultaneously depressing demand and returns in the 'real economy'. The imbalance between the necessity of continuous investment – whether productive or not – and falling returns will eventually lead to interruptions in the normal circuit of capital that even compensating trends, such as faster turnover of capital or work speedups, cannot prevent. This is at the root of increasing tendencies towards economic crises, intensified by the speculative dynamics generated by financial markets.

When a crisis does hit, markets become even more centralized. Small firms are more likely to struggle during economic downturns than large ones, which may have access to substantial pools of previous earnings and close relationships with financial institutions that can provide them with credit to keep them afloat.[17] Without these relationships, and with much lower margins and often much higher debt levels, smaller firms are often the first to be culled during a recession. And when they go under, their assets are bought up on the cheap by their larger rivals. As Marx wrote, '[c]apital grows in one place to a huge mass in a single hand, because it has in another place been lost by many'.[18]

If centralization leads to crisis, and crisis leads to centralization, where is the state in this cycle of monopolization? The average neoclassical economist might have expected greater levels of state intervention to correct for the 'market failure' of rising market concentration. But state intervention is never neutral – capitalist states construct and act within markets in the interests of capital. As capitalism has become more concentrated, supporting both the interests of capital and the efficient functioning of free markets are goals that increasingly seem at odds with one another. Rather than attempt to construct competitive markets that discourage centralization, almost all states take actions that actively encourage market concentration.

Intellectual property law permits large firms to buy up smaller, more innovative ones simply for the purposes of acquiring patents, sometimes without even developing the technology that has been patented.[19] Accounting standards allow large firms with greater brand recognition and deeper relationships with investors to benefit from 'goodwill' against which they can borrow.[20] Planning laws in some states allow large developers with close relationships with financial institutions and local government to buy up large plots of land in the hope of gaining planning permission and acquiring the 'hope value' associated with the increase in land values. Government procurement often explicitly favours large firms over small ones as only firms of a certain size are permitted to take on state contracts.[21] Large procurement firms often develop expertise in winning government contracts before subcontracting the work to other firms.

In part, these policy biases stem from the proximity between state actors and large multinational corporations – as capitalism has become more concentrated, power has increasingly rested in a small number of hands, making it easier for these individuals to cooperate in pursuit of their mutual interests.[22] But these biases are also a reflection of the logic of centralization inherent within capitalism – large firms boast higher returns than smaller ones, are more efficient, and are far less risky, making it easier for states, as well as banks, to invest their trust in them.

States are paying closer attention to competition policy today than they were during the waves of merger and acquisition activity that brought the global economy to the levels of centralization we see now. However, high profile competition cases conceal two important points: firstly, competition law has become much less interventionist in recent years; and, secondly, states are more likely to take action against foreign than domestic firms. The transition from Keynesianism towards supply-side economic policy in the 1980s was associated with a shift in the foundation of competition law away from a measure of consideration of the 'public interest' and toward a more exclusive focus on 'market efficiency'.[23] On the one hand, this narrowed the focus of competition law to only the impact of market concentration on prices and consumer choice. On the other hand, the emphasis of supply-side economists on 'government failure' (as opposed to market failure) increased the burden of proof on those attempting to enforce competition law and therefore reduced caseloads among many competition authorities.

It is true that the enforcement of competition law has become a political tool for many states seeking to increase the power of their domestic corporations relative to foreign multinationals. Most of the high-profile competition cases heard in the European Court of Justice, for example, have dealt with US multinationals like Facebook and Google.[24] While attempting to control the market power of US multinationals operating in the EU, eurozone leaders are also wary of the impact growth of large, Chinese state-owned enterprises operating in European markets, and have also been considering the need to relax competition law for European firms to allow for greater market concentration in some sectors to compete with China and America.[25] Foreign takeovers of large domestic corporations – particularly those in strategically important sectors like energy or weapons manufacturing – have also become subject to much closer scrutiny of late, as in the UK where the government is considering introducing new laws against foreign takeovers.[26]

The emergence in recent years of so-called zombie firms that can only afford to repay the interest on their outstanding loans initially served to constrain market concentration by keeping unviable firms alive for longer but has recently begun to create more centralization. Ever since the 'Greenspan put' that followed the tech bubble, investors have counted on the fact that policymakers will cut interest rates in the wake of a market crash. This process has deepened in recent years with the introduction of quantitative easing, which has further reduced the costs of market financing for many firms.[27] Low interest rates have allowed large firms to buy up other firms on the cheap, or to buy-back their own shares and pay out large dividends, further increasing their attractiveness to investors. But with the massive economic downturn triggered by Covid-19, falling revenues have had an immediate impact on these firms' delicate balance sheets, pushing many to the brink of insolvency.[28] When these firms go under, large firms are able to buy up their assets on the cheap – a process made easier by the availability of cheap credit now guaranteed once again by central bankers.

PLANNED CAPITALISM VERSUS DEMOCRATIC PLANNING

As capitalism has become more centralized in the twenty-first century, the defining neoclassical economists' claim that competition between firms promotes the most efficient use of society's scarce resources has become less and less convincing. It would seem absurd to argue today that the forces of competition have driven the global economy towards a state of general equilibrium and the optimal use of our scarce resources. Instead, modern capitalism is subject to frequent crises and upheavals – along with deepening secular crises – that threaten to erode the ideological and material foundations of its existence. When these upheavals take place, the only thing that stands between capitalism and chaos is the state. Yet as states attempt to reduce the losses suffered by capital and to restart accumulation when the crisis is over in the interest of 'capital as a whole', market competition is again substantially eroded.

The responses of states to the pandemic have included extraordinary fiscal and monetary measures – just as during the financial crisis of 2008 – but now these measures are aimed at the entire domestic private sector. Almost all businesses, from the large monopolies to small businesses, are being offered state-backed loans; and workers' wages are being subsidized through furlough schemes that maintain workers' dependence upon firm or emergency benefits plans. Moreover, monetary policy has become looser than at any other point in history: interest rates have been slashed to zero; central banks have revived and expanded post-crisis asset purchasing programmes; and the Fed has brought back its network of swap lines to provide the world's major central banks with access to dollar liquidity.[29] Without this extraordinary support from the state in defence of capital accumulation, entire economies would be on the brink of collapse.

Of course, capitalist corporations do not – and cannot – simply rely on states to plan in their interests: they actively engage in planning themselves. Economists are generally content to treat firms as a 'black box', leaving questions of corporate governance and business strategy to organizational theorists. But even the latter usually fail to recognise that the structure of the world's largest monopolies support socialist arguments for economic planning, as Michal Rozworski and Leigh Phillips show in their book, *The People's Republic of Walmart*.[30] Large firms that have attempted to introduce 'internal markets' to determine the allocation of capital between different outputs and functions (the example used in the book is that of the US retail chain Sears) have struggled to compete with competitors who centralize processes of resource allocation. The direct allocation of resources by firms like Amazon and Walmart has, in fact, become all the more effective in recent years as their command over the data produced by consumers allows them to more accurately forecast – and therefore plan – for future demand. Rozworski and Phillips argue that the technologies developed by these firms to allocate resources internally could be repurposed by socialists to coordinate processes of democratic planning.

It is indeed possible to detect at least two additional ways in which capitalist planning might contribute to the de-legitimation of capitalism as a system while boosting the capacities of those seeking to build a socialist alternative. As state intervention in markets has become more prevalent and more obvious, it has also become harder to legitimize. The free market ideology which serves as a defence of the type of government intervention that supports the interests of capital and prohibits state interventions that might increase the power of workers has become more and more incoherent and discredited. The foundation of this ideology is a sharp separation between politics and economics – the state and the market.[31] For this ideology to retain its credibility, economic policy must be naturalized and its distributive implications hidden so that social outcomes are seen as the inevitable result of the operation of market forces. The idea that there is a 'natural' rate of interest determined by demand and supply for money, as well as a 'natural' rate of unemployment, legitimated central bank independence and the technocratic determination of monetary policy after the crisis of the 1970s.[32] But retaining this distinction of states and markets as separate spheres with their independent logics has become much harder in an era where state intervention is necessary to ensure the continued functioning of markets in the general interest of all capitalists.

When states are sustaining asset prices, providing wholesale bailouts to private corporations and buying up substantial portions of their own debt, it becomes far harder to argue that state interventions that might promote the public good are undesirable because they might disrupt the operation of the market mechanism. Coordinated action to tackle poverty, inequality, and climate breakdown becomes far harder to oppose in the context of an already politicized and interventionist state. Moreover, as the global workforce is exploited by an ever-shrinking number of ever-growing monopolies, the potential for, and impact of, worker organizing increases. Organizing vertically through supply chains has always been fraught with difficulties. But organizations like the Tech Workers Coalition (TWC) have documented many successful examples of solidarity between workers within large tech companies.[33] Horizontal organizing between workers subjected to similar conditions in different companies have also shown signs of success, like the recent strikes by Amazon, Instacart, and Target workers in the US. The concentration of economic activity in a small number of large firms means that such strike action could ultimately prove highly effective – the impact of shutting down Amazon for just a day would be huge.

The ideological and material weaknesses of global capitalism will be compounded as centralization increases the likelihood, and impact, of further economic crises. Indeed, the global labour force is already beginning to contract, even as employment has become more precarious or 'informal'.[34] With monopolies hoarding profits and failing to invest, employment will continue to shrink. The high profits generated by monopolistic firms will continue to be redirected into financial markets, supported by a manic financial sector in which investors are increasingly 'reaching for yield'. If the combination of loose monetary policy and relatively tight fiscal policy continues, further boosting asset prices while suppressing demand in the 'real' economy, this will only intensify the crisis tendencies in contemporary capitalism. Falling demand associated with rising inequality and lower state spending, accompanied by a sustained slowdown in world trade and growing geo-economic rivalries, will make it harder to recover from these crises, and lead to political instability once they hit. The imperial struggles that manifest themselves during this time are likely to exacerbate the underlying issues of economic fragility, even as they support certain states trying to out-compete their rivals. The growing power of the tech monopolies, meanwhile, will stand in contrast to the weakening legitimacy of many advanced capitalist states.

It is now easier than ever for socialists to demonstrate the irrationality and inefficiency of capital allocation under capitalism – especially since the financial crisis and in the context of an accelerating climate emergency and the current pandemic. The emancipatory potential of democratic planning contrasts favourably – a rational, democratic system of production and allocation counter-posed to the anarchy and oligarchy of the 'free market'. Democratic planning, however, requires much more than beefing up economic regulation and setting up state investment banks. These could be useful first steps towards both improving living standards and constructing necessary alliances with progressive liberals. But democratic planning cannot evade confronting the socialization of the means of production *and* the means of capital allocation – in other words, it requires the nationalization of monopolies and the socialization of finance.[35]

NOTES

1 Matt Phillips 'Investors Bet Giant Companies Will Dominate After Crisis', *New York Times,* 28 April 2020.

2 Ibid.

3 See 'Section 2: Relative Diminution of the Variable Part of Capital Simultaneously with the Progress of Accumulation and of the Concentration that Accompanies it' in Chapter 25 of Karl Marx, *Capital*, Volume I, London: Penguin, 1976.

4 Karl Marx, 'Chapter 25: Section 2: Relative Diminution of the Variable Part of Capital Simultaneously with the Progress of Accumulation and of the Concentration that Accompanies it' in *Capital*, Volume I, p. 777.

5 Karl Marx 'Chapter 32: The Historical Tendency of Capitalist Accumulation' in *Capital*, Volume I, pp. 929.

6 See, e.g., Jonathan Taplin, 'Move Fast and Break Things: How Google, Facebook and Amazon Cornered Culture and Undermined Democracy', New York: Hachette, 2017, in which the author makes the now well-known claim that 'Data is … the new oil'.

7 Rana Foroohar, *Don't Be Evil: The Case Against Big Tech*, London: Allen Lane, 2019; Martin Wolf, 'Why rigged capitalism is damaging liberal democracy', *The Financial Times*, 18 September 2019.

8 Matthew Vincent, 'Loss-making tech companies are floating like it's 1999', *The Financial Times*, 16 June 2019.

9 Michael Moritz, 'Investment banks are losing their grip on IPOs', *The Financial Times*, 18 August 2019.

10 Eric Platt, Andrew Edgecliffe-Johnson, James Fontanella-Khan and Laura Noonan, 'WeWork turmoil puts spotlight on JPMorgan Chase and Goldman Sachs', *The Financial Times*, 24 September 2019.

11 Eric Platt, Laura Noonan, Nicole Bullock and Shannon Bond, 'Morgan Stanley, Goldman and JPMorgan's grip on tech IPOs under threat after Uber', *The Financial Times*, 22 May 2019.

12 Martin Wolf, 'Corporate surpluses are contributing to the savings glut', *The Financial Times*, 17 November 2015; Peter Chen, Loukas Karabarbounis, and Brent Neiman, 'The global corporate saving glut: Long-term evidence', VOX CEPR Policy Portal, 5 April 2017.

13 Rana Foroohar, 'Tech companies are the new investment banks', *The Financial Times*, 11 February 2018.

14 Zack Cope, *The Wealth of (some) Nations: Imperialism and the Mechanics of Value Transfer*, London: Pluto, 2019.

15 Nick Shaxson, *Treasure Islands: Tax Havens and the Men Who Stole the World*, London: Palgrave Macmillan, 2012; Richard Murphy, *Dirty Secrets: How Tax Havens Destroy the Economy*, London: Verso, 2017.

16 Jonathan Tepper and Denise Hearn, *The Myth of Capitalism: Monopolies and the Death of Competition*, New York: Wiley, 2018.

17 Grace Blakeley, 'By Letting Small Businesses Fail, the State is Handing Power to Corporate Giants', *Novara Media*, 2 April 2020, available at: novaramedia.com.

18 Karl Marx, 'Chapter 25: Section 2: Relative Diminution of the Variable Part of Capital Simultaneously with the Progress of Accumulation and of the Concentration that Accompanies it', in *Capital*, Volume I, p. 777.

19 Zia Quereshi, 'Intellectual property, not intellectual monopoly', Brookings Institute 11 July 2018.

20 Adam Leaver, 'Out of time: The fragile temporality of Carillion's accumulation model', Sheffield Political Economy Research Institute [SPERI], 17 January 2018, available at: speri.dept.shef.ac.uk.

21 See: Grace Blakeley, 'Carillion's missing millions', *Red Pepper*, 19 January 2018, available at: www.redpepper.org.uk.

22 C. Wright Mills, *The Power Elite*, Oxford: Oxford University Press, 1956.

23 Sean McDaniel and Craig Berry, 'Digital Platforms and Competition Policy: A literature review' Sheffield Political Economy Research Institute [SPERI], 2017, available at: speri.dept.shef.ac.uk.

24 See the European Commission's report 'Competition Policy for the Digital Era' for an analysis of the effectiveness of EU competition law and recommendations for targeting the power of big tech.

25 Grace Blakeley, 'The European project has far bigger problems than Brexit', *The New Statesman*, 29 March 2019.

26 Sebastian Payne, 'UK to tighten takeover rules for groups vital to virus response', *The Financial Times*, 21 June 2020.

27 Guy Steer, 'Big drama in corporate bonds could be closer than you think', *The Financial Times*, 18 February 2020; Matthew Watson, 'Re-establishing What Went Wrong Before: The Greenspan Put as Macroeconomic Modellers' New Normal', *Journal of Critical Globalisation Studies* 7, 2014.

28 Mark Vandevelde 'The Leveraging of America', *The Financial Times*, 10 July 2020; Michalis Nikiforos, 'When Two Minskyan Processes Meet a Large Shock: The Economic Implications of the Pandemic' Levy Economics Institute POLICY NOTE 2020/1, 2020.

29 See Nathan Tankus, 'The Federal Reserve's Coronavirus Crisis Actions, Explained', Parts 1-4, March-April 2020, available at: nathantankus.substack.com.

30 Michal Rozworski and Leigh Phillips, *The People's Republic of Wall Mart*, London: Verso, 2018.

31 Eleanor Meiskins Wood, *Democracy Against Capitalism: Renewing Historical Materialism*, London: Verso, 2016.

32 Peter Mair, *Ruling the Void: The Hollowing of Western Democracy*, London: Verso, 2013.

33 See the TWC website for more information (techworkerscoalition.org).

34 Aaron Benanev, 'Automation and the future of work—2', *New Left Review* 120, Nov/Dec 2019; Gargi Bhattacharyya, *Rethinking Racial Capitalism*, Washington D.C.: Roman and Littlefield International, 2018.

35 For a discussion of policy proposals aimed at the socialisation of finance, see my *Stolen: How to save the world from financialisation*, London: Repeater, 2019; for a discussion of options for nationalising tech companies, see Wendy Liu, *Abolish Silicon Valley: How to Liberate Technology from Capitalism*, London: Repeater, 2020.

SOCIALISTS ON SOCIAL MEDIA PLATFORMS: COMMUNICATING WITHIN AND AGAINST DIGITAL CAPITALISM

TANNER MIRRLEES

Bertolt Brecht, in the 1932 essay 'The Radio as an Apparatus of Communication', made a 'positive suggestion' to transform radio into a dialogical medium for many-to-many communications. 'Radio is one-sided when it should be two' said Brecht, and 'The radio would be the finest possible communication apparatus in public life ... if it knew how to receive as well as transmit, how to let the listener speak as well as hear', and thereby bring many 'into a relationship' with many others, 'instead of isolating' them.[1] Brecht saw the state as the only entity capable of remaking radio in this way, but because radio's 'proper application' might make it a 'revolutionary' medium, Brecht concluded the bourgeois state would have 'no interest in sponsoring such exercises'. Whether built as a commercial venture or a national public broadcaster, the institutions of radio in the twentieth century were for the most part designed as a one-way communication system, used by corporations and governments to transmit messages to listeners separated by geographical distances. Radio shows were made to inform, entertain, and sell, not to let every listener speak and hear. TV's path was similar: when tuned in to TV shows, viewers could see but not be seen, nor could they share what they thought about what they saw with everyone else watching.

Brecht's 'positive suggestion' for a many-to-many communications system seems to have come to fruition with the internet, and more recently, with the spread of social media platforms such as Facebook, Twitter and YouTube. Socialists around the world are now using these platforms to produce, distribute, exhibit, and consume socialist media and cultural works, and they are openly building events, movements, and organizations within digital capitalism, to go beyond it.[2] That said, the internet and social media platforms are surrounded by all kinds of deterministic, optimistic, and pessimistic rhetorics that cloud a clear view of what they give to *and* take from socialist communicators, especially as compared to the twentieth century's mass media industries, whose state and corporate owners tended to filter out and vilify socialist ideas. While digital platforms are enabling socialists to communicate in ways that were not possible in the pre-digital world of mass media, they are supplements to – not substitutes for – building democratic and sustainable socialist organizations and militant working-class movements. Taking it as axiomatic that communications underpins any possibility for socialist organization and politics, this essay contextualizes the 'brave new world' of digital capitalism, historicizes socialist communications from the 'old media' world of the nineteenth and twentieth centuries to the 'new digital media' world of the early twenty-first, and then maps 'another world' of socialists on social media platforms, with an eye to the novelties, limitations, and challenges.

THE BRAVE NEW WORLD OF DIGITAL CAPITALISM

The postwar American state brought the internet system of interconnected computer networks into being, initially for reasons of national security, and only much later, for capital accumulation. Indeed, the internet's commercial use was illegal up until 1992. Massive US Department of Defense outlays fostered the Advanced Research Projects Agency Network (ARPANET), supported the development of the Transmission Control Program/Internet Protocol TCP/IP suite (joining separate computer networks into a network of networks) and interlinked with university-based researchers aligned with the National Science Foundation to seed and cultivate the core infrastructural hardware and software of the digital age.[3] It was only in the mid-1990s that ownership of the internet was transferred to private hands, when the Clinton administration oversaw the internet's reconfiguration by new high-tech companies into the motor of a US-led 'digital capitalism'. This medium's potentially revolutionary 'message' was massaged to grease the reproduction of market order. The futurist Alvin Toffler joined others in penning 'Cyberspace and the American Dream', a venture-capital-ready 'manifesto' that championed a US-centered global internet as 'renewing the American dream and enhancing its promise'.[4] A 1994 *New York Times* story titled 'US Begins Privatizing Internet's Operations', aptly quoted Jordan Becker, one of the internet's prime innovators at the interface between the state and capital: 'I see the commercial users of the Internet to be the big winners here … [as] the Internet enters this brave new world.'[5]

It was on the heels of this that software initially developed for public use by researchers at the University of Illinois was turned by Marc Andreesen into Netscape, the first big for-profit web browser. And even bigger winners soon followed with the passage of the 1996 Telecommunications Act, the legal centerpiece of the decade of massive internet speculation, 'New Economy' exuberance, the overvaluation of start-ups like Netscape and Yahoo, and the wave of mergers that led to AT&T, Comcast, and Verizon forming the Internet Service Provider (ISP) oligopoly.[6] At the same time, the Washington Consensus was refashioned for the internet. David Rothkopf captured the American empire's 'realpolitik of the Information Age': it was 'strategically crucial' that the US 'do whatever is in its power' to shape the global internet's 'infrastructure, the rules governing it, and the information traversing it'. This involved 'setting technological standards, defining software standards, producing the most popular information products, and leading in the related development of the global trade in services'.[7]

Although cyber-optimism lost some of its luster due to the burst of the dot-com bubble at the turn of the millennium, the launch of new social media platforms such as Facebook (2004), YouTube (2005), and Twitter (2006) amidst much hype about a shift from Web 1.0 to Web 2.0 soon re-infused the 'New Economy' hubris with further revolutionary pretensions.[8] An innovated and better internet that was more user-friendly, interactive, and participatory than ever before would disrupt the power of Big Government, Big Capital, and Big Mass Media, effectively democratising society. Facebook would 'give people the power to share and make the world more open and connected'. YouTube would abide by Google's 'Don't Be evil' motto when inviting everyone to 'Broadcast Yourself'. Twitter would let the world 'create and share ideas and information instantly without barriers' and overturn autocracies along the way. Grifters of the 'Californian ideology'[9] that emerged in the 1990s now lauded these Web 2.0 corporations as revitalizers of popular sovereignty. Embracing the hype from the peddlers of Silicon Valley snake oil, *Time Magazine* named the 2006 Person of the Year, 'You'.[10] The little tech guys became the darlings of Wall Street financiers and Democratic Party politicos at the same time as they enchanted the masses with their promises of cyber-empowerment, only to become the world's most powerful corporations.

The 'Big Five' – Google, Apple, Facebook, Amazon and Microsoft (the 'GAFAM') – rule much of the internet today and preside over its most significant social media platforms.[11] For the past decade, the Big Five's market capitalization, scale of operations, and user base have grown immensely. Valued at more than $5 trillion, the GAFAM now influence the global internet's technological infrastructure, accumulation logics, laws, policies, and regulations, and the ideological orientation of the digital media environment as a whole. Due to their ownership of numerous subsidiaries, the GAFAM rely on a mix of business models to turn a profit, but they are most frequently associated with the exploits of 'platform capitalism' which are built for the collection, algorithmic sorting, processing, commodification, and circulation of user data.[12] Their mechanisms of 'datafication' (surveilling, rendering into and capturing data about aspects of social life), 'commodification' (transforming data about the social relations, emotions, and ideas of users into commodities for sale to advertisers), and 'selection' (steering user interaction and attention with algorithms that select or curate the content users are exposed to apropos inferences about their personal interests, desires, and wants) have helped to make the GAFAM's owning and CEO class incredibly rich.[13] Facebook's Mark Zuckerberg and Microsoft's Bill Gates are worth more than the total GDP of more than half of Africa. Amazon's Jeff Bezos, soon to be the world's first trillionaire, possesses a fortune greater than Morocco's $119-billion-dollar GDP, and every hour, he takes approximately 315 times the $28,466 median annual pay to Amazon workers.[14]

Backed by lobbies such as the Internet Association, the Computer & Communications Industry Association, and the Information Technology Industry Council, the GAFAM spent more than half a billion dollars from 2005 to 2018 cajoling Congress.[15] From the Bush Administration's Global Internet Freedom Task Force to Obama's International Strategy for Cyberspace: Prosperity, Security and Openness in a Networked World (ISCPSONW), the GAFAM have been central actors in crafting bilateral and multilateral free trade agreements to their benefit. The National Security Agency, the Department of Defense, and the CIA's tech investment arm, In-Q-Tel, all support GAFAM research and development as well as procure their hardware and software for surveillance and cyber-warfare; and the Department of State uses their advert-targeting services for public diplomacy campaigns that aim to organize consent to US foreign policy across borders.

In addition to thus being political as well as economic entities, the GAFAM are significant cultural entities, interwoven with daily ways of life in myriad forms. It now seems habitual for billions of people spanning different countries, class positions, racial ascriptions, sexual orientations, ethnicities, creeds, and lifestyles to spend an average of 144 minutes each day doing things on platforms: signing in; scrolling, viewing, and reviewing; writing, posting, and reading; liking, sharing, deleting; signing out. In 2005, just 5 per cent of American adults were using social media platforms, but by 2011, nearly 50 per cent were; in 2020, over 75 per cent were doing so each day. In 2020, about 4.5 billion people worldwide were using the internet, and 3.8 billion of these were using at least one social media platform. Each second, 8,952 tweets are sent on Twitter and 83,831 videos get viewed on YouTube. Every sixty seconds, Facebook users make 317,000 status updates, upload 147,000 photos and share 54,000 links to everything from 'baby yoda' graphic images to the *Manifesto of the Communist Party*.[16] Evidently, the GAFAMs are using their platforms to privatize, marketize, and commodify more and more of cultural life. They are in the process of restructuring the way billions of people work, live, learn, create, and play.

Of course, the very same GAFAMs which are 're-inventing a capitalistic future'[17] are at the same time more and more the objects of 'ruthless criticism'.[18] They are variously described as: monopolists[19] profiting from a 'gig economy' that degrades labour and precaritizes work;[20] 'surveillance capitalists'[21] that turn people into exploitable 'prosumers' while monitoring, accumulating, commodifying and selling their data;[22] imperialist servants of the US war machine and military-industrial-complex;[23] destroyers of the public service function that journalism ought to play in democracy;[24] generators of far right 'filter bubbles' that perpetuate hate, disinformation and 'fake news';[25] and, anti-union solicitors of dog-eat-dog entrepreneurialism and egotistical self-branding.[26]

In fact, all these types of issues have been on the radar of critical studies of the communications and mass media industries for a long time.[27] These studies address these issues not in terms of the novel properties of newfangled technologies, but as stemming from the social forces and relations of communications technologies and media made for and put in the service of capitalism. They show how the news, advertising and PR, radio and TV broadcasting, and entertainment played a double role for capitalism, first, as a profit-making machine, and second, as a means of legitimizing the system. Even if they did not always directly uphold 'ruling class ideas', and even reflected class antagonisms,[28] the mass media industries engaged in mass socialization for consumer-capitalism. By transmitting commercial messages and images to millions of working people spread across vast distances, many media products took part in normalizing certain ways of being working class that aligned with the status quo, while ignoring or caricaturizing the socialists, unionists, and militant workers who fought for things to be otherwise.[29] As Ralph Miliband put it over 40 years ago: 'whatever else the immense output of the mass media is intended to achieve, it is also intended to help prevent the development of class consciousness in the working class, and to reduce as much as possibly any hankering it might have for radical alternatives.'[30]

But if it is indeed here that the critical study of the industries of 'digital', 'communicative', or 'platform' capitalism today also needs to *begin*, this is not where it should end. For something else is happening that was inconceivable for most of the second half of the twentieth century, when socialists in the West were largely kept out of the mass media's one-to-many communications regime. Digital technologies and social media platforms are today being used by socialists for communicating within and against digital capitalism, and for socialism on a remarkably large scale.

SOCIALISTS ON SOCIAL MEDIA PLATFORMS: MAPPING ANOTHER WORLD

Socialists always have tried to harness each new communications technology into a new means for producing, distributing and consuming socialist media and cultural works.[31] Karl Marx was, after all, the mid-nineteenth century's most significant socialist media communicator. On commission to the Communist League, Marx in the first two months of 1848, with dip pen in hand, wrote the *Manifesto of the Communist Party*. This was published anonymously by the London-based German Workers' Educational Association, which used its own printing press to mechanically reproduce and bind its inked pages into a thousand or so book copies, and then it administered the work's translation from German into Polish, Danish, Swedish, and French language editions.[32] The League's German newspaper *Neue Rheinische Zeitung* (edited by Marx) serialized the *Manifesto*, but its first English-language version was published in the late 1850s by *The Red Republican*, an English socialist newspaper. Exiled to London after the failure of the 1848 revolutions, Marx made his way between 1852 and 1863 with modest pay from *The New York Tribune* for his op-eds, which reached its 200,000 readers.[33] An advocate of press freedom, Marx would have kept writing for the *Tribune* had he not been fired for refusing to cow to its editors' calls for peace between the Union and the Confederacy, but without abolishing slavery. To most Americans of the day, Marx was known as a rabble-rousing journalist, not a historical materialist philosopher. After all, the first English language version of the *Manifesto* only appeared in the United States in 1871 as a serial in *Woodhull & Claflin's Weekly*, a socialist feminist magazine. *Capital*'s first full English volume appeared in 1888, five years after Marx's death. In socialism's germinal period, Marx created 'content', and organizations – socialist and bourgeois – circulated it.

The German Social Democratic Party (SPD) launched *Vorwärts* ('forward') in 1876. The Italian Socialist Party released the first issue of *Avanti!* on 25 December 1896, which was later co-edited by Antonio Gramsci, who had previously written for *Il Grido del Popolo* ('to tell the truth is revolutionary'). The Section Française de l'Internationale Ouvrière (SFIO) launched

L'Humanité in 1909, and in England, the Social Democratic Federation published *Justice* in 1884 and the Socialist League launched *Commonweal* in 1885.[34] Across the Atlantic, the burgeoning Socialist Party of America, which in 1912 got nearly 900,000 votes for its presidential candidate Eugene Debs, was running mass newspapers such as *Chicago Daily Socialist* (1906-1912), *New York Call* (1908-1923), and *Milwaukee Leader* (1911-1938).[35] Produced by a staff of sixty and circulated to half a million readers each week, *Appeal to Reason* (1895-1922) was the biggest American socialist newspaper of the day. A plurality of socialist media and cultural works were read and seen by tens to hundreds of thousands of people.[36]

By the spoken word, or by mechanically or digitally reproducible newspapers, pamphlets, books, and posters, as well as with motion pictures, radio and TV programmes, socialist parties, organizations, and activists have always engaged in multi-media communications. Their freedom to express themselves in capitalist societies has ebbed and flowed, as the major means for communicating on a massive scale has mostly been owned by the bourgeoisie, whose accumulation interests were facilitated and legitimized by states. As a consequence of being marginalized, socialists have mostly tried to speak to one another and to the working class through media made by themselves or made with the support of small non-profit or for-profit operations. The first three decades of the twentieth century represented the high point of mass socialist parties, and relatedly massive socialist media and cultural production and consumption. For the next seven decades, successive generations of committed socialists continued to produce and circulate print and other forms of media, but their societal influence experienced a long decline.

In the Cold War decades in the West, the Communist parties continued to run their media outlets, but as with those founded by Trotskyist political organizations, these usually reached a much smaller audience than in the heyday of socialist media. The 1960s New Left's challenge from the grassroots to higher education to both the US and Soviet propaganda regimes (epitomized in the US by Michael Harrington's *New America* and Paul and Mari Jo Buhle's *Radical America*) gave rise to the vibrant scholar-activist communities which also birthed *New Left Review* and the *Socialist Register* in the UK.[37] Alongside the independent socialist journal *Monthly Review* established earlier in 1949, these three academic-political crossover journals became especially vital in keeping the socialist tradition alive in hard times, and still do, in ours.

The New Left also reconfigured tape recorders, cameras, video recorders and TV sets for non-profit and community media initiatives.[38] For example, in 1971, Michael Shamberg's 'Guerrilla Television' manifesto inspired countercultural TV projects such as TVTV, Broadside TV, and University Community Vide.[39] In 1981, Dee Dee Halleck launched *Paper Tiger Television* (PTTV), a New York City-based non-profit public access TV show featuring 'Herb Schiller Reads the *New York Times*'. Inspired by the Situationist International's *détournement* of the society of the spectacle, artist-activists of this era devised tactics such as culture jamming, satirical parody, and pranking, and put all kinds of creativity into the service of vibrant 'cultural resistance' against the superstructures of capital.[40] Theses scrappy media and cultural activities tended to exhibit small teams of producers, shoestring budgets, limited distribution and niche audiences, and they could not achieve the influence once wielded by the century's earlier socialist parties and working-class organizations, nor slow the mass media industries' growth or counter the sway of its ideology. By the early 1980s, *Radical America*'s readership was about 4,100 and *Monthly Review*'s was 10,000,[41] while Henry Luce's *Time Magazine* had about four million subscribers. Guerrilla TV never captured close to the mass attention channelled by CBS TV hits such as the 'Who Done It?' episode of *Dallas*, which was watched by 90 million people on one evening.

Yet even the relatively modest diffusion of the internet by the late 1990s provided socialists with a new and powerful means of many-to-many mass transmissive and dialogical media communications that we are only beginning to grasp. Having given rise to a new 'Cyber Left' and Indymedia organizations,[42] the internet became not only a salient means for socialists to speak, get seen, and be heard, but even came to be viewed as 'representing a qualitatively different way of organizing the social processes of communication'.[43] The anti-globalization 'movement of movements' protests, beginning with the 'Battle of Seattle' in November 1999 and the disruption of IMF and World Bank meetings in Washington in April 2000, cheered as the dawn of an altogether 'new' form of mass politics, were prepared via the internet.[44] The NGOs, unionists, students, and anarchists on the front lines of these 'rhizomatic rebellions' used the web 'to do everything from cataloguing the latest transgressions of the World Bank to bombarding Shell Oil with faxes and emails, to distributing ready-to-download anti-sweatshop leaflets for protests at Nike Town'.[45]

While these netcentric street protests often fuelled the mass media's spectacle of the Left as violent, disruptive, freakish, ignorant, or incoherent,[46] this was countered by the embrace of this new 'Cyber Left' in the North of Subcomandante Marcos and the Zapatista Army of National Liberation to inspire international socialist solidarity. Yet as Judy Hellman argued in the *Socialist Register* volume on 'Necessary and Unnecessary Utopias' in 2000,[47] this 'virtual Chiapas' not only gave its Northern supporters too much information (some of it, disinformation) but also created virtual communities that were exclusionary (due to the digital divide), illusory (because so much cyber-interaction is solitary and low stakes), and inorganic (as effect of no face-to-face encounters). At worst, the internet gave 'electronic militants' a way to 'to communicate to downtrodden people around the world that we have them in mind without actually having to bestir ourselves to climb out of our ergonomically correct computer chair to leave the house!' This prescient critique would later be taken up more broadly in terms of the limits of 'clicktivism' or 'slacktivism', that 'feel good activism' which fosters the 'illusion of having a meaningful impact on the world without demanding anything more than joining a Facebook group'.[48]

Yet as 9/11 spawned the War on Terror and the invasion of Afghanistan and then Iraq after the turn of the millennium, millions of people in every major city on the planet were the using the internet for anti-war activism, and climbing out of their computer chairs to join in the largest ever global marches for peace in history.[49] By the time of the Arab Spring and the *Adbusters*-initiated Occupy protests of 2011, a new type of technological determinism led journalists to coin terms like 'Facebook revolution', 'Twitter Revolution', and 'YouTube Revolution'. Democratic Party innovation guru Alec Ross touted the social internet as the 'Che Guevara of the 21st century'.[50]

But smartphones did not make the new protest movements and social media platforms did not build the uprisings, human organizers did.[51] In that regard, the digital technologies have not brought about a totally 'new means of and a new meaning of being political'[52] and the people using them did not stop the Global War on Terror or nationalize Wall Street. They certainly did help activists to put the problems of empire and war, as well neoliberal capitalism's social class antagonisms, on the public mind. Yet the failure of these networked protests to bring about the massive social changes they demanded was a valuable object lesson in how and why the rabble of the streets needs to also rebuild organizations and even remake parties capable of intervening in and transforming the state.

In the first decade of the twenty-first century, socialists were on the internet, linking with others near and far, participating in and posting to discussion forums, and arguing with one another about history, theory, strategy, and tactics on email listserves (Louis Proyect's Marxmail was among the first of these).[53] New socialist organizations were also emerging, and putting themselves online. As early as 2005, the Toronto-based Socialist

Project launched *The Bullet*, a digital magazine; and in 2008, it built a YouTube channel called LeftStreamed, which grew to become a massive open online archive of hundreds of digitized public talks by socialist educators from all over the world. But it was in the second decade of the twenty-first century that a new US-centered yet globalizing socialist media really took off. Bhaskar Sunkara launched *Jacobin* online in 2010, and by 2020, it had 50,000 paid subscribers to its print magazine and two million monthly visitors to its website (a much wider audience than the *Daily Worker* had in its heyday of the 1930s).[54] Significant as it is, *Jacobin* is just one of the many new flourishing twenty-first century socialist media outlets that have helped to make a new generation of socialists, from the millennials that were 'early adopters' of digital technologies, to those in 'Generation Z' who came of age when social media platforms were already interwoven with their everyday lives.[55]

In North America and elsewhere, the internet, computers and smartphones, and platforms have reached a critical mass, making a rigid binary between online and offline, virtual and real, disembodied and embodied communications less pertinent. Drawing a hard line between what socialists are doing on social media and what they are doing off of them may be misguided given how embedded they have become in society and how often online and offline political experiences merge. There are plenty of socialists whose work in communities and organizations blends seamlessly with their social media interactions. They may be physically present at a socialist meeting or rally while logged into Facebook and communicating to the rest of the world in real-time about what's being done. And they may attend an event or demo, and then return home and start chatting about it on Twitter, or turn this experience into a new article or video to be shared with the world later on. In any case, across generations – 'Boomer, X, Y, and Z'–socialists with smartphones in hand and Facebook and Twitter profiles open for ideological battle are by now spreading pro-socialist messages and images that would never have passed through the old gatekeepers and filters of the mass media industries and reached a mass audience of readers, viewers, and listeners.

To be clear, capitalist social media platforms are not the cause of this socialist communications ferment. They do not produce socialist media. Socialists themselves create the content – the manifestos, news and magazine articles, pamphlets and statements, books and book excerpts and reviews, interviews, videos, ads, pages, events, posts, tweets, and comments – and spread them across these platforms. Left publishing houses and journals all have their own pages and profiles on platforms, and use these to publicize and build audiences for their authors and works. For example, Verso Books is followed by 98,016K on Facebook, 98,100 on Twitter, and 11,600 on YouTube. *Jacobin* is followed by 345,000 on Facebook, 276,000 on Twitter and 23,500 on YouTube. Apart from the many small socialist organizations that publish online magazines and news,[56] Bernie Sanders and Jeremy Corbyn's leadership campaign teams hired numerous social media publicists to spread content out across all the major platforms.[57] Spun out of the 2016 Bernie Sanders campaign, 'Our Revolution' launched with a YouTube live-stream to push Democrats leftward, while the Democratic Socialists of America grew online as well as off.[58] Momentum, launched in 2015 in support of Jeremy Corbyn's attempt to push the Labour Party toward socialism, made a big social media presence for itself, spreading low-budget but punchy videos such as 'Daddy, why do you hate me?' to millions on Facebook, and operating Twitter and YouTube channels as well. Closely associated with this development, Novara Media emerged in the UK to take on 'the issues that are set to define the 21st century, from a crisis of capitalism to racism and climate change'.[59] Like the US-based Means TV – 'the world's first post-capitalist, cooperatively run streaming service' – it employs or contracts socialist media makers to this end. [60]

Across all major social media platforms, socialist media producer roles may fluctuate, as one may be a party member, movement participant, organizer, editor, author, educator, journalist, interviewer, and interviewee. Many socialist media creators operate their own podcasts and YouTube channels to creatively combine their knowledge with digital technologies to innovate or emulate new media forms with the goal of making ends meet through their work and moving people to socialism. Over the past decade, hundreds of socialist podcasts – scripted and improvised shows featuring one or more recurring hosts – have launched. The names of these range from earnest (e.g., 'The Sensible Socialist') to the guffaw-inducing ironic (e.g., 'Southern Fried Socialist') to the cyber-savvy (e.g., 'The BlockChain Socialist'). Some podcasts are affiliated with socialist organizations and publishers, but most often, they seem to be run by an individual or small group of entrepreneurial socialists who script, feature in, produce, edit, and publicize their own work. With over 35,000 subscribers and anywhere from 150-200,000 downloads of its bi-weekly episodes, Chapo Trap House is the biggest socialist podcast gig going these days. Crowdfunded through Patreon, this flashpoint of the 'Dirtbag Left' adopts a reflexively 'politically incorrect' and irreverent tone to distinguish its style from what its creators chastise as much of the Left's 'humorlessness', 'upper-middle-class smugness', and 'self-righteousness'.[61] Smaller but still significant socialist podcasts include Dead Pundits Society

(DPS), whose goal is to 'spread accessible socialist politics far and wide in order to contribute to the expanding socialist media ecosystem'. Red Scare (subtitled 'The Ladies Make a Podcast') is a socialist 'cultural commentary podcast' hosted by self-described 'bohemian layabout' women. Season of the Bitch (SotB) is a socialist feminist podcast whose hosts refer to themselves as The Coven. Working People is a podcast 'by, for, and about the working class today'; in the spirit of 'history from below', each episode features interviews with a diversity of working-class people from across the US that shed light on their histories, jobs, pleasures and pains, hopes and fears, and struggles to understand and change their conditions with the goal of 'build[ing] a sense of shared struggle and solidarity between workers around the country'. Hundreds more socialist podcasts spread out across the internet and platforms.

Socialist media creators and entertainers are also growing in numbers across YouTube. 'BreadTube'[62] – often used interchangeably with 'LeftTube' – is a loose network of Leftist YouTube creators and channels who argue for a variety of left and socialist traditions and positions, while advancing a radical critique of capitalism and the ideas of conservative and neoliberal ideologues.[63] With over 972,000 subscribers, Natalie Wynn's Contrapoints is by far the most popular of these, and her videos such as 'The Left', 'What's Wrong with Capitalism', and 'Decrypting the Alt-Right: How to Recognize a F@scist' regularly garner up to two million views.[64] With 586,000 subscribers, 'hbomberguy' is a channel run by an articulate yet self-effacing young socialist gamer who debunks right-wing conspiracy theories (e.g., 'Cultural Marxism: A Measured Response') and has live chats with left politicians (e.g., 'Alexandria Ocasio-Cortez Says Trans Rights' is a live-stream of him playing Donkey Kong while talking 'strategy' with this 'democratic socialist' US Congresswoman). With 335,000 subscribers, 'Shaun' does video critiques of popular culture (e.g., 'Is *Black Panther* Alt-Right?'), white nationalist ideology (e.g., 'The Great Replacement Isn't Real- ft. Lauren Southern'), and neoliberal policy (e.g., 'How Privatization Fails: Railways'). With 271,000 subscribers, Peter Coffin's channel is home to sharp witted videos ranging from 'How Bernie Sanders Won' and 'The Road to Socialism' all the way to '*Joker*, The Culture War, and Pure Ideology'. Renowned for winning live-streamed debates with alt-right propagandists, 'Vaush' describes himself as a 'Dirtbag leftist & revolutionary LARPer' and has over 180,000 subscribers to his channel, which features video take downs of far right Tubers (e.g., 'Debating Sargon of Akkad and Exposing Him as a White Nationalist') and contentious topics (e.g., 'Socialism, Free Speech & Sex Work' and 'Addressing the Drama – Black Nationalism').

With 'Total Liberation' as her tagline and over 53,000 subscribers, 'Mexie' is a Toronto-based Tuber who creates slick informative videos on topics such as 'Capitalism Does Not Give a Damn About Disabled People', 'Climate Barbarism and Eco-Fascism', and 'On Strategies for Post-Capitalism'. The PhD student Tom Nicholas' 60,000-subscribed 'What the Theory' (WTF?) series features Marxist humanities explainer videos (e.g., 'Cultural Materialism: WTF? Raymond Williams, Culture and Structures of Feeling' and 'Marxist Literary Theory: WTF? An Introduction to Marxism and Culture'). A self-described Iraqi Marxist called Hakim who 'makes videos from time to time', offers his nearly 32,000 subscribers 'book recommendations under such labels as 'Down with the Bourgeoisie' as well as videos like 'Marx's Wage Labour and Capital Explained - Part 1 - What Are Wages?') and challenges to capitalist 'misconceptions' like 'No Innovation Under Socialism'. Xexizy, another 'Marxist youtuber determined to bring about the social revolution through the internet, somehow', is subscribed to by 23,000 viewers who take in fare such as 'Jordan Peterson Doesn't Understand Marxism' and 'Why New Leftists Are Stuck in the Supermarket of Ideology'.

A more earnest channel subscribed to by nearly 16,000 viewers is DemocraticSocialist01 whose videos take on alt-light pundits (e.g., 'Ben Shapiro has no idea what he is talking about + not worth debating') and take down conservative philosophers (e.g., 'Rightwing Socialism and the Lies of Hayek'). With over 10,000 subscribers, 'Flea Market Socialist' envisages 'Communism as a direction, not a goal' and creates videos that teach socialists how to create propaganda (e.g., 'Socialist Screen Printing: For Cheap'), and remix advertising formats with tongue-in-cheek socialist propaganda (e.g. 'It's Time for Guillotines'). Some other notable Leftist Tuber channels and videos are: Angie Speaks (e.g., 'Exit The Vampire Castle: A Commentary on Cancel Culture' and 'Loneliness & Capitalism: Inside Angie Speaks'); Philosophy Tube (e.g., 'Why the Left Will Win' and the 'Mad Marx series in 4 parts on capitalism, exploitation, labour, and the working class'); the anarcho-commie Re-Education (e.g., 'Capitalism vs Socialism: Who's Better at Propaganda' and '3 Ways to be Revolutionary Every Day'); YUGOPNIK (e.g., 'Is it hypocritical for leftist YouTubers to make a lot of money?' and 'How consumerism presents itself as activism - Does watching leftist YouTube contribute to anything?'); Red Star Videos (e.g., 'Hal Draper and the Anatomy of the Microsect' and 'Popular Wobbly Music Video'); Brendan Mccooney (e.g., 'The Law of Value') and The Swoletariat (which has launched some live-stream debates such as 'Democratic Socialism vs Leninism').

Interlinking with socialist podcaster sites and LeftTuber channels are a number of other platforms where socialists hang out, chat, debate, and learn from one another. For example, Reddit (/r/Socialism) features thousands of threads about all kinds of socialist questions and answers such as: 'Am I Too Young to Be a Socialist?', 'What are the Best Books on the Economic Aspects of Socialism?', and 'My grocery store is ending 'hazard pay' of a measly two extra dollars an hour tomorrow. How can I advocate or spread agit prop in my store without drawing attention?' Also, on live chat and game streaming platforms such as Discord, socialists from all over the world meet in real time to hash out socialist politics on servers with names like 'Leftist Bunker', 'Left Union Collective', and 'Discord Done Left'. On Twitch, a live-streaming service subsidiary of Amazon, the self-identified socialist gamer Hasan Piker frequently 'goes live' before 90,000 followers around the world. On TikTok, socialists post funny music videos and political pitches (Joshua Collins, a 26-year-old socialist truck driver, launched his Congressional campaign @ joshua4congress). On the Facebook-owned photo sharing site Instagram, 'demsocialists', 'sassysocialistmemes', and 'socialism_memes' post and spread humorous and angsty images. One is a photo of the Sesame Street Elmo doll cut with the caption 'We are all puppets of the bourgeoisie!'

Intersecting with these organizational and individual sources of socialist media influence are innumerable people who, from their own profile pages, whether logged in via personal computer or smartphone, produce their own content, consume the content produced by others, and then produce more content in relation to it. These socialist 'prosumers' may: consume and affirm content created by other socialists (by reading published articles, listening to podcasts and watching videos, perhaps indicating their approval by clicking 'like' or leaving a positive comment); reproduce and amplify content (by captioning, retweeting, or sharing it with friends or followers in their personalized network); augment content (by offering some pithy remark or substantive commentary, extending the discussion or starting an altogether new one); and, remix content (by taking something from the initial work and then mixing it up with other found materials – some from the commons and others from the copyright world – to create a new piece of content, a socialist 'meme' for example).[65]

For most of the twentieth century, the socialist left was largely kept out of the mass media industries, but all of the above examples demonstrate how in the twenty-first century socialists are logged in to massively populated social media platforms, and communicating their ideas from everywhere, to anyone, at any time. From within digital capitalism, socialists have found a way to use social media platforms to produce, circulate, and consume abundant socialist media and cultural expressions in opposition to capitalism. Across platforms that expand across borders flow: digital versions of books, book excerpts and reviews; peer reviewed scholarly articles, magazine and news articles and op-ed pieces; sound and video interviews with socialist intellectuals, movement leaders and cadre; live-streamed debates and video recordings of public events, book launches, rallies and demonstrations; coverage of and commentary on current events and popular culture; text, sound and video speeches by socialist politicians, and assessments of these; photos, live game-streams, creative remixes and memes; and user-generated commentary on nearly every piece of content that moves.

Social media platforms are enabling socialists to undertake forms of mass-mediated transmissive and dialogical communications that were not possible in the previous age of the mass media industries, when 'barriers to entry' were so high. Socialists tend to be very resource poor: they are not financed by Wall Street, do not own big studios, and do not have major cross-national distribution networks and exhibition venues. But with digital media production software acquired at little to no cost from the internet ('shareware' and 'freeware'), and the 'freemium' service of platforms acting as efficient distribution and exhibition networks, socialists, so long as they have an internet connection, a computer, and rudimentary digital literacy skills, can now create and spread their media far and wide. In effect, socialists are becoming mass media communicators, and they are using platforms to become positively visible, audible and readable to hundreds, thousands, even millions of people. Given the lack of such abundant, widespread and incredibly fast-moving socialist media in the age of the mass media industries, this is a novel development. Socialist media content is no longer scarce or hard to find, but widely available and searchable to almost anyone using the internet right now.

POSSIBILITIES AND LIMITATIONS

Whether 'to be or not to be' a socialist communicator on social media platforms has been a question taken up in two recent *Jacobin* articles – Benjamin Fong's 'Log Off',[66] and Meagan Day's 'Unfortunately, We Can't Log Off'.[67] Fong urges socialists to log off, saying these platforms foster in users 'an obsession with self-perception', 'a disturbing lack of empathy', and 'atomization' that reinforces the 'loneliness' and 'inhumanity' of life in neoliberal capitalism. Bemoaning these negative psychosocial effects, Fong describes social media platforms as an 'imminent threat' to a viable socialist left and proposes we try to abolish them all together. Day validates Fong's concerns, but declares she is 'not sure' if she 'would've become a socialist without social media'. While she prefers 'listening to a rousing speech on a picket line or taking in the crowd at a well-attended socialist meeting' than tweeting about socialism all day, Day sees platforms as helpful to the twenty-first century socialist project. Recognizing that social media platforms are where billions of working-class people are at, Day says socialists 'face a choice: we can either relinquish the social media sphere to our class enemies, or we can attempt to infuse it with our own political perspective'. Day chooses to wield platforms 'for collective political education and agitation' with the goal of winning people to socialism. These platforms can 'suck', says Day, but they might 'be the best propaganda tool socialists have ever had'. Day's assessment of these possibilities rings true, and Day's article itself 'had legs', thanks in part to social media platforms.[68]

In the postwar heyday of the mass media industries, the mainstream media space was the TV set, and corporate self-censorship and governmentalized anti-socialism ensured that socialists would not appear, at least not in a positive way, to anyone tuned in to the TV shows broadcast to millions. On platforms, the new mainstream media space, socialists are shifting the connotative meanings attached to the sign of socialism away from the negative (the dystopian history of Stalinist gulags and authoritarian terror regimes) toward the positive (the future prospect of an equal, just and democratic society). Socialists are using platforms to reclaim and remake the word 'socialism' into something cool, attractive, reasonable, and viable to more and more people. They popularize the idea that there is an alternative to capitalism called 'socialism' among working-class people, young and old. Capitalist crisis and organized politics created an opening for this rearticulation of socialism, and socialist media producers are contributing to this effort by making a 'socialism' (in one formulation or another) seem 'common sense' to more people. For what they are worth, public opinion polls indicate that 'socialism' is indeed trending in a positive direction.[69]

In addition to being a powerful propaganda tool, social media platforms are political 'battle-spaces' where individuals, groups, and organizations across the spectrum spread their ideologies with the goal of shaping perceptions, influencing opinions, and winning people to their way vis-à-vis similar attempts by others. On platforms, the alt-light and alt-right often got the jump on the socialist left, and on YouTube and elsewhere, they malign and attack socialism. For example, Steven Crowder is a Christian conservative who sometimes wears Che Guevara t-shirts that say 'Socialism is for f*gs' [sic] and from his 4.42 million subscribed YouTube show 'Louder with Crowder', he releases videos such as 'Socialism is Evil: Change my Mind' and 'Why Democratic' Socialism Doesn't Work'. The 1.17 million subscribed Ben Shapiro Show channel streams videos such as 'Even if you ignore that socialism is evil, it's also unworkable'. The neoconservative Heritage Foundation's YouTube channel bashes socialists with videos such as 'Millennials do not know the true evils of socialism' and 'Telling the Truth about Socialism'. Far from capitulating to these far right smears, socialists are directly battling right-wing intellectuals and their ideas on platforms. This is an asymmetrical fight, as the powers-that-be continue to wield far greater resources than socialists for setting social media agendas, framing reality, and reaching mass audiences. Yet socialists have not ceded this battle-space to the right. They are on platforms directly challenging dominant media agendas and frames with the goal of connecting with working-class people 'where they are at' with the hope of winning them to socialism.

Beyond empowering socialists in the 'culture wars', social media platforms play a positive role in the everyday lives of socialists, as they provide a way for socialists to construct socialist identities for themselves, and convey these to the world. The mass media industries had the power to under-represent and misrepresent socialists, but on social media platforms, socialists are representing themselves. To convey their socialist identities, they sometimes include the word 'socialist' in their username or bio statement, or add a relevant emoji. For example, on Twitter, people often identify themselves as 'democratic socialists' by placing a rose emoji next to their username. On platforms, representing oneself as a 'socialist' and being recognized by peers and strangers alike as one is a way to positively differentiate one's identity from neoliberals and conservatives, and assert one's identification with an alternative to the status quo. Importantly, representing oneself as a socialist is a way to proudly express this identity and be recognized for it, which is an important symbolic act given the long history of anti-socialist shame campaigns. Social media platforms let socialists make their private political identities public, and this is a significant way to delineate 'who they are' from 'who they are not' in a mostly bourgeois world.

Relatedly, social media platforms enable self-identified socialists to search for and participate in virtual socialist communities. Physical locations are still important places of socialist interaction, as much socialist organization and political action is very local (e.g., the workplace, the union hall, the café, the classroom, the streets and the public square). But platforms such as Facebook, Twitter, YouTube, ZOOM and Google Hangouts unbind socialist interaction from the constraints of propinquity, and are new meeting spaces for socialists spread across cities, regions, and countries. This is especially the case in the context of the Covid-19 pandemic and physical distancing rules. Friending and following other socialists and joining virtual socialist groups, pages, forums, and live-stream events enable isolated socialists to commune, form comradely links, and make connections. In these virtual spaces of interaction, socialists can be close to one another while far away and engage in meaningful discourse about everything from socialist history to current events. While no substitute for socialist organizing in face-to-meetings, platforms can help bridge territorial gaps between many far-flung socialists who may have never had a chance to meet, see and be seen, speak and be spoken to, listen and be heard, if bound by place.

Social media platforms are turning into massive open online means of making and keeping socialists (not least by enabling socialists to educate themselves). Flesh and blood educators will always play a vital role in agitating and educating for socialism in a shared place, but platforms are helping them connect with far away learners. A learner might 'friend' a leading socialist public intellectual on Facebook or follow them on Twitter. On YouTube, a learner can subscribe to free courses such as 'Reading Marx's Capital with David Harvey', engage with over a decade's worth of recorded public lectures featuring hundreds of educators on the Socialist Project's LeftStreamed channel, and read Vivek Chibber's 'The ABCs of Capitalism' pamphlet series alongside *Jacobin*-supported Covid-19 'Stay at Home' live-stream videos. The algorithmic 'selection' and 'personalization' mechanism of each platform may also semi-automate the work of socialist education by exposing learners to content that it deems will be relevant to them based upon the data it has gathered and inferences it has made about their interests (e.g., their search history, viewing history, channels subscribed to, and click behaviour). The more a learner searches for, views, and clicks through socialist posts, stories, pages, groups, channels, playlists, and videos, the more platform algorithms recommend and expose learners to these. While socialist learners may self-educate on platforms, this is a supplement not a substitution for the important living labours of socialist educators, as well as of collective organization and action.

Significantly, social media platforms have helped socialists to be recognized and platformed by the mainstream media outlets that once marginalized them. Perhaps recognizing the appeal of the 'democratic socialist' Bernie Sanders and 'the Squad' (Alexandria Ocasio-Cortez, Ilhan Omar, Ayanna Pressley, and Rashida Tlaib), and acknowledging the popular flow of socialist ideas on platforms, various mass newspapers, TV news networks, and magazines have made some space for socialist content – possibly as a way to capture a youthful socialist 'audience commodity'. In any case, *The Washington Post* ('This is not Your Grandfather's Concept of Socialism'), *The New York Times* ('The New Socialists'), and *The Globe and Mail* ('Is

There a Marxist Revival'), as well as CNBC ('Why Democratic Socialism is Gaining Popularity in the United States'), NBC News ('Analyzing the Rise of Democratic Socialism') and even FOX TV News ('What is Democratic Socialism?') have given some space and time to 'democratic socialists' such as Bhaskar Sunkara and others. *Teen Vogue* regularly publishes pro-socialist articles ('The Deep Socialist Roots of the U.S. Labor Movement', 'Socialism is the Answer to Corporate 'Girl Boss' Feminism', and 'International Women's Day is Rooted in Socialist Feminism'). Given the mass media industries' history of repressing or demonizing socialists, all this is significant.

But optimism about socialists on social media platforms should be tempered by attention to the limitations. In the past, socialists might distinguish themselves and their media from the mass media industries by their autonomy from and oppositional stance toward corporate capital. But when logged in to and using social media platforms, socialists get used by what Jodi Dean long ago conceptualized as 'communicative capitalism'[70] and what Nick Srniceck recently called 'platform capitalism'.[71] To use these platforms, we must first consent to their owners' conditions, and when 'clicking to accept', we become 'users' subject to the corporation's terms of service, policies, and community guidelines, including its right to collect data about everything we say and do while logged in. In this regard, socialists may be doing a form of unpaid 'digital labour' and functioning as an exploitable 'prosumer commodity'[72] for the GAFAM and other platform corporations.

This integration is also politically risky because the relationship between platform owners and users is authoritarian, not democratic. Platforms are accountable to their shareholders first, advertisers second, and users third. These corporations possess the power to decide what counts as 'appropriate' and 'inappropriate' user interaction and user-generated content, and if socialism ever became a real threat to their interests or to digital capitalism more generally, they could block, suspend, or ban the accounts of socialists. Also, platform capitalism's data-veillance of prosumers is converging with state surveillance of citizens, and so while platforms have made socialists more visible to the mainstream, they also potentially put every socialist that uses them in the security state's surveillance crosshairs. If the socialist left ever one day became a serious challenge to the capitalist status quo, the FBI agent and NSA officer would only need to turn to social media platforms for a registry of the 'who's who' of twenty-first-century socialism. For these reasons, it is imperative for socialists to maintain their own independent digital media sites while also using the corporate platforms as long as they can to educate, agitate and organize.

Another limitation is the digital divide. Far from encompassing humanity as a whole, the diffusion, use, and impact of social media platforms is unevenly developed and unequally accessible. About 60 per cent of the total world population is currently online and able to access the internet, and the countries of North America and Europe are home to the most internet users (as a percentage of the population). If the incredible growth in the number of people around the world using American social media platforms is an indication of future trends, current initiatives to shrink the 'digital divide' will help the GAFAM enlarge its already gigantic global footprint. Also, many leading Western platform socialists are young, male, white, and possess socialist cultural and digital capital. Their online (and offline) followings may replicate the problem of small groups: conditions of entry may alienate the 'newbie' to socialist politics, especially those already experiencing generational, gendered, and racial forms of oppression and exclusion in society. In response, socialists might push for 'public service internet platforms'[73] that 'put people before profit' and do much better than platform capitalism to be genuinely accessible and inclusive of all people.[74] The American state made the internet and then gave it to capital, and given all the problems with digital capitalism, perhaps there is good reason to take the internet back. Not to be put in the service of the military-industrial-complex or the consumer demand creation exigencies of advertisers, but to be put to work for the widest and deepest democratization of social life.

A further limitation are the exploitative conditions of work and labour in the digital technology and social media industries. Platforms have been useful to some worker self-organizing campaigns and wildcat strikes,[75] but the corporations that own them are no friends to the working class. In 2020, Facebook tinkered with a content moderation tool that would let its corporate clients deter unionization drives on its platform by suppressing the word 'unionize', but then stopped this 'innovation' in response to an AFL-CIO backlash, which made headlines eventually reposted to the union's Facebook page.[76] In any case, Silicon Valley workers are unionizing to confront precarious and low wage work, racism, sexism, and neo-Taylorism.[77] Collective organization might be especially beneficial to so many individual socialist media creators and influencers trying to become the next Left Tube star or micro-celebrity. They invest their own money, time, and energy into the production of channels, pages, programmes, and content, build and interact with audiences, and cross-promote their work with the hope of getting paid (and sometimes just enough to make next month's rent). They rely upon advertising revenue sharing arrangements with Google Ads (they get paid about $4 for every 1,000 views) and other firms, tiered Patreon subscriptions, donations, and merchandise sales. Some socialist creators make it big, but the many who do not may experience work-related hardships, from precarity to poverty to being trolled and suffering burnout.[78]

In an ideal world, socialist media creators would shift gears from competing to cooperating in a collective and democratic socialist communications project, but given the dearth of organizations with the resources to provide good jobs for these influencers, their attempt to make ends meet, win people to socialism and defeat the alt right on platforms is commendable. Socialists should keep using the platforms while also supporting the class struggles of digital media and tech workers *and* subscribing and donating to as many socialist media creators as they can. Given the power of the GAFAM, even the most reasonable proposals to collectivize and democratize today's digital technology industries and social media platforms will be fiercely resisted by the powers-that-be. The left is nowhere prepared to take up this fight. But socialist media communicators can help catalyze support for these politics, and their chances of success may increase when they are articulated to the rebooting of democratic socialist organizations oriented to rebuilding a militant, diverse, and energetic working-class movement within digital capitalism, that aims to go beyond it.

NOTES

1 Bertolt Brecht, 'The Radio as a Communications Apparatus', in Marc Silberman, ed., *Bertolt Brecht on Film & Radio*, New York: Bloomsbury, 2001, pp. 41-6.

2 See Christian Fuchs, ed., 'Communicative Socialism/Digital Capitalism', Special Issue, *tripleC: Communication, Capitalism & Critique*, 18(1), 2020.

3 See Dan Schiller, *Digital Capitalism: Networking the Global Market System*, Cambridge, MA: MIT Press, 1999; *How to Think About Information*, Champaign: University of Illinois Press, 2007; and, *Digital Depression: Information Technology and Economic Crisis*, Champaign: University of Illinois Press, 2014. Schiller is a foundational political economist of 'digital capitalism' who coined the term in 1999 and has traced the system's development from the postwar era through the neoliberal era to the global economic crisis of our time. See also: Robert McChesney, *Digital Disconnect: How Capitalism is Turning the Internet Against Democracy*, New York: The New Press, 2013; and, Nick Dyer-Witheford, *Cyber-Marx: Cycles and Circuits of Struggle in High Technology Capitalism*, Champaign: University of Illinois Press, 1999.

4 Esther Dyson, George Gilder, George Keyworth and Alvin Toffler, 'Cyberspace and the American Dream: A Magna Carta for the Knowledge Age', *Future Insight*, 1994, available at: www.pff.org.

5 Peter H. Lewis, 'U.S. Begins Privatizing Internet's Operations', *New York Times*, 24 October 1994.

6 Robert McChesney, 'Between Cambridge and Palo Alto', *Catalyst* 2(1), 2018, pp. 7-33.

7 David Rothkopf, 'In Praise of Cultural Imperialism?', *Foreign Policy*, 1997.
8 See Doug Henwood, *After the New Economy*, New York: New Press, 2005.
9 Richard Barbrook and Andy Cameron, 'The Californian Ideology', 1995, available at: www.imaginaryfutures.net.
10 Lev Grossman, '*Time*'s Person of the Year: You', *Time*, 13 December 2006.
11 For a definitional qualification and snapshot of the immense economic and political power wielded by 'GAFAM', see Jacques Fontanel, 'GAFAM, a progress and a danger for civilization. Financial Architecture: Forced Economic Development in the Context of External Shocks and Internal Inconsistencies', 2019, available at: hal.univ-grenoble-alpes.fr.
12 Nick Srnicek, *Platform Capitalism*, London: Polity, 2016.
13 Jose van Dijck, Thomas Poell, and Martijn de Waal, *The Platform Society: Public Values in a Connective World*, New York: Oxford University Press, 2018, pp. 31-48
14 Hillary Hoffower, 'We did the math to calculate how much money Jeff Bezos makes in a year, month, week, day, hour, minute, and second', *Business Insider*, 9 January 2019.
15 For the specifics of this lobbying effort, see Gaya Polat, 'The Issues that Matter to the Big Tech Lobby', *vpmMentor*, 30 April 2019, available at: www.vpnmentor.com.
16 John Clement, 'Daily social media usage worldwide 2012-2019', *Statista*, 26 February 2020, available at: www.statista.com; 'Internet World States: Usage and Population Statistics', available at: www.internetworldstats.com; Pew Research Center, 'Social Media Fact Sheet', 12 June 2019, available at: www.pewresearch.org; 'Internet Live Stats', available at: www.internetlivestats.com; Salman Aslam, 'Facebook by the Numbers: Stats, Demographics & Fun Facts', *Omnicore*, 22 April 2020, available at: www.omnicoreagency.com.
17 Naomi Klein, 'Screen New Deal', *The Intercept*, 8 April 2020.
18 Karl Marx, 'Letter from Marx to Arnold Ruge', September 1843.
19 See Tim Wu, *The Curse of Bigness: Antitrust in the New Gilded Age*, New York: Columbia Global Reports, 2018.
20 See, for example, Ursula Huws, *Labor in the Global Digital Economy*, New York: Monthly Review Press, 2014; Trebor Scholz, *Underworked and Underpaid: How Workers are Disrupting the Digital Economy*, London: Polity, 2017.
21 See John Bellamy Foster and Robert W. McChesney, 'Surveillance Capitalism', *Monthly Review*, 1 June 2014.
22 See Lee McGuigan and Vincent Manzerolle, eds., *The Audience Commodity in a Digital Age: Revisit a Critical Theory of Commercial Media*, New York: Peter Lang, 2014.
23 See Shane Harris, *@War: The Rise of the Military-Internet-Complex*, New York: Houghton-Mifflin-Harcourt, 2014; Yasha Levine, *Surveillance Valley: The Secret Military History of the Internet*, New York: PublicAffairs, 2018.
24 See Victor Pickard, *Democracy without Journalism? Confronting the Misinformation Society*, Oxford: Oxford University Press, 2020.
25 See Yochai Benkler, Robert Faris and Hal Roberts, *Network Propaganda: Manipulation, Disinformation, and Radicalization in American Politics*, Oxford: Oxford University Press, 2018.
26 See Matthew Flisfeder, 'The Entrepreneurial Subject and the Objectivization of the Self in Social Media', *South Atlantic Quarterly* 114(3), 2015, pp. 553-70.
27 See for example Oscar H. Gandy Jr., *The Panoptic Sort: A Political Economy of Personal Information*, Boulder, CA: Westview Press, 1993; Ursula Huws, *The Making of a*

Cybertariat: Virtual Work in a Real World, New York: Monthly Review Press, 2003; Vincent Mosco, *The Digital Sublime: Myth, Power and Cyberspace*, Cambridge, MA: MIT Press, 2004; Kevin Robins and Frank Webster, *Times of the Technoculture: from the Information Society to the Virtual life*, New York: Routledge, 1999; Herbert Schiller, *Information Inequality*, New York: Routledge, 1995; Reg Whitaker, *The End of Privacy: How Total Surveillance is Becoming a Reality*, New York: The New Press, 1999; Nick Dyer-Witheford, *Cyber-Marx: Cycles and Circuits of Struggle in High Technology Capitalism*, Illinois: University of Illinois Press, 1999.

28 See Fredric Jameson, 'Reification and Utopia in Mass Culture', *Social Text* 1(1), 1979, pp. 130-48; and, Stuart Hall, 'Notes on deconstructing the popular', in Richard Samuel, ed., *People's History and Socialist Theory*, New York: Routledge, 1981, pp. 227–41.

29 For poignant studies of the mainstream media's underrepresentation and 'symbolic violence' against the working class and organized labour interests for more than five decades, see Christopher R. Martin, *No Longer Newsworthy: How the Mainstream Media Abandoned the Working Class*, Ithaca and London: Cornell University, 2019; see also, Diana Kendall, *Framing Class: Media Representations of Wealth and Poverty in America*, New York: Rowman & Littlefield, 2011.

30 Ralph Miliband, *Marxism and Politics*, Oxford: Oxford University Press, 1977, p. 50.

31 For a global overview of radical media, see John. H. Downing's magisterial *Encyclopedia of Social Movement Media*, Thousand Oaks, California: SAGE Publications, 2011.

32 See Eric Hobsbawm's material history of the Manifesto, in *How to Change the World: Reflections on Marx and Marxism*, New Haven and London: Yale University Press, 2011, pp. 3-15, 101-120; also see Leo Panitch and Colin Leys, eds., *The Communist Manifesto Now: Socialist Register 1998*, 1997, London: Merlin Press.

33 See Karl Marx, *Dispatches for the New York Tribune*, New York: Penguin RandomHouse, 2008.

34 For a comprehensive overview of English socialist media-culture of that era, see Deborah Mutch, *English Socialist Periodicals, 1880-1900*, Burlington, VT: Ashgate Publishing Company, 2005.

35 See Rebecca Flores, 'Socialist Newspapers and Periodicals 1900-1920', Mapping American Socialist Movements Project, available at: depts.washington.edu.

36 For a deft historical study of the pre-WWI radical press in the United States, see Linda J. Lumsden, *Black, White, and Red All Over: A Cultural History of the Radical Press in Its Heyday, 1900-1917*, Kent, Ohio: Kent State University Press, 2014.

37 Some see the academicization of the New Left's best and brightest as a political defeat. See for example, Perry Anderson, *Considerations on Western Marxism*, New York: Verso, 1976.

38 For the long view of radical media, see John Downing, Tamara Villarreal Ford, Genéve Gil, and Laura Stein, eds, *Radical Media: Rebellious Communication and Social Movements*, Thousand Oaks, CA: Sage, 2001.

39 See Deirdre Boyle, *Subject to Change: Guerrilla Television Revisited*, New York: Oxford University Press, 1997.

40 See Stephen Duncombe, ed., *Cultural Resistance Reader*, New York: Verso, 2002; Stephen Duncombe, *Dream or Nightmare: Reimagining Politics in an Age of Fantasy*, New York: O/R Books, 2019.

41 Christopher Phelps, 'Introduction: A Socialist Magazine in the American Century', *Monthly Review*, 1999, pp. 1–21.

42 Todd Wolfson, *Digital Rebellion: The Birth of the Cyber Left*, Champaign: University of Illinois Press, 2014.

43 Derek Hrynyshyn, *The Limits of the Digital Revolution: How Mass Media Culture Endures in a Social Media World*, Santa Barbara: Praeger, 2017, p. 44.

44 Naomi Klein, *Fences and Windows: Dispatches from the Front Lines of the Globalization Debate*, Toronto: Random House of Canada, 2002, p. 17.

45 Klein, *Fences and Windows*, p. 19

46 Jules Boykoff, 'Framing Dissent: Mass-Media Coverage of the Global Justice Movement', *New Political Science*, 2006, pp. 201-28.

47 See Judith Adler Hellman, 'Real and Virtual Chiapas: Magic Realism and the Left', in Leo Panitch and Colin Leys, eds., *Socialist Register 2000: Necessary and Unnecessary Utopias*, 1999, London: Merlin Press, pp. 161-86.

48 Evgeny Morozov, 'The brave new world of slacktivism', *Foreign Policy*, 19 May 2009.

49 Kevin Gillan, Jennifer Pickerill, and Frank Webster, *Anti-War Activism: New Media and Protest in the Information Age*, New York: Palgrave Macmillan, 2008.

50 Josh Halliday, 'Hillary Clinton adviser compares internet to Che Guevara', *The Guardian*, 22 June 2011.

51 For a rejoinder to the idea that digital technologies *determine* political change, see Zeynep Tufekci, *Twitter and Tear Gas: The Power and Fragility of Networked Protest*, New Haven, CN: Yale University Press, 2017. For the best book on the smartphone for digital capitalism (and for resisting it), see Nicole Aschoff, *The Smartphone Society: Technology, Power and Resistance in the New Gilded Age*, Boston: Beacon Press, 2020.

52 Natalie Fenton, 'The Internet of Radical Politics and Social Change', in James Curran, Natalie Fenton, and Des Freedman, *Misunderstanding the Internet*, New York: Routledge, p. 174; for a materialist anchor to digital political theory, see Natalie Fenton, *Digital, Political, Radical*, London: Polity, 2016.

53 Louis Proyect, 'Marxmail: The Marxism Mailing List', available at: www.marxmail.org.

54 *Jacobin*, 'About Us', 10 June 2020, available at: jacobinmag.com.

55 See Emily Vogels, 'Millennials stand out for their technology use, but older generations also embrace digital life', Pew Research Centre, 9 September 2019.

56 For insight into the potentials and risks of the fusion of digital media and political parties, see Paolo Gerbaudo, *The Digital Party: Political Organization and Online Democracy*, London: Pluto Press, 2019.

57 Emily Stewart, 'Bernie Sanders is winning the internet. Will it win him the White House?', *Recode*, 5 July 2019; Ben Tarnoff, 'Social Media Saved Socialism', *The Guardian*, 12 July 2017.

58 For an original study of the Democratic Socialists of America (DSA) on platforms, see Christopher C. Barnes, 'Democratic Socialists on Social Media: Cohesion, Fragmentation, and Normative Strategies', *tripleC* 18(1), 2020, pp. 32-47.

59 www.novaramedia.com.

60 www.means.tv.

61 Jason Rhode, 'Chapo Trap House are the Vulgar, Brilliant Demigods of the New Progressive Left', *Paste Magazine*, 29 July 2016.

62 For a thoughtful study of some BreadTubers, see Dmitry Kuznetsov and Milan Ismangil, 'YouTube as Praxis? On BreadTube and the Digital Propagation of Socialist Thought', *tripleC* 18(1), 2020, pp. 204-218.

63 This assemblage's name is attributed to Peter Kropotkin's anarchist classic *The Conquest of Bread*.

64 See Andrew Marantz, 'The Stylish Socialist Who Is Trying to Save YouTube from Alt-Right Domination', *The New Yorker*, 20 November 2018.

65 See, for instance, the 'Sassy Socialist Meme' page on Facebook, followed by over a million people, available at: www.facebook.com/sassysocialistmemes.

66 Benjamin Fong, 'Log Off', *Jacobin*, 29 November 2018.

67 Meagan Day, 'Unfortunately, We Can't Log Off', *Jacobin*, 12 June 2018.

68 After publishing Day's article, *Jacobin*'s publicists used the magazine's Facebook page to circulate it to the 345,143 people who 'like' and the 353,649 people who 'follow' it, some who then went on to share it such as Chapo Trap House Shitposting 'private group' page which linked it with its 3,897 members. @jacobinmag also tweeted this article to its 270,000 followers, some of which retweeted it.

69 Rasmussen Reports, 'Just 53% Say Capitalism Better Than Socialism', 9 April 2009; Andy Gregory, 'More than a third of millennials approve of communism, YouGov poll indicates', *The Independent*, 17 November 2019.

70 Jodi Dean, 'Communicative Capitalism: Circulation and the Foreclosure of Politics', *Cultural Politics* 1(1), 2005, p. 56.

71 Nick Srniceck, *Platform Capitalism*.

72 Matthew Flisfeder, 'Digital Labour and the Internet Prosumer Commodity: In Conversation with Christian Fuchs', *Alternate Routes* 27(1), pp. 267-78.

73 Christian Fuchs, *Marxism: Karl Marx's Fifteen Key Concepts for Cultural and Communication Studies*, New York: Routledge, 2020, p. 232

74 Daniel Joseph, 'Platforms for People, not Profit', *Briarpatch Magazine*, 23 December 2019; see also for contrast, Evan Malmgren, 'Socialized Media', *The Baffler*, 19 September 2018.

75 See Eric Blanc, *Red State Revolt*, New York: Verso, 2019, p. 175, on the significance of Facebook to worker self-organizing. Blanc writes: 'Without social media, there's no chance that the red state revolt would have developed as it did. Facebook made it possible to communicate easily with large groups of people and to widely disseminate calls to action without, as in the past, having to undertake the arduous work of building up a well-resourced, formal organizational infrastructure'.

76 Lee Fang, 'Facebook Pitched New Tool Allowing Employers to Suppress Words Like 'Unionize' in Workplace Chat Product', *The Intercept*, 11 June 2020.

77 For pertinent research and analysis of worker organizing and union campaigns in the digital media and technology sectors, see: culturalworkersorganize.org; see also, Nicole Cohen and Greig de Peuter, *New Media Unions: Organizing Digital Journalists*, New York: Routledge, 2020.

78 Todd Frankel, 'Why almost no one is making a living on YouTube', *The Washington Post*, 2 March 2018.

IMAGINING PLATFORM SOCIALISM

DEREK HRYNYSHYN

President Donald Trump presented his 'Executive Order on Preventing Online Censorship' of 28 May 2020 as the opening shot in a war against social media platforms, signaling his willingness to stand up to powerful interests that he and his supporters saw as obstacles to his agenda:

> A small handful of social media monopolies controls a vast portion of all public and private communications in the United States ... They've had unchecked power to censor, restrict, edit, shape, hide, alter, virtually any form of communication between private citizens and large public audiences.[1]

Not long ago, it would have been assumed that anyone making this claim would be on the far left. But recently, not only Trump, but also many moderate politicians have expressed their opposition to the creeping commercialization of the formerly open public space that was the internet. Especially since the revelations of how widely the internet was used to promote disinformation in the 2016 campaigns for the US presidency and the Brexit referendum, concern about the dangers to democracy from unregulated social media have been widely discussed.[2] How these platforms distribute information, and how they moderate the political discussions for which they provide space, are clearly of great interest in the context of a highly polarized polity.

That the dominant platforms seem particularly effective at promoting the spread of false, misleading, sensationalist, and otherwise malicious claims became evident in the wake of the Cambridge Analytica revelations in early 2018.[3] Propaganda and negative campaigning in elections were nothing new, of course, but the ease with which claims that had no basis in reality spread, and the involvement of foreign actors, constitute a fundamentally new threat to democracy. The concerns about fake news added to concerns about violations of privacy. Earlier revelations by Edward Snowden about the extent of surveillance by the US national security apparatus had made clear the potential for unprecedented quantities of personal information to be collected in massive databases,[4] but the Cambridge Analytica scandal also revealed that the purpose of the non-consensual collection of the same kind of data by private firms was to support campaigns of disinformation and sway very significant political decisions.[5]

Investigations have also demonstrated the ways that the operations of the algorithmic processes that select and sort information for users of YouTube, Facebook, and Twitter not only distribute such malicious content, but also amplify its effects. In order to hold the attention of users, platforms tend to recommend increasingly controversial and sensationalist suggestions, leading users quickly into rabbit holes of conspiracy theories and extremist views that undermine attempts at informed and reasoned debate.[6] Other studies showed that Google's search engine was capable of exhibiting serious racist bias,[7] and that the platforms' attempts to limit access to hate speech and misinformation were of limited effectiveness.[8]

These problems came to light as the corporations that owned the platforms were becoming the most profitable and wealthiest in the world, while traditional sources of political information were falling into a state of financial crisis.[9] That the production and distribution of serious journalism can't compete economically with social media platforms indicates a need to reconsider the economic process behind the flow of information.

But at the same time, the monopolistic digital platforms are undeniably of great use to activists working for a more democratic world, including socialists. The events that triggered Trump's demands for stricter platform regulation were part of a mobilization of dissent that came to be known by its Twitter hashtag, 'Black Lives Matter', and numerous other examples could be found of activists raising awareness in ways that would not be possible with mass media.[10] Social media empowers individuals to participate in the distribution of their own ideas, although this empowerment is limited by the mediation of the flow of information by the owners of the platforms in ways that can have direct effects on how mobilizations are informed.[11]

This makes it all the more necessary to explore the contradictions between our expectations of social media and the reality of its use, and determine if there are ways to avoid the harms done to democracy while preserving the benefits. The purpose of the present essay is to inquire whether and how social media could be organized more democratically, so that they allow our expressive capacities to be developed freely and not under conditions determined by capital.

THE LIMITS OF REGULATION

Given that platforms are relatively new, it does not appear unreasonable to suggest that, properly regulated, the existing platforms might come to mitigate the threat to democracy. Governments have been, in fact, developing regulations in recent years. But knowing that such efforts are likely inevitable, the major platforms have already started to impose some limits on their own behavior in order to prevent harsher forms from being imposed. Facebook has agreed to censor content that promotes violence, and Twitter, as mentioned above, has recently shown willingness even to mark some of the US President's tweets as requiring fact checking. Both platforms have for many years censored what they distribute in order to conform to local laws in a number of countries.[12]

Like most self-regulation, however, this is likely to have limited effect. It does not appear that there are effective ways to ensure that the massive quantities of content constantly being distributed through these platforms could be adequately examined in order to stop messages deemed harmful.[13] But even if such means could be found, the decision of where to draw the line is an inherently political one, and leaving this judgment up to the owners of the platforms is not a democratic way to ensure communication serves the public. Mark Zuckerburg's decision not to follow Twitter's lead and restrict Facebook's distribution of Trump's messaging in the wake of the Black Lives Matter protests in June 2020, which even provoked public protests by Facebook employees, is a case in point.[14]

The weakness of self-regulation can also be seen in the privacy settings that platforms provide to users. These allow users to determine to what extent content they supply is seen by different categories of other users, but they do nothing to prevent personal information of users from being used by the platforms themselves. In the case of Cambridge Analytica, third parties with whom a platform does business were able to make use of personal data in ways that most users would most likely choose to reject if they were given a chance.

The other obvious difficulty with platform self-regulation is that the platforms operate on a global basis, yet are managed from within the US. The decisions about regulating platforms, what content to prohibit, and how algorithms should prioritize different kinds of content, which affect users around the world, are made in Silicon Valley by decision makers who are simply not accountable in any way to those users. This has resulted in many conflicts with regulators, particularly in France and Germany.[15] These examples demonstrate that there is a need for some external power to impose limits on the way platforms work.

A number of governments have already assumed this role. The recent European law known as the General Data Protection Regulation (GDPR), designed to protect the privacy of individuals, is an attempt to impose regulation above the level of the nation state, and the state of California has followed suit with the California Consumer Privacy Act.[16] And Germany 's Network Enforcement Act imposes very heavy fines on platform operators that fail to remove hate speech quickly.[17] While the global scale of the internet makes attempts at regulations by national or regional bodies difficult, platforms have been required to prevent distribution of forms of content that are already illegal in different jurisdictions.[18] This is made possible by the fact that while the networks on which these platforms are built are in fact global, platforms are capable of manipulating traffic into and across specific territories.[19] But this only deals with issues that are specific to nation states, and does not prevent users from undermining these national limits through Virtual Private Networks and other such measures. And it does little to prevent activity in one country designed to undermine democracy in another, as was the case in the Trump 2016 campaign.[20]

The negotiation of global standards on these matters remains necessary for regulation to succeed. This has in fact been recognized enough to make the first steps in this direction, as shown by the 'International Grand Committee on Big Data, Privacy and Democracy'. Spearheaded by Canadian and British MPs in the wake of Cambridge Analytica revelations, this brought together other parliamentarians from various other countries in meetings in London in 2018 and Ottawa in 2019 to 'discuss how governments can protect citizen rights in the age of big data'.[21] But these meetings ended without recommending the establishment of the kind of permanent institution with enforcement power that would be required to be effective. Even if one eventually were, negotiations among the states involved would be very difficult. Governments would need to reach agreement on the appropriate limits of free speech, the line between falsehoods designed to influence elections and mere exaggeration, and a number of other thorny philosophical questions. Given the US dominance in global cultural industries, and its tradition of insisting on free speech rather than any kind of regime to manage global communications, the prospects of successfully regulating platforms globally would appear exceedingly slim.

Even if we set aside those difficulties, the immense complexity of the systems involved and the inequality of information about processes between regulators and states would present a serious obstacle to the effectiveness of any regulatory schema not only for setting global standards, but also even for making national regulations very effective. Platform algorithms are very complex, making it difficult to verify that algorithms are complying with regulations that restrict the way they sort content, or that restricts the tendency towards polarizing information. Algorithms create unique feeds for each user, and do so without making the process visible. This makes it much more difficult to ensure compliance with regulations by social media platforms than by broadcasters.

A regulator would therefore need to have access to the details of the code in the algorithm.[22] Regulators would require access to the insides of the algorithms, which so far have been 'black boxes'. They are likely to resist strongly such measures, for three reasons. First, algorithms for search engines or social networking platforms are kept secret because the platforms' value depends on their ability to distribute information to each user that is unique to that platform. The secrecy of algorithms is part of their value, making platform operators very reluctant to allow the details to be known by others.

Secondly, allowing regulators to enforce laws that would alter the algorithms would mean limiting the power of the network owners to target specific users, which (as is discussed in the next section) is the basis of the value of the platforms. Regulating algorithms to promote other values, such as political neutrality, for instance, would be in direct opposition to the process that generates profit for the platform.

Thirdly, platforms also regularly update algorithms, in a continuous search for greater value. The notorious 'emotional contagion' experiment conducted by Facebook in 2014 is an example of the process by which platforms constantly seek to improve their ability to extract value from the user's communicative activity, without informing users.[23] Regulation of constantly changing algorithms would need to be highly intrusive and would require constant oversight of private business activity. Capitalist platforms, in other words, inevitably require the hidden operation of algorithms in ways that enable the social harms that regulation is intended to counter. Platforms would have every incentive to not co-operate with regulators, and regulators would have little ability to ensure compliance. Regulatory approaches, therefore, are unlikely to succeed in limiting the social harms of existing platforms.

The highly oligopolistic structure of the platform industry also makes it difficult for users to hold platforms to account. Platforms do not work in ways that competitive markets do, and their services do not need to satisfy the users of the service the way firms in competitive markets need to satisfy consumers. This is because the services offered by each of the monopolistic platforms are essentially unique, and Facebook, Twitter, and YouTube have no effective competition. Like other telecommunications services, they are governed by 'network effects', meaning that they simply work much better if there is a single service to which individuals can turn to connect to all others.[24] Not only would users dissatisfied with the way the platforms work have few alternative choices, but in the case of Facebook and Twitter, it is increasingly difficult to opt out of their use without incurring significant social costs. These factors give monopolistic corporations a significant ability to ignore the interests of users. That ability is amplified by the platform economy in which users are not paying customers, and thus are not a source of demand to which platforms need to respond. Since the public who makes use of platforms is not the source of their funding, they are not ones primarily empowered by them.

THE ROOT OF THE PROBLEM

This relation between the users, the platforms and the funding that supports their operation is key to understanding the exercise of power over the communicative space they offer. In order to imagine how platforms could operate more democratically, we need to examine this relationship more closely. The crucial factor most ignored in discussion of the politics of platforms is that while platforms empower individuals by providing a space in which they can express themselves to each other, their operation is almost entirely funded by advertising. Platforms provide a communicative space for users, but they must structure that space in ways that serve the needs of the advertisers, rather than those of the users. Ensuring that their services are valuable to the advertisers is thus always the first priority.

This became evident in June of 2020, when Facebook came under criticism, even from its own precariously employed moderators, for failing to prevent the spread of racist hate speech.[25] However, the platform only altered its policies – and then only slightly by promising to include labels on harmful content – after a large number of major advertisers were persuaded by the 'Stop Hate for Profit Campaign' to participate in a boycott of Facebook.[26] YouTube, Reddit, and Twitch soon followed suit with increased restrictions on hate speech.[27]

The relation between advertisers and the users of social media platforms is the subject of much theoretical discussion. Some have applied Dallas Smythe's theory of the mass media audience commodity to social media, arguing that users engage in labour, and that their labour power is commodified by the media platforms, which profit by selling that commodified labour power to advertisers.[28] A similar but less critically oriented line of thought suggests that platforms, like all commercial media, are engaged in an 'attention economy'.[29] Others argue that the profit of the platforms is earned through rent payments or some other form of return on speculative investment.[30] Yet another interpretation suggests that platforms' profits are earned through the extraction and sale of data generated by users through their social media activity, or, in Zuboff's term, the 'surplus behaviour' of users as they are measured and tracked by platforms.[31] However complex and important are the debates around these various perspectives, what is common to all of them is the understanding that the platforms are in the advertising business, rather than in the business of providing internet users with opportunities to share ideas and content with others. Which content is promoted, recommended, prioritized, and emphasized so that it goes viral, and which is made irrelevant by being relegated to the bottom of a news feed, depends entirely on decisions made by the platforms with advertisers in mind. Therefore, the conditions under which we communicate with each other on these platforms, as is the case for commercial mass media, are shaped to meet the needs of advertisers.

And like commercial mass media, the interest of the advertisers is to attract the attention of users in order to alter their behaviour, usually related to consumption but also often to voting. Because social media platforms apply complex algorithmic processing to the content seen by each user, they are able to attract attention much more powerfully than even the mass media, and they are able to target advertising at specific users in much more effective, persuasive ways. Social media advertising can be targeted to specific users, meaning that it can be associated with exactly the 'right' content, which supports the advertising message's ability to persuade. The algorithmic targeting of advertising is all but invisible to the users, but it is presumably much more effective at changing attitudes towards brands and personalities than is the case with mass media.

A democratic socialist platform for communicative engagement must be disconnected from this imperative. The ability to manipulate the way users are provided with the information they use to make sense of the world around them, of themselves, and of their own needs and desires cannot be put in the hands of powerful monopolistic corporations if communications are to be organized democratically. More than a different 'business model' must be found to support this activity: what is needed is a different mode of provisioning service, entailing a different mode of organization and governance.

In theory, a service like Facebook or Twitter could, instead of relying on advertising, turn to subscription-based services along the lines of Netflix and Apple's streaming services.[32] However, as long as platforms are able to sell advertising, they most likely will do so, and use the revenue to reduce costs to the users. This would mean that the incentives to use algorithms to manipulate the flow of information in ways that do not serve the user public would persist. This might not be a problem in a competitive market for social networking services, for instance, but it is unlikely that such markets would remain competitive.

The 2020 Sanders campaign for the US presidency challenged the power of platforms by proposing the use of anti-trust laws to break up the monopolies into smaller companies, each of which would only be allowed to operate one of the services they control.[33] This would limit their political power, but would not change the incentives to operate as they do, or solve the problems discussed here. Solving the problems of fake news and algorithmic bias requires more than the issuing of limits on the size of companies or providing public infrastructure. Intervention is needed at the level of algorithmic mediation of content. And this is a problem that would not even be solved by the more radical policy proposals for 'digital democracy' advanced under Jeremy Corbyn's leadership of the Labour Party, which included nationalizing and publicly funding the broadband internet infrastructure so as to make it much more broadly available to all, regardless of regional location or who can afford to pay for service. This is surely a necessary first step to any agenda that would provide equal access for all to the advantages of a democratic communication medium, and it would seem relatively easy to argue that it could work at a national level. To consider the internet as the same sort of public utility as an electricity grid or water supply system, and thus to operate it as a public utility, would seem an obvious beginning for any socialist approach to internet services. However, the physical infrastructure is one thing, and the platforms that run across it are another. Since the platforms are global rather than national, they could not be nationalized as the infrastructure could be. As long as social media platforms are under the control of private owners and operated as for-profit businesses, they will be unlikely to support the democratic organization of communication. The spread of disinformation, the fragmentation of the public into polarized segments that are unable to deliberate together, and the violation of privacy, is likely to continue. For platforms to serve the public, they must be removed from private operators, and an alternative source of financial support must be found. It may be very difficult to envision the exercise of legal or state power putting an end to the private operation of networking platforms, but if we are to believe in the possibility of a more democratic form of communication, then we need to imagine how platforms could be socialized so as to serve the needs of the public rather than the needs of private capital.

Conventionally, the alternative to advertising revenue for supporting media systems is public funding. While public media corporations like the BBC have often enjoyed broad support as a response to the inability of markets to meet public needs, they have operated alongside private corporations, and this has obviated fears of the depressing effects on democracy of a state media monopoly. Moreover, given the appeal, and the benefits, of more decentralized means of communication which platforms now provide, the kind of state funding provided for large centrally controlled services, with a single network under the administrative control of even the most liberal democratic states, would hardly be satisfactory to realize the full democratic potential of a socialized media. Although public broadcasters are insulated from direct political influence by the guarantees of an 'arm's-length relationship' with state power, the need of public authorities to be accountable to majoritarian tastes and values would most likely limit the openness that is the value of social media platforms. It is likely that the imperatives of the state – whether they are seen as the defense of some particular notion of national interests, 'community standards', or some other values – will ultimately end up undermining the diversity and openness that characterizes the use of social networking platforms to which we have become accustomed. Even if outright censorship is never imposed on communication over such a network by state funders, the ability of users to trust in the openness of the interactions could be undermined by reliance on centralized decision making.

A further difficulty is the need for such decisions to be imposed at a global level; the public funding and administration of a single global network would present serious difficulties for the maintenance of the trust that would be required for the exercise of freedom of expression. For these reasons, it would be preferable if the operation of social media systems, even while brought into the public domain, could look more like 'the commons' and remain more thoroughly separated from state power.

NEW PLATFORMS WITH OLD PRINCIPLES

Fortunately, there is no need to imagine new communications platforms along the lines of the organization of public broadcasting media. Different media possess different potentials, and the centralized control typical in public broadcasting is unnecessary in the world of digital media. From its origin, the internet has functioned on structural principles that are very different from those of other media, and those original principles supported, and could still support, non-capitalist platforms. Existing platforms represent a form of colonization by capital of that space, imposing a centralizing and commercial logic on it.

The basic design of the internet's infrastructure is one that avoids reliance on centralized administrative control. Social media networks operating over this infrastructure are highly centralized, but there is no need for this to be the case. Applications like the world wide web, email, or peer-to-peer file-sharing networks like BitTorrent, can operate and reach users anywhere using shared protocols without a central point from which services are offered or where content is stored. All of the services the internet offered in its early days operated this way, which made it difficult to find ways to engage in commercial activity.[34] Even the basic service of access to the network was, until the late 1990s, often free.[35]

As Zuboff notes, it was only after the 'dot com' crash of 2000 that the providers of major online services began to search for a way to systematically monetize their offerings. This led to, as she describes it, the 'discovery' of the potential value of users to advertisers, and led to the emergence of monopolistic platforms that have shaped the internet's development ever since.[36] Yet, the original idea of distributed development of services has not been completely abandoned, and its presence is still evident in the operation of a number of common applications. In fact, much of the basic operation of the internet and the servers that host information runs on software that is freely available to anyone to install and customize.

Perhaps the most common application through the history of the internet operates on these principles and serves as a helpful illustration of how social media platforms could operate. E-mail, one of the very first uses of the internet, requires no central administrative point, can be funded in ways that require no advertisers, and allows individual users to structure their own communicative activity. That everyone uses the same kind of programming code to send and receive email messages across the internet is possible because those protocols were designed to be open to anyone to install and run on their own computers.

Of course, e-mail, like the rest of the internet, has come to be dominated by the same platform giants that offer other services. Services like Google's Gmail, however, are not fundamentally different from that of any small internet service provider, operating on the same open protocols. Typically in the early days of popular internet use, e-mail service was offered as part of access to the internet, and this is still the case with most providers today. There is no reason why such services need to be dominated by monopolistic corporate giants.

Once the corporate giants were socialized and their social media platforms brought into the public domain, their services could be made available the same way, on the basis of a set of common, open, and universal protocols running on a local server that would connect to other servers to produce the flows of information that users are looking for. Content that users post to their accounts could be stored locally, and could be made accessible to other account holders that have been recognized as followers or friends, and no central agency would be needed to store all of the contents of all users, as is the case with capitalist platforms. Developing the protocols for connecting users would require a significant amount of labour, but software development of projects on this scale takes place without centralized control in the case of open-source projects such as the Linux operating system, the Firefox browser, and the LibreOffice productivity suite. These projects are generally developed by volunteers helping to improve existing code outside the context of a formal employment relationship, and then distributed freely.[37]

Attempts to develop platforms along these lines have already been made. But open source projects like Diaspora*, Friendica, and Mastodon have not been able to attract a significant user base, and remain relatively unknown. Since open source projects operate largely without the exchange of commodified goods, it is not likely that private capital will promote or invest in most such projects. For an open-source platform to be adopted widely, some kind of resources must be devoted to promoting it, and to coordinating its production and development; otherwise different versions of the code proliferate and the common protocols that are required will not be agreed upon. But having an open, coordinated project supports the development and improvement of different versions, unlike proprietary software that cannot be legally altered. This offers an opportunity for governments to play a role supporting, coordinating, and promoting platform development. Contributors to the program would not need to be accountable to the state, but could be encouraged to help develop a platform that respects both the privacy and communicative freedom of the users.

An open source social media platform could serve users as well as the monopolistic platforms do now, without needing to serve the interests of advertisers or corporate owners. It would allow users to customize their own access to information, so that users could control the conditions in which they communicate, rather than having those conditions chosen for them. And it could integrate forms of moderation that could be democratically chosen by the users who access the service provided in a locality, rather than imposed on the entire user base around the world by a single corporation.

Any platform on this scale, usable by all members of the public, would still require financial resources to operate and maintain. Social networking processes are more complicated than e-mail, and work would need to be done by the local host of the service to ensure its smooth operation, and also to moderate content and deal with new developments as they arise. There would be a large role for local authorities here as well. Since a more fully democratic platform would allow local service providers to customize the platform for local needs and interests, some of this work would need to be accountable to local communities. There would also be legitimate roles for national or regional level funding for certain kinds of work moderating content flows and ensuring the operation of larger-level networks that could be configured into the platform as a project. And democratic decision-making could be facilitated online, through mechanisms deliberately coded into the platform through the same open-source development process.

DEMOCRATIC SOCIALIST COMMUNICATION

Interacting over an open, decentralized platform need not be a radically different experience from using commercial platforms, apart from the lack of advertising. But since it would allow communication between large numbers to take place under more democratic conditions, it would be completely new. It will be helpful to describe the advantages in more detail.

Privacy is one of the most discussed issues when dealing with existing capitalist social media platforms. But with decentralized platforms, users would retain control of their own information and determine who is able to have access to it, thus resolving most of the privacy problems in a simple manner. With no centralized agency collecting, storing, and processing everyone's data, the manipulation of behaviour through the exploitation of personal information would no longer be a threat. Access to the contents of a user's account would be limited to those with whom the user chooses to interact, and differing levels of access would be possible. Users would be able to choose how private to keep different kinds of information, and the settings to control this feature could be designed to maximize its simplicity.

Existing platforms allow users to alter privacy settings, but this provides a false sense of user control, since they do nothing to limit the extent to which the corporation behind the platform can exploit user data, and in reality are often highly complex and difficult to navigate. The contractual arrangements, to which users are required to consent, typically grant platforms rights to surveil, sell, sort, and analyze personal data in nearly unlimited ways.[38] There would be no reason to make this happen if user account information was not centralized in large databases of all users. State surveillance on the scale that exists now would be similarly be impossible, although law enforcement would still be able to gain warranted access to the personal information about specific users.

Decentralizing and distributing social media platforms across the internet would also provide better ways to deal with fake news and propaganda campaigns. Platform protocols could incorporate ways for users to set their own account to prioritize the information that they find most reliable, or to connect to independent services for fact checking and rating content. Essentially, each user could have their own algorithm, which they could manipulate themselves, without relying on the platform operator to select and prioritize information for them. Users who prefer to expose themselves to controversial and provocative ideas could choose to do so, while others could choose to restrict themselves to ideas that are already widely popular. Users could make their own choice of fact-checking service, or not use one, while others could place priority on seeing updates from family and entertainment recommendations from friends. Algorithmic control in the hands of the users would open up possibilities that are entirely closed by the need to use algorithms to maximize value for advertisers.

This is not to argue for an individualism that only values letting each user have unlimited ability to create, distribute, and receive any kind of messages. In fact, the lack of restrictions of certain kinds of content that spread quickly across the internet in existing problems is a serious problem. Defining exactly what constitutes 'fake news' or 'hate speech', or whether to prevent the distribution of misinformation about public health crises, for instance, might always be controversial. But there are many forms of communication, such as online harassment, threats of violence, child pornography, and other forms of expression that are universally seen as undesirable and for which freedom of expression is not considered adequate justification, and these forms of content could be stopped by protocols built into platforms at the highest level.

But what constitutes hate speech, harassment, or incitement to violence is not possible to determine universally, and a democratic system would allow different communities to establish these lines on their own. Open platforms could allow content to be blocked at the level of local service providers, and this would also allow each local network to customize the criteria for blocking content, or to rely on more widely shared criteria. In all likelihood, there will always be some dissatisfied with the way that such content is blocked; this is probably unavoidable. Reconfiguring platforms won't solve all problems around censorship, and it would not be realistic to intend it to do so. But the idea that communication could happen under democratic conditions requires us to believe that, at some level, communities could establish their own limits on what information should be allowed to circulate.

The problem of the algorithmic promotion of polarizing and extremist content could be solved in similar ways. This problem results from the actions of algorithms that analyze patterns in data collected on large numbers of users to determine what is most likely to continue to attract attention. Without centralized databases, this becomes much less effective, and without commercial incentives, it is not necessary. User control over algorithms would, in any case, minimize this tendency. Some users of social media might prefer to prioritize content that confirms and amplifies tendencies in their thinking, and so would set their account to show them more sensational and extremist content; this is also probably inevitable. But it would be possible to design a platform that allows users to sort information using different values, such as reliability or the diversity of other users to whom content appeals. A platform in which users would have control over the flow of information would have no necessary bias towards the shallow and superficial engagement that is promoted by consumerist ideology; critical thinking could be supported more effectively. This might be a key factor in allowing social platforms to escape from the worst tendencies of mass media culture.[39]

The development and implementation of communicative and cultural infrastructure organized according to democratic socialist principles is not likely to happen in the near future, but this is not because of any lack of technological capacities. Everything required already exists to reorganize our communication systems to support collective discussions as a public good. What is lacking is a strategy for building popular support to confront the power of the existing giant capitalist firms that own and operate today's platforms, and insist that they be socialized by being brought into the public sphere and their services transformed. Imagining a plausible alternative to the capitalist configurations of the technologies involved is only be a first step, but is necessary before such a project can be promoted more widely.

NOTES

1 Timothy B. Lee and Kate Cox, 'Trump Is Desperate to Punish Big Tech but Has No Good Way to Do It,' *Ars Technica*, 29 May 2020.

2 Jonathan Taplin, *Move Fast and Break Things: How Facebook, Google, and Amazon Cornered Culture and Undermined Democracy*, New York: Little, Brown and Company, 2017; Shoshana Zuboff, *The Age of Surveillance Capitalism: The Fight for a Human Future at the New Frontier of Power*, PublicAffairs, 2019.

3 Soroush Vosoughi, Deb Roy, and Sinan Aral, 'The Spread of True and False News Online', *Science*, 359, 9 March 2018, pp. 1146–51.

4 Glenn Greenwald and Ewen MacAskill, 'Boundless Informant: The NSA's Secret Tool to Track Global Surveillance Data', *The Guardian*, 11 June 2013.

5 Carole Cadwalladr, '"I Made Steve Bannon's Psychological Warfare Tool": Meet the

Data War Whistleblower', *The Guardian*, 18 March 2018.

6 Zeynep Tufecki, 'YouTube, the Great Radicalizer', *New York Times*, 10 March, 2018.

7 Safiya Umoja Noble, *Algorithms of Oppression: How Search Engines Reinforce Racism*, New York: New York University Press, 2018.

8 Ariana Tobin, Madeleine Varner, and Julia Angwin, 'Facebook's Uneven Enforcement of Hate Speech Rules Allows Vile Posts to Stay Up', *ProPublica*, 28 December 2017.

9 Matt Phillips, 'Apple's $1 Trillion Milestone Reflects Rise of Powerful Megacompanies', *New York Times*, 2 August 2018.

10 Manuel Castells, *Networks of Outrage and Hope: Social Movements in the Internet Age*, Cambridge, UK: Polity Press, 2015; Clay Shirky, 'The Political Power of Social Media: Technology, the Public Sphere, and Political Change', *Foreign Affairs*, 90(1), 2011, pp. 28–41.

11 Zeynep Tufekci, 'What Happens to #Ferguson Affects Ferguson: — The Message', *Medium*, 14 August 2014.

12 Ronald Deibert et al., *Access Denied: The Practice and Policy of Global Internet Filtering*, Cambridge, MA: MIT Press, 2008.

13 Kevin Roose, 'Social Media Giants Support Racial Justice. Their Products Undermine It', *New York Times*, 19 June 2020; Tech Transparency Project, 'White Supremacist Groups Are Thriving on Facebook', Campaign for Accountability, 21 May 2020.

14 Zeynep Tufekci, 'Why Zuckerberg's 14-Year Apology Tour Hasn't Fixed Facebook', *Wired*, 6 April 2018.

15 Alex Hern, 'Google Fined Record £44m by French Data Protection Watchdog', *The Guardian*, 21 January 2019; Associated Press, 'Germany Fines Facebook $2.3 Million under Hate Speech Law', 2 July 2019.

16 Annegret Bendiek and Magnus Römer, 'Externalizing Europe: The Global Effects of European Data Protection', *Digital Policy, Regulation and Governance*, 21(1), 1 January 2019, pp. 32–43; Kari Paul, 'California's Groundbreaking Privacy Law Takes Effect in January. What Does It Do?', *The Guardian*, 30 December 2019.

17 Philip Oltermann, 'Tough New German Law Puts Tech Firms and Free Speech in Spotlight', *The Guardian*, 5 January 2018.

18 Ronald Deibert, John Palfrey, Rafal Rohozinski, and Jonathan Zittrain, eds, *Access Denied: The Practice and Policy of Global Internet Filtering*, Cambridge, MA: MIT Press, 2008.

19 Jack L. Goldsmith and Tim Wu, *Who Controls the Internet? Illusions of a Borderless World*, Oxford University Press, 2006.

20 Julia Carrie Wong, 'Facebook Discloses Operations by Russia and Iran to Meddle in 2020 Election', *The Guardian*, 21 October 2019.

21 Jesse Hirsh 'What you need to know about the grand-committee on big-data, privacy and democracy', Centre for international Governance Innovation, 29 May 2019; Billy Perrigo, 'Mark Zuckerberg Slammed After Failing to Show for Grilling by Global Lawmakers', *Time*, 27 November 2018.

22 For discussion, see the proposal in Andrew Tutt, 'An FDA for Algorithms', *Administrative Law Review*, 69(1), 2017.

23 Adam D. I. Kramer, Jamie E. Guillory, and Jeffrey T. Hancock, 'Experimental Evidence of Massive-Scale Emotional Contagion through Social Networks', *Proceedings of the National Academy of Sciences*, 111(24), 2014; Robinson Meyer, 'Everything We Know About Facebook's Secret Mood Manipulation Experiment', *The Atlantic*, 28 June 2014.

24 Bertand Belvaux, 'The Development of Social Media: Proposal for a Diffusion Model Incorporating Network Externalities in a Competitive Environment - Bertand Belvaux, 2011', *Recherche et Applications En Marketing (English Edition)*, 1 September 2011.

25 Alex Hern, 'Facebook Moderators Join Criticism of Zuckerberg over Trump Stance', *The Guardian*, 8 June 2020.

26 Alex Hern, 'How Hate Speech Campaigners Found Facebook's Weak Spot', *The Guardian*, 29 June 2020.

27 'YouTube Bans Prominent White Supremacist Channels', *BBC News*, 30 June 2020.

28 Dallas Walker Smythe, *Dependency Road: Communications, Capitalism, Consciousness and Canada*, Norwood, N.J.: Ablex, 1981; Nicole Cohen, 'The Valorization of Surveillance: Towards a Political Economy of Facebook', *Democratic Communique*, 22(1), 2008; Christian Fuchs, 'Dallas Smythe Today - The Audience Commodity, the Digital Labour Debate, Marxist Political Economy and Critical Theory. Prolegomena to a Digital Labour Theory of Value', *TripleC: Communication, Capitalism & Critique. Open Access Journal for a Global Sustainable Information Society*, 10(2), 19 September 2012, pp. 692–740; Lee McGuigan and Vincent Manzerolle, *The Audience Commodity in a Digital Age: Revisiting a Critical Theory of Commercial Media*, New York, NY: Peter Lang Publishing Inc., 2014.

29 Philip M. Napoli, *Audience Economics: Media Institutions and the Audience Marketplace*, Columbia University Press, 2003; James G. Webster, *The Marketplace of Attention: How Audiences Take Shape in a Digital Age*, Boston: MIT Press, 2014.

30 Ursula Huws, 'The Underpinnings of Class in the Digital Age: Living, Labour and Value', in Leo Panitch and Greg Albo, eds., *Socialist Register 2014: Registering Class*, London: Merlin Press, 2013; Adam Arvidsson and Elanor Colleoni, 'Value in Informational Capitalism and on the Internet', *The Information Society* 28(3), 1 May 2012, pp. 135–50; Greg Elmer, 'Prospecting Facebook: The Limits of the Economy of Attention', *Media, Culture & Society*, 41(3), April 2019, pp. 332–46.

31 Zuboff, *The Age of Surveillance Capitalism.*

32 See Zeynep Tufekci, 'Mark Zuckerberg, Let Me Pay for Facebook', *New York Times,* 4 June 2015; as well as Bregtje van der Haak, Michael Parks, and Manuel Castells, 'The Future of Journalism: Networked Journalism', *International Journal of Communication*, 6, 30 November 2012, p. 16.

33 Bernie Sanders, 'Bernie Sanders on His Plan for Journalism', *Columbia Journalism Review*, 26 August 2019.

34 Janet Abbate, *Inventing the Internet,* Cambridge, MA: MIT Press, 1999.

35 Pierre Bourque and Rosaleen Dickson, *FreeNet: Canadian Online Access, the Free and Easy Way*, Toronto: Stoddart, 1996.

36 Zuboff, *The Age of Surveillance Capitalism*, pp. 71–4.

37 Yochai Benkler, *The Wealth of Networks: How Social Production Transforms Markets and Freedom*, New Haven, CT: Yale University Press, 2006.

38 Jonathan A. Obar and Anne Oeldorf-Hirsch, 'The Biggest Lie on the Internet: Ignoring the Privacy Policies and Terms of Service Policies of Social Networking Services', *Information, Communication & Society*, 23(1), 2020.

39 Derek Hrynyshyn, *The Limits of the Digital Revolution: How Mass Media Culture Endures in a Social Media World*, Santa Barbara, CA: Praeger, 2017.

WORKING-CLASS CINEMA IN THE AGE OF DIGITAL CAPITALISM

MASSIMILIANO MOLLONA

The story of cinema starts with workers. The film *Workers Leaving The Lumière Factory In Lyon* (*La Sortie des Usines Lumière à Lyon*, 1895) by the brothers Louis and Auguste Lumière, 45 seconds long, shows the approximately 100 workers at a factory for photographic goods in Lyon-Montplaisir leaving through two gates and exiting the frame to both sides.

But why does the story of cinema begin with the end of work? Is it because, as has been suggested, it is impossible to represent work from the perspective of labour but only from the point of view of capital, because the revolutionary horizon of the working class coincides with the end of work?[1] After all, the early revolutionary art avant-garde had an ambiguous relationship with capitalism: it provided both a critique of commodification whilst also reproducing the commodity form.[2] Even the cinema of Eisenstein, which so subverted the bourgeois sense of space, time, and personhood, at the same time standardized and commodified working-class reality with techniques of framing and editing that molded images on the commodity form.[3]

Such dialectics between art and the commodity form continue to be played out in today's digital capitalism, as exemplified by so-called 'debt-artists', like the hackers collective Robin Hood, who appropriate the techniques and modes of sociality of financial capitalism to generate spaces of reciprocity and cooperation with the aim of disrupting their commodity logic, but who in fact end up reproducing it.[4] The tension between critique and commodification is no less in play as the digital medium erases the specificity of cinema, the relation between its material bases and its poetics, opening up as it does to other relations – intertextual, lateral, and cross-media – that recall the synchronic aesthetics of the avant-garde. As well as disrupting the materiality of the film medium, digital film disrupts the temporality of classical cinema, suspended in-between movement and stillness and experienced in the expanded duration of the time-image.

Susan Sontag famously lamented the decay of cinema in her 1996 *New York Times* article on the occasion of cinema's 100th anniversary.[5] She argued that the commercial logic of Hollywood blockbuster movies – based on short-term profits, stellar budgets, and simplified narratives – was killing people's love for cinema (cine-philia), which revolved around the ritual of going to the movie theatre. In the magical zone of the movie theatre, she felt kidnapped and transported and 'learned how to dress, how to smoke and how to love'. But the contemporary movie business, she argued, made film consumption individualistic, disengaged, and voyeuristic – akin to the 'possessive spectator' described by film critic Laura Mulvey. A similar grim assessment of the death of cinema was recently made by filmmaker Martin Scorsese,[6] who blamed it on superhero movies with Computer Generated Image aesthetics, parasitical economies linking advertising, gaming, and social media, and online streaming and private video consumption that all undermine the economies and representational style of traditional cinema. Under the regime of platform capitalism, the home spectator is also a 'prosumer'[7] of digital content for the big tech monopolies such as the media service provider and film producer Netflix. Boosted even more during the Covid-19 pandemic, Netflix increased its base of subscribers to 183 million, acquiring a market value of $190 billion even as other mainstream streamers such as Disney+ and Warner Media were nearly going under.

Notably, Mulvey disagrees with such grim assessments of the effects of digital video consumption.[8] Since in the digital image there is no interval – movement happens within the frame and is patterned, complex, and coded – it is in this new field of electronic complexity, information overload, and glimmering digital capital that the 'emancipated spectator'[9] learns to recognize new patterns of meaning.[10] As Mulvey put it, digital technology enhances the 'pensive spectator's' concerns with multiple consciousness and temporalities, thereby increasing in turn the modernist function of cinema as a key repository of collective historical memory – an imaginary museum, where the great events of the past are stored.[11] (Take Godard's *Historie(s) du Cinéma*, which explores world history through a nine-hour long cinematic detour.)[12] For Mulvey, the digital spectator operating from home is more curious, critical, inquisitive, and 'pensive' than the male and bourgeois 'possessive spectator' of modernist cinema, who was voyeuristically absorbed in stereotypically female stars and narcissistically identified with the main male protagonist. The pensive spectator skips and repeats sequences, overturns hierarchies of privilege, and sets up unexpected links that dissolve the chain of meaning invested in cause and effect. In their anti-hierarchic and horizontal and synchronic aesthetics, the digital spectator is a new type of avant-garde artist.

Yet, because the proletarian condition will not disappear with the death of cinema, we must ask whether, and in what ways, these very developments are reproducing the old dialectics between avant-garde art and the commodity form, or whether they are fostering films which transcend these dialectics in ways that contribute to working-class emancipation.

WORKING-CLASS CINEMA FROM GRIERSON TO LOACH

In the UK, this tension between critique and commodification in working-class cinema was played out in the early documentary movement associated with John Grierson, who gave voice to the working class for the first time in cinema's history. But by the 1970s social realist films were under attack from both feminist and black film collectives for several reasons: their voyeuristic distance, rooted in uneven class relations between the filmmaker (often male, white, and middle class) and the subjects (often 'the poor', 'the marginal', or 'the working class'); their victimizing approach; their lack of intersectional narratives; and their excessively materialistic and productivist focus on work, poverty, and inequality. At the same time, the Third Cinema movement in the Global South radicalized cinema, using it as a tool of political mobilization against military regimes and colonial powers. Refusing the imperialist forms of the commercial Hollywood films (first cinema) and of the European authorial cinema (second cinema), 'Third Cinema' devised democratic and participatory film processes, a popular and non-elitist visual grammar, grassroots forms of production and distribution, and a powerful realist style that reflected 'allegorically' the condition of underdevelopment of the Global South.[13] At the same time, media projects among indigenous communities in the Global South opened new uses for cinema, which went beyond the mere aesthetics and function of the documentary.

In the 1980s, it was paradoxically the commercial *Channel Four* that gave voice to black and women realist film-makers in the UK and the Global South.[14] Their representation of the British working class was infused with a new sense of hope, openness, and radicalism associated with a new left multiculturalism. The impact of this was such that when 'social realism' was revived in the 1990s as the brand of the British film industry, the British working class was represented as a national cultural subject rather than as a class formation. Unlike the militant multiculturalism of Stuart Hall, this culture was the branded cultural capital controlled by the financial classes, the 'cool' Britannia of Tony Blair, Britpop, and young British artists designated as the YBAs – entrepreneurs from working-class backgrounds who, endorsing

New Labour's Third Way, took their distance from both the old power elites and the 'uncool' working class of the previous generations.

The realist aesthetics of New Labour emerged from deindustrialization, an epochal and traumatic change for the working class. As the materiality of manual jobs and lives was replaced by immaterial labour, debt-fuelled lifestyles, and social relations marked by precarity, anger, and fear, these precarious working-class lives proved difficult to conceptualize and represent – unlike the ghostly materiality of post-war society represented so well by Italian neo-realist cinema in the 50s which, as Mulvey has pointed out, was able to reflect the spirit of reconstruction precisely by engaging the new 'pensive spectator' attuned to 'temporal delays'.[15]

Within the broader context of the commercialization and depoliticization of working-class cinema and the parallel emergence of commercial TV, art galleries, and film studies departments – three different locales of cultural reification and engines of the post-industrial economy – the epic cinema of Ken Loach was an exception throughout the 1990s, masterfully capturing and staging the tragic struggle between working-class solidarity and the alienating and disintegrative forces of capitalism. Yet as Marxist critical theory gravitated towards Althusserian and Lacanian abstract approaches, Marxist cinema turned over-intellectualizing and self-reflexive too, first in the form of the film essay, and then through its post-modernist appreciation of popular culture.[16]

In television, Loach's allegorical storytelling, depicting working-class lives as symbols of labour's struggle against the mighty forces of capital, was replicated in the popular genre of soap operas such as *EastEnders* – which is still ongoing. Here, women and marginal social constituencies are given voice in the heightened emotional register of the melodrama, through twisting and baroque storytelling and dramatic plot-reversals driven by passionate love, envy, and revenge. Traditionally aimed at a female audience, eventually soap operas captured the entire social demographic as male breadwinners were made redundant and joined the rest of the family watching TV on the couch. The series *The Royle Family* takes place entirely on a sofa of a typical working-class family whose members watch TV continuously whilst gossiping, arguing, and caring for each other.

Reality TV, most famously in the *Big Brother* series, was the other form of mainstream working-class entertainment. It pushed the techniques of classical observational cinema – the non-professional actors, the unedited footage, the powerful *mise-en-scene* and working-class subjects caught in their everyday lives – to its limit. In fact, its surveillance aesthetics, the extreme voyeurism, the sadistic manipulation, the invisible scripted editing, the human captivity, the controlled environment, the inflated and artificial egos, and the productivity of social relations of reality television embodied the alienated subjectivity of capitalism best described by Lukács[17] as a detached and passive spectatorship of one's life. In fact reality TV, by invisibly re-editing and manipulating the contestants' lives and involving the audience in the co-production of stories (as 'prosumers'), anticipated the productive and political regime of late capitalism based on post-produced reality, fake news, production-as-consumption, and the transformation of the Internet into a space of virtual citizenship and an e-public.

Steel Lives

It was the spirit of that time that I wanted to capture with my own film *Steel Lives* (2001).[18] Suspended between Thatcherism and New Labour, a new imaginary of a classless, individualist, and post-industrial society was erasing previous forms of working-class history, solidarity, and livelihood, and at the same time resurrecting Victorian forms of work and labour relations. Living in Sheffield during the 1990s, when profitable steel companies were closed down or downsized by venture capitalists, it seemed that the expansion of the cinema industry and the collapse of the steel industry almost went hand in hand. Big EU structural funds went into the development of the Sheffield Film Festival, the Showroom cinema complex, art galleries, and luxury industrial lofts on the sites of abandoned Victorian steel factories. While my steelworker friends battled against management every day, the spectacle of working-class decline, defeat, and unemployment was being played out in local cinemas showing Loach's latest film *The Navigators*,[19] which tells the stories of five railway workers made redundant after the privatization of British Rail in 1995.

Loach's emphasis on the catastrophic social consequences of privatizations clearly resonated with the lives of my co-workers. But by historicizing working-class struggles that were still unfolding, the film made the triumph of neoliberalism seem not only inevitable, but already present. The immense beauty and empathy that Loach is able to evoke from simple working-class stories seemed to pull the viewer into a state of passive witness. Perhaps had *The Navigators* followed the path of advocacy rather than of realism and beauty, it would have achieved a different effect amongst my friends – perhaps prompting them to want to tell their stories in their own voices? In making my film *Steel Lives* I wanted to engage with working-class representation as a site of political struggle. Unlike the archetypical outsider/observer/film-maker who reifies the working class as a homogeneous political subject, I wanted the film-making process to bring into the open, to catalyze and socialize the contradictions, power imbalances, and structural violence that were implicated in working-class Sheffield. In other words, I wanted the camera to trigger new social relations of production around a process of collective self-representation, rather than documenting a section of the otherwise disappearing working class.

With *Steel Lives*, I wanted to experiment with the politics of film-making, explore so-called 'non-western' ways of telling, to interrogate the double nature of cinema as both an abstract commodity and a materiality. I wanted to make the tension between these polarities present and transparent, and to create a space of both capitalist critique and of active construction of a working-class imaginary. I wanted to tell a story that did not reach the spectator already completed but that, instead, pulled the viewer inside a dialogic, polyvocal, and multi-layered space of resonance in which the diverse affective, imaginative, and material facets of working-class identity would all come alive and coexist in the fragile space in between the autobiographical, the fictional, and the historical.

The aesthetics of *Steel Lives* reflects the egalitarian structure of the film process, our joint commitment to a low-budget and DIY ethics – to find out things together, socialize the process, and pool resources – and our defiant attitude of wanting to narrate a story about the working class that was neither romantic nor cynical, as in mainstream media representations, but showed the grounded and resilient point of view of the steelworkers, a social category that was believed to have disappeared a long time ago. I was interested not so much in realism as a pure ontological class position embodied in a specific aesthetic form. Instead, I was interested in realism's internal tensions, contradictions, and articulations, particularly as they were played out in the frictions and entanglements between identification and critique. By setting up a DIY, improvized, and egalitarian process of production based on co-editing and co-research, and grassroots forms of distribution and screenings in labour organizations branches, companies, underground art galleries, and film clubs – I created a space for the working class to come together in solidarity, as an autonomous and self-producing subject and at the same time as a pensive and militant spectator.

Steel Lives ends with a close-up of a reflection of a derelict Victorian workshop floating on the surface of the river Don. Wildflowers and litter are scattered along the riverbank and a small red poppy stands out from a hybrid landscape of electric wires and grass. My voiceover says: 'Is this what the economists call immaterial economy? Is this the future? And if so, what will come next?'

ARTISTS' LABOUR AND THE NEW EXPERIENCE ECONOMY

In the 1990s the decline of manufacturing in Europe and the US, associated with economic financialization and extreme subcontracting, led to what Negri called the crumbling of 'the factory walls' and the rise of the general intellect – a new invisible, dispersed, and biopolitical productive regime associated with post-industrial capitalism.[20] The fragmented, heterogeneous, fluid, and invisible working class emerging from such new capital articulation challenged traditional forms of working-class representation. As artists and cultural workers became the new lumpen within the expanding media and cultural industries, and of the particularly exploitative system of the gallery-factory,[21] they took up the challenge of working-class representation.

Initially, it was performance artists who, following the genre of 'occupational realism', shaped their practices 'like labour', or, supported by the methodology of ethnographic fieldwork, became 'real workers' especially in the service economy.[22] But in the early 2000s the field of visual art went through a re-politicization. Amidst capitalist globalization, where the spread of digital technology accompanied the massive growth of an industrialized working class in the Global South, a new working-class cinema was being born.

Western Deep

Steve McQueen's *Western Deep* (2002)[23] is a twenty-five minute long film, shot with a Super-8 camera and later transferred to video, of work in the Tautona Mines in Johannesburg, the world's deepest gold mine (3.9 km). Tautona ('The Great Lion') was built by the British multinational Anglo-American Corporation[24] in 1957, as part of Britain's forced industrialization of the colonies. Today AngloGold is the world's second biggest mining corporation with a dismal social record of environmental pollution in Ghana, repression of workers' strikes in Colombia, and generalized debt peonage and anti-black violence across the four continents where it operates. Nearby seismic activities force the management to constantly revise the mine's layout and mining methods, creating even more precarious working conditions. With 800 km of tunnels, the mine is an underground city, inhabited by 5,600 miners. The Nigerian curator Okwui Enwezor commissioned *Western Deep* for the international exhibition *Documenta XI*. Enwezor justified the commission by saying that the film rendered 'the terrible nearness of distant places that global logic sought to abolish and bring into one domain of deterritorialized rule'.[25]

The first five minutes of *Western Deep* is nearly entirely black and silent, occasionally punctuated with shrieking mechanical noises and red, blurred flashes on the miners' faces. We are in the 'cage' with the miners, descending with them down the shaft. We don't know how many miners are around the camera. Some double deck cages can fit up to 120 workers. The gate suddenly opens, the sound disappears and an artificial green light invades the field of vision. The sequences that follow are de-structured and sensorially overwhelming. We pass through dark tunnels, miners drilling into the walls, water spilling, wet faces occasionally hit by cones of light, and human flesh coming in and out the camera's visual threshold. The soundtrack alternates between drilling noise and silence. Images of labour are intercut with images of miners relaxing in a workers' lounge.

Next, we witness a surreal medical examination. Two rows of miners in blue boxer shorts perform a step exercise while monitored by doctors. They continuously step up and down, following a loud mechanical sound synchronized with blinking red lights. They have thermometers in their mouths. We experience the mechanical time of Taylorism. Miners become machines in human flesh. Slowly, the red light accelerates its rhythm to the point of flashing chaotically. Sound and image become detached from each other. The bodies of the miners gather speed, as if out of control. We are experiencing a terrifying ritual of dispossession. The surrealist style of Jean Rouch's 1955 film 'Mad Masters'[26] – focused on a possession ritual in post-colonial Accra – comes to mind. The sequence ends with a close-up of the red light of the buzzer, an expanded and abstract red zone.

The issue of scale is central to industrial films such as this. How to represent the vast expanse of the mine, the extreme heat (140 degrees Fahrenheit), and the immense value of small grains of gold?[27] The strategy chosen by McQueen, based on a multisensory aesthetics, is to bring the viewer to imagine what cannot be shown, rather than to provide visual evidence. In darkness, it is the soundtrack that leads the action, so that we can 'listen to images' before we see them.[28] Art historian T. J. Demos[29] argues that *Western Deep*'s 'aesthetics of opacity' is representative of a new current of documentary practice in art that challenges the false assumption of neutrality and unmediated representation and embraces 'instability' as a new political register. McQueen solves the political dilemma of the impossibility of representing work from the point of view of labour by shifting from realistic representation to abstraction. Bright red, artificial green, electric blue, all cast on a dark background produce different hues of 'blackness', intended not as representation of an absence but rather as a 'chromatic force' or an 'undercurrent movement'.[30]

The notion of blackness and opacity as a form of resistance and 'counter movement' is central to postcolonial Marxism and black radical philosophy.

In Marxist terms, every working-class representation quantifies, objectifies, dis-embeds, and reifies the un-representable and unique experience of labour. Thus, black Marxism embraces abstraction to resist the commodity form and the representation of the working class 'as a single being'.[31]

The destabilization of black identity is a central trope in McQueen's work, resonating with the diasporic narratives of the Sankofa Film and Video group and the Black Audio Film Collective in London whose critique of the Thatcherite politics of race and class, as well as of the Eurocentric mode of documentary representation, inspired him. But the focus of *Western Deep* is neither on labour nor on race or class. Rather, it is on the dis-identification and disorientation experienced by the viewer in encountering opaque images, which like ghosts, represent the un-representable. In this sense the film produces not so much a new form of realist aesthetics, but a form of subversive biopolitics, locating the viewer in a zone of doubt and sensory dislocation in which they are able to connect with the subaltern.

West of the Tracks

With the emergence of affordable digital video (DV) cameras in the 1990s, Chinese independent film-makers, avoiding state censorship, started to address the inequalities associated with the post-socialist transition in China.[32] In its representation of the exploitative *hakou* migration regime, working-class poverty in rust-belt areas, and the dehumanizing subcontracting system in the apparel and electronic industries, the so-called Chinese 'new documentary movement' went beyond traditional forms of filmic class representation. The independent DV movement embraced a specific amateur and improvised DIY ethics and a realist aesthetics – described as *xianchang*, which translates as 'live' and 'on the scene' – based on the ethnographic method of spending long periods of time with film subjects, shooting in real settings and with no crew. It organized private screenings, informal and online distribution of cheap and pirated DVDs that reached out to disenfranchised counter-publics consisting of ethnic and religious minorities and LGBTQ communities.[33]

Wang Bing's *West of the Tracks* (2002)[34] is an epic, nine-hour long film document-ing the decay of the industrial district of Tiexi in the city of Shenyang, and the struggles of its industrial workers to exist in the liminal zone of post-socialism. For fifty years, Tiexi has been China's largest industrial base and the embodiment of socialist planning. During the Reform Era, the Tiexi complex resisted the country's shift to the market economy, and up until the 1980s it still employed around a million workers. By the early 1990s, the district started to decline, and by the end of the decade most of its factories were closed. In 2002, the 16th Congress of the Communist

Party announced the transformation of the area into a high-tech industrial hub. But the promise was never delivered, and the Tiexi district now lies in ruin. As mass unemployment rises in the area, so do mass protests and labour demonstrations.[35]

The film is divided into three parts. The first part, 'Rust', follows a group of factory workers in three state-run factories: a smelting plant, an electric cable factory, and a sheet metal factory. When they are not struggling with sub-standard equipment, poisonous waste, and hazardous labour, workers spend their time in idleness, waiting for raw material that will never arrive. By the time the film is finished, the three plants have closed. The second part, 'Remnants: Pretty Girls Street' follows the working-class families of the old state-run housing block *Rainbow Row*, focusing on teenage children who struggle to see a future beyond unemployment. The third part, 'Rails' narrows its focus to a single father and son who scavenge the rail yards and sell raw parts to local factories in order to survive.

As a young film student who had never shot a film before, Wang Bing arrived in Tiexi in 1999 with a borrowed DV camera. He left two years later with more than 300 hours of footage. Critics have described *West of the Tracks* as a rumination on post-socialist modernity, a melancholic tribute to the working class, and 'an act of mourning'.[36] As per McQueen, Wang's observation of the slow dissolution of the industrial working class in China is not rendered through visual evidence, but rather through an imperfect, opaque, and reflexive mode of witnessing. For film critic Ramos-Martinez,[37] the aesthetics of *West of the Tracks* is marked by a process of oxidation, of rusting of images. Rusts creeps along the factory walls, along train trucks and even in domestic spaces. Rust makes disbanded industrial tools and machines 'vibrant' with matter,[38] and at the same time, shows the imperfection, decay, and fragility of images. It creates zones of intensity and invisibility inside the frame. Paradoxically, this enhanced sense of materiality derives from the pixelated quality of the digital medium, which is, by its very nature, immaterial. Especially at low visual thresholds and in scenes filmed at night, blobs, forms, and patterns seem to emerge from nowhere, attacking and distorting the image, whilst human bodies disappear into the digital flow, engulfed in electronic surfaces that 'are screen for other luminous entities'.[39] Indeed, as the camera in *West of the Tracks* wanders through industrial ruins, scavenges for waste, and witnesses the workers floating in steaming baths, it pulls the viewer into a mesmerising wandering, akin to the surrealist *derive*.

The oxidation of *West of the Tracks*, in addition to producing an aesthetics of opacity, constructs a more-than-human temporality allegorically questioning the linear logic of the planned economy, of working-class history, and even of the film experience. This temporal challenge comes from the violent and unexpected intrusions of natural elements inside the film – not only of rust, but also of snow, earth, rain, and dust – which disrupts the workers' agency as well as that of the film-maker who, through his camera movements, we feel struggling against extreme environmental conditions. We experience nature's contribution to the slow collapse of a socialist workplace – as an active force – and the fleeting and random movements of rain, dust, and snow being more effective than human actions in eroding the structural ground of socialism. We 'feel' the end of socialism and the beginning of the new cycle of the market economy through the flow of nature, and in the form of corrosion of the monumental – in anti-monumental style.

Bitter Money

Wang's subsequent film *Bitter Money* (2016),[40] shown in Documenta 14, is a masterful description of the lives of rural migrants working in the booming garment factories of Huzhou. Using a small digital video camera with an autofocus lens, Wang filmed between 2014 and 2016, producing more than 2,000 hours of footage, which he then edited down to two-and-a-half hours. The film starts with a 15-year-old girl and her older cousin talking and fantasizing about the future on the evening before their long journey to Huzhou. Their sense of hope quickly dissipates in the journey – first by bus, then by train, then again by bus, and terminating with a long walk under the rain into the grey building block of their dormitories. During the journey, which lasts twenty minutes in the film, we learn of the desperate working conditions these migrant workers are leaving behind.

Once in Huzhou, Wang's filming becomes more directed and less observational, as it moves from workshop to workshop, closely documenting the manual skills of these supposedly unskilled subcontractors (their weaving, cutting, and folding), tracking down the movement of value across invisible production chains (from the production of the garment to its packaging), and sketching a visual narrative of re-composition, reconstruction, and reparation that goes against the workers' material alienation, fragmentation, and separation. Following the gentle weaving and threading of the camera around simple human gestures, we learn the architecture of the flat/workshop where every room has at least three working stations; we overhear workers talking of hourly piece rates, their bosses' profits, and the wealth they will accumulate before returning home. We overhear one of them: 'they say you will earn 10.4 million in three months. Who falls for that roams around like a lost soul and behaves like a ghost'. We witness women working hard and being resilient and men getting drunk, defeated, and abusive. At one point, a worker, Liu, describes her rift with her husband and her wish to split from him. Her cousin warns her, 'You are too tiny to defeat him. What woman can overpower a man?'

As in *West of the Trucks*, we feel the film-maker's dwelling in the flow of relations – sweeping past in crowded rooms, standing by beds at night and even passively observing Liu's abusive husband beating and harassing her for ten minutes. In a sequence such as this, we wonder why the angry husband allows the film-maker to film, and we question the clinical detachment of the film-maker. Towards the end of the film, a traffic accident leads the workers to congregate on their balcony, half absorbed in the scene of the accident and half in a beautiful sunset. From the street, a police officer shouts at them: 'What are you looking at? Go away'. As the workers return to their rooms the camera takes another quick peek down as if to acknowledge its voyeuristic presence all along.

Bitter Money ends with some workers packing garments into giant plastic bags in a busy backstreet at night. Amongst them we recognize Liu and her husband. That the film ends with the last phase of the production process unfolding in real time (the scene lasts ten minutes and is nearly unedited) makes us realize that the process of filming and the process of producing garments have been running in parallel all along. Besides, we know that these garments will be exported to some European countries for foreign consumption, and we also know that Wang's film will be seen only outside China. Perhaps the title *Bitter Money* means that as well as alienating the working class, money also has alienated Wang from his native country? In the last sequence, the workers finish packing and run into different directions, seeking shelter from heavy rain. As in *West of the Tracks*, it is a random natural event that drives the visual narrative. But just before the end, Liu appears from nowhere, runs towards the packed merchandise, checks the label on it, and disappears again.

Miners, Grooms, Pneumoconiosis

We have seen how, in the case of the Chinese documentary movement, digital production and distribution reflected the strategic needs of an increasingly young and precarious working class, and new modes of critical investigation and political assembly. But digital technology per se cannot explain the resurgence of working-class cinema in China or elsewhere. Take for instance the film *Miners, Grooms, Pneumoconiosis* (2019)[41] by Jiang Nengjie. Shot over eight years, the film investigates illegal coalmining in the central province of Huan, and the fatal lung diseases that affect most local miners. Jiang was born in the mountains of rural Hunan and many of the characters in the film are his relatives. It is because of the social proximity to his subjects that the camera is allowed into the forbidden space of illegal mining. We see miners working at night to avoid state inspectors and officials digging pits on mountain tops, taking shelter in makeshift huts under the snow, talking about corrupt and lazy state bureaucrats. We witness children watch their fathers dying in a dilapidated rural clinic.

Jiang, whose income mostly relies on wedding videos, did not submit the film for state approval nor enter it in national or international festivals. Instead he distributed it online, sending instructions to anonymous individuals on how to download it for free from the internet. The film became a sensation after going viral on YouTube, where it got more than 10,000 downloads. But *Miners, Grooms, Pneumoconiosis* also received heavy criticism from nationalist party cadres and the film-making community, who argued that it exposed illegal miners to the threat of legal persecution. Indeed, the individualistic character of the film process, the lack of consultation with the subjects despite (or because of) their familiarity with the film-maker, and its distribution according to the logic of social media all beg the question of whether this film really speaks for the working class.

American Factory

It is against the background of Wang's films that the significance of the workplace documentary *American Factory* (2019),[42] made by Steven Bognar and Julia Reichert and produced by Barak and Michelle Obama for Netflix, can best be appreciated for what it tells us about the working-class experience in today's global cyber-capitalism. During her early career, film-maker Julia Reichert was part of the group of experimental film-makers associated with Jonas Mekas and Stan Brackage and the radical film collective *Newsreel* in New York City. True to her working-class background (her father was a unionized butcher), Reichert produced militant feminist films, which she considered as a means of labour organizing rather than just aesthetic experimentation or working-class representation. Snubbing commercial distribution in cinema theatres, she distributed her films instead in schools, unions, and community groups. Reichert's shift from militant to mainstream cinema is therefore an unexpected departure.

American Factory documents the painful transformation of the General Motors car plant in Dayton, Ohio, which had been closed since 2008, into the new Chinese auto glass manufacturer Fuyao, opened in 2014, and alongside this, the struggles of American workers against the exploitative Chinese regime of production. The film starts with a celebration of the reopening of the plant, when the residents of Dayton warmly welcome the management of Fuyao and its chairman Cao Dewang – referred to as 'chairman Cao'. But the good mood soon fades as the Chinese management starts to regiment the American workforce to a harsh labour regime in order to increase productivity. Salaries are just $27,000 per year – a supervisor tells us that his daughter earns $40,000 working in a nail salon – and unpaid overtime on weekends is the norm. Despite the management's clear determination to crush any attempt to unionize, activists from the local 696 UAW start a unionization campaign on the shop floor, and eventually organize a ballot. Some militant workers are fired. The ballot ends with a humiliating defeat: less than 40 per cent of the workers support the unionization of the plant.

Throughout the film, the conflict between the management and the workforce is described as a culture clash. US workers seem lost vis-à-vis the Chinese corporate rituals – the inaugurations, the cutting of ribbons, the misspelled company values, the logos and the flags, and the ritualistic group meetings before the morning shifts. On the other hand, the paternalism of the Chinese management is filled with cultural stereotyping of the Americans. An empathic supervisor commiserates with the Americans for having two jobs at a time. At a Human Relations training meeting, Chinese managers are told that Americans are simple, bluntly honest, and childlike, that 'they want to be pleased' and 'made feel important'. It is touching to see muscular working men adapting to make fragile auto glass. As these shatter and break in the background, a Chinese manager tells us 'Their fingers are so fat ... we have to keep on training them'. Eventually, the American management is entirely replaced by a Chinese one and the culture gap widens. 'We need to use all our intelligence to help them,' says a concerned manager.

Towards the end of the film, in the crowded company auditorium, chairman Cao announces that the company has a $40 million deficit, and it may soon close. The workforce is terrified. In the next sequence, chairman Cao, while being driven to the airport, ponders, 'In the past few decades I have built so many factories. Have I taken the peace away and destroyed the environment? I don't know if I am a contributor or a sinner.' In the film's final sequence two engineers walk with chairman Cao through the empty workshop, explaining the heavy work reorganization ahead. The working stations are filled with robotic arms. One engineer tells Cao, 'Here there used to be one worker'. At the next working station, he says, 'Here I am going to get rid of four workers'. In the end credits, we learn that the company is still open and operates at a profit.

Sorry We Missed You

The central message of Ken Loach's latest film, *Sorry We Missed You,*[43] comes already in the opening credits, when we hear the main character Ricky being interviewed for the job of parcel delivery driver:

> BOSS: Let's get a few things straight: you don't get hired here, you 'come on board', we call it 'onboarding'; you don't work for us you 'work with us'; you don't drive for us, you 'perform services'; there is no employment contract there is no performance target, 'you meet delivery standards'; there is no wages but 'fees'; no clocking on, but you 'become available'; if you sign with us you become an 'owner driver franchisee', masters of your own destiny, separated from the fucking losers and one of the warriors. Are you up for that?
> RICKY: Yes, I have been waiting for an opportunity like this for ages.

The remainder of the film deals with the consequences of Ricky having signed such a Faustian contract, and his slow descent to hell together with his wife Abbie, who is subject to a similar exploitative labour regime as a contract nurse and in-home carer. In her soul-destroying affective labour of looking after disabled, elderly, and vulnerable people, Abbie struggles to reconcile the inhuman laws of capital – the zero hours contract, the unpaid transfers, and the piece-work rates — with the intense emotional needs of her 'clients' who constantly push her into uncomfortable physical interactions and maternal 'tuck-ins' in baths, toilets, and beds.

As in previous films, Loach's social realist style – the non-professional actors, the working-class locations, and the hyper-realistic dialogue based on real-life ethnographic observations – draws the spectator into a detached and alienated (in Lukács terms) observation of working-class life, enhanced by the soft and melancholy light engulfing Newcastle's hilly working-class suburbs.

The first alienating effect comes from Paul Laverty's well-researched script, which provides a constant sociological and historical contextualization of the characters' lives, as if they were mere illustrations of the workings of capitalism. 'We lost our house when Northern Rock crashed ten years ago' says Abbie to one of her patients; 'he ended up with £75,000 in debts and now works in a call centre', says the rebellious son Seb about a friend's university experience, to Ricky who is attempting to discourage him from playing truant; and 'I need to work!' screams Ricky to Abbie and Seb who are trying to keep him safe at home, in a melodramatic final scene that recalls De Sica's *Bicycle Thieves*. The second alienating effect is triggered by the occasional glitches of the non-professional actors – Kris Hitchen who plays Ricky is a plumber in real life; Abbie is played by real-life teaching assistant Debbie Honeywood; Seb is a graffiti artist; and all of Ricky's colleagues are real-life delivery drivers. As with reality television and epic theatre,[44] in this film the perceived artificiality of acting draws the spectator's attention to the absurdity of the overarching framework – a capitalist system that disposes with the uniqueness of human beings and turns them into mere ciphers.

Historically, the melodramatic genre in cinema has been used to deconstruct middle-class morality, typically in Douglas Sirk's depictions of the catastrophic consequences of the patriarchy and racism of the affluent bourgeoisie.[45] But Loach's turning of the reflective gaze upon the very working class – upon Ricky's initial sin of wanting to be like a capitalist – ends up reproducing the power of capital vis-à-vis labour, as it forces the working class either to identify with 'a fucking loser' or restricts the restorative power of drama to those middle classes who can afford the noble refusal. 'Sorry we missed you' is the standardized message stamped – as if handwritten – on the postcards delivery drivers leave to customers who are absent, and which Ricky uses to write a love message to Abby just before the film's final dramatic scene. This absence can be read in several, possibly conflicting, ways, and it is precisely the gap between the openness of the meaning and the clarity of the message that ultimately tells us that we are stuck with just one reality: capitalism is here to stay.

It has been said that Loach is the most European amongst the British filmmakers, if anything because his films are heavily financed by European companies and EU film funds. But there is no mention of Brexit in the film, which deals mainly with the white working class. Whether it comes from Loach's personal views or from the need to reach out to European audiences, this silence is another way in which the point of view of the working class has gone missing.

Labour in a Single Shot

The pensive spectator will have a very different kind of film experience roaming in the online digital archive of the *Labour in a Single Shot* project,[46] containing videos of one to two minutes in length of work of any kind – of cobblers, cooks, waiters, farmers, window cleaners, surgeons, nurses, tattoo-artists, or garbage workers – taken in a single shot. Set up by filmmakers Antje Ehmann and Harun Farocki, the archive contains around 150 films from the video production workshops they led in fifteen cities worldwide between 2011 and 2019.

The scope of the project is not only to uncover and render visible contemporary forms of labour but also to reflect on the labour of the film-maker. How to capture labour as an event, in all its integrity and its fluid internal choreography? How to valorize it, rather than objectify it?

As in all of Farocki's oeuvre, *Labour in a Single Shot* (1995) reflects on the kind of consciousness generated by cinema since its beginning:

> early films such as the Lumière brothers' *Workers Leaving the Lumière Factory* and *Arrival of a Train at La Ciotat* were made in a single continuous shot and implied that every detail of the moving world is worth considering and capturing. They were forced by the immobile camera to have a fixed point of view, whereas the documentary films of today often tend towards indecisive cascades of shots. The single-shot film, in contrast, combines predetermination and openness, concept and contingency.[47]

Farocki's own film, *Arbeiter Verlassen die Fabrik* (*Workers Leaving the factory*) (1995)[48] refers to the Lumieres' film. It consists of compiled film sequences of workers leaving the workplace, sourced from documentaries, industrial and propaganda films, newsreels, and features. The compulsive reproduction of images of workers leaving the factory reflects the impossibility of representing the agency of labour due to its dispersed, immaterial, and fragmented nature, especially today. Composed as an unfolding visual archive, the film interrogates and re-enacts such fragmented labour agency. As Farocki put it:

> The film montage had a totalizing effect on me. With the montage before me, I found myself gaining the impression that for over a century cinematography had been dealing with just one single theme. Like a child repeating for more than a hundred years the first words it has learned to speak in order to immortalize the joy of first speech.[49]

It is paradoxical that the pristine qualities of the single shot, its magical power of capturing movement, ends up being enhanced by the cut, the moment in which movement is arrested, and in the compositional space of the visual archive, where the labour of the film-maker overpowers that of the worker. Yet this nostalgic wandering in the visual archives in search of labour's original movement feels more uplifting than the nationalistic recasting of class struggle in terms of cultural difference in *American Factory*, or the downcast stories of the British proletariat in Loach's working-class films.

CONCLUSION

What does this survey tell us about working-class cinema today? First, revolutionary cinema is not about specific technologies, aesthetics, or social processes, but emerges from the encounter between specific conditions of production, circulation, and consumption, contingent working-class struggles and forms of radical imagination. Second, the notion of militant cinema is historically specific. The politics of the modernist film-maker was to gather visual evidence in order to improve working-class conditions; that of the diasporic artist is to bring the viewer to endorse the point of view of the subaltern, achieved through an aesthetics of opacity and dis-identification, whereas the contemporary video maker is engaged in direct advocacy and campaign – as in Jang's advocacy against illegal mining and, to a certain extent, *American Factory*, which I read as a 'nationalistic' call for unionization. Thus, to Mulvey's typologies of spectatorship – the 'possessive spectator' who is fetishistically absorbed in the spectacle of images, and the self-reflexive and historically minded 'pensive spectator' – a third should be added: that of the tactical spectator who 'takes cinema entirely as an instrument, complement or support of a specific political goal'.[50] But in treating film just as epistemology, ontology, or advocacy, respectively, each of these three modalities of militant cinema lacks an essential dimension of working-class life and therefore is alienated. A working-class cinema made by the working class remains a distant utopia.

The new ethnographic genre of labour representation developed by artists working in digital formats such as Wang and McQueen – characterized by an extremely high shooting ratio, opaque aesthetics, irreversible temporality, and a sensuous camera presence – reflects not only the new conditions of production and distribution associated with digital film, but also new modes of consumption and access, specifically the format of the film installation in the art gallery, in which Wang's and McQueen's films are primarily shown. According to T. J. Demos, the format of the film installation forces audiences to actively register the materiality and physical presence of film – 'haptically as well as optically'.[51] The spectator's experience of *West of the Tracks* in the gallery is nearly mystical. In the liminal space 'between video projection and exhibition', as the bodies of the miners disappear in darkness, spectators are touched by the light of film. Existing between materiality and immateriality – luminosity and darkness – viewers are destabilized and sensorially overwhelmed, and at the same time, they engage in an active process of self-transformation. From passive and sovereign observers, they become immaterial, sensuous, and image-like.

From the discussion above, it can be argued that working-class cinema made by artists has the following characteristics: (1) a pensive mode attuned to temporality, memory, and history; (2) individual film-making in which the film-making process is set up as a process of self-discovery, and where cinematic time and real time tend to converge; (3) a new aesthetics of opacity, fragmentation, and multi-perspectivism; and (4) gallery distribution, under the curatorial mode of production and in the exhibition format, often in the context of group shows and biennials. Demos' mystical appreciation of artists' film installations fits well with art historian Boris Groys' description of the logic of the contemporary art museum. Unlike traditional museums of historical art, which functioned as mechanisms of neutralization of time and abolition of history, the contemporary art museum embraces the flow of time. Unlike the former, which gave spectators a sovereign gaze, the latter pushes the spectator right inside 'the curated event', where images interact with objects, images, texts, and documents, as well as with the architecture of the space, sound, and light. Thus, according to Groys,[52] the contemporary art museum 'stages and enacts its own precariousness'.

With Jameson,[53] I would argue that the curatorial mode of production of the contemporary art gallery reflects the experience economy of late capitalism, based on the valorization of precariousness, and in which the precariousness of the public that activates the artwork – as 'prosumer', that is, as both producer and consumer – is an instance of the precariousness of labour in general. In fact, if the opacity and the sensuous and durational quality of artists' films about the working class push the spectator into an emancipated and inquiring posture, that spectator's insertion into the curated event ultimately disempowers them and neutralizes their curiosity. In the space where the image-spectator meets the 'abstract real' presence of the workers, the destabilized art spectator lacks the empathy, or the time, to identify with the destabilized worker, despite their common deterritorialized and subterranean existence.

But less opaque modes of labour representation are similarly problematic for how, by turning the gaze back to the working class, they end up reifying it as either a dehumanized cipher of capital, as in *Sorry We Missed You,* or as an identitarian and particularistic social formation, as in *American Factory*. If the ontological approach of the curatorial mode of production, by focusing on the pensive spectator, disavows the subject of representation – the working class – the documentary approach pulls the focus back to it but only to 'please' (as per Mulvey's notion of visual pleasure) the possessive spectator.

Besides, the horizontal, creative, and experimental approach of the digital spectator, highlighted by Mulvey, relies on the film-maker validating the viewer with some 'emancipatory power'. The simple nationalistic message of *American Factory* doesn't leave much room for creative interpretation, whereas Farocki's *Labour in a Single Shot* online archive does open up a pensive space of memory, reparation, and experimental reconstruction of the future of cinema though a glance to its early beginning. It is also telling that these different forms of online distribution – Netflix's streaming is by subscription only, whereas Farocki's archive can be freely accessed – imagine different forms of social aggregation: isolated, private, and lonely in the former; collective, dialectical, and playful in the latter – another insight into how cinema doesn't just reflect existing social relations, but also creates them anew.

NOTES

1 John Roberts, 'The Missing Factory', *Mute*, 2012; available at: www.metamute.org.
2 Claire La Berge, *Wages Against Artwork: Decommodified Labor and the Claims of Socially Engaged Art*, London and Durham: Duke University Press, 2019.
3 Jonathan Beller, *The Cinematic Mode of Production. Attention Economy and the Society of the Spectacle*, Hanover and London: University Press of New England, 2006.
4 Max Haiven, *Art after Money, Money after Art*, London: Pluto Press, 2018.
5 Susan Sontag, 'The Decay of Cinema', *New York Times*, 25 February 1996.
6 Adam Epstein, 'The Movies are Dead According to Two Distinguished Moviemakers', *Quartz*, 4 January 2017.
7 Nick Dyer-Whiteford, *Cyber-Proletariat: Global Labour in the Digital Vortex*, London: Pluto, 2015.
8 Laura Mulvey, *Death 24X a Second: Stillness and the Moving Image*, London: Reaktion Books, 2006.
9 Jacques Rancière, *The Emancipated Spectator*, London: Verso, 2008.
10 Hito Steyerl, 'A Sea of Data: Apophenia and Pattern (Mis-) Recognition,' *e-flux journal* 72, April 2016.
11 For the relationship between cinema, memory and history, see Sigfried Krakauer, *Theory of Films*, Oxford: Oxford University Press, 1960.
12 Jean-Luc Godard, *Histoire(s) du Cinéma,* (4h27'), 1998.
13 Octavio Getino, 'The Cinema as a Political Fact', *Third Text* 25(1), 2011, pp. 41-53; and Ismail Xavier, *Allegories of Underdevelopment: Aesthetics and Politics in Modern Brazilian Cinema*, Minneapolis and London: University of Minnesota Press, 1995.
14 Such as the series *Eleventh Hour,* which included political and personal documentaries and low budget fiction from the Global South, or the seasons *New Cinema in Latin America* and *Africa on Africa* in 1982.
15 Mulvey, *Death 24X a Second*, p. 160.
16 For an insightful reconstruction of the history of Marxist cinema, see Scott Forsyth, 'Marxism, Film and Theory: From the Barricades to Postmodernism', *Socialist Register: Ruthless Criticism of All that Exists*, London: Merlin Press, 1997.
17 Gregory Lukács, *History and Class Consciousness*, trans. Rodney Livingstone, London: Merlin Press, 1974.
18 Mao Mollona, *Steel Lives* (50'), 2001.

19 Ken Loach, *The Navigators.* (1h 36'), 2001.

20 Antonio Negri, *Marx Beyond Marx: Lessons on the Grundrisse*, London: Pluto, 1991.

21 Hito Steyerl, 'Is a Museum A Factory?', *e-flux Journal* 7, 2009.

22 Julia Bryan-Wilson, *Art Workers: Radical Practices in the Vietnam War*, Berkeley, Los Angeles and London: University of California Press, 2009; and Hal Foster, *The Return of the Real*, Cambridge: MIT Press, 1996.

23 Steve McQueen, *Western Deep*, (24'12"), 2002.

24 Anglo American was established in Johannesburg by Ernest Oppenheimer who also founded De Beers in 1917.

25 Okwui Enwezor, The Black Box, *Documenta 11, Platform 5: Exhibition Catalogue*, Ostfildern- Ruit: Hatje Cantz, 2002, p. 44.

26 Jean Rouch, *Le Maitres Fous (Mad Masters)*, (28'), 1955.

27 Gold is so expensive that a mine such as Tautona only needs to extract 0.35 ounces from a ton of rock to be profitable. It produces 209,000 ounces per year.

28 Black philosopher Tina Campt calls 'listening to images' the multisensory and non-fetishistic approach to images, especially with regards to representation of people of color. Tina Campt, *Listening to Images*, Durham: Duke University Press, 2017.

29 T. J. Demos, 'The Art of Darkness: On Steve McQueen', *October Magazine* 114, 2005, MIT Press, pp. 61-89.

30 Kirk Varnedoe, *Pictures of Nothing: Abstract Art since Pollock*, Princeton: Princeton University Press, 2006. Black philosopher Fred Moten argues that Fanon's post-colonial philosophy embodies movement. Fred Moten, 'The Case of Blackness', *Criticism* 2, 2008 Wayne State University Press, pp. 177-218.

31 Moten refers to the relational politics of French Caribbean writer and philosopher Edouard Glissant. Fred Moten, *The Universal Machine*. London and Durham: Duke University Press, 2018.

32 Chris Berry, Lu Xinyu, Lisa Rofel, eds, *The New Chinese Documentary Movement: For the Public Record*, Hing Kong: Hong Kong University Press, 2010.

33 As well as DV filmmakers, the Chinese new documentary movement included filmmakers working with film such as Jia Zhangke whose stories also deal with the conditions of the Chinese working class in the context of post-socialism. For instance, like *West of Track*, Jie's *24 City* (2008) describes the closure of a state-run factory – in this case Factory 420, a military factory built in Chengdu, Sichuan Province, in the late 1950s in the context of the Cold War. In the 1980s and 1990s Factory 420 struggled to adapt to the new market of television sets and refrigerators, and eventually it closed down. The film describes its final liquidation, purchase by private real estate developers and demolition. 'Part documentary', 24 City mixes together documentary footage and fictional performances by four professional actors to produce a form of staged remembering of life under socialism. Zhang Zhen and Angela Zito, *DV-Made China: Digital Subjects and Social Transformations after Independent Film*, Honolulu: University of Hawai'I Press, 2015.

34 Wang Bing, *Tie Xi Qu: West of the Tracks*, (9h). France, 2002.

35 In the Liaoning province alone, there are 2.5 million unemployed.

36 Chris Berry, Lu Xinyu, Lisa Rofel, eds, *The New Chinese Documentary Movement: For the Public Record*, Hing Kong: Hong Kong University Press, 2010, p. 20.

37 Manuel Ramos-Martinez, 'The Oxidation of the Documentary: The Politics of Rust in Wang Bing's Tie Xi Qu: West of the Tracks', *Third Text* 29(1-2), 2015, pp. 1-13.

38 This is a reference to Janet Bennett's book *Vibrant Matter*, which emphasizes the active role that material objects have on social and political life. Jane Bennett, *Vibrant Matter: A Political Ecology of Things*, Durham: Duke University Press, 2010.

39 T. J. Demos, 'The Art of Darkness: On Steve McQueen', p. 67.

40 Wang Bing, *Ku Qian: Bitter Money*. (2h32'), 2016.

41 Jiang Nengjie, *Miners, Grooms, Pneumoconiosis* (1h22'), 2019.

42 Steven Bognor and Julia Reichert, *American Factory*, (110'), USA, 2019.

43 Ken Loach, Sorry We Missed You, (100') UK, France, Belgium, 2019.

44 For a discussion of Brecht's epic theatre, see Walter Benjamin, *Understanding Brecht*, London: Verso, 1988.

45 Laura Mulvey, 'Notes on Sirk and Melodrama', *Visual and Other Pleasures*, London: Palgrave Macmillan, 1989.

46 The archive is available at: www.labour-in-a-single-shot.net.

47 Antje Ehmann and Harun Farocki, Labour in a Single Shot. www.labour-in-a-single-shot.net/en/project/concept/.

48 Harun Farocki, *Workers Leaving the Factory* (Arbeiter verlassen die Fabrik), (36'), 1995.

49 Harun Farocki, 'Workers Leaving the Factory', *NachDruck/Imprint,* Berlin: Verlag Vorwerk, New York: Lukas & Sternberg, 2001, p. 32.

50 Octavio Getino, 'The Cinema as a Political Fact', p. 43.

51 T. J. Demos, 'The Art of Darkness: On Steve McQueen', p. 70.

52 Boris Groys, 'Entering the Flow: Museum between Archive and Gesamtkunstwerk', *e-flux journal* #50 December 2013, p. 8.

53 Frederic Jameson, 'The Aesthetics of Singularity', *New Left Review*, 92, March April 2015, p. 110.

THE SURVEILLANCE OF SERVICE LABOUR: CONDITIONS AND POSSIBILITIES OF RESISTANCE

JOAN SANGSTER

When workers in retail outlets in North America go to work every day, they no longer punch a clock like the women in *Nine to Five*. Instead, a computer records their biometric fingerprint, leaving no way to evade managerial scrutiny or punch in for a late fellow worker. One cannot fake or borrow a body part. Once at work, workers' physical movements and sales are monitored through CCTV and digital data collection. The latter facilitates tracking of cashiers' speed and frequency of sales, which are linked to their personnel record, making anxiety about error and the pace of work more intense. Video cameras focus especially on the till, but also track one's movements across the floor and in the storage rooms, leaving a record for discipline that can be presented as more scientific, exact and infallible. Not only performance and productivity, but subjective attributes, attitudes, and the most personal of health information are tracked by employers, who claim this information enhances innovation and productivity or protects workers and the public. The increasingly panoptical gaze of technological surveillance conjures up fears of a dystopian future of work, confirmed by employers who dismiss worker privacy as 'illusory', or boast about their omniscient power to 'measure everything that moves'.[1]

The technological possibilities for, and managerial uses of, surveillance have undoubtedly intensified in recent years with computer programs that collect, store, share, and interpret massive amounts of data. Productivity apps, electronic sensors, fitness trackers, facial recognition, biometrics, FRID [radio frequency identification data], DNA testing, thermal and location sensors, to name a few tactics, have become more accessible and affordable for employers. Since the 1980s, women, immigrants, and minorities in 'high volume' service and manufacturing jobs considered less skilled, and often non-unionized, have experienced the heaviest brunt of this intensified, invasive surveillance.[2]

As surveillance continually modernizes its forms, there are deleterious effects on the cultural and material dimensions of workers' lives within worksites and beyond, including their work cultures, health, wellbeing, subjectivity, and life choices. However, labour historians have long cautioned against technological determinism: political and economic conditions, the specificities of the work, and changing power relations, not technology as a 'pure' phenomenon, shape how surveillance is applied, experienced, modified, or jettisoned. Feminist 'surveillance studies' scholars echo this caution: technologies are also gendered, shaped within and often reinforcing gender inequalities.[3] Historically, the surveillance of workers has varied according to spatial contexts, political economies, labour law regimes and work processes, as well as the gender and racial make-up of the workforce and extent of unionization.

The *capabilities* of employer surveillance are not the same as how and when technologies are applied, how workers respond, or even the basic raison d'être of surveillance. The monitoring of service labour may be shaped by multiple factors, including the search for solutions to technological problems, new management thinking, changing capitalist organization and competition within business sectors, even the aggressive marketing of new 'wonder' technologies, but at its very heart, it involves the organizing of labour and control of workers in order to enhance the pace, production, predictability, and profit of work.

Understanding this is central to a materialist and feminist analysis of the conditions of surveillance and resistance to it. A feminist eye for highly asymmetrical power relations of gender and race and a materialist concern with the 'kernel of human relations' at the heart of capitalism, namely the lived experience of exploitation, will guide my exploration of the surveillance of working women's bodies in this essay. Women's work reflects the 'determining logic' of accumulation and the expropriation of surplus value – with all the instabilities and contradictions involved – that structures capitalist social relations, but these relationships are simultaneously lived through cultural and ideological processes that explain, naturalize, legitimize, and sometimes reassure us as we negotiate life on and off the job.[4]

Surveillance is not only tethered to the logic accumulation, it also shapes the nature of alienation associated with the labour relationship under capitalism. For Marx, alienation was the consequence of the estrangement of humans from their bodies, from the products of their labour, from external nature, and indeed from other humans. While alienation is often depicted with examples drawn from the production of material commodities, service labour also produces a commodity, though one that is created and consumed somewhat differently. Service workers bodies are used, their human traits or 'essence' mobilized for profit, leading to estrangement from their own bodies, from other workers, and from consumers.[5] The varying modalities of surveillance have physical and psychological effects on how estrangement is understood, experienced, and negotiated by workers. Whether surveillance involves rote or emotional labour, is random or expected, on or off site, personal or machine-based – and so on – conditions the sensory, bodily, lived experience of alienation.

If women's bodily labour is shaped by alienation, it is also a conduit for agency and resistance, however remote the latter concept appears in the current moment of technological escalation. Taking into account the logic of accumulation does not mean capitulation to the inevitability of an ever-intensifying panoptical workplace. However limited or constrained, workers have responded to the most invasive surveillance with informal and formal strategies intended to temper or even reject employers' disciplinary gaze.

After a brief discussion of the history of surveillance at work, this essay looks specifically at private sector service labour, historicizing the work processes, experience, and resistance of two groups of women workers: flight attendants and retail workers in the US and Canada.[6] Both are subject to intense surveillance as the labour process involves face-to-face customer interactions, in which the mode of delivering service is itself part of the product sold. Both occupations were historically dominated by women and remain feminized; aesthetic and emotional labour are also intrinsic to both occupations. Yet, they diverge in their work processes, bargaining power, unionization, and success in resisting unwelcome surveillance.

SURVEILLANCE IN HISTORICAL PERSPECTIVE

If surveillance is perennial, though always shifting in the history of capitalism, the topic has taken on new urgency over the last two decades, in concert with structural economic change, the emergence of new occupations, neoliberal ideology, and academic theories. The consolidation of neoliberal capitalism privileged the market over human needs and rights, flexible over stable employment, insecurity over security. Individualization and the exaltation of the market, two pillars of neoliberalism, have made workplace surveillance more ideologically 'common sense' and more difficult to challenge (and indeed, the growth of the security state after 9/11 also played an important role). The changing spatial organization of labour across the globe, including e-work such as freelance telecommuting, created the incentive and rationalization for remote monitoring; employers can photograph workers at their computer screens, access their work at random, counting keystrokes and mouse clicks.

Moreover, intellectual trends, particularly the seduction of Foucauldian studies, made surveillance a preoccupation in academic analyses of modern institutions ranging from the prison to the factory (perhaps without enough distinction between these).[7] Foucault, the 'preeminent theorist' of surveillance studies,[8] is a ubiquitous presence in organizational studies of service labour, particularly those exploring the serving body as a discursive social script, a conduit for normalization and self-management. Surveillance is the means to power knowledge, the linkage between bureaucratic and professional expertise and forms of discipline and punishment. Unfortunately, postmodern scholarship often positioned Foucault as a superior alternative, rather than complement to Marx: the resulting fascination with the malleable, fragmented, flexible, self-regulating body, and indeed the 'libidinal body', meant that the labouring body was obscured and de-materialized, abstracted from the social processes and relations in which all labour is situated. If Foucauldian insight into the processes of normalization was gained, less attention was paid to historical and materialist structures of class, centralized power, and human agency and resistance.[9]

Notwithstanding the recent emergence of 'surveillance studies',[10] surveillance has in fact been central to the history of work over the nineteenth and twentieth centuries. If, as Christopher Dandeker argues, surveillance is the 'gathering of information about and the supervision of subject populations' in order to monitor, modify, and discipline, then work and surveillance are inextricably linked in modern capitalist economies.[11] Notions of hierarchy, supervision, and the exchange and measurement of labour for reward, are almost 'universal' in these 'contract-based employment relations'.[12]

Surveillance lies at the heart of Marx's description of factory organization, and it underpins Marxist discussion of changes in capitalist managerial strategies. Surveillance was central to Harry Braverman's explication of scientific management as a strategy to monitor work flows in order to segment, deskill, and speed up production, exemplified by his evocative description of the foreman 'overseer' timing Schmidt's brute physical labour.[13] Marxist expositions on work were cognizant of both the 'hard' technical surveillance done through clocks, measurements, and other purportedly scientific techniques, as well as 'soft' surveillance strategies that involved managers and personnel professionals observing and recording workers' interactions with managers and each other, even probing their lives away from work. Surveillance might involve direct observation, record keeping, and quantification, as well as peer pressure and moral suasion. Data, both qualitative and quantitative, was not only used to discipline and punish, but also to modify behaviour, attitudes, and customary work cultures, even to predict future problems. Fordism was born not just on the assembly line, but through the indirect surveillance of Ford's Sociological Department that spied on workers at home in order to re-shape the working-class family and curb their oppositional political views.

Studies of service labour, more attuned to gender and sexuality, drew on Braverman's insights; as clerical labour became feminized, it was also more forthrightly surveyed, centralized and monitored, typified by the strictly-supervised typing pool. The gendered division of labour accompanying the rise of the modern department store went hand-in-hand with new surveillance tactics directed at lower-paid, supposedly less skilled female sellers assumed to be temporary workers. Pei-Chia Lan's contemporary study of retail sellers in the beauty industry explores how bodies and identities are part of a work process in which surveillance encompasses the body, presentation, and emotion as much as the measurement of sales. The uneven global development of such service 'body work' has created different sensibilities and restrictions for racialized migrant women. Many find it difficult to escape proscribed emotional roles and racial stereotypes intrinsic to the work process, as they are constrained by the lack of work alternatives, citizenship rights and their financial responsibilities in their home country.[14]

As this last example indicates, situating workplace surveillance within the geographies of global power, political economy, and cultural contexts is critical. The increase in service labour since the 1970s was a global phenomenon; service work now comprises the largest sector of many national workforces. The massive increase in women's paid work since the seventies in western countries has been correlated with a growing service economy, and service work remains profoundly gendered and racialized. This contingent labour force also reflected the structural shift to flexible accumulation. Over the course of the 1980s, *Business Week* noted, the number of contingent employees had almost doubled, with most of these female workers.[15]

However, service work is an immensely variegated category that includes both well-established occupations and forms of labour only recently commodified as they moved from home to the market, as well as jobs linked to new leisure, hospitality, caring, and intimate services.[16] Distinctions between public and private sector work are significant; public sector employees often have more tools available to object to unwanted surveillance. Some 'interactive' service jobs, in which provider and customer are present in the same space, involve emotional and aesthetic labour; the former involving both intentional and unconscious emotional work of client care, the latter the cultivation of employees' embodied attributes as an advertisement of the service being sold. Both are often naturalized as inherent to women workers' personalities and desires, and as such they are not easily quantified, recognized, and rewarded.[17] Emotional and aesthetic service work often involve more invisible forms of 'body work': labouring on one's own body to be 'workplace ready'; labouring on the emotional or physical bodies of others; or 'the management of embodied emotion or display as part of the job'.[18]

Many scholars identify radical shifts in surveillance tactics in all workplaces in the 1980s, as employers turned to computerized information technologies. Computer programs promised objectivity, precision, and certainty – not just recording, but also intelligently and immediately interpreting worksite data. Although work became 'measurement saturated', the outcome of computerization, suggested Shoshana Zuboff in 1984, was not predetermined: information technology might 'automate', work, intensifying employer control, but it could also 'informate' or empower employees if they had access to, and a dialogue with, new IT systems.[19] The notion that workers – particularly those without professional bargaining power – might utilize the same technology designed to enhance profit to instead extend control over their own conditions of work always seemed overly optimistic, and soon was proved to be a miscalculation amidst the escalation of invasive computer control in the 1990s.

Indeed, through that decade, corporate self-reporting showed an intensification of technological surveillance practices, especially the purchase of CCTV.[20] Studies of team work and just-in-time labour linked surveillance strategies to changes in capitalist production, arguing that new forms of 'chimerical control' replaced top-down Taylorism with a combination of electronic surveillance, peer group pressure, and self-regulation. These new 'Foucauldian' tactics eschewed the direction of 'compliant bodies' from above, instead using workers' minds and initiative to alter their subjectivity, while convincing them this offered enhanced personal autonomy. If this 'microscopic policing of subjectivity'[21]was different in form from Fordist Taylorism, it had similar goals. The apparent devolution of decisions downwards did not alter structures of ownership: the 'superstructure of surveillance and the information collected' was still firmly in the employers' hands.[22]

Indeed, as Paul Thompson points out, the goal of many forms of surveillance is, in the last resort, Taylorist: 'squeezing labour and its costs through the intensification of measuring, monitoring and surveillance'.[23]

With good reason, one commentator on current surveillance strategies sums them up with 'long live Taylorism!'[24] Some long-established service occupations have simply integrated electronic surveillance into existing routines to verify measurement and rules, from fast food workers whose Hygiene Guard 'smart badges' measure washroom hand washing to hotel 'maids' who use hand-held computers to remotely transmit information on their cleaning routines – though employers are less inclined to provide them with smart technology that might protect them against assaults and harassment.[25]

Other new enterprises of the late twentieth century did, by their very nature, advance technological oversight. The connection of telephone and computer technologies in call centres facilitated quantitative and qualitative surveillance of service delivery by this new, often female cybertariat; pace and timing, success in service or sales delivery, even workers' vocabulary and demeanour could be closely monitored. Surveillance of these lower-paid jobs may be off-site, hidden from view, executed randomly, leaving workers lacking autonomy and control; this also facilitated the spatial relocation of jobs from higher-waged economies to lower-wage ones.[26] With good reason, surveillance experts cite telecommunications work as an instance of the invisible digital panopticon on a global scale, though some researchers also point to traces of individual resistance and occasionally collective organizing.

Finally, computerized surveillance has had a multiplying effect on occupations as well as the intensification of labour. Professional and managerial work has been altered by new surveillance capabilities and the labour of surveillance itself has expanded, taking in, for instance, workers monitoring, archiving, and quantifying electronic surveillance, IT workers fixing it, supervisors assessing and manipulating it, and technical professionals designing countless new programs and apps.

Yet, the application of new technologies is not simply the product of scientific advances. Urinalysis drug testing at work, as Jeremy Milloy shows, emerged in the 1980s in the US not because of medical testing advances, but because earlier union and management human resources efforts to 'aid' addicts were hijacked, reinvented as forced drug testing in a changing political and economic context. Neoliberal management techniques promoting the 'individualization' of employees, political fear mongering about drug wars (described by Abbie Hoffman in *Steal This Urine Test*), and declining union power and will to challenge testing all contributed to this invasive surveillance. Urinalysis, as Milloy shows, combines new scientific testing with old-fashioned intrusive humiliation. Not surprisingly, this 'scientific' test proved to be neither error-proof, nor did it eliminate addiction.[27]

Surveillance may also come in the guise of aid and protection, just as it did in some early twentieth century paternalist welfare schemes. Addiction counselling, for instance, has been integrated into corporate wellness programs. Supposedly voluntary (but often not really voluntary), these programs collect data on workers, ostensibly to provide a health benefit, but in reality are also used to enhance worker productivity and to predict future risks for the employer. The burgeoning multi-billion dollar business of wellness programs may use the latest electronic fit bits, but they also rely on older personnel information gathering. Surveillance in the wellness industry is explained not just by technology, but also by political economy. Wellness providers in the US were aided into existence by Obamacare provisions, and serve as corporate strategies – on the one hand advertising employer 'care', and on the other offering a means to constrain employer health benefits costs.[28]

More recently, a preoccupation with 'surveillance capitalism' of the tech giants has inspired academic and journalistic exposés of their invasive mis/use of private data. Shoshana Zuboff's *The Age of Surveillance Capitalism* does situate surveillance within changing modes of accumulation: after 2008, capital sought new areas of accumulation, just as it had once colonized and commodified new land and resources. Human communication was turned into a marketable resource, a form of 'behavioural surplus' that could be sold and manipulated in projects of behaviour modification. It is telling, however, that the Google Glass project – proposing massive public data collection through glasses worn by individuals in public – was so reviled that the company reassigned it for development *only* in the workplace, where surveillance had become so completely 'normalized' it might attract less opposition.[29]

Contemporary discussions about the need to protect digital privacy rightly identify the obscene misuse of power by Facebook and its corporate cohort, but defenses of individual privacy (in which the individual is all too often abstractly imagined as white, affluent, and male) may obscure class relations and the realities of the workplace. We should not overlook the illiberal history of privacy. Privacy has never been equally enjoyed by all citizens, as workers, the homeless, criminalized, marginalized, and the welfare recipient can attest. Reformist legal strategies to protect worker privacy may falter not only on this liberal mythology of individual privacy, but also on the shoals of the hegemonic ideology of the market as progressive, innovative and fair. After all, employers claim, why would workers not welcome surveillance to improve efficiency, maintain group norms, or prevent other workers from slacking off? The promise of enhanced compensation through increased productivity associated with surveillance is also understandably enticing for workers.

The recent intensification of digitalized welfare surveillance in many countries suggests how easily claims of enforcing 'fairness' become intrusive infringements on the human rights of those with less power. Even informational surveillance *intended* to aid welfare recipients with fairer distribution of resources became unintended, intensified, invasive, and discriminatory social control. It is not surveillance technologies per se, but how they are used and co-opted in a society that normalizes and pathologizes inequality that is the problem.[30]

SURVEILLANCE IN THE AIR

Publicity concerning the most outrageous employer surveillance, from 'smart toilets' to secret internet monitoring of worker's private lives, is alarming, but may not be the mundane, everyday norm. There are also assumptions about the current trajectory of workplace surveillance that accompany discussions of computerized monitoring: that surveillance will inevitably follow 'lockstep' with technology, that it is becoming more, not less technically based, and that it moves from 'predictable' authoritarian control to invisible and individualized solutions, including more 'participatory' methods in which workers use apps to monitor themselves.[31]

Yet all service labour does not fit these patterns. Combinations of tactics are more common: older bureaucratic personnel surveillance tactics, both direct and indirect, may overlap with more technologically sophisticated ones, or even outpace them. Flight attendant work arguably fits the latter scenario. Surveillance of flight attendants evolved from an era of intense sexist and racist surveillance of the body, appearance, and demeanour in the 1950s and 1960s to some limits on such surveillance by the 1980s due to union and feminist resistance. Current efforts of airlines to enhance flexibility and cheapen the costs of labour circle back to some of the same monitoring techniques employed decades ago, suggesting continuities with older management tactics of surveillance as much as much as the emergence of new ones.

One could hardly imagine a more surveyed occupation than the largely feminized work of flight attendants in the 1950s and 1960s. Surveillance followed from the interview through training to their daily labour. Height, weight, age, body attributes, and a subjective notion of white attractiveness, politeness, and good humour were assessed in recruitment and ongoing observation.[32] Historical studies reveal how women's bodies were both a form of labour power and mobilized as a feminine image that was packaged, commodified, and sold as part of airlines' service and brand. By the 1970s, when airlines altered written guidelines to avoid charges of sexism, there were still unwritten methods of surveillance: as one union activist recalls, she was told to stand up and 'turn around' by her male interviewer so he could look at her body.[33] Rules that airlines claimed were safety based, such as disallowing eyeglasses or flying when pregnant, were critiqued by flight attendants as further efforts to create a conventionally attractive body. Awareness of safety regulations, their unions complained, was less important than knowledge about eye shadow.

Male flight attendants were also subject to grooming surveillance, but employer monitoring was asymmetrical, encouraged in part by a gendered division of labour that positioned men as pursers/supervisors until the 1970s. The airlines' projected image of flight attendant heterosexual masculinity was different from the 'sexy stewardess': women were more obtrusively surveyed, their bodies more rigidly assessed. While this bodily policing is common knowledge, there is significance in the enduring tactics of employer surveillance over many decades. From the 1950s to the 1980s manuals for female attendants laid out countless pages of rules about every detail of their appearance, and a highly developed system of observational checks and inspections, both expected and random, was used to survey women's bodies, attitudes, and demeanour.[34]

Surveillance had serious consequences. Promotion was tied to a good appearance record and warnings and discipline were invoked for infractions of dress codes as well customer complaints about attitude – for example, not smiling enough. Surveillance also followed workers into public spaces: flight attendants could be censured if their public appearance in terms of dress or demeanour was 'unbecoming' to the airline brand. The same still applies, though now they can be fired for their blog posts that the airline takes exception to.[35] Employer monitoring of appearance was relentless, but as one former flight attendant union activist put it: at heart, 'it was all about controlling the worker'.[36]

Employer methods also included team and self-surveillance. Employees were encouraged to labour on their own bodies to keep them beautiful and presentable, to take pride in an image they were told was of great value, and to encourage fellow attendants to keep up appearances so that the occupation maintained its prestige – otherwise everyone would lose. Aesthetic labour also required workers to subsidize their service work with time spent on body care, makeup, and so on. Individualization and self-policing techniques, in other words, were part of the employers' arsenal long before academics noted a turn to Foucauldian management of the self.

Flight attendants were aware that their emotional labour was also assessed, even before the term was used. In oral histories, those working in the 1960s list emotional tasks (calming, flattering, reassuring, joking, socializing, etc.) as just part of their job; so too was elder and child care during flights, according to airline advertising and promotion.[37] Nonetheless, Arlie Hothschild's exposition of emotional labour in the 1980s was a feminist breakthrough that still resonates in studies of women's service labour. Hothschild argued emotional labour was intrinsic to flight attendant work, and though it was portrayed as natural to women, it was commodified for the airlines' benefit. Encouraged first through intensive training, then through ongoing employer demands and oversight, emotional labour might involve surface or deep acting: the former could be feigning emotion, but the latter involved altering your emotional state, literally separating oneself from one's own subjectivity, resulting in a process of transmutation that could lead to burnout and alienation.[38]

The concept was soon deployed, debated, and also critiqued in studies of service labour. Some scholars countered that flight attendants, like other service workers, derived satisfaction from emotional work and could disentangle different 'sets of feelings and rules'; others criticized Hothschild's 'absolutist' view of management control.[39] If Hothschild downplayed negotiation and resistance, the concept nonetheless had important materialist and feminist insights. First, employers like the airlines commodified affect; they expropriated value from women's emotional labour, though this work often went unrecognized and unrewarded. Workers' emotions and subjectivity were and are 'colonized', plundered by service industries for profit.[40] Second, emotional work is tied to alienation, creating a disjuncture between the job requirements and suppressed personal feeling and needs. Even presuming workers do negotiate or resist the emotional demands of their job, the cumulative toll that the lived experience of work potentially takes on the body is important to Hothschild's definition.

In keeping with the turn towards Foucault and Bourdieu, by the 1990s scholars focused more on aesthetic labour: the mobilization, cultivation, and commodification of pre-existing class and gender cultural dispositions by employers in order to use attributes of style, presentation, and speech to 'sell' the service encounter.[41] Emotional labour, critics claimed, ignored the 'corporeal body' and erroneously assumed one could artificially separate an inner and outer consciousness, identifying an authentic, true 'interiorality'.[42] Aesthetic labour is useful in describing the process of scrutinizing beauty, grooming, and speech styles in service work, the commodification of aesthetics for profit, and how social meanings attached to appearance reinforce race and class barriers to certain jobs. However, most studies eventually rejected a hierarchy of concepts, noting the entanglement of emotional and aesthetic labour. It is revealing that in interviews, flight attendants 'recognized instantly' emotional labour as part of their work process and the toll it took on their physical and psychic lives.[43] They seemed to know what 'interiorality' felt like: anxiety, burnout, exhaustion, frustration. They also recognized that employer scrutiny was embedded in unequal power relations, so managerial strategies to survey emotional responses could not be easily ignored.[44] By 2000, one study showed, competition in the industry led to intensified management surveillance of service performance so that flight attendants were pressed to respond even more positively to 'demanding publics' (basically the customer is always right) no matter the emotional cost. The encouragement of customer entitlement / attendant subservience, combined with the historic sexualization of female flight attendants, meant that sexual harassment and verbal abuse were routine occurrences on the job.[45]

As neoliberal capitalism consolidated, many airlines periodically pressed for both government deregulation and employee concessions; the industry favoured two tier contracts, part-time labour, and the creation of subsidiary budget airlines paying budget wages. The contemporary methods of on-the-job surveillance, however, have remained relatively stable. Even if employee data is more quickly available and malleable through computer tracking, surveillance has less to do with advanced information technologies than with more of the same: recruitment, training, and ongoing direct, qualitative (and thus subjective) observations by supervisors and customers to create a bodily image, inculcate values, and encourage emotional and aesthetic labour.

Surveillance also continues to elicit resistance. In Canada, flight attendants in the Canadian Union of Public Employees (CUPE) filed a complaint with the Canadian Human Rights Commission (CHRC) in 1987, alleging a 'pervasive policy problem' in the airlines due to overly judgmental sexist standards of appearance and the sexualization of flight attendants. Thirty years later, CUPE filed another complaint with the same CHRC, on behalf of 8,500 Air Canada attendants, contending that workers are subject to 'rampant sexual harassment and discrimination', forced to participate in a 'sexualized fashion show' to display new uniforms, 'lined up and graded on appearance',[46] and instructed on what kind of undergarments and makeup to wear.[47] Senka Dukovitch, the feminist union activist who filed the 1987 complaint (and was disciplined by her employer for her comments to the press about it) felt she had 'déjà vu … when I heard about the recent human rights complaint. It's just like in the 1970s and the systemic complaint I filed as head of the CUPE Women's Committee that I was interviewed about and punished for. It's almost identical'.[48] A recent campaign by flight attendants in the budget Air Canada Rouge airline similarly protested the subjective surveillance of appearance and demeanour requirements, though in a more gender neutral manner: unappealing, uncomfortable uniforms coupled with flight attendants being forced to take a Disney course on service labour – even footing part of the bill from their own wages.[49]

The filing of these complaints, decades apart, suggests why and how flight attendants continue to contest intrusive surveillance. First, their work process mitigates some forms of electronic surveillance. Timing and speed up are problems, as are reduced numbers of attendants per plane, but flight attendants maintain a small measure of autonomy within their workplace – a hunk of steel hurtling through the skies – where they must exercise some decision making and collaborative work. They can also lay claim to a professional status. However much the airlines encourage Disneyization, most of us are primarily interested in whether a flight attendant can get us out of a burning plane, not the colour of their lipstick. While emotional labour remains a key part of their work, the public may judge aesthetic labour as less important.

Perhaps most significant, flight attendants have strong union and activist roots, traditions all the more interesting as this was a feminized occupation with a geographically scattered, mobile workforce, and one generally hired to be agreeable not oppositional. However, in the US and Canada, unions developed early and by the late 1960s, some were quite militant; they included feminists in leadership positions who made strong alliances with the women's movement. Resistance to unreasonable surveillance and calls for women's bodily autonomy and dignity emerged through flight attendant unions, which used multiple tactics: grievances, collective bargaining, court cases, and human rights claims. Transparency in bargaining rounds and publicity about legal challenges became educational moments for rank-and-file members, including those uninterested in feminist ideas, but who nonetheless could be persuaded that professional know-how, not super surveillance of appearance, was most important to a job well done.

Flight attendants also have a history of appealing directly to consumers, most recently with blogs (both informational and ironic) and public statements; US union leaders, for example, publicly criticized mandatory drug testing, claiming these would penalize flight attendants whose work often requires the use of sleeping pills and weight loss drugs.[50] During the recent Covid-19 pandemic, Sara Nelson, the president of the American union of flight attendants, delivered one of the most impassioned and militant trade union appeals for solidarity, calling for state financial support for *all* workers remotely linked to air travel, as well as limits on executive compensation.[51]

SURVEILLANCE ON THE GROUND

Retail workers in the US and Canada have far less robust union protection than flight attendants, and their work process lends itself to more intense surveillance. Retail workers, to be sure, are a more diverse category than flight attendants; they include those working in small and large businesses, selling vastly different products, but even a focus on larger stores indicates the continuities as well as changes in modes of surveillance. Customer service, shaped by emotional and aesthetic labour, is an essential part of the work process; women especially are expected to inhabit the job, becoming part of the product sold.

The overall trend in large retail after the 1920s involved the replacement of male with female labour, particularly as work was de-skilled, made part-time, and changed to self-service. By mid-century, retail work had become a feminized occupation, though one in which a gendered division of labour, justified by a male breadwinner ideology, streamed men into higher-paid selling jobs and a track to management, and most women, even 'career' sellers, into lower-level clerical and sales positions.[52] Within this hierarchy, women were more strictly surveyed than men, in part because more men were in jobs that allowed them mobility within the store, while women were ever-visible behind counters, but also because managers saw women as more psychologically problematic: more emotional, less reliable and in need of direction. Ironically, women's emotional labour was appropriated by the employer, but their 'emotional' character used against them; many supervisors psychologized women workers, commenting critically on their personalities, complexes, motives, and so on.[53]

In the postwar period, one department store's personnel files show, surveillance took multiple forms: there was indirect pressure exerted through employee organizations, newsletters and co-worker informal networks, most of which had a management presence. Often, these forums stressed the need to self regulate, creating the proper persona for the job and personal identification with consumption, the store, and managements' goals.[54] Most surveillance involved direct, personal, and persistent observational monitoring. Sellers were evaluated repeatedly through standard forms and written commentary that judged them in terms of appearance, language, initiative, quality of work, attitude, and collaboration, with assessments redoubled during sales and holiday periods. Obviously, financial mistakes and lateness were concerns, but women were told to correct their hair, dress, attentiveness, politeness, tone of voice, 'time theft' (talking to family on the phone), clumsiness, tardiness, gossiping, lack of cooperation, and a host of other sins. Nor was surveillance necessarily scheduled: in retail, a long tradition of random floor walking, or later 'surprise shoppers' kept workers expectant and on their best.[55]

Women's proper deployment of emotional and aesthetic labour was – and still is – integral to the work process, and customer complaints have played an important role in justifying management surveillance. Retail selling is based on a presentation of the self that involves displays of deference, good humour, sympathy, commiseration, and many other emotions performed as work. Sellers' emotions were deployed to provide clients with reassurance, flattery, nurturing, delivered in the appropriate tone, striking a balance between sellers' knowledge and deference to the customer. Aesthetic presentation – manner, body, attire – was also critical, and had to be a match for the 'brand' being sold, in terms of the store's overall brand and within stores, the objects being sold, whether it was furs, children's clothing or appliances. Aesthetic labour mobilizes class dispositions, but in retail, not necessarily to mimic but reassure the customer, perhaps reaffirming the worker's subordinate role. Remember, lectured a supervisor to female sellers, you must, 'not have a hair out of place, but never be more elegant than the customer'.[56] The demand to be impeccable assumed that women's off hours work on their bodies – caring for one's appearance, clothes, etc. – was part of the job.

Direct, qualitative observation that was persistent and personal was thus the primary mode of surveillance until the 1970s, even if it had the patina of quantitative oversight as infractions were tabulated in personnel files. Like flight attendant work, surveillance was gender asymmetrical, with different emotional and aesthetic expectations for men and women. Surveillance also had concrete, if graduated consequences; discipline started with corrections and lectures before moving to demotions, moves to less desirable departments (like the bargain basement) or dismissal. Both women and men retail workers rebelled against employer monitoring in individual ways, suggesting the exercise of agency more than resistance: workers ignored orders, pilfered, fought customer rudeness with rudeness, shared information on bad managers, evaded observation, or complained about their individual mistreatment. Collective organizing and unionization were attempted, though with rare exceptions they were unsuccessful, remaining a persistent theme in retail today. With a few exceptions, retail is not unionized globally, even though on average about 10 per cent of the global workforce is involved in retail. Despite the seeming proliferation of brands and stores, large corporate empires are the dominant players, allowing them to use their inordinate power to stave off unions, even closing large stores that do unionize.

One could argue that retail work, at least for women, never involved secure jobs, but since the 1980s, it has become even more economically precarious. Just-in-time production associated with flexible accumulation is extended to just-in-time selling. Surveillance has adapted to these conditions, though even the more digitally advanced stores utilize an assemblage of tactics: direct observation, reviews of camera footage, and invisible digital assessments. Efforts to create a personal identification with the brand or store and peer pressure – co-worker surveillance – are utilized, as are undercover or 'surprise' shoppers and supervisors' subjective assessments, even if through reviewing CCTV tapes. Direct observation, though, remains important, and managers' ability to ferret out wrongdoers may mean promotion for the ambitious. As Barbara Ehrenreich recalls of her work at Walmart, invasive monitoring came from the assistant manager's floor walking. She and a fellow worker hid to avoid him seeing them speak to each other, as socializing was considered an egregious form of time theft: 'here were two women of mature years, very hard working women, dodging behind a clothing rack to avoid a twenty-six-year-old management twerp'.[57]

Many retail employers also begin surveillance before hiring: in the US (though not Canada), many states allow compulsory drug testing and pre-employment personality tests are common, though intelligence/aptitude/personality tests existed since the turn of the last century, and have long been challenged as less than scientific. Personality screening tests for lower-level positions (created by yet another surveillance industry) are supposed to find the right character for the job but employers often interpret that 'fit' by examining attitudes towards authority. As Ehrenreich found, the Walmart test question for her interview, 'Rules have to be followed to the letter of the law at all times,' required the response 'very strongly'. Just 'strongly' was a failing answer.[58]

If women sellers historically comprise an emotional and aesthetic service workforce with little influence over the work process, the increased application of information technologies has intensified store surveillance, promising management even more control over a workforce characterized by the 'short termism' of flexible accumulation.[59] Covert but constant digital surveillance guarantees a measure of employee self-discipline: the psychological impact of always being watched is an effective mode of employee control. Admittedly, there are still immense differences within retail, but computer surveillance has become common, in part because software firms have developed all-purpose programs that track inventory, customer choices and personal information, and workers' efficiency. These new technologies are themselves an industry, not unlike the proliferation of scientific management efficiency firms in the early twentieth century. Programs like RetailNext advertise point of sale monitoring, tracking the sales of each worker, their till balances, returns, and speed of sales, as well as many other tasks. Workers' individual sales records are measured against aggregates in order to weed out underperformers.

The use of 'just in time staffing' (last-minute hour assignments) to cut labour costs, as one study showed, led to the proliferation of digital surveillance. Irregular schedules and more employees created a larger, fluid workforce and the 'propensity to treat workers like potential criminals'.[60] Biometric fingerprinting and point of sale monitoring were thus deemed all the more essential in order to keep an eye on workers. Digital information collection can lead to 'data or function creep' as new uses are found for excess, collected information. Technologies originally introduced as theft prevention in retail, for example, had 'unexpected bonuses' for management, ushering in new forms of control over workers.[61] Yet, there was not a rule of automatic ever-increasing digital surveillance in retail: what mattered was the 'dynamic relationship of technologies with one another', matching monitoring with the workforce, the work process and the products sold.[62] Indeed, the proliferation of data can lead to employers 'drowning in data', without the resources to review it all.[63] Workers can only hope that employers' fascination with covert monitoring will become a burden as much as a benefit for management.

Technology is not infallible. Computerized monitoring, including biometric tracking, sometimes malfunctions, and retail workers find ways to occasionally circumvent the finger print punch-in or deal with computer oversight. If you are required to put in a customers' email with each sale and you don't have time, just put in your own multiple times.[64] Nor is technology neutral. Supposedly scientific monitoring has not obviated race and gender biases in retail: in some stores, workers of colour are still relegated to the inventory room, aesthetic appearance standards keep racialized or trans groups out of some jobs, and when workers are taught how to 'profile' shoplifters with CCTV video, the usual race and gender biases in profiling are simply repeated.

The experience of covert surveillance elicits costs for employee health and morale: it creates a stressful work environment as workers adjust their emotions to the ever-present eye of management. Stress is exacerbated by last-minute work assignments that require constant juggling of childcare and family responsibilities. Algorithm-produced schedules, like other big data workplace 'innovations', are often designed without attention to women's work, including their balancing of unpaid care and paid work.[65] Alienation, in other words, is experienced in particularly stressful ways. When surveillance becomes ideologically normalized, part of the 'common sense' of the job, resistance becomes more difficult, and is often expressed in informal acts, from quitting to tricking the surveillance technology. Workers may resort to unplanned, mundane reactions to employer control, such as disruptiveness, circumventing or mocking of the rules.[66] These are coping strategies or forms of subversion but they are not the same as conscious critique or collective organizing against exploitation, inequality, and unfairness.

Service sector workers do use digital technology to 'hit back' at management, for example with anonymous web exposés of bad bosses, practices or illegalities – all in the hopes that public exposure matters. Organizing in retail has assumed non-union forms, facilitated by the reach of the internet, used as a virtual space to share ideas, education, and tactics, including store-based networks, sector associations, and sporadic protests. Organizations like the Retail Rights Project take up specific causes such as unpaid overtime pay, whether there is a union or not.[67] Class action court cases have intermittently challenged gender discrimination in retail, but such legal strategies are politically limited and cumbersome, with disappointing outcomes.

Ultimately, though, the almost non-existent unionization – combined with the nature of the work process, precarious labour, and the workers' lack of claims on skill – make challenges to surveillance extremely difficult. Workers simply have fewer human and material resources to counter managerial resources. Without traditions and practices of solidarity and collective resistance, workers' inclination to challenge surveillance is constrained. Though the media often celebrates digital rebellion as a tactic, networking efforts by workers may prove transitory, ignore on-the-ground organizing, and lack a deeper analysis of the underlying causes of capital's seemingly unchecked power to survey.[68] Celebrating sporadic forms of resistance through short term or one-time, focused protests is important to workers' morale and sense of possibility, but collective organizing promises the hope of more long-term change. Labour studies scholars who refer to trade unionism and strikes as 'clichés of Fordism'[69] are perhaps overly cynical about collective forms of protest. The absence of such mobilizations may reflect the doldrums of the labour movement, but such strategies have proven effective, and may open up avenues to more thoroughgoing critiques of waged labour that go beyond the workplace to capitalism itself.

CONCLUSION

Historicizing flight attendant and retail work suggests that surveillance has not followed 'lockstep' with technological advances, nor do current strategies necessary move automatically from visible, authoritarian to more invisible control, or from top down to more 'participatory' self-regulation. Older tactics of subjective observation overlap with new computer tracking, and the particular recipe for surveillance in each workplace or industry is shaped by the work processes, workers' claim on knowledge, and the collective ability of workers to hinder, temper or resist surveillance. Flight attendants, in contrast to retail workers, have benefited not only from a different work process and claim on skill, but long traditions of unionization. Using multiple forms of resistance, from grievances to human rights cases, they have tried to keep surveillance in check. Retail workers, lacking the same collective traditions and protections, have turned to other, non-union means of sporadic issue-based and sector-based resistance, though often of a fleeting nature.

In both retail and flight attendant work, emotional and aesthetic labour are connected elements of the work process that are not readily rewarded by employers, yet they are nonetheless surveyed and monitored by them. Whether an employer relies on aesthetic dispositions of appearance that are cultivated for the brand being sold or emotional labour that elicits customer reassurance, both are key to interactive service delivery, a measure of the employers' success and profitability – and as such, they are also part of the process of commodification, expropriation of their labour, and exploitation. While both forms of labour are important, the concept of emotional labour in service work has continuing theoretical resonance; resting on feminist and materialist suppositions, it assumes the conscious, feeling self of workers, the expropriation of the labour for capital, and the potential for alienation. Emotional labour has been disproportionately expected of women workers, naturalized as part of their character rather than their jobs – though again this could shift in the future.

This emphasis on expropriation and accumulation does not deny worker choices, agency, or desires. Enjoyment, accommodation, and manipulation were all part of how flight attendants dealt strategically with beauty and emotional demands of the job. Retail employees also draw satisfaction, incentive, and dignity from emotional and aesthetic aspects of their jobs. It simply recognizes that there is a major discrepancy between worker and owner in terms of that core political economy question: 'who benefits?'

Surveillance is also implicated in how alienation is experienced. Women's service work, which requires the 'value added' of aesthetic and emotional labour, reinforces the significance of connecting surveillance and alienation in a historical, materialist, and feminist analysis in which interactive service work is understood within the prevailing relations of power in which labour is expended. Employers' confiscation of emotion for profit is part of the process of accumulation, but this expropriation also opens up questions of worker agency, feeling, and consciousness. Bodily service labour is 'an accumulation strategy' for capital but it may also be the 'locus of agency and potential political resistance'[70] to the indignities of surveillance.

The declarations in the 1990s by postmodernists as well as post-Fordists that advanced western societies were 'post-Panoptical' seemed out of touch with the reality of labouring lives. In the first world at least, the argument went, the Panopticon model describing a 'clockwork' society with 'armies of workers and infantrymen who were shaped by policing and indoctrination', was no longer appropriate; these were now 'societies shaped by consumption and enjoyment imperatives', by mobility, and especially self surveillance.[71] Yet by the 1990s the use of information technologies designed to enhance control over workers had become more sophisticated and widespread, especially so with e-workers and precarious labour. If the metaphor of the Panopticon is an overstatement in describing contemporary worksites, the intensification of surveillance remains a concerning element of labour relations.

Surveillance has been central to the history of modern labour, structured into and by capitalist accumulation, management ideologies of efficiency, competence and control, and the hierarchical relations of class, gender, and race. From Karl Marx's description of factory discipline in the mid-nineteenth century, to Frederick Winslow Taylor's writing on scientific management at the beginning of the twentieth, to the naming of emotional labour much more recently, work has been analyzed, recorded, timed, standardized, modified, deskilled, and reorganized using changing surveillance strategies that are both indirect and direct, some claiming objective measurement, others subjective assessment. In the latter case, the goal is often to change attributes, attitudes, and inner motivations, with the rationalization that shared norms and practices are better for the common good of the enterprise, the workforce, or the public.

At the same time, surveillance continually modernizes its forms, adapting to the political economy, technologies available, spatial context, and the precise nature of the work being observed. In many areas of service labour, new information technologies using massive data collection and manipulation, and biometric and spatial tracking, have recently augmented surveillance capabilities. This sophisticated use of informational data has engendered an understandable concern with the corporate invasion of our private lives, often without our knowledge or permission. Digital surveillance that is covert, continuous, and comprehensive, aimed at service workers who have less bargaining power – disproportionately women and minorities – is particularly alarming. These may also be migrant workers circulating across borders, doubly precarious due to their lack of citizenship rights in increasingly punitive anti-migrant nationalist contexts.

Worksite surveillance is also entangled with the labour of social reproduction, disproportionately shouldered by women, whether they are performing paid care work or unpaid familial labour. While the connection between surveillance and social reproduction needs more analysis, we know women patching together at-home child care and remotely-monitored paid labour (often piece or part-time computer work) are under stress to do two jobs that can have unlimited hours. The ever-diminishing welfare state has also forced some women to assume more unpaid care work for incapacitated family members, yet governments have enhanced surveillance of this work to make sure they are performing it 'adequately'.[72] For personal care workers looking after the elderly and ill in their homes, time surveillance encourages work intensification and speed-up: workers are paid only for designated tasks, not for travel or for the minutes of emotional labour (such as talking to a lonely patient) necessary for the 'caring' part of caring labour.

An analysis of the surveillance of all these varieties of service work requires more than a liberal call for worker privacy or a focus on the runaway possibilities of panoptical technologies. A critique of capitalist and neoliberal ideologies legitimating surveillance and the gender and race hierarchies sustaining them are both essential. Discussion of surveillance capabilities should not avert our eyes from its most elemental raison d'être: it lies at the heart of capitalist accumulation and hierarchical power relations inherent in contract employment. It is imagined, designed, and used to organize the labouring body, control worksites, and monitor relations between workers and between workers and managers. A heightened awareness of the way in which surveillance strategies have been gendered and racialized is also important, not only because of the intractability of gender and racial divisions of labour, but also because gender and race, as structures and ideologies, are fused with the process of class formation. Historically, surveillance has been shaped within and often reinforced unequal gendered and racial relations, but this could shift over time with different work arrangements, and it is to be hoped the class struggles in the twenty-first century will increasingly be directed at ensuring this is the case.

NOTES

My thanks to Bryan Palmer for commenting on an earlier draft of this paper and Jeremy Milloy for sharing his unpublished work.

1 American Management Association quoted in Ifeoma Ajunwa, Kate Crawford, Jason Schultz, 'Limitless Worker Surveillance', *California Law Review*, 105(3), 2017, p. 743; Bank of America executive quoted in Gary Marx, *Windows Into the Soul: Surveillance and Society in an Age of High Technology*, Chicago: University of Chicago Press, 2016, p. 179.

2 Marx, *Windows*, p. 189; Kirstie Ball, 'Workplace Surveillance: an Overview', *Labor History*, 51(1), pp. 87-106. Legal scholars – in the US at least – suggest that the fundamental legal logic of 'at will employment' (put simply: once you accept the contract there is no escape from management rights) spells the almost 'limitless', unchecked scope of employer surveillance, its current inevitable 'lockstep' advancement with technology. See Ajunwa, Crawford, Schultz, 'Limitless Worker Surveillance', p. 743. Note that they point to more privacy protection for EU workers; there are significant differences across borders.

3 Rachel E. Dubrofsky and Shoshana Amielle Magnet, 'Introduction', in Rachel Dubrofsky and Shoshana Magnet, eds., *Feminist Surveillance Studies*, Durham: Duke University Press, 2015, pp. 1-17.

4 Rosemary Hennessy, *Profit and Pleasure: Sexual Identities in Late Capitalism*, New York: Routledge, 2000, p. 27.

5 George Novak, 'The Problem of Alienation', in Ernest Mandel and George Novak, eds., *The Marxist Theory of Alienation*, New York: Pathfinder Press, 1970, p. 62.

6 Examining male workers raises different questions about masculinity and emotional and aesthetic labour. For example, see 'I Can't Put a Smiley Face On: Working-Class Masculinity, Emotional Labour and Service Work in the New Economy', *Gender, Work & Organization* [*GWO*], 16(3), 2009, pp. 300-322; Dennis Nickson and Marek Korczynski, 'Aesthetic Labour, Emotional Labour and Masculinity', *GWO*, 16(3), 2009, pp. 291-99.

7 For criticism of Foucault's elision of surveillance in different kinds of institutions see Christopher Dandeker, *Surveillance, Power and Modernity: Bureaucracy and Discipline From 1700 to the Present Day*, Cambridge: Polity Press, 1990; and Paul Thompson, 'Fantasy Island: a Labour Process Critique of the "Age of Surveillance"', *Surveillance and Society*, 1(2), 2003, p. 148.

8 Greg Elmer, 'Panopticon – Discipline – Control', in Kirstie Ball, Kevin Haggerty and David Lyon, eds., *Routledge Handbook of Surveillance Studies*, New York: Routledge, 2012, p. 21.

9 Terry Eagleton, *The Illusions of Postmodernism*, Oxford: Blackwell, 1996, p. 71. Though recent writing by Carol Wolkowitz and others has altered this trend, Eagleton's observation still has validity. In a 2020 issue of *Gender, Work & Organization* on aesthetic service labour, the editors list the cutting edge theories used: 'feminist philosophy, phenomenology, actor network theory, multispecies and more than human perspectives and queer theory'. Neither this, nor their second list of 'useful' theories mentions Marxism or historical materialism. Leanne Cutcher, Karen Dale, Melissa Tyler, 'Editorial: Emotion, Aesthetics and Sexuality at work: Theoretical Challenges and Future Directions', *GWO*, 27(1), 2020, pp. 1-2.

10 See, for example, the journal *Surveillance and Society*, launched in 2002. On our 'new' age of surveillance, see Shoshana Zuboff, *The Age of Surveillance Capitalism: The Fight for a Human Future at the New Frontier of Power*, New York: Hachette Book Group, 2019.

11 Christopher Dandeker, *Surveillance, Power and Modernity*, p. vii. There is debate about the difference between monitoring and surveillance, the former seen more 'neutrally', the latter more 'dystopian'. See Kirstie Ball, 'Workplace Surveillance', p. 87. However I see them on the same continuum.

12 Graham Sewell, 'Organization, Employees and Surveillance', in Kirstie Ball, Kevin Haggerty and David Lyon, eds., *Routledge Handbook of Surveillance Studies*, p. 303.

13 Karl Marx, *Capital: A Critique of Political Economy*, New York: The Modern Library, 1936, chapter 15, section 4 ("The Factory"), pp. 457-465; Harry Braverman, *Labor and Monopoly Capital: The Degradation of Work in the Twentieth Century*, New York: Monthly Review Press, 1974, chapter 4.

14 Pei-Chia Lan, 'Working in a Neon Cage: Bodily Labour of Cosmetics Saleswomen in Taiwan', *Feminist Studies*, 29(1), 2003, pp. 21- 45; Miliann Kang, *The Managed Hand: Race and Gender in the Body and Beauty Service Work*, Berkeley: University of California Press, 2010.

15 Donald Lowe, *The Body in Late Capitalist USA*, Durham: Duke University Press, 1995, p. 26. See also David Harvey, *The Condition of Postmodernity: An Enquiry into the Origins of Cultural Change*, Cambridge, Mass: Blackwell Publishing, 1990.

16 Linda McDowell, *Working Bodies: Interactive Service Employment and Workplace Identities*, Oxford: Wiley-Blackwell, 2009.

17 The classic statement on emotional labour is Arlie Hochschild, *The Managed Heart: Commercialization of Human Feeling*, Berkeley: University of California Press, 1983. On aesthetic labour: Anne Witz, Chris Warhurst, Dennis Nickson, 'The Labour of Aesthetics and the Aesthetics of Organization', *Organization*, 10(1), 2003, pp. 33-54; C. Warhurst, D. Nickson, A.Witz, A.M. Cullen, 'Aesthetic labour in interactive service work: Some case study evidence from the "new" Glasgow', *The Service Industries Journal*, 20(3), 2009, pp. 1-18.

18 Granted, all labour is bodily labour, as recognized by Marx when he described bodies as both the source of labour and its product. Writing on sociology of the body has placed more emphasis on other theoreticians, such as Foucault and Bourdieu, and until recently has also concentrated less on work than on sexuality and other topics. Debra Gimlin, 'What is Body Work? A Review of the Literature', *Sociological Compass*, 1(1), 2007, pp. 353-70; Carol Wolkowitz, *Bodies at Work*, London: Sage, 2006.

19 Shoshana Zuboff, *In The Age of the Smart Machine: The Future of Work and Power*, New York: Basic Books, 1984, pp. 57, 303.

20 Gary Marx, 'Measuring Everything That Moves: The New Surveillance at Work', in Ida Harper Simpson and Richard L. Simpson, eds., *Deviance in the Workplace*, JAI Press Inc.: Stamford, Conn, 1991, pp. 165-90. For an overview of shifts in Canada at the same time, Susan Bryant, 'Electronic Surveillance in the Workplace', *Canadian Journal of Communications* 26(4), 1995.

21 G. Sewell, 'The discipline of teams: the control of team-based industrial work through electronic and peer surveillance', *Administrative Science Quarterly*, 43, 1998, p. 422; A. McKinlay and P. Taylor, '"Through the looking glass": Foucault and the politics of production', in A. McKinlay and K. Starkey, eds., *Foucault, Management and Organization Theory*, London: Sage, 1998, pp. 180-81.

22 Graham Sewell and Barry Wilkinson, 'Someone to Watch Over Me: Surveillance, Discipline and the Just-In-Time Labour Process', *Sociology*, 26(2), 1992, pp. 271-89.

23 Paul Thompson, 'Fantasy Island', p.146.

24 Michele Beck, 'Working for Them', *Surveillance and Society*, 1(2), 2003, p. 233.

25 Gary Marx, 'Measuring Everything That Moves'; Emily E. TB. Twarog, 'Gender Violence in the Hospitality Industry: Panic Buttons, Pants, and Protest', in Jeremy Milloy and Joan Sangster, eds., *Violence at Work: New Essays in Canada and US Labour History*, Toronto: University of Toronto Press, 2020, forthcoming.

26 Ursula Huws, *The Making of the Cybertariat: Virtual Work in a Real World*, New York: Monthly Review Press, 2003.

27 Abbie Hoffman with Jonathan Silvers, *Steal This Urine Test: Fighting Drug Hysteria in America,* New York: Penguin, 1987. 'Pulling workers pants down lets 'em know who is boss. It threatens their jobs and their dignity', p.159; Jeremy Milloy, 'High Priority: Businesses' War on Drugs and the Expansion of Surveillance in the United States', in Josh Lauer and Ken Lipartito, eds., *Surveillance Capitalism: From Slavery to Social Media,* Philadelphia: University of Pennsylvania Press, forthcoming.

28 Ifeoma Ajunwa, Kate Crawford, Jason Schultz, 'Limitless Worker Surveillance', p. 769. These examples also point to regional and national differences; the US is more permissive in terms of employer power over worker privacy than other nations.

29 Zuboff, *The Age of Surveillance Capitalism*, p. 157.

30 United Nations General Assembly Report on Extreme Poverty and Human Rights, A/74/493, 11 Oct. 2019. For the American study: Virginia Eubanks, *Automating Inequality: How High-Tech Tools Profile, Police and Punish the Poor*, London: St. Martin's Press, 2017.

31 Ifeoma Ajunwa, Kate Crawford, Jason Schultz, 'Limitless Worker Surveillance', pp. 738-39.

32 Age, marital status and race were also barriers to employment. The literature on flight attendants is massive. Two US examples which address appearance are Kathleen Barry, *Femininity in Flight: A History of Flight Attendants*, Durham: Duke University Press, 2007; Dorothy Sue Cobble, '"A Spontaneous Loss of Enthusiasm": Workplace Feminism and the Transformation of Women's Service Jobs in the 1970's', *International Labor and Working-Class History*, 56, 1999, pp. 23-44. Two Canadian examples are Jill Newby, *The Sky's the Limit: The Story of the Canadian Air Line Flight Attendants' Association*, Vancouver: Mitchell Press, 1986; and Joan Sangster and Julia Smith, '"Beards and Bloomers": Flight Attendants, Grievances and Embodied Labour in the Canadian Airline Industry, 1960s-1980s', *GWO*, 23(2), 2016, pp. 183-99.

33 Interview by Joan Sangster and Julia Smith with Senka Dukovitch, 29 January 2014.

34 At the same time, in the words of one union activist in the 1980s, women flight attendants were inspected as if they were 'five year olds'. Senka Dukovitch quoted in Alanna Mitchell, 'Wardair employee defends remarks', *Toronto Star*, 18 August, 1988; *Wardair Flight Attendant Manual*, revised April 1985.

35 Christina Negroni, 'Fired Flight Attendant Finds Blogs Can Backfire', *New York Times*, 16 November 2004. Delta accused the flight attendant of posting suggestive pictures on her blog, Queen of the Sky.

36 Conversation of Joan Sangster with Marilyne White, former CALFAA and CUPE activist, 11 January, 2020.

37 Canadian Union of Public Employees (CUPE) Air Canada component, transcripts of interviews done for Newby, *The Sky's the Limit* [papers held by the union, uncatalogued]. The airlines portrayed female flight attendants caring for children and the elderly on flights. Joan Sangster and Julia Smith, 'From Career Girl to Sexy Stewardess: Popular Culture and Women's Work in the Canadian and American Airline Industries', *Women: A Cultural Review*, 30(2), 2019, pp. 141-61.
38 Hothschild, *The Managed Heart*.
39 C. Wouters, 'The Sociology of Emotions and Flight Attendants: Hothschild's Managed Heart', *Theory Culture and Society*, 6(1), 1989, pp. 95-123. See also S. Bolton and C. Boyd, 'Trolley Dolly or Skilled Emotional Manager? Moving on from Hothschild's Managed Heart', *Work, Employment and Society*, 17(2), 2003, pp. 289-308.
40 Jason Hughes, 'Bringing Emotion to Work, Emotional Intelligence, Employee Resistance and the Reinvention of Character', *Work, Employment and Society*, 19(3), 2005, p. 606.
41 Christine L. Williams and Catherine Connell, '"Looking Good and Sounding Right": Aesthetic Labor and Social Inequality in the Retail Industry', *Work and Organization*, 37(3), 2010, pp. 349-77.
42 Witz et al, 'The Labour of Aesthetics'.
43 C. Williams, 'Sky service: The demands of emotional labour in the airline industry', *GWO* 10(5), 2003, p. 528.
44 One study of flight attendant labour which places it in the context of managerial control is Steve Taylor and Melissa Tyler, 'Emotional Labour and Sexual Difference in the Airline Industry', *Work, Employment & Society*, 14(1), 2000, pp.77-95.
45 Williams, 'Sky Service', p. 513.
46 Jessica Vomiero, 'Air Canada flight attendants say they were lined up, graded on appearance: union complaint', *Global News*, 31 March 2018.
47 Tamar Harris, 'Air Canada flight attendants allege harassment, discrimination', *The Toronto Star*, 29 March 2018.
48 Email from Senka Dukovich to Joan Sangster and Julia Smith, 4 April 2018.
49 'Air Canada rouge defends partly-employee-paid Disney training', *Yahoo Finance*, 29 May 2013.
50 Milloy, 'High Priority'.
51 Sarah Anderson, 'How to Make the Airlines Bailout Work for Workers, Not Just CEOs', *Common Dreams*, 17 March 2020.
52 Nona Glazer, *Women's Paid and Unpaid Labour: the Work Transfer in Health Care and Retail*, Philadelphia: Temple University Press, 1993; Susan Porter Benson *Counter Cultures: Saleswomen, Managers, and Customers in American Department Stores, 1890-1940*, Urbana: University of Illinois Press, 1986; Donica Belisle, *Retail Nation: Department Stores and the Making of Modern Canada*, Vancouver: UBC Press, 2011.
53 Université de Montréal, HEC [*École des hautes études commerciales de Montréal*] Archives, Dupuis Frères fonds [HEC, DF], employee files, Box 21656.
54 Donica Belisle, 'Negotiating Paternalism: Women and Canada's Largest Department Store, 1890-1960', *Journal of Women's History*, 19(1), 2007, pp. 58-81; Joan Sangster, 'Souriez Pour Les Clients, Retail Work, Dupuis Frères and Union Protest', in *Transforming Labour: Women and Work in Postwar Canada*, Toronto: University of Toronto Press, 2010, pp. 108-44.
55 HEC, DF, Employee files, Box 21656.

56 *Le Duprex*, employee magazine quoted in Sangster, 'Souriez', p.119.

57 Barbara Ehrenreich, *Nickel and Dimed: On (Not) Getting by in America*, New York: Henry Holt and Co., 2001, p. 181.

58 Ibid, p. 124.

59 On short termism and emotional labour, Hughes, 'Bringing Emotion to Work', p. 606.

60 Madison Van Oort, 'The Emotional Labour of Surveillance: Digital Control in Fast Fashion Retail', *Critical Sociology*, 45(7-8), 2019, p. 1175.

61 Michael McCahill and Clive Norris, 'Watching the Workers: Crime, CCTV and the Workplace', in Pamela Davies, Peter Francis, Victor Jump, eds., *Invisible Crimes*, London: Macmillan, 1999, pp. 208-31.

62 Van Oort, 'The Emotional Labour', p. 1168.

63 Marx, 'Measuring Everything That Moves', p. 197.

64 Van Oort, 'The Emotional Labour', p. 1175.

65 Caroline Criado Perez, *Invisible Women: Exposing Data Bias in a World Designed for Men*, London: Chatto &Windus, 2019, pp. 135-36.

66 Anshuman Prasad and Pushkala Prasad, '(Unwilling) to Resist? The Discursive Production of Local Workplace Opposition', *Studies in Culture, Organization and Society*, 7, 2001, pp. 105-25; Graham Sewell and Peter Fleming, 'Looking for the Good Soldier, Švejk: Contemporary Alternative Modalities of Resistance in the Workplace', *Sociology*, 36(4), 2002, pp. 857-73.

67 Kendra Coulter, 'Raising Retail: Organizing Retail Workers in Canada and the United States', *Labor Studies Journal*, 38(1), 2013, p. 65.

68 Nick Dyer-Witherford, *Cyber-Proletariat: Global Labour in the Digital Vortex*, London: Pluto Press, 2015.

69 Sewell and Fleming, 'Looking', p. 859.

70 David Harvey, 'The body as an accumulation strategy,' *Environment and Planning D: Society and Space*, 16(4), 1998, pp. 401–21.

71 Roy Boyne (in a critique of Zygmunt Bauman), 'Post-Panopticism', *Economy and Society*, 29(2), 2000, pp. 285-307.

72 Susan Braedley, '"Someone to Watch over You": Gender, Class, and Social Reproduction', in Kate Bezanson and Meg Luxton, eds., *Social Reproduction: Feminist Political Economy Challenges Neo-Liberalism*, Kingston and Montreal: McGill Queens University Press, 2006, pp. 215-30.

FROM NEOLIBERAL FASHION TO NEW WAYS OF CLOTHING

JERÓNIMO MONTERO BRESSÁN

The past four decades have seen a tremendous transformation in how we clothe ourselves. The way clothes are produced, traded and sold today around the world reflects many of the problems capitalism poses to the working classes, with deleterious consequences on the environment as well. Global supply chains, in which non-finished goods flow back and forth around the world so that brands and retailers can increase their profits, dominate the landscape of this industry. The liberalization of trade between 1995 and 2005 allowed companies to pit workers worldwide against each other, providing the former with enormous savings in labour costs. Growing competition and problems in the sphere of realization after the 2008 financial crisis forced companies to continuously expand their marketing strategies, notably by incorporating expensive digital technologies. But on the manufacturing side costs were squeezed to the limit. The deregulation of labour markets through neoliberalization allows companies not only to employ cheap labour in far away countries, but also to subcontract production to 'local sweatshops' employing migrants in situations of debt-peonage, forced labour and the like in the proximity of the end markets, so that fast fashion retailers and brands can replenish their stores quickly and cheaply. The rise of fast fashion, based on quick turnover times, the rapid obsolescence of clothing and low prices, has made all these problems worse, and also led to unprecedented levels of waste creation.

THE TRANSFORMATION OF THE CLOTHING INDUSTRY

The transformations the clothing industry has undergone were a direct outcome of how companies in the different segments since the 1970s adopted a series of strategies to face stagnating demand. A first strategy was the expansion of fashion propaganda, which ultimately created a massification of fashion. A second was the flexibilization of labour relations in the production and supply chains through subcontracting, which provided the savings needed to fund marketing propaganda. The massification of fashion coupled with the industry's high elasticity of demand to intensify the worst aspects of seasonality – the continuous segmentation of markets (i.e. small batches of constantly changing items, which increases unit costs) and the sales of superfluous products (consumers stop buying when faced with income constraints). This resulted in further pressures for greater flexibility in the labour supply. Today, the importance given to the exchange value through fashion propaganda results in a market structure by which companies are forced to understand their manufacturing expenditures as mere costs of doing business, while it is their marketing expenditures which are regarded by them as their real investments.

The way the sector is structured globally not only allows but actually forces all companies to save on production costs by squeezing their suppliers.[1] As we shall see, large retailers and brands do so through offshoring and the development of global supply chains, increasingly using arms-length subcontracting rather than direct investments. At the same time, as we shall show with particular attention to Italy and Argentina, other manufacturers in core countries and in peripheral countries who were not linked to these chains but were affected by cheap imports, reconverted their businesses to selling higher value-added items like fashionwear, shutting down their factories, and subcontracting production locally to homeworkers and migrant-run workshops usually employing informal labour. In other words, offshoring and local/national subcontracting were parallel movements, resulting in an international competitive race to the bottom, often with dire consequences for old and new workers in the industry.

In its endless search for growth, capital creates new needs, wants and desires. Fashion is the mechanism invented by capital in order to expand clothing consumption by means of augmenting the exchange value embodied in certain clothing items and detaching them as much as possible from their use value. Until the 1970s fashion remained limited to the upper classes, although its success in fostering consumption always enabled it to expand to other parts of society. The crisis of the 1970s laid the ground for the massification of fashion through an expansion of propaganda.[2] While high fashion houses continued to differentiate themselves through the selling of luxury clothing and accesories, there was an ever broader dissemination of fashion, paralleled by the massive incorporation of women in the labour market which created bigger and bigger markets for cheaper fashionwear.[3] The logic of fashion, with its clearly segmented markets, spread across clothing consumption. Furthermore, fashion was increasingly mobilized to accelerate the rate of turnover of capital by fostering the consumption of clothing that runs out of fashion quickly.

The intensification and massification of this competitive logic resulted in the emergence of fast fashion by the early twenty-first century. Although fast fashion is now a *process* that, to one degree or another, encompasses the entire fashion industry, it is as a *market segment* that fast fashion most vividly illustrates the contradiction between the production of clothing as use value and as exchange value. Together with the widespread adoption of planned obsolescence, a fundamental change has taken place in consumption habits through the massification of fashion, by which the quality of the clothes is not considered as an important variable. Consumers' buying decisions depend on the look of the items, the brands' 'values', prices, and the facility to get the clothes – be it home delivery, point of collection, or shops located in places concentrating considerable offers. This has affected the cost balance between the production of the use value and the production of the exchange value added to clothing. If the quality of the product is the least important when we pay for our clothes at the counter, more money goes to fashion expenditures and less to manufacturers – and their workers. Companies find themselves forced to continuously improve and fund their marketing strategies (including renting expensive stores and adopting digital technologies) to the detriment of the quality of what they sell. While marketing expenditures are understood as investments, resources dedicated to manufacturing are deemed mere costs.

The massification of fashion required a series of transformations in the labour process and in the broader political and economic conditions which allowed these transformations. In fact, the resources dedicated to fashion marketing came partly from the savings in labour costs through flexibilization of labour relations. Compared with the manufacturing of more basic garments (like t-shirts and plain jeans), producing fashionwear is more expensive. The fashion business is based upon selling highly differentiated items which give the customer a sense of exclusivity, as opposed to basic and sports garments produced in mass in large factories. Fashionwear, therefore, must be produced in smaller batches, which increases the unit cost because economies of scale do not adjust to many of these items. The more complicated and detailed seams a fashionwear item includes, the more minutes per item are required to producing fashionwear than to producing basic apparel. Labour costs are therefore higher.

An example to illustrate this point is that of Zara. It could be argued that Zara manufactures large enough orders to achieve economies of scale, in which case the argument that producing fashionwear is more expensive because it does not allow economies of scale would not hold true. However, the Spanish firm subcontracts the production of the most fashion-sensitive items to factories and workshops in Spain and Portugal, where the average size of the companies is much smaller than that in Asia, where it subcontracts the production of basics: 42 workers per factory in Portugal, 1,780 in Bangladesh and 736 in India.[4] Labour costs increase even more due to the need for speedy delivery, meaning that fashion-sensitive garments must be produced in proximity to the end markets, where salaries are usually much higher. However, if these clothes are to be discarded quickly, offering low prices is a necessary condition. Fast fashion retail stores are therefore replete with extremely cheap garments. These prices are not only achieved by the use of cheaper fabric, but also through an extensive process of restructuring that allowed an immense savings in labour costs.

THE GLOBALIZATION OF SUBCONTRACTING: SWEATSHOP WORLD

As a major remapping of the industry took place through the massive shift of manufacturing to peripheral economies, more and more companies in both former industrialised economies and in peripheral countries not linked to global supply chains, faced increasing competition from cheap imported garments. Some manufacturers were forced to shut down their factories, while others reduced their capacities and continued their businesses by subcontracting the bulk of production to migrant-run workshops and (female) homeworkers. Subcontracting, then, became the main strategy to enhance competitiveness for every firm, as it allowed savings in labour costs that contributed to funding investments in branding and marketing.

Subcontracting has historically provided companies with a way to control the high labour costs involved in this industry and to navigate the instability of demand and the seasonality, which creates peaks of high and low labour demand that make permanent jobs a complicated matter. From the sweatshops in London's East End in the late nineteenth century to Tazreen and Rana Plaza in Bangladesh in our own time, the industry has always relied on the employment of informal workers and migrants in subcontracted workshops, and women homeworkers.[5] The textiles and clothing industries actually provide one of the earliest experiences of international offshoring, as was already seen with the manufacturing of Bangladeshi jute in British-owned factories in Bengal in the second half of the nineteenth century.[6] Towards the mid-twentieth century, German companies started to offshore clothing production,[7] with Japanese companies following on in the 1960s and 1970s and US firms widely adopting offshoring since the late 1970s.[8] By the 1980s, offshoring had allowed established large retailers and brands to challenge their smaller competitors by selling significantly cheaper garments, which further reinforced more and more concentration amongst retailers, and in turn forced those retailers and brands which remained independent to adopt offshoring so as to remain competitive.[9]

In a parallel move, luxury fashion companies adopted massively local subcontracting. During the 1970s, when clothing consumption declined in several core economies,[10] leading firms decided to shore up sales by adopting the 'brands without factories' strategy that was proving so successful for sportswear companies like Nike. For example, the high-end fashion house Gucci reduced operations in its headquarters in Florence by cutting down its labour force to 20 per cent.[11] Production was therefore subcontracted to its former workers, who continued working for the same employer from home, and to migrant-run workshops that offered lower prices through recruiting fellow migrants informally. The resulting savings in labour costs allowed luxury brands to fund marketing propaganda to expand their markets.

Concentration in retail led to a major shift in power relations between brands and retailers, on the one hand, and manufacturers, on the other. Today, the clothing industry is a typical example of a buyer-driven chain, where rather few 'global' buyers with vast purchasing power manage to impose contracting prices and conditions to myriad producers in several countries.[12] The increasing power of retailers and brands allowed them to push through the end of the Multi-Fiber Agreement (MFA). The MFA had since 1974 protected local textiles and clothing manufacturers in core countries from imports from peripheral economies through an intricate system of bilaterally negotiated quotas and the selective implementation of tariffs. The phasing out of the MFA allowed brands and retailers to chase cheap labour around the world much more freely.

The economic liberalization in China since the mid-1980s as well as the collapse of the Soviet Union created the opportunity to incorporate millions of new workers into these supply chains, triggering global auctions for the orders of powerful global buyers between manufacturers involved in a worldwide competitive race to the bottom. This led to a significant deflation in clothing prices based primarily on the reduction in production costs, as cheap clothing produced in peripheral countries flooded the world's markets. This made it impossible for old-established manufacturers to continue business as usual, and drove them to shut down their factories in the core countries. They joined the offshoring club and became 'global buyers', while reorientating their home-based operations to design, marketing, and retail. Adidas shut down its last factory in Germany in 1993; Levi's started to reduce its operations in US and Europe in the late 1980s, and in 2003 it shut down its last remaining factories in the US; Hugo Boss and other leading British clothing firms followed suit around the same time.[13]

When cheap basic garments made in Asia flooded the world's markets, it also hit smaller manufacturers lacking the capacity to develop offshoring strategies. Those in many core economies and in dozens of peripheral countries not linked to global supply chains were forced to 'reconvert or die'. Taking advantage of the surging market for fashionwear, created by the expansion of fashion propaganda, and of their proximity to the end markets, they shut down their factories and became branded manufacturers of fashionwear. In so doing they concentrated in the higher value-added processes of design, marketing and retail, while supplying their businesses through a mix of imports and locally subcontracted production.

Thus, in Brazil, for instance, the giant textile firm Hering, faced with the competition of cheap imported basics from Asia by the mid-1990s, shifted to selling fashionwear for the middle and lower-middle classes, strengthening its branding and opening up brand name stores.[14] In so doing, it shut down a significant part of its textiles and sewing factories and moved to a mix of offshoring of some basics to China and subcontracted to a number of regions, supplying stores in large cities (like Brasilia and Manaus) directly from subcontracted workshops located in the proximity of these cities.

Similarly, in Argentina, where industrial production in general is overwhelmingly aimed at the internal market and labour costs are relatively high by Latin American standards, many of the owners of textiles and clothing factories, and most notably their heirs, decided to shut down their unviable factories. They shifted their capital instead to the emerging fashionwear market, creating new trendy local brands with a strong presence in shopping malls and high streets, and achieving rapid success. A thorough process of labour informalization through subcontracting accompanied these shifts, allowing savings in production costs that helped to fund investments in design, marketing and renting expensive store properties. The two largest brands now design their collections and cut the fabric in their own offices (using expensive laser cutting technology) and subcontract all of the sewing and assembly to small local workshops, the majority of which are migrant-run workshops employing informal workers, mainly from Bolivia, a practice so common that unregistered labour accounts to 60-70 per cent of the labour force.[15] The lack of factory inspections is understood by those who study the fashion sector as a subsidy to the entrepreneurs that were forced to adapt to the new international context in the 1990s.[16] As a result of this restructuring of local companies and the permissive state policies, sweatshop working conditions became widespread.[17]

This mimics what occurred in Italy. Manufacturers of both clothing and textiles focused on marketing, design, and the like, while keeping either no production premises at all or only small workshops to produce prototypes and carry the cut-and-trim process. They proved able to take advantage of national policies of support for 'artisan' firms (those with up to 15 workers), even if they had a large number of subcontractors which supply their businesses either with imported garments or with a mix of imported and locally-produced garments. The bulk of local production, in turn, is subcontracted to small workshops that in many cases employ irregular migrants, mainly from China.

All this occurred while in cities in peripheral countries concentrating export-led production, companies working as subcontractors of the largest suppliers proliferated with the flow of international orders by covering the higher demand with seasonal labour sewing the least profitable items.[18] Indeed, international offshoring and national 'nearshoring' through local subcontracting are parallel movements in the clothing industry, dividing workers by fostering competiton between them all around the world. The combination between high labour costs in core economies and the need to increase speed-to-market, explains the demand for cheap informal labour in the proximities of large cities/markets. In recent years, this demand has been covered by 'local sweatshops'[19] like those found in Buenos Aires and Prato in Italy. They mushroomed in both core countries and in peripheral countries which were not linked to global supply chains.[20] These sweatshops supply local and international brands with quick orders of constantly changing garments at low prices, based on the exploitation of migrant workers in conditions of forced labour in dangerous workshops. In both Argentina and Italy this has led to factory fires, like those which killed eight workers in Buenos Aires in 2006 and 2015 and seven workers in Prato in 2013.

THE CLOTHING INDUSTRY AFTER 2008

By fine-tuning their marketing strategies to tell consumers that it is embarrassing to wear the same clothing for long or that new models and colours are waiting for them at the shops to provide them with a quick – and short-term – satisfaction, a larger and larger field of ephemeral consumption has very recently come to provide a major field of capital accumulation in the clothing industry. Insofar as the clothes we wear reflect certain aspects of our personalities, marketing propaganda telling consumers to change their clothes as quickly as possible and throw away the 'old' ones promotes ephemeral ways of being and living. By adopting quick turnover of its merchandise as its main competitive advantage, fast fashion has taken this ephemerality to unprecedented levels, leading as well to accelerating levels of waste-creation, including non-biodegradable microfibers.

With the recession that followed the 2008 financial collapse, a combination between increased competition and stagnated consumption – which in fact provides evidence to argue that the industry is undergoing a crisis of overaccumulation – has taken the clothing industry to a point in which companies increasingly resort to the acceleration of product turnaround in order to expand their sales. This trend is not exclusive to the fashion industry. In consumer electronics, for instance, Asian manufacturers are settling new production facilities closer to the end markets, including plants in Eastern Europe (like those of Foxxconn[21]) and the US (e.g. Quanta, the world's largest manufacturer of notebooks[22]), in order to supply these markets with products like mobile phones or computer printers that need to be changed every two to three years due to planned obsolescence. Yet, with its constantly changing styles and designs, and the renewal of merchandise several times a month, the fast fashion industry epitomizes the search for escaping a crisis of overaccumulation through accelerating turnaround times.

These trends, again, have enormous consequences for the organization of supply chains. Companies have been forced to make huge investments in technology to secure speedy delivery from the shop floor to the customer. The incorporation of robotics and automation for reducing labour costs and delays in warehouses is widespread amongst the largest brands and retailers. For example, Fast Retailing (Uniqlo) replaced 90 per cent of its labour force with robots in its main warehouse in Tokyo, reducing the lead time between order and dispatch from 8–16 hours to 15 minutes.[23] Furthermore, the fine-tuning of marketing also drives companies to invest in new and expensive digital technologies that help secure 'just-in-time personalization, digital customer relationships, and emotional connection'.[24] These technologies include smart barcode tags, new software, the internet of things, and artificial intelligence in order to forecast projected demand for new products, improve customer fidelity and social media performance, and influence the buying behaviours of consumers. The latter are targeted according to their previous purchases, and by responding to enquiries and offering conversation about products and services through chatbots, etc. All of this data reveals, as noted by the ILO in a recent report, 'how consumers shop, when, and through which channels'. [25] While the use of digital technologies to these ends yields advantages to the fashion firms, it also brings with it the constant threat of major disruptions in labour markets from production shifts, even in core countries.

The vast resources invested in these types of new technologies contrast starkly with the antique technology used in the sewing and assembly processes – which account for 80 per cent of total labour costs.[26] Although these high-tech investments put further pressure on labour costs, the development of labour-saving technology in the assembly and sewing stages is poor and only incipient. The lack of significant technological developments in these areas since the appearance of the sewing machine in the mid-nineteenth century may be explained by the fact that the industry has always managed to renew its labour force with cheaper workers.

In fact, in the early 1980s progress was made towards the development of *sewing robots*, but in the context of increasing offshoring, the technology was quickly discarded given the availability of low-wage labour in peripheral economies. Only in 2012, when labour costs in China were increasing steadily, did new investments in labour-saving technology developed by the Department of Defense lead to the appeareance of 'sewbots' that can manufacture t-shirts while using only a small workforce. Despite announcements by the Chinese company Tian Yuan about the planned incorporation of these machines in a factory in Arkansas to supply Adidas t-shirts, the technology is still extremely expensive and has not been widely deployed in the industry. Yet, its potential to change the industry and destroy millions of jobs in peripheral countries in the mid-term, needs to be considered, especially in the post-Covid-19 context, given the disruption of long supply chains scattered around the globe.

While the structure of this industry requires increasing labour exploitation, the legalization of flexibility worldwide has led to a return to situations of debt peonage, forced labour, and the like, not as marginal practices but as critical to the workings of the apparel industry, which as presently constituted is 'exploitative at its core'.[27]

THE POST-COVID FASHION INDUSTRY

The fashion industry has been strongly hit by Covid-19. Consumption has plummeted and for this year is set to be between 27 and 30 per cent behind last year's figures.[28] The impact on the manufacturing side has been strong, illustrating in a matter of weeks the very nature of international subcontracting: commercial relations developed over decades were suddenly scrapped by Western buyers through the cancellation of orders and the non-payment of orders already sewn and shipped,[29] forcing Asian manufacturers to shut down and, in some cases, go bankrupt. In Bangladesh, the country most hit by the disruption of consumption in the West, thousands of workers were left without pay for months, and their protests have met, as usual, police violence. Almost 10 per cent of the 4,500 factories operating in the country have shut down during the lockdown in the largest Western markets, including about 150 factories that have already gone bankrupt.[30]

Low consumption levels are likely to continue, not least because the lack or the reduction of dressing occasions will impact the fashion industry. Industry insiders like Matthijs Crietee, Secretary-General of the International Apparel Federation, argue that the 'Coronacrisis' will basically accelerate the trends that were already in the retailers and brand's agendas: nearshoring and the growing adoption of digital technologies.[31] Companies like Li & Fung, the world's largest supplier of clothing, are using the opportunity to restructure their supply chains and reduce their workforce across Asia. The adoption of digital technologies will accelerate, putting further pressure on labour costs, and especially in regards to the strengthening of online retailing, which implies fewer stores and more automated warehouses around the world.

The main consequence of this crisis will be the long overdue 'Darwinian shake-out' that will now take place, albeit only sooner rather than later, through mergers and acquisitions across all segments of the industry.[32] Growing competition and timid demand growth over the last decade were already setting the context for a thorough restructuring. With the current crisis, 'the bigger players, unfortunately, are gonna get bigger and stronger'.[33]

If the future of this industry is set to be marked by more concentration on the retail end and more digitalization and automation in production, the need to strengthen workers' organizations so that the crisis is paid for by capitalists is clear. In this context, the left needs to take the opportunity of this crisis to develop its own agenda to move beyond resistance and accommodative responses.

WHAT'S THE ALTERNATIVE?

The liberalization of trade has taken global supply chains to such a bizarre point that it is not uncommon to see a Swedish retailer like H&M asking its Asian supplier to bring fabrics from the US and labels from China to be assembled at a factory near Dhaka in Bangladesh and then tranported to the port of Chittagong on the Bay of Bengal to be shipped to Germany. Given that US textiles firms are the most effective in producing the fabric that H&M wants the supplier to use, Chinese firms provide the majority of clothing inputs (like the labels) in Asia at high quality and low prices, and as Bangladeshi workers are the cheapest in Asia, this way of organizing production is highly efficient for H&M's profit-making objectives. In fact, this kind of practice is part of the daily life of many global supply chains in all economic sectors. However, if we step back and look at supply chains thus organized, it is hard to believe that this is efficient for the societies involved, not least because of its environmental effects. If we detach efficiency from the goal of profit-making, and build a new conception of it based on the minimization of socially needed time, the capacity to satisfy needs and the minimization of environmental effects, then emphasizing the need to produce fabrics and clothes at the closest possible locations comes to the fore.

Protecting local firms would automatically help avoid international subcontracting. Although foreign investments provide millions of workers in peripheral economies with the opportunity to earn salaries significantly higher than those in jobs locally available to them, labour over-supply and the possibility to chase the cheapest labour around the world is a problem for labour at large, as it turns the balance more favourable to capital. Therefore, for all the benefits that foreign investments may bring to local communities, the exploitative structure of the global garment industry must be dismantled.[34]

In this sense it is important to remind ourselves that offshoring never gained serious political legitimacy.[35] The current political support for discourses of reshoring certainly reflects this, and it could be taken as an opportunity to push a political agenda that seeks self-sufficiency of clothing needs in cities and regions across core countries. This would require contesting the present use of right-wing anti-globalization discourses calling for a type of reshoring that would rely on removing labour market and other regulations. At the same time, opposition amongst liberal-minded political leaders that reject the current protectionist impulse adopted by right-wing governments in core countries highlights how deeply the discourse of free trade has permeated progressive circles. This is why it is all the more important for alternative radical voices to be heard highlighting the madness of current trade flows, their role in uneven development, and their environmental consequences.

As in all economic sectors in a capitalist economy, it is the producers who decide what clothes are to be produced and how many. Problems at the point of *realization* are solved through end of season sales, a few bankruptcies a year (resulting in the devaluation of the labour force as well), and by throwing away a 20 per cent of the world's output into landfills.[36] What is above all needed is to reverse the relationship between production and realization; as Harvey has aptly put it, 'realization should be replaced by the discovery and statement of the use values needed by the population at large and production should then be orchestrated to meet these social needs'.[37]

If the sector is undergoing a crisis of overaccumulation despite – or owing to – the success of fashion in fostering consumption in recent decades, a rather obvious conclusion is that the world produces too many garments. The consequence of taking this conclusion to the real world would be the unemployment of millions around the world. In fact, when discussing alternatives to existing ways to produce and consume clothing with cooperatives in Buenos Aires (in the preparation of this essay), the idea that there are too many manufacturing companies in the sector is fiercely rejected and taken as an attack on them. In the same vein, workers' unions also oppose the plan to reduce the industry's output due to the shrinking labour force they target. However, it is clear that labour surplus strengthens the power of brands and retailers who can open auctions for their orders to several competing manufacturers who squeeze their workers in order to 'win'. In sum, building the alliances to plan production according to needs is a major challenge for militants embedded in this sector. Political conditions should be created for reducing labour surpluses by eliminating sweatshops, firstly, and other private firms later on.

Planning production according to needs requires first identifying the bulk of wants and needs of a certain community, and then developing vast inventories of the available resources to cover these needs. Local or regional committees could be formed, involving all textiles and clothing factories, in order to carry out this task. Scientific research and technological development should serve these purposes by helping to calculate what clothing items, and how many of these, will be needed during a certain season. To be sure, while some core countries would in principle have little trouble in developing inputs and technology in order to secure self-sufficiency, peripheral economies would need to fund scientific research aimed at this goal. This would require efforts at the national and maybe even macroregional scales, in order to also allow the exchange of the necessary raw materials. Certainly, some places would be more dependent than others – especially considering the uneven distribution of minerals – but dependency in one economic sector could be balanced with surplus in others. Here, the search for self-satisfaction of clothing needs is a horizon towards which it is worth moving.

A key mechanism by which capital gained power during the neoliberal era is the upscaling of attributes (and ultimately of power) from national states to macroregional or multilateral agreements and institutions.[38] These upscaling processes were motivated by the fact that it is easier for employers than for workers to make decisions – or to influence decision-making – at larger scales.[39] The creation of multilateral trade disciplines enforced by the WTO, supplemented by regional free trade and investment agreements, opened the field for companies to move freely across national borders while securing safer investment environments. Opposition to this upscaling movement has been timid, coming from weakened labour unions in some cases – like the failed attempts to stop NAFTA. There also exist a number of initiatives by international unions and NGOs that claim that these agreements should include regulations on the protection of workers' rights and the free movement of people between countries participating in these. A more interesting initiative is the Asia Floor Wage Global Alliance, which seeks to establish a floor wage at the continental level, specifically targeting clothing manufacturers. Although this is in principle an interesting proposal, because it could stop brands and retailers from using and reproducing uneven geographical development within Asia, it still accepts passively the processes of upscaling, which were engineered by capital to facilitate its movement across space.

If the upscaling of state powers was a key mechanism to strengthen the power of multinational companies, a thorough counter movement of downscaling – i.e. strengthening local, regional, and national decision-making powers – would ease conditions for labour and local activists to participate more actively in these processes. The rescaling of state powers has been a tremendously important element in the process of international capitalist neoliberalization; it should be clear that alternatives benefiting workers globally will require them to develop their own scalar political strategies.[40]

Insofar as these strategies will have to involve bringing the key decisions on economic activity to the smallest convenient scales, it will at the same time be vital to avoid reactionary and nationalist sentiments. In fact, as we have seen, the movement of devolution which paralleled upscaling processes did not provide any opportunities for workers, but was instead complementary to the upscaling by easing conditions for foreign investment and leading to a strong inter-local and inter-regional competition for foreign investments.[41] A radical alternative downscaling would have to involve the building up of strong workers' organizations and their coming together into federations at larger scales for planning economic activity according to the needs, wants, and desires of the people. Seizing the means of production, perhaps starting with foreign companies, would have to take place at some point, always depending on context. Downscaling and leaving to local communities the decisions on how to best satisfy the needs, wants, and desires of its people, does not mean contenting ourselves with a landscape of isolated local/regional communities, but rather limiting the power of institutions acting at larger scales than is strictly necessary. The underlying idea is that closer is fairer, meaning that the more decisions are taken at the lowest levels, the easier they are controlled and supervised by those affected by these.

It is important to acknowledge, of course, that any movement in this direction would be contingent upon building up a social base capable of protecting local producers and stopping local subcontracting, while advancing democratic planning capacities for alternative production according to needs. The first step for this would surely be to build a broad and diverse group of committed consumers, workers, and activists that could push these and other ideas forward. Although around the world, and especially in core countries, public knowledge about the profound impacts of this industry on workers and the environment is widespread, and criticism involves even mainstream media and industry insiders, this needs to be taken much further. Boycotting fashion events and fast fashion brands and retailers, as well as those companies using sweatshop labour and even those contracting out all the manufacturing, would help raise visibility and awareness about what is wrong with this industry. Social pressure should also be brought to bear on famous models and sports stars contracted by companies for advertising, so that they use their power to influence consumers for furthering workers' rights. Pro-labour advocates, anti-sweatshop and environmental activists, students of clothing design and staff teaching them, as well as professionals working in this sector – designers and IT and administrative workers – should be part of this movement. That said, a broad movement of people organized behind the idea that this industry needs radical change, must have garment workers in the frontline. In this sense, it is essential to overcome existing tensions between social movements and unions. As Leo Panitch contends:

> … the enormous potential of the new social movements for social transformation will only be realized if labour finally takes enthusiastically on board the key emancipatory themes raised by the other movements. But at the same time, the new social movements themselves can hardly ignore their own need for strategy for labour.[42]

The criticisms of union strategies often made by radical social movements must be taken seriously.[43] Not only North American 'service' trade unionism, but even the European social democratic unions, who embraced 'the illusions of the humanization of capitalism' have largely failed to stop the neoliberal counterattack.[44] Rethinking union strategies and priorities is, therefore, critical. Many leaders of unions in the clothing industry have spent the last decades prioritising the well-being of local employers facing international competition instead of that of workers, and have done little in protecting informal and migrant workers. Furthermore, in places like Mexico and Cambodia, where there are thousands of company-based unions, changes in labour legislation are needed to forbid the formation of branch-based unions.

With a powerful social base, demands to protect local producers by strictly regulating imports – including intermediary goods – might in fact secure the support of local manufacturers and unions, although brands and retailers would fiercely oppose it. It is not hard to imagine that several countries could move in this direction in the current context of regression of free trade, not least since the liberalization of textiles and clothing industries took place later than in other sectors, so protection is not a distant memory.

The search for an alternative needs to include the progressive elimination of fashion, or its reduction to its minimal expression. However, this does not mean eliminating diversity. Living in a place where everyone uses the very same clothes is definitely not desirable. However, the massification of fashion has taken us to a point in which wearing the same jumper as someone else – not to mention the same dress at a party – is shameful, and this diversity comes at a high cost due to its consequences on the production line (see above). It is vital to gather groups of designers who could facilitate a movement that promotes diversity, art, or communication of ideas and values through clothing, working with teams in which a clear knowledge is developed about the consequences of the designers' ideas and conceptions over the production process, costs and trade balance.

A militant agenda to create the political conditions to put technological developments and specialized knowledge at the service of these strategic directions is needed if we are to radically transform an industry long based upon the worst forms of workers' exploitation.

NOTES

1 John Smith, *Imperialism in the Twenty-First Century*, New York: Monthly Review Press, 2013, p. 80.

2 Gilles Lipovetsky, *The Empire of Fashion*, Princeton: Princeton University Press, 2002.

3 Jerónimo Montero Bressán, 'Local Sweatshops in the Global Economy', in M. Atzeni and I. Ness, eds, *Global Perspectives on Workers' and Labour Organisations*, Singapore: Springer, 2018.

4 Víctor Garrido Sotomayor, *Informe de reunión de trabajo con los sindicatos y proveedores de la cadena de suministro de Inditex en India*, Comisiones Obreras: Madrid, 2019; Víctor Garrido Sotomayor, *Proyecto de formación y sensibilización en el área de seguridad y salud laboral en la cadena de suministro de Inditex en Portugal*, Madrid: Comisiones Obreras, 2019; Víctor Garrido Sotomayor, *Informe de visita y reunión de trabajo con los sindicatos de la cadena de suministro de Inditex en Bangladesh*, Madrid: Comisiones Obreras, 2019.

5 Edna Bonacich and Richard Appelbaum, *Behind the Label: Inequality in the Los Angeles Apparel Industry*, Berkeley: California University Press, 2000; Nancy Green, *Ready-to-Wear and Ready-to-Work*, London: Duke University Press, 1997; Robert Ross, *Slaves to Fashion*, Ann Arbor: University of Michigan Press, 2004.

6 Smith, *Imperialism*, p. 40.
7 Folker Fröbel, Jurgen Heinrichs and Otto Kreye, *The New International Division of Labour*, Cambridge: Cambridge University Press, 1980.
8 Peter Dicken, *Global Shift*, 5th edition, London: Sage, 2007, p. 265..
9 Richard Appelbaum, 'Giant transnational contractors in East Asia', *Competition & Change* 12(1), 2008; Dicken, *Global shift*.
10 Mirjana Morokvasic, Annie Phizacklea and Hedwig Rudolph, 'Small firms and minority groups: Contradictory trends in the French, German and British Clothing industries', *International Sociology* 1(4), 1986.
11 Jerónimo Montero, *Neoliberal fashion: The Political Economy of Sweatshops in Europe and Latin America*, PhD thesis, University of Durham, 2011, p. 157.
12 Gary Gereffi, 'The organisation of buyer-driven global commodity chains: How US retailers shape overseas production networks', In G Gereffi and M Korzeniewicz, eds, *Commodity Chains and Global Capitalism*, Westport, Praeger, 1994.
13 Dicken, *Global shift*, pp. 265-6.
14 Renato Garcia, 'Uma Análise dos Processos Recentes de desconcentração regional nas industrias têxtil e de calçados e a importância dos sistemas locais de produção' in *Revista Econômica do Nordeste* 41(1), 2010; A. S. Leite, A. M. Barco, J. M. Rosa, D. R. Pereira, M Costa and N. B. Trindade, 'Análise estructural da industria textil' in *proceedings of the 2do Congresso Científico Textil e de Moda*, São Paulo, 20-22 May 2014.
15 Ariel Lieutier, *Esclavos*, Buenos Aires, Retórica, 2010.
16 Lieutier, *Esclavos*; Montero, *Neoliberal fashion*.
17 Andrés Matta and Cecilia Magnano, *Trama productiva urbana y trabajo decente. Análisis y estrategias para la cadena productiva textil de indumentariaen Áreas Metropolitanas. Buenos Aires*, Buenos Aires, ILO, 2011; Montero, *Neoliberal fashion*.
18 Alessandra Mezzadri, *The sweatshop regime*, New York: Cambridge University Press, 2017.
19 Jerónimo Montero Bressán and Ayelén Arcos, 'How do migrant workers respond to labour abuses in 'local sweatshops'?', *Antipode*, 49(2), 2017.
20 For Medellín see Karina Camacho Reyes, *Las confesiones de las confecciones*, Medellín, Escuela Nacional Sindical, 2008; for Sao Paulo see Silvana Cristina da Silva, *Circuito espacial produtivo das confeccoes e exploracão do trabalho na metrópole de São Paulo*, PhD thesis, Universidade Estadual de Campinas, 2012; and Siobhán McGrath, *The Political Economy of Forced Labour in Brazil: Examining Labour Dynamics of Production Networks in Two Cases of 'Slave Labour'*, PhD thesis, University of Manchester, 2010; for Durban, see Skinner and Valodia , 2001.
21 Rudvika Andrijasevic and Devi Sacchetto, 'Il just-in-time della vita: Reti di produzione globale e compressione spazio-temporale alla Foxconn', *Stato e Mercato* 111, 2017.
22 Cheng Ting-Fang, 'Taiwanese companies see 'Made in USA' opportunities'. *Financial Times*, 18 May 2016.
23 Tana Inagaki, 'Uniqlo: Fit for the future', *Financial Times*, 14 March 2019.
24 Boston Consulting Group, 'Three Personalization Imperatives During the Crisis', available at: www.bcg.com.
25 International Labour Organization, *The future of work in textiles, clothing, leather and footwear*, Working paper Nr 326, Geneva, International Labour Office, Sectoral Policies Department, 2019.
26 Dicken, *Global shift*, p. 259.

27 Bonacich and Appelbaum, *Behind the Label*, p. 22.

28 Achim Berg and Imran Amed, *Uncovering the State of Fashion: Coronavirus Update*, London: McKinsey and Business of Fashion, 2020.

29 Bangladesh Garment Manufacturers and Exporters Association (BGMEA), 'Listen to Rubana Huq, BGMEA president sit down with BBC', YouTube, 2020.

30 BGMEA, *Listen to Rubana Huq*.

31 'Reboot – Rebuild – Rebound: Fashion industry ready for Resurrection?' YouTube, 10 June 2020.

32 Achim Berg and Imran Amed, 'Uncovering the state of fashion', The McKinsey Podcast, 13 March 2020.

33 'Fashion's Darwinian Shakeout with Scott Galloway,' YouTube, 28 May 2020.

34 In a recent note in *The Bullet* ['Will the Pandemic Set Women Back?', 17 May 2020, available at socialistproject.ca], Beth English and Kelly Pike highlight the 'potential for gender empowerment' and 'the promise of independence, skills development, mobility and [the] better quality of life' that come with the incorporation of certain countries in global garment production networks. However, although the authors do mention the 'rampant' exploitation in the industry, their view tends to justify – perhaps unintentionally – the whole exploitative structure of the industry rather than point to alternatives that could be developed by other – long term – means not dependent on foreign capital.

35 Jamie Peck, *Offshore*, Oxford: Oxford University Press, 2017.

36 Berg and Amed, *Uncovering the State of Fashion*.

37 Harvey, *Seventeen Contradictions*, p. 85.

38 Bob Jessop, *The Future of the Capitalist State*, Cambridge: Polity Press, 2002; Erik Swyngedouw, 'Authoritarian governance, power, and the politics of rescaling' *Environment and Planning* D 18, 2000; Jamie Peck, 'Political economies of scale: Fast policy, interscalar relations, and neoliberal workfare', *Economic Geography*, 78(3), 2002.

39 Costis Hadjimichalis, *Crisis Spaces*, London: Routledge, 2017.

40 Neil Smith, 'Homeless/global: Scaling places', in J. Bird, B. Curtis, T. Putnam, G. Robertson, L. Tickner, eds, *Mapping the Futures: Local Cultures, Global Change* (87-109), London: Routledge, 1993.

41 Jamie Peck and Adam Tickell, 'Neoliberalizing space', *Antipode* 34(3), 2002.

42 Leo Panitch, 'Reflections on strategy for labour', in Leo Panitch and Colin Leys, eds, *Socialist Register 2001: Working Classes, Global Realities*, London: Merlin Press, 2000, p. 369.

43 Maurizio Atzeni and Juan Grigera, 'The Revival of Labour Movement Studies in Argentina: Old and Lost Agendas', *Work, Employment & Society*, 33(5), 2019, p. 871.

44 Panitch, 'Reflections'; see also Harvey, *Seventeen Contradictions*; Kim Moody, *On New Terrain: How Capital is Reshaping the Battleground for Class War*, Chicago: Haymarket Books, 2017.

SHIFTING GEARS: LABOUR STRATEGIES FOR LOW-CARBON PUBLIC TRANSIT MOBILITY

SEAN SWEENEY AND JOHN TREAT

The outbreak of the Covid-19 pandemic has unleashed a complex, multi-dimensional, and arguably unprecedented crisis. Although the world has experienced pandemics in the past, the 'Covid crisis' has unfolded in the context of a world economy that is much more complex, and much more vulnerable to disruption, than ever before in history. Of course, just as the impacts of the current pandemic are being felt very differently around the world, generally hitting poorer countries and communities much harder, so the impacts of the coming economic contraction are likely to have dramatically more severe impacts on those same countries and communities – and especially if the current arrangement of social, political, and economic forces remains unchallenged.

At this point, nearly everything about the ultimate impacts of the crisis unleashed by the Covid-19 pandemic remains in question. It has thrown wide open a range of questions about possible futures. Public health, food systems, education, leisure activities, and most everything else have been changed dramatically by the pandemic crisis. This is especially the case with the transportation of people and things. As a result of the pandemic and ensuing lockdowns, public transport systems have seen ridership numbers collapse to barely a fraction of their pre-pandemic levels. Work habits have changed in ways that, for the 'Zoomer' strata at least, require less personal mobility, although many 'essential workers' have had no choice but to continue to use public transport even under lockdown conditions. Some of the pandemic-related shifts in the way people move around – or don't – may turn out to be temporary, but others may be longer lasting or even permanent. For now, it seems reasonable to conclude that the current economic contraction may impede the growth of some modes of transport, but it could increase others.

Before the pandemic, global transport-related emissions were growing faster than any other sector, with annual emissions expected to rise by 55 per cent by 2030 as compared with 2010 levels. But even if global GDP were to return to 2010 levels – which would be an unprecedented depression-like contraction of around 24 per cent – this would still mean annual emissions that are wildly out of step with climate targets like those adopted under the Paris Climate Agreement.[1] Put differently, the Covid crisis on its own does nothing to reduce the threat of climate change, or to alleviate the other aspects of ecological disruption towards which the world's current patterns of production and consumption are leading us.

We have argued elsewhere[2] that reaching the emissions-reduction targets established under the Paris Agreement will not happen without a major shift in transport policy – a shift that breaks with the model of development centered on providing 'on-demand personal mobility' at almost any cost, and that places mass public transport at the center of future passenger mobility. The current approach has relied on incentives and assurances to private investors in the hope of 'unlocking private finance to help governments achieve their climate goals'[3] (including for transport), but has failed miserably. Although under such an approach public transport has grown in many places, that growth has not been sufficient to even *slow* the rise in transport-related emissions – let alone help bring them down. Similarly, the reliance in mainstream climate policy on small electric vehicles (EVs) as a 'replacement technology' for internal combustion engine (ICE) cars and trucks has led to a situation where there is currently too little emphasis on pursuing ways to minimize unnecessary or unwanted mobility. In fact, not only is the mass displacement of ICE vehicles by EVs far from inevitable, the potential emissions benefits of doing so have often been exaggerated.

In this essay, we take a global look at road transport, and more specifically how we might begin to imagine (and then organize around) a long-term political effort to establish urban transport systems that are organized on a 'public goods' basis. We assess some current trends, and consider some of the challenges that such a transition will likely need to confront. We argue that the incursions of private corporations such as Uber and Lyft into the territory traditionally occupied by public transport systems could be repelled, at least partially, by improved access to high quality public transport. At the same time, given the car-dependent development of peri-urban and rural areas, and the likely expansion of urban space in the coming decades (especially in the Global South), advocates of public transport – and that includes unions and the left in general – will want to explore how what we call 'occupying the platforms' through public car sharing schemes might meet these needs as part of municipal or communally owned fleets. Reclaiming and expanding public transport can and should be part of a broader project to re-imagine neighborhoods, cities, ecosystems, systems of production, and circulation.

WORKING WITH TRANSPORT WORKERS

At the World Congress of the International Transport Workers Federation (ITF) in Mexico City in 2010, two thousand delegates from the ITF's 700 affiliates in some 150 countries adopted a document titled *Transport Workers and Climate Change: Towards Sustainable, Low-Carbon Mobility*. This document looked at the transport sector's contribution to emissions, explained why transport-related emissions were rising, and outlined steps to reduce them. Its key component was a 'Reduce, Shift, Improve' (RSI) framework that aimed to guide efforts by transport unions interested in taking action on climate change in ways that could advance transport justice and equality by: first, *reducing* the unnecessary movement of goods and people; second, *shifting* the ways in which people and goods move (sometimes called 'modal shifts') away from high-carbon to low-carbon modes of transport; and, third, *improving* technologies to promote energy efficiency.

In 2019, the ITF launched its new *People's Public Transport Policy* (www.OPTPolicy.org) consisting of 28 policy demands in six key areas: public ownership, public financing, employment and decent work, women in public transport, worker control of technology, and climate change. As part of this broad effort, the ITF has attempted to initiate a discussion on how web-based platform technologies might be incorporated into modern public transport systems.[4] The idea is to find practical ways to respond to the challenges posed to public transport systems by 'transport network companies' like Uber in a way that extends public ownership over ride sharing and similar services while maintaining a clear commitment to conventional modern public transport systems. The ITF has also stressed that any public transport projects, existing or new, be subjected to community and worker review in order to guarantee decent jobs and conditions, improve their design, ensure a quality service, control costs, and to strike the best possible balance between levels of passenger demand and the availability of the specific service.

It is not possible here to do justice to the analysis developed by the ITF or to even begin to discuss the various features of its approach as it pertains to aviation, shipping, road transport, and other mobility modes. But it provides a useful framework for socialist discussions on transport, in that it takes a global view, is aware of key trends and challenges, and has the support of a significant section of organized labor. The ITF works closely with representatives of informal workers' organizations, such as those representing taxi and minivan drivers in large cities of the Global South.

The ITF's important, foundational work has the potential to inspire broader and more detailed investigation into transport possibilities. At the same time, the complexities around transport, land use and city planning are such that the ITF's general assessments and schematic solutions can only go so far, while most transport unions themselves have limited research capacity. It is important to acknowledge, moreover, that not all of the ITF's affiliates are able to actively promote the ITF's approach. Currently, the top priority of unions representing workers in aviation and shipping is to protect the jobs of their members; meanwhile, the loss of revenues due to falling public transport ridership levels amidst the pandemic could also lead to significant job losses, at least temporarily. Understandably, many transport unions are preoccupied with these concerns.

THE ACTUAL PRESENT: MASS MOTORIZATION AND PRIVATE PLATFORM MOBILITY

Whatever the future holds, one thing is clear: the challenges facing any serious effort to establish sustainable, low-carbon public mobility will continue to be formidable. There are too many private cars on the roads, public transport is not keeping up with urban population growth, and transport-related emissions have been on a steady upward trajectory for years. As the ITF rightly emphasizes, public transport should be liberated from the neoliberal obsession with 'full cost recovery'. This should be accompanied by putting an end to public-private partnerships (P3s), which are designed to ensure profits to investors. P3s introduce the requirement for profit, entail higher borrowing, transaction and competition costs, and can often result in higher prices for those using the service. P3 arrangements also favor 'megaprojects' that suit the needs of developers, but that are often out of step with – or even undermine – the mobility needs of working-class communities, and the employment needs of transport workers in the informal sector.[5]

Neoliberalism has propagated the idea that private sector investment is key to the future of public transport. But public funds remain the main source of finance, both for infrastructure and for operating costs to keep transport affordable. This is the case in both developed and developing countries.[6] According to the World Bank, there is not a single public transport system that operates without subsidies for passengers or through preferential financing extended to private contractors.[7] But as a recent report by the 'Sustainable Mobility for All' coalition acknowledges, 'The pace of change is making it hard for companies to anticipate demand, adapt to the market, or plan long-term investment in research, development, and production.'[8] Despite this set of glaring failures, the 'engage the private sector' policy discourse plods on regardless. The World Bank bemoans the fact that public transport suffers from an 'underfunding trap', but the trap itself was invented by the Bank and its regional operations and is kept in force by them.[9]

The need for a shift away from 'full cost recovery' directives was already urgent before the pandemic, and is even more urgent now, given that many public transport operators face sharp declines in fare-based revenues. Europe is likely to face a loss of EUR 40 billion as a result of Covid-19.[10] Transit agencies in the United States are reportedly facing revenue shortfalls of $26 to $38 billion.[11] A policy shift is therefore needed – one that can restore government budgets so that public transport can be adequately funded. But this shift is not a cure-all. Moving beyond neoliberal prescriptions such as these will not alter the fact that, in many countries, much of the built environment reflects the availability, and presumed permanence, of motor vehicles – something that will take decades to change. In the US, 45 per cent of residents have no access to public transport, and almost half of US residents need to walk a mile or more to get to a bus or train station.[12] Even in densely populated Europe, where public transport is very well developed by international standards, the steady depopulation and rising poverty levels in rural areas has coincided with the neglect of public transport services. In France it was these same conditions – and the decision by the Macron government to introduce a 'pollution tax' on diesel fuel – that ignited the Yellow Vests movement in late 2018.[13]

In the Global South, the 'internal migration' away from rural areas towards cities has proceeded at a staggering pace. According to one study, 'The first 30 years of the 21st century is highly likely to experience more urban land expansion than all of history'.[14] According to UN Habitat's latest data (June 2020), a third of the world's population now live in just 2,000 metropolitan areas. These are home to around 60 per cent of the world's urban population. It is projected that almost one billion people will become metropolitan inhabitants in the next fifteen years and there will be 429 new metropolises by 2035.[15] Given the pace of urbanization globally, even the most progressive national or municipal governments committed to high quality public services are likely to struggle to provide city-wide, high-capacity public transport. The challenge becomes even more intimidating when one considers that cities are also growing *spatially* as they become more crowded with cars and people.

The great expansion of urban populations has coincided with a rapid rise in private vehicle ownership. In many cities of the Global North in particular, bike lanes, pedestrian-only streets, and new public transport systems are being developed, and car ownership is falling, at least among younger people. But this does not reflect the overall picture. Globally, nearly 95 million cars and light commercial vehicles were sold in 2018 – roughly four times the number sold in 1965.[16] Prior to the pandemic, the total number of vehicles on the world's roads was projected to *double* by 2030, and to *triple* by 2050 – truly staggering statistics.[17] Helped along by low oil prices, some countries have also seen a trend towards larger, less fuel-efficient vehicles. In the US, the share of SUVs and light trucks is currently around 60 per cent of total sales [2017 figures].[18] Sales of SUVs are also rising in China, Australia, and elsewhere.[19]

The massive increase in motorization, particularly in the South, has resulted in hundreds of the world's largest cities becoming death traps. In 2019, there were 1.35 million traffic-related fatalities globally. But 93 per cent of those fatalities occurred in low- and middle-income countries. More than half of those killed annually are pedestrians, cyclists, or motorcyclists. For children under ten years old, road accidents are the largest single cause of death globally. Around 50 million people are also injured on the world's roads every year.[20] Meanwhile, the World Health Organization estimates that two million people die every year from outdoor air pollution, with vehicles being a major contributor alongside industry and agriculture. Over 90 per cent of the world's inhabitants live in areas where air pollution exceeds safe levels.[21]

Studies by UN Habitat have shown that the limited availability of public transport is a major factor driving the rise of private vehicle ownership and motorization more broadly.[22] As we will see, it is also helping the platform-based ride-hailing companies gain an even firmer foothold. Of course, both car ownership and the use of ride-hailing are skewed towards the better off. As the IPCC notes, just 10 per cent of the world's population is responsible for 80 per cent of motorized travel; large numbers of people rarely use any motorized transport.[23] And because private cars often share infrastructure with public buses and trams, the resulting congestion impedes the smooth running of public transport systems.

A more recent feature of the 'actual present' is the proliferation of 'new mobility services' provided by so-called 'transport network companies' (TNCs) using internet-based platforms. These companies have grown rapidly in just a few short years. Uber reached one billion trips worldwide by the end of 2015, and two billion by mid-2016;[24] by the end of May 2017, the total had risen to five billion.[25] As of the end of 2018, Uber's fleet of drivers totaled 3.9 million.[26] The number of Uber-like companies has also proliferated, including in the global South. In 2017, China's 'DiDi' reportedly carried out up to 25 million daily trips across 400 cities for a total of 7.3 billion rides for the year.[27] In Southeast Asia, 'Grab' (formerly 'MyTaxi') out-competed Uber, buying the latter's business in key countries and 'driving the ride-hailing giant out of several fast-growing markets such as Indonesia and Thailand'.[28]

Comprehensive studies have shown that as many as one-third of rides with companies like Uber and Lyft were due to poor or infrequent public transport services, while the impact of TNCs on existing public transport systems has invariably been negative, not only in terms of reduced ridership levels on public mass transit even before the pandemic, but also by increasing surface transport congestion which often slows down public buses in situations where dedicated bus lanes do not exist.[29] Some local authorities are even looking to companies like Uber and Lyft to provide mobility as an alternative to maintaining 'low ridership' public transport routes – and they are willing to subsidize the process.[30] Had these public transport services been maintained, expanded, and improved over the years instead of being starved of resources, the rise of private companies like Uber and Lyft could have been significantly curtailed.[31]

ADDRESSING CLIMATE CHANGE

Transport's contribution to the climate crisis already shows signs of being out of control. Transport is the fastest-growing carbon emissions sector globally, accounting for 23 per cent of global CO2 emissions currently; this is predicted to increase by 70 per cent by 2050 under a business-as-usual scenario.[32] Transport currently accounts for roughly 14 per cent of all global GHG emissions.[33] Emissions from international aviation essentially doubled during the period 1990 to 2016, up 98.3 per cent, while those from shipping rose by 13 per cent during the same period.[34] However, road transport – cars, trucks, motorbikes, etc. – still accounts for almost 70 per cent of transport-related emissions. The movement of people by road accounts for around 67 per cent of road transport's share. Freight – essentially, the movement of stuff – accounts for almost a third.[35] Prior to the COVID crisis, global freight volumes were expected to increase by 69 per cent from the period 2015 to 2030.[36] These projections may soon be revised downward, but road freight already accounts for almost 10 per cent of annual energy-related CO2 emissions globally.[37] Neoliberal policy has for decades promoted the kind of trade-led growth that has caused emissions to skyrocket. Meanwhile, these same policies have impeded the growth of public transport even though it is widely accepted by the policy mainstream that public transport is clearly a 'climate solution' of immense significance and enormous potential.

If the world was hoping the 2015 Paris Agreement would turn out to be a 'turning point for humanity' in terms of reducing emissions levels, then it is fair to say that an unconscious virus has accomplished more in five months than was achieved by armies of government negotiators in the five years since the agreement was adopted. Most of the G20 countries are currently not on target to meet their 'nationally determined contributions' (NDCs) to either reducing emissions or, in the case of many developing countries, slowing their increase.[38] The overwhelming majority of NDCs submitted by governments (113 of the 164 total national submissions) include commitments to sustainable mobility, but barely one-third of those make specific reference to transport-related emissions, and only 15 country submissions give any indication of plans to address their upward course.[39] The willingness to acknowledge the problem merely draws attention to the lack of any clear ideas on the part of countries regarding what, exactly, should be done about it.

Policies dedicated to the decarbonization of road transport have thus far had little effect.[40] The same is true of aviation and shipping. For many on the left, this lack of progress is often attributed to the political power of the large car companies, oil companies and their various allies, some of which have actively promoted climate change denial. But regardless of the behavior of these companies, it remains the case that reducing transport-related emissions presents a massive headache for climate scientists and engineers. Transport today is almost completely dependent on petroleum products, and, when it comes to finding alternative forms of energy, there is no 'low hanging fruit' that, if harvested, might begin to produce significant results.[41] In other words, today's transport systems are both socially inequitable and ecologically unsustainable, and even a sharp pandemic-induced economic contraction will not alter that basic reality. In its *Global Mobility Report 2017*, the World Bank itself concluded, 'The world is off track to achieving sustainable mobility. The growing demand for moving people and goods is increasingly met at the expense of future generations. It is urgent to reverse this trend. The costs for society … are simply too high.'[42]

ELECTROMOBILITY: PUBLIC VERSUS PRIVATE

This explains in part why electric vehicles have become the primary mitigation option for many policymakers. While public transport's potential contribution is acknowledged, it is the electric car that makes headlines. Its advocates point out that the prices of EVs are falling and the technologies are improving, so why not simply phase out ICE vehicles and replace them with EVs?[43] But even leaving aside some of the anticipated environmental impacts that might result from intensive lithium extraction (for EV batteries) in countries like Argentina, Bolivia and Chile,[44] there are several major problems with this approach.

First, EVs are not replacing ICE vehicles. Global sales of EVs reached 1.1 million in 2017.[45] And while the recent annual growth rates have been impressive, in 2018 EVs (which are heavily subsidized and tend to appeal to wealthier consumers) accounted for just a little over 2 per cent of total annual vehicle sales.[46] Second, when electricity used to charge EVs is generated by either coal or gas, the mile-for-mile CO2 reductions compared to ICE vehicles of similar size are often quite insignificant.[47] Speaking from the World Economic Forum in Davos, Switzerland, in early 2019, the International Energy Agency's Executive Director, Fatih Birol, noted that even if the number of EVs on the road was increased by 60 times (to 300 million), the impact on global CO2 emissions, given the current global power generation mix, would be minimal.[48] Third, a mass deployment scenario is only possible if charging infrastructure grows alongside the use of EVs. But private investment in such infrastructure depends on confidence that usage will dramatically increase to ensure returns on investment, and these conditions are not in place.[49] A UK study summed up the fundamental problem of a market-led approach: 'Electric transport requires an infrastructure of charging points. It is a classic infant infrastructure problem: the network is economic only when there are lots of EVs charging from it; and the EVs are worth buying only if the infrastructure is in place.'[50] The EU's 'European Green Deal' (EGD) proposes to 'boost considerably the uptake of clean vehicles and alternative fuels', by 'supporting and financing the deployment of recharging and refueling points'.[51] But such infrastructure support is just another form of subsidy for private vehicle ownership.

In addition to all this, mass deployment of EVs would have a massive impact on demand for electricity. If EVs were to grow quickly while the world is trying to decarbonize electricity generation, the pressure on renewables to keep up with that rising demand would increase accordingly. By one estimate, 'One EV can double the total consumption of residential energy. Thus, 10 per cent of households charging EVs would be the equivalent of growing the residential customer base by 7 per cent'.[52] Moreover, the mass deployment of EVs on the basis of a one-for-one swap will do nothing to address the problems of traffic congestion and accidents. Currently, the prospect of motorization continuing to grow alongside urbanization evokes disturbing images of a big 'civilizational crunch', with private vehicles increasingly in physical competition for space with the growing ranks of the urban poor. Pedestrians and cyclists hit by cars will take little consolation from the fact that their injuries were caused by electrical vehicles.

At this point, it should be obvious that the policy emphasis on the mass deployment of individually owned EVs is misplaced, and the reasons why the illusion is sustained are more a reflection of short-term political considerations than a display of genuine confidence in the idea that, one day, there will be 'an EV in every garage' (or driveway). By contrast, there *can* be a public approach to the full electrification of mobility, operating on the principle that every vehicle on the road will be electric, and that all vehicles on the road should be part of a system of public mobility, and should serve a social purpose.

Indeed, despite the disturbing trends in the present and the formidable challenges ahead, public transport is thriving in many parts of the world. The main problem is that it has been unable to keep up with the enormous increase in urban populations and rising mobility needs. The expansion of public transport has been especially impressive in China, India, and other major developing countries. Globally, the availability of mass public transport – buses, metro systems, light rail, etc. – has nearly doubled (measured in passenger journeys) during the last 25 years. In the EU, the use of public transport reached a total of 57.9 billion journeys in 2014, its highest level since 2000.[53] Urban metro and light rail systems serve the daily mobility needs of tens of millions of people around the world. According to the UITP, urban systems served nearly 54 billion passengers in 2017 – 9 billion more than in 2012, with most of the increase in Asia and the Middle East-North Africa region. As UITP notes, 'At the end of 2017, there were metros in 178 cities in 56 countries, carrying on average a total of 168 million passengers per day.' Between year 2000 and 2017, 75 new urban metro systems were opened, mostly in Asia – an increase of 70 per cent.[54]

Passenger travel by long-distance rail (both conventional and high-speed) has also grown dramatically, led by a massive expansion of conventional rail in India, where such travel has tripled during this period.[55] India accounts for 37 per cent of global conventional passenger rail travel, China 29 per cent, and Japan 11 per cent [2016 data].[56] According to the IPCC, rail transport accounts for 28 billion passenger journeys globally, covering roughly 2,500 billion person kilometres per year. By way of contrast, aviation provides far less than one-tenth as many passenger journeys – 2.1 billion per year, covering 3,900 billion passenger kilometers. As with passenger rail systems, buses have also historically served as a cornerstone of urban passenger transport, and bus use has also grown in recent years.

These are encouraging data, but to maximize public transport's contribution to improved health and climate protection, public transport modes should be both modernized and electrified. Rail transport in urban areas already runs almost exclusively on electricity. In the last decade, passenger rail transport has decreased its energy consumption by 22 per cent.[57] The electrification of public bus fleets, however, still has a long way to go – although it is worth remembering that, from a climate and health perspective, even partially filled diesel buses are far more efficient in terms of energy use than fossil fuel-powered cars.[58] Electric public buses will be even more efficient, especially if the electricity used for charging the buses is generated from low carbon sources (wind, solar, hydropower or nuclear).

As of 2018, there were an estimated 425,000 electric buses in use globally[59] – roughly 14 per cent of the total 3,000,000 municipal buses in service around the world.[60] But roughly 99 per cent of the global fleet is operating in China. The city of Shenzhen – often called 'China's Silicon Valley'– operates more than 16,000 electric buses and 19,000 EV taxis. These 35,000 vehicles are charged at more than 5,000 public charging points located throughout the city.[61] Battery-electric buses already offer emissions advantages (2.5 times cleaner than diesel buses, on average) even in situations where the share of renewable power generation is still quite small.[62] Contrast China's bus fleet with that of the US, where public transportation agencies are using buses (as well as railcars and other infrastructure) that are well beyond their useful lives.[63] For buses, the average fleet age has increased in recent years. Of the 123,000 transit buses and vans, almost one in five is not in a state of good repair. For rail transit vehicles, the average fleet age is close to 20 years. In 2019, the New York City transit system retired the last of its 'R-42' subway cars – 51 years after they entered service.[64]

Facts like these suggest that conventional public transport systems can and should be improved (especially where they have been neglected and starved of public funds), scaled up further (particularly in the Global South), and electrified (which should be done in tandem with the planned decarbonization of electricity generation). Of course, different transport modes have their own infrastructure needs and requirements. For example, Bus Rapid Transit (BRT) systems require dedicated road lanes that cannot be used by vehicles other than large buses. BRT involves building new roads, interchanges, terminals, and modern stations along the routes. It is, in essence, a light rail system, but one that runs on tires rather than rails.[65] Transport planners have encouraged governments to develop BRT infrastructure as a means of relieving congestion and reducing accidents. Yet, sometimes these systems are introduced without regard to the impact on drivers of taxis and minivans that had hitherto provided mobility for working people. In countries like the Philippines and Kenya, the ITF has worked with leaders of various driver cooperatives on a 'just transition'. In fact, there is no reason why major travel corridors cannot continue to be served by efficient conventional bus and BRT systems. And smaller buses, with 8 to 16 seats, have been shown to be capable of providing point-to-point services and can be summoned to locations near specific residences. Major cities continue to build rail systems for the busiest travel routes. In other words, conventional public transport systems with new electric right-sized vehicles could play a major role in providing mobility that is both *public* and *low-carbon* – if the forces of motorization, private vehicle ownership, corporate control over land use decisions, and so forth, can be brought under control.

OCCUPY THE PLATFORM

Of course, socialists are not alone in believing that public transportation systems should be developed to a point where most day-to-day travel, whether for work or leisure, can be accomplished via mass transportation. We know that such systems already have a proven track record in terms of their social and environmental benefits. And in the debates on climate change, public transport is already regarded as a crucial 'mitigation option', in that it can help control and eventually reduce transport-related greenhouse gas emissions (GHGs). But while conventional forms of public transport remain central to a socialist approach to mobility, they are not sufficient on their own. Efforts to promote public transport must be part a broader transitional agenda for transport as a whole – one that can, in turn, reinforce transitions in other key sectors, such as power generation, food and agriculture, building and construction, and so on. But that agenda must also work to *limit* certain types of socially damaging and ecologically destructive mobility.

Municipal authorities must get control over private ride-hailing companies like Uber, through strenuous regulation or even outright bans. Indeed, some municipalities already have. It is worth remembering that the roads that these companies use were paid for, and are maintained by, public funds. The rider and route data that Uber and others claim to own would not exist without satellites and other publicly funded communications infrastructure. Public transport authorities have the capability of generating and storing passenger data as a means of improving service, and many of them are probably already doing so. But all private transport network companies should be required to release existing stores of data so that public transport systems can be further improved. Travel data should be part of 'the commons' and can be used to improve public transport and generally serve the public good, and not – as data are used today – to the detriment of public systems. Therefore the fight for public transport will involve a struggle for ownership and control over these technologies, so that they can be used to complement and improve the public transport services of the future rather than displace or undermine them.

But there is no reason that a public transport authority cannot immediately incorporate publicly owned ride-sharing services in a wider system of public transport aimed squarely at the shared public good. In the context of strict limits on private vehicle ownership and use, public authorities can establish public car sharing services.[66] A managed 'public goods' approach to car sharing could complement and help grow public transport, rather than competing with it.[67] If properly integrated into an overall public transport system, 'Zipcars' and other managed fleets of shared vehicles can likely help reduce emissions; if these fleets are powered by renewable energy, their contribution to climate protection can increase still further.[68]

Not only would such a system be easier to coordinate, but it would allow public vehicle fleets to be standardized and fully electrified, and charged in public spaces using public charging stations or at a central depot, with (over time) the power coming from a modern grid transmitting and distributing electricity generated from low-carbon sources.[69] In this respect, the future of urban mobility stands at a crossroads. If pre-pandemic trends in new mobility and 'Uberization' resume, the challenge to decarbonize road transport will become even more formidable than it already is.

As Leo Panitch and Sam Gindin put it in the *Socialist Register 2000: Necessary and Unnecessary Utopias,* socialism is 'a movement linking the present with the possible'.[70] From this we can postulate the following: our assessment of the possible (as well as the impossible or very unlikely) will become more grounded and credible if it is based on a clear grasp of the *actual* present. Having a vision of low-carbon public mobility is better than not having one, but that vision must be informed by a thorough, rigorous and continually improving body of knowledge and experience. Socialists have the conceptual tools to develop a 'transitional program' for transport, but the link between the present and the possible must be both strong and flexible. Neoliberal policies have undermined public transport in many countries of the North and impeded its growth in countries of the South, and if those policies disappeared tomorrow, and socialist policies were immediately adopted, new possibilities would certainly open up. But achieving those possibilities – and knowing which ones to pursue – will likely be a decades-long process that will require changing the built environment, managing population flows, and adapting technological change in ways consistent with achieving our socialist goals.

NOTES

1. Partnership on Sustainable Low, Carbon Transport (SLoCaT), *Implications of 2DS and 1.5DS for Land Transport Carbon Emissions in 2050*, November 2016, available at: www.ppmc-transport.org.
2. Sean Sweeney and John Treat, *The Road Less Travelled: Reclaiming Public Transport for Climate-Ready Mobility*, TUED Working Paper #12, May 2019, available at: unionsforenergydemocracy.org.
3. Tom Kerr and Aditi Maheshwari, 'Unlocking Private Finance to Help Governments Achieve their Climate Goals', NDC Partnership, 14 May 2017, available at: ndcpartnership.org.
4. ITF, Urban Transport / 'Our Public Transport', available at: www.itfglobal.org.
5. World Bank, 'Private Participation in Infrastructure', 2017 Annual Report, available at: documents.worldbank.org.
6. Tomás Serebrisky et al, 'Affordability and Subsidies in Public Urban Transport: What Do We Mean, What Can Be Done?', Policy Research Working Paper No. 4440, December 2007, World Bank, available at: openknowledge.worldbank.org; see also, National Conference of State Legislatures, *On Track: How States Fund and Support Public Transportation*, 16 February 2017, available at: www.ncsl.org; IEA, *The Future of Rail: Opportunities for energy and the environment*, 30 January 2019, available at: webstore.iea.org.
7. World Bank, 'Private Participation in Infrastructure'.
8. Sustainable Mobility for All, 'Global Roadmap of Action Toward Sustainable Mobility', 2019, available at: sum4all.org.
9. Arturo Ardila-Gomez and Adriana Ortegon-Sanchez, 'From Sidewalk to Subway - Achieving Sustainable Financing for Urban Transport', World Bank, 25 May 2016, available at: www.worldbank.org.
10. Kevin Smith, 'UITP projects €40bn hit for European public transport in 2020', *International Railway Journal*, 13 May 2020, available at: www.railjournal.com.
11. Jenna Fortunati, 'COVID-19 will cost transit agencies $26-$38 billion, TransitCenter estimates', *Transportation for America Blog*, 24 March 2020, available at: t4america.org.
12. Census Bureau, *American Housing Survey*, 2013
13. Michael Kimmelman, 'France's Yellow Vests Reveal a Crisis of Mobility in All Its Forms', *New York Times*, 20 December 2018.
14. Karen C. Seto, Burak Güneralp, Lucy R. Hutyra, 'Global forecasts of urban expansion to 2030', *Proceedings of the National Academy of Sciences* 109(40), pp. 16088.
15. UN Habitat, *Global State of Metropolis 2020 – Population Data Booklet*, 2020, available at: unhabitat.org.
16. Automobile industry portal, 'LMC Automotive Global Light Vehicle Sales Update (December 2017)', available at: www.marklines.com.
17. Global Fuel Economy Initiative, *Delivering Sustainable Development Goal* 7, July 2018, available at: www.globalfueleconomy.org.
18. IEA, *Global Energy & CO2 Status Report* (GECO) 2017, available at: www.iea.org.
19. Hiroko Tabuchi, 'The World Is Embracing S.U.V.s. That's Bad News for the Climate.', *New York Times*, 3 March 2018.
20. WHO, 'Global Status Report on Road Safety 2018', December 2018, available at: www.who.int.

21 WHO, '9 out of 10 people worldwide breathe polluted air, but more countries are taking action', 2 May 2018, available at: www.who.int.

22 United Nations Human Settlements Programme, 'Planning and Design for Sustainable Urban Mobility: Global Report on Human Settlements 2013', available at: unhabitat.org.

23 IPCC Working Group 3, 'Chapter 8: Transport', *Fifth Assessment Report (AR5): Climate Change 2014: Mitigation of Climate Change*, available at: www.ipcc.ch.

24 Heather Somerville, 'Uber reaches 2 billion rides six months after hitting its first billion', *Reuters Technology News*, 18 July 2016.

25 Rachel Holt, Andrew Macdonald and Pierre-Dimitri Gore-Coty, '5 Billion Trips', Uber News Room, 29 June 2017, available at: www.uber.com.

26 Uber News Room, 'Facts and figures as of December 2018', available at: www.uber.com.

27 Xinhua, 'DiDi completes 7.43b rides in 2017', 9 January 2018.

28 Michelle Toh, 'Grab beat Uber in Southeast Asia. It's just getting started', *CNN Business*, 27 April 2018.

29 Eric Hannon, Stefan Knupfer, Sebastian Stern, and Jan Tijs Nijssen, 'The road to seamless urban mobility', *McKinsey Quarterly*, January 2019; Regina R. Clewlow, Gouri Shankar Mishra, 'Disruptive Transportation: The Adoption, Utilization, and Impacts of Ride-Hailing in the United States', Institute of Transportation Studies, University of California, Davis, October 2017, available at: trid.trb.org.

30 Mark Wilding, 'Private companies want to replace public transport. Should we let them?' *The Guardian*, 29 March 2018.

31 ITDP, *Ride Fair: A Policy Framework for Managing Transportation Network Companies*, March 2019, available at: www.itdp.org.

32 IPCC Working Group 3, 'Chapter 8: Transport'.

33 IPCC, 'Chapter 8: Transport'; See also: IEA, *Tracking Transport 2019*, May 2019; E360 Digest, 'Transportation Replaces Power in U.S. as Top Source of CO2 Emissions', Yale School of the Environment, 4 December 2017, available at: e360.yale.edu.

34 UNFCCC, *National greenhouse gas inventory data for the period 1990–2016. Report by the secretariat*, 21 September 2018, available at: unfccc.int.

35 IEA, *Energy efficiency indicators: Highlights*, 2018, p. 2.

36 World Bank, *Global Mobility Report 2017*, available at: sum4all.org.

37 IEA, *Energy efficiency indicators: Highlights*, 2018, p. 3.

38 UNFCCC, Paris Agreement, Article 4; United Nations Environment Program (UNEP), *The Emissions Gap Report 2017*, www.unenvironment.org.

39 UN Habitat, *Sustainable Urbanization in the Paris Agreement*, 2016, available at: unhabitat.org.

40 Nicholas Stern et al, *The Stern Review: The Economics of Climate Change*, Cambridge University Press, 4 January 2007, available at: webarchive.nationalarchives.gov.uk. The landmark study known as the *Stern Review* acknowledged that market mechanisms – most importantly, carbon pricing – could be effective in shaping the behavior of investors and business owners in key sectors, but markets, thought Stern, may not be able to deliver the kind of radical changes needed in the transport sector.

41 IPCC Working Group 3, 'Chapter 8: Transport', *Fifth Assessment Report (AR5): Climate Change 2014: Mitigation of Climate Change*, available at: www.ipcc.ch.

42 José Luis Irigoyen, Senior Director of Transport & ICT Global Practice, at the launch; *World Bank Global Mobility Report 2017*, available at: www.worldbank.org. Similarly, the Intergovernmental Panel on Climate Change (IPCC) – the leading scientific body advising governments on the climate threat and how it can be met – has also warned that continuing growth in passenger and freight transport could more than offset emissions reductions made in other economic sectors, making it difficult if not impossible to reach the emissions reduction targets consistent with the Paris targets. See: IPCC WG3 AR5, Chapter 8, p. 603.

43 IEA/IRENA, *Perspectives for the Energy Transition: Investment Needs for a Low Carbon Energy System*, 2017, available at: www.irena.org; IEA, *Global EV Outlook 2017*, available at: webstore.iea.org.

44 Thomas Wilson and Thomas Biesheuvel, 'Mad Scramble for Lithium Stretches From Congo to Cornwall', *Bloomberg*, 24 October 2017.

45 LMC Automotive, *Global Light Vehicle Sales Update*, December 2018, available at: www.marklines.com.

46 Colin McKerracher, 'BP's Energy Outlook and the Rising Consensus on EV Adoption', *Bloomberg New Energy Finance*, 23 February 2018.

47 UITP, Towards low/zero-carbon urban mobility in Europe, 2011, available at: www.uitp.org. In the case of the EU, 'GHG emissions of electric cars range from 76 to 262 grams per passenger-kilometre (138g for the so-called EU electricity mix) and are not significantly different from today's diesel or gasoline cars. With emissions between 17 and 48 grams per passenger-kilometre, public transport is unbeatable.'

48 Fatih Birol, speaking on the panel, 'Strategic Outlook on Energy', World Economic Forum, 22 January 2019, available at: www.weforum.org.

49 Constance Douris, 'Who Should Pay For Electric Vehicle Chargers? Who Should Profit?' *Forbes*, 8 November 2017.

50 Dieter Helm, *Cost of Energy Review*, October 2017, available at: www.gov.uk.

51 European Commission, 'Sustainable transport: What do we want to achieve?' *Mobility and Transport*, available at: ec.europa.eu.

52 Doug Houseman, 'Our grid must be strong, smart and sustainable', *Powergrid International*, 24 March 2020, available at: www.power-grid.com.

53 UITP, *Declaration on Climate Leadership: Update on Implementation 2016*, available at: www.uitp.org.

54 UITP, *World Metro Figures 2018*, September 2018, available at: www.uitp.org.

55 IEA, *The Future of Rail: Opportunities for energy and the environment*, 30 January 2019, available at: webstore.iea.org.

56 IEA, *The Future of Rail.*

57 UITP, *Towards low/zero-carbon urban mobility in Europe*, 2011, available at: www.uitp.org.

58 Marcy Lowe, Bengu Aytekin, and Gary Gereffi, 'Public Transit Buses: A Green Choice Gets Greener', *Manufacturing Climate Solutions: Carbon-Reducing Technologies and U.S. Jobs*, Center on Globalization, Governance & Competitiveness, Duke University, 26 October 2009, Chapter 12, available at: gvcc.duke.edu; see also Eric Jaffe, 'Can We Please Stop Pretending Cars Are Greener Than Transit?' 21 November 2012.https://www.citylab.com/transportation/2012/11/can-we-please-stop-pretending-cars-are-greener-transit/3960/

59 Linda Poon, 'Why U.S. Cities Aren't Using More Electric Buses', *Bloomberg*, 27 June 2019.

60 BNEF, *Electric Buses in Cities: Driving Towards Cleaner Air and Lower* CO_2, 29 March 2018, available at: about.bnef.com.

61 Zigor Aldama, 'Powered by the state, China takes charge of electric buses, with Shenzhen taking the lead', *South China Morning Post*, 18 January 2019.

62 Jimmy O'Dea, 'Electric vs. Diesel vs. Natural Gas: Which Bus is Best for the Climate?' *Union of Concerned Scientists Blog*, 19 July 2018.

63 Testimony of Paul P. Skoutelas, President and CEO, American Public Transportation Association, Hearing on 'Surface Transportation Reauthorization: Public Transportation Stakeholders' Perspectives', available at: www.apta.com.

64 Staff, 'NYCT retires 1960s rail cars', *Progressive Railroading*, 13 February 2020, available at: www.progressiverailroading.com.

65 ITF, *Bus Rapid Transit (BRT) and the formalisation of informal public transport: a trade union negotiating guide*, 25 November 2019, available at: www.itfglobal.org.

66 Sven Teske, ed., *Achieving the Paris Climate Agreement Goals: Global and Regional 100% Renewable Energy Scenarios with Non-energy GHG Pathways for +1.5°C and +2°C*, Springer International Publishing, 2019.

67 PPMC, *Global Macro Roadmap Outlining an Actionable Vision Towards Decarbonized, Resilient Transport*, November 2017, available at: www.ppmc-transport.org.

68 Elliot Martin and Susan Shaheen, 'Greenhouse Gas Emission Impacts of Car Sharing in North America', *IEEE Transactions on Intelligent Transportation Systems* 12(4), December 2011; See also Adam Millard-Ball, *Car-Sharing: Where and How It Succeeds*, Washington, DC: The National Academies Press.

69 Diego Canales et al, 'Connected Urban Growth: Public-Private Collaborations for Transforming Urban Mobility', World Resources Institute, available at: www.wri.org.

70 Leo Panitch and Sam Gindin, 'Transcending Pessimism: Rekindling Socialist Imagination', in Leo Panitch and Colin Leys eds, *Socialist Register 2000: Necessary and Unnecessary Utopias*, London: Merlin Press, 1999.

COMMUNITY RESTAURANTS: DECOMMODIFYING FOOD AS SOCIALIST STRATEGY

BENJAMIN SELWYN

Even before the Coronavirus (Covid-19) pandemic, the Inter-Academy Partnership characterised the world's food system as broken. Over 800 million people were hungry, 600 million suffered from obesity and another 2 billion people were overweight, while one third of food produced globally (about 1 billion tons) was wasted every year.[1] The outbreak of Covid-19 has exacerbated many of the system's worst aspects. In the UK, the birthplace of free wage-labour based capitalist agriculture, the pandemic has exacerbated existing food inequities. Five million people were food insecure in mid-2020, with BAME people disproportionately at risk.[2] The pandemic has stimulated discussions about how to remedy the world's corporate-dominated food system. The most popular alternative visions propose shifting production and consumption away from meat increasingly to plant-based diets produced according to agro-ecological principles.[3] Whilst these approaches could be part of a broader solution, so far they have tended to eschew explaining the food system's inequities in class-relational terms.

This essay argues that the root problems of the contemporary food system are three-fold: (1) it is rooted in, and depends upon, the commodification of labour, food, and natural resources (including land); (2) that these commodities are subordinate to capitalism's endless drive of exploitation-based accumulation; and (3) that the food system itself incorporates, and contributes to reproducing, these dynamics throughout the wider capitalist system. Facilitating healthy, increasingly plant-based diets should be part and parcel of a socialist agenda.

The commodification of food serves to reproduce labouring class market dependence under capitalism. Accessing food via the market necessitates money, wages, employment, and subordination to capital inside and outside the workplace – the former where surplus value is generated, the latter where subsistence goods are purchased and surplus value realised. Much food preparation is predicated upon unpaid, gendered, domestic care work. Given that food is arguably the most essential wage good, its availability and affordability for labouring classes is an important determinant of wage rates. Cheap food can enable low wages and thus cheap workers while expensive food can lead to upward wage pressures and/or political instability.

While sufficiently available food is necessary to feed capitalism's labouring classes, high-energy food is required to facilitate capitalisms intense labour process.[4] For these reasons the cost and content of energy in food has been a concern for capitalists and their states since at least the industrial revolution. Since capitalism's early days food has been increasingly commodified – produced as an exchange-value for sale onto markets using inputs purchased on markets – rather than as a use-value for self-consumption. Commodity fetishism, the ideological expression of commodification, hides ways in which food becomes available for purchase through the market, such as exploitative labour and environmentally destructive practices. This generates 'food from nowhere' – the mass production, distribution and sale of cheap, undifferentiated and often highly processed foodstuffs.[5]

Gøsta Esping-Andersen refers to decommodification as 'the degree to which individuals, or families, can uphold a socially acceptable standard of living independently of market participation'. While decommodification exists in various settings (some more amenable to the reproduction of capitalism than others), '[w]hen work approaches free choice rather than necessity, de-commodification may amount to de-proletarianization'.[6] For alternative food systems to facilitate a shift from decommodification to de-proletarianization, means thinking about how individuals are transformed from market-dependent worker-consumers to what Jennifer Wilkins calls 'food-citizens'. These citizens engage in 'food-related behaviours that support, rather than threaten, the development of a democratic, socially and economically just, and environmentally sustainable food system'.[7]

What might an emergent alternative food system look like? How could it decommodify food in order to reduce labouring class market dependence while enhancing workers' health? How could it increase workers' democratic control over its production, distribution and consumption? How could it reduce race and gender inequalities? How could the construction of such an alternative system facilitate political alliance building amongst oppressed and exploited groups? How could it enable workers' organizations to encroach upon the power of capital? This essay suggests that community restaurants, serving free and cheap food, represent a socialist demand that can fulfil the above criteria.

THE COMMODIFICATION OF FOOD

World food production has undergone long-term commodification as food is increasingly produced as exchange values for sale on to markets. Far from entailing the establishment of free markets in food, as in liberal ideology, these production and exchange relations have required the continual presence of leading capitalist states. As Karl Polanyi noted:

> The road to the free market was opened and kept open by an enormous increase in continuous, centrally organised and controlled interventionism … the introduction of free markets, far from doing away with the need for control, regulation and intervention, enormously increased their range.[8]

The rise of an increasingly globalized capitalist agriculture was achieved through long term, state-directed social restructuring across four key world historical moments. From the sixteenth century enclosures in England gave rise to the first form of wage-labour based agricultural capitalism. In the emergent United States, 'unproductive' land was seized and cleared of indigenous populations, while both states promoted transatlantic plantation slavery and the triangular trade. In the nineteenth century, Britain organized the first world market for food through free-trade imperialism. The US granted land-rights to railroad companies to expand the North American frontier, imposed tariffs and protection, and encouraged the mass production of grains and livestock in the mid-west based on family agriculture. From the mid-twentieth century, the US and the emerging EU regulated trade and subsidized systematic over-production. The US rolled-out the Green Revolution, used buffer stocks to protect farmer income, and implemented a grain disposal system (PL480) designed to establish relative food dependence in emergent post-colonial states. Late-twentieth century structural adjustment programmes encouraged so called Non-Traditional Agricultural Exports from the Global South to Global North, boosting the power of giant retail capital.[9]

Capitalist food systems rest upon the simultaneous commodification and externalization of nature – where its use and destruction are either not incorporated as a cost into production, or is done so very cheaply. The word's agricultural system, generating between 20-35 per cent of anthropogenic greenhouse gasses, is a major contributor to the sixth mass extinction of wildlife.[10] Far from being financially self-sustaining as in liberal mythology, industrial food production relies upon extensive state support. Approximately $530 billion of an annual $700 billion of global public funds to agriculture is paid to farmers engaged in high-input, chemically intensive, mono-crop based farming.[11] Often brutal labour exploitation is central to the reproduction of global agriculture:

> [O]f the 1.3 billion people employed in agriculture … there are some 450 million waged workers, over half of whom are women. Seventy per cent of child labour globally takes place in agriculture … and agriculture produces over 170,000 work-related deaths annually. Agricultural workers are twice as likely to die at work than in any other sector. Between three to four million pesticide poisonings occur each year, some 40,000 of them fatal … chronically high rates of malnutrition occur among agricultural workers.[12]

Rather than a system orientated to meet human need through environmentally sustainable and socially equitable practices, the global agro-industrial system is one where 'people, animals, plants and the environment [are] controlled in order to maintain order, authority and predictability'.[13]

FOOD INEQUALITY AND LABOUR EXPLOITATION IN THE UK

From production, distribution and marketing, to preparation and consumption, contemporary food systems are built upon, and facilitate directly, intense social inequalities and labour exploitation. Such polarizing dynamics are particularly visible in the United Kingdom, the birthplace of wage-labour based capitalist agriculture. They have been exacerbated by the Covid-19 pandemic.

Ownership of land in the UK is highly concentrated. Less than one per cent of the UK's population, around 25,000 individuals and corporate entities, own around half of the land. Owners of the largest swathes of English land include members of the aristocracy and gentry which own approximately 30 per cent, corporations 18 per cent, oligarchs and city bankers 17 per cent. The public sector owns 8 per cent and homeowners 5 per cent.[14] In Scotland just 432 landlords own half of private land.[15] Meanwhile, Britain's farming sector accounts for around 9 per cent of national CO_2 emissions, with its livestock sector responsible for the majority of these. In terms of human calorie provision the UK's livestock sector is grossly inefficient. While sheep occupy four million hectares, roughly equivalent to all crop land, they account for around one per cent of calories in the UK diet.[16] One study estimates that if the UK's population consumed a plant-based diet, around 15 million hectares of land (currently used for livestock and feed crops) would be freed up.[17]

Working conditions on British farms have always been more precarious than in other economic sectors. Average farm workers' earnings are about two thirds of those in the rest of the economy. Trade union representation and collective bargaining has only a minimum impact on workers' wages, especially since the abolition of the Agricultural Wages Board in 2011. Because much of the sector is seasonal, farms rely upon highly flexible, often short-term migrant labour forces. Farming is the most dangerous place for workers, with a higher number of deaths at work than in other sectors.[18] In the spring of 2020, at the height of the Covid-19 pandemic, thousands of Eastern European migrant workers were employed in the UK's fruit and vegetable sector. They were housed in cramped temporary accommodation, often four to a room, in breach of the government's social distancing directions and at risk to their health.[19] Under the Covid-19 crisis, supermarket workers – already disproportionately suffering from zero-hours contracts compared to workers in other sectors of the economy – became 'key workers', risking exposure to the virus as they carried out their duties.

Digital technology – which could be used to lighten worker's loads – has been used by segments of capital to generate new forms of labour exploitation. Platforms like UberEats and Deliveroo offer multi-restaurant food-delivery services. These 'match and coordinate interactions between workers, restaurants and consumers via their digital eco-systems while retaining flat organisational structures'.[20] These platforms classify their workers as independent contractors rather than employees, thereby avoiding employer responsibilities such as health and safety provision, health insurance and pension contributions. Workers must purchase, and are responsible for, their own equipment (smartphones with data, bicycles/motorbikes/cars, delivery bags). Workers are paid predominantly by piece rate. Some platforms have 'core' workforces that are guaranteed a minimum number of jobs per shift, while non-core workers hustle for work from the platform by accepting jobs as quickly as possible. Workers are not paid as they wait for jobs or wait at restaurants to collect meals. As one Deliveroo driver put it:

> You log in to work at about 6pm or 6.30 p.m. for the evening rush, and you find that there are already 20 other people at the branch waiting for work. You often sit around waiting for an order. By 7.30 p.m. there might be 50 people logged in. All you end up getting is about £20 to £25 a day. I only work for Deliveroo. I used to do work for UberEats but they blocked me after a customer complained that I hadn't delivered something, when I had.[21]

Even prior to the Covid-19 crisis around four million children in the UK lived in households that struggled to afford to buy enough healthy food to meet official nutritional guidelines.[22] In the decade prior to the pandemic, food inequality as indicated by food bank use increased massively across the UK. The Trussell Trust, responsible for around 60 per cent of food banks, reported that three-day food parcel provision increased from 61,000 in 2010/11 to 1,583,000 in 2018/19.[23] Buying cheap, highly processed but unhealthy food often represents a survival strategy for these households. These combined pressures have accelerated problems of child and adulthood obesity derived from the consumption of empty calories contained in high-energy, low nutrient foods. As Jane Dixon puts it, working classes in the global north 'may now be portrayed as … over-consumers, but their overweight bodies are the result of insufficient incomes to consume fewer, less energy dense foods'.[24]

Patterns of domestic food preparation reproduce gender norms and inequality. Most of this care work is done by women, contributing to their double burden of paid work and unpaid domestic work. In the UK prior to Covid-19 approximately 9.1 million people (mostly women) undertook unpaid care work for relatives. Since the onset of the pandemic an additional 4.5 million people have become unpaid carers of which the vast majority are women.[25] The pandemic has also knocked out a large swathe of independent local restaurants.

COMMUNITY RESTAURANTS

What kinds of institutions, organizations and policies could be implemented in the UK to begin to overcome the unsustainability of the current food system – poverty wages in production, widespread mal- and under-nutrition, social inequalities of class, race, and gender, massive levels of unpaid care work and the disappearance of many local eateries? There is a simple answer that addresses all of these maladies: community restaurants, financed by progressive taxation, sourcing local produce, serving healthy plant-based dishes and providing a combination of free and cheap meals. Such restaurants should represent a core socialist demand, as part of the quest for democratization of social life.

The legitimacy of such a political demand could flow from Article 25 of the UN Declaration of Human Rights: 'everyone has the right to a standard of living adequate for the health and well-being of themselves and their families, including food …' As a socialist demand, the idea of decommodifying food through community restaurants could build upon, and then extrapolate from, prior and already existing moves in this direction.

During the Second World War, Community Feeding Centres, later renamed 'British Restaurants' at Churchill's behest (because he deemed the word community as socialistic), were established by the Ministry of Food. They helped people who had been bombed out of their houses, had run out of ration coupons, or were too poor to afford to buy food. By 1943 over 2,000 such restaurants were serving around 600,000 meals a day for today's equivalent of £1.26. They were disbanded in 1947.[26]

Much more recently, the Sheffield Food Hall project was established in 2015, 'for the community, by the community', in response to rising food bank use under Tory government imposed austerity. It intercepts and uses food waste from local traders to produce food on a 'pay what you can' basis.[27] The project also contributed to establishing the National Food Service in 2018, which by early 2020 had 13 branches across the UK. The NFS is rooted in solidaristic conceptions of food equity:

> Imagine a social eating space in every street and high-rise made by people from all backgrounds, created in common. Places free at the point of entry, use and delivery. Social equality integrated into the very fabric of urban life and with people able to live happily in their city and community. Around the dinner table barriers are broken down and real change is made, these spaces should be at the heart of every city.[28]

NFS restaurants' ability to generate food equity through decommodification in the UK is strictly limited, however, as they are run by unpaid volunteers and rely on food provided by local traders, such as supermarkets off-loading surplus food. It was significant, therefore, that the idea of the NFS was adopted by Jeremy Corbyn's Labour Party, as part of its Green New Deal agenda prior to the 2019 general election campaign. Although Labour lost that election, and has since shifted away from explicit socialist rhetoric and policies under Keir Starmer, the issue of food equity has not disappeared. In fact, the Covid crisis is keeping food poverty and equity in the public eye.[29]

A campaign for community restaurants providing decommodified food would combine demands for centralized funding with decentralized management. Local councils could be funded by central government to buy up closed restaurants, pubs, and other vacant retail properties for conversion into community restaurants. The funds for such a venture could be raised through progressive taxation. If the UK Treasury were to tax UK-based wealth at the same rate as income, it could raise up to £174 billion a year.[30] One study, based on assumptions of a 48 per cent participation rate for seven meals a week averaged across the population, estimates:

> This option would have a total [annual] cost of around £21.2bn, with values to households ranging from £45/week in the lowest deciles to £1.63/week in the highest deciles. Our cursory distributional analysis assumes lower take up rates in higher deciles, with 5 per cent of those in the highest decile only using the service for 0.5 meals/week, while those in the lowest deciles would use 14 meals/week.[31]

Such restaurants could represent regenerative hubs for communities battered by austerity, poverty, and rampant individualism. They could start by providing a set number of free meals to community members, to be increased over time. Electronic meal coupons would be allocated to families and individuals on a 'use-it-or-lose-it' basis, to avoid creating parallel coupon markets. Diners could pre-order electronically to facilitate preparation, and once established, demand could be predicted in order to prepare sufficient food and minimize waste. Subsidies would ensure that, in addition to free meals, such restaurants could produce and sell cheaper food than local junk food outlets, contributing further to a healthy dietary shift. Like other state provisions, such as the National Health Service, there would be no obligation to dine at these restaurants, and people who want to eat at fast-food chains could do so. What would change would be that the economic pressure to eat cheap, health-damaging food, would be reduced.

Community restaurants could be locally run, with neighbourhood-wide elected management teams coordinating supply with regional farms and alternatives-to-meat producers. Staff would be employed by local councils. Communities' different dietary preferences (vegan, vegetarian, diverse world cuisines) could be catered to through participatory planning. For decommodified food to be readily available to working-class communities, corresponding delivery networks would have to be established. While already-existing networks such as Deliveroo and UberEats are profit-orientated, part of the demand for community restaurants would be their regulation, or the establishment of parallel community-orientated delivery networks. As Callum Cant, a former Deliveroo rider argues, 'a platform-based worker-run "meals on wheels" service could begin to provide the needs of an ageing population and expand the support available to those with additional temporary or permanent care needs'.[32]

State funds could enable the establishment of large-scale production units of alternatives-to-meat to supply community restaurants with cheap high quality ingredients. The government should legislate that wages in agriculture should be living wages. Agrarian reform and the establishment of increasingly publicly owned and run agriculture must be part of the project of decommodifying food. Community owned and run farms, supported by research and development extension services, could coordinate production and provision with community restaurants. Following the UK's exit from the EU and the ending of the common agricultural policy, farms could receive replacement subsidies to produce specific crops – seasonal food crops under open skies and counter-seasonal and non-native crops in greenhouses. A new subsidy regime that prioritises human food over animal feed crops would shift market signals, pushing up the price of meat while reducing the price of plant-based food, further encouraging a healthy dietary shift.

Capital's ability to exploit workers rests, in part, upon the latter's dependence upon the market for their daily reproduction. Market dependence operates through the continued and increased commodification of social life. The struggle for socialism is, simultaneously, the struggle for workers' power in production and collective democratic control over resource allocation across society. Decommodifying food through community restaurants, subsidized initially by progressive taxation, should be a core socialist demand in the current context of pandemic, environmental breakdown, and intense social inequalities. Such a demand could act to integrate socialist, gender, racial, and environmental justice movements. It would have the strength of raising a concrete demand that opens political doors from socialist to other, potentially allied, movements. Through this demand – free and affordable good food for all – it facilitates a broader, systemic critique of capitalism.

The global food system is a pillar of capitalism's structural domination of labour. Not only does it incorporate capitalist social relations of subordination and exploitation, but it also heightens these relations in the wider economy through the mass production and provision of food as a cheap wage good. The reduction of food to an exchange-value, orientated to keeping down wages rather than serving as a foundation for human freedom, underpins many of the maladies associated with the food system. Its contributions to climate change, obesity, hunger, and malnutrition, its reliance upon unpaid care work, underpaid agricultural, delivery and preparation work, and its exacerbation of gender and race inequalities, are all indications of its failure to facilitate genuine human development.

NOTES

A shorter version of this article was published in *Le Monde Diplomatique*, 12 May 2020.

1 Damian Carrington, 'Global food system is broken, say world's science academies', *The Guardian*, 28 November 2018.

2 Covid-19 tracker: latest impact on food, foodfoundation.org.uk.
3 W. Willett, J. Rockström, B. Loken, M. Springmann, T. Lang, S. Vermeulen, T. Garnett, D. Tilman, F. DeClerck, A. Wood, M. Jonell, 'Food in the Anthropocene: the EAT–Lancet Commission on healthy diets from sustainable food systems,' *The Lancet* 393, 2 Feb 2019, pp. 447-92; Greenpeace, 'Manifesto for a Green Recovery', 4 June 2020, available at: www.greenpeace.org.uk.
4 Sidney Mintz, *Sweetness and Power: The Place of Sugar in Modern History*, New York: Penguin, 1986.
5 Philip McMichael, 'A food regime genealogy,' *The Journal of Peasant Studies* 36(1), 2009, pp. 139-69.
6 Gosta Esping-Andersen, *The Three Worlds of Welfare Capitalism*, Princeton: Princeton University Press, 1990, p. 37.
7 Jennifer L Wilkins, 'Eating right here: Moving from consumer to food citizen', *Agriculture and human values* 22(3), 2005, pp. 269-73.
8 Karl Polanyi, *The Great Transformation: The Political and Economic Origins of Our Times*, Boston: Beacon Press, 2001, pp. 146-7
9 Ellen Wood, *The Origin of Capitalism: A Longer View*, London: Verso, 2002; Eric Williams, *Capitalism and Slavery*, Chapel Hill: UNC Press, 2014; Harriet Friedmann, 'The political economy of food: a global crisis', *New Left Review* 197, 1993, pp. 29-57.
10 Jennifer Clapp, Peter Newell, and Zoe W. Brent, 'The global political economy of climate change, agriculture and food systems', *The Journal of Peasant Studies* 45(1), 2018, pp. 80-88.
11 Food and Land Use Commission, *Growing Better Report 2019,* p. 54, available at: www.foodandlandusecoalition.org.
12 Peter Rossman, 'Food workers' rights as a path to a low carbon agriculture', in N. Räthzel and D. Uzzell, eds, *Trade Unions in the Green Economy,* Abingdon: Routledge, 2012, p. 61.
13 Tim Lang and Michael Heasman, *Food Wars: The Global Battle for Mouths, Minds and Markets*, Abingdon: Routledge, 2015, p. 279.
14 Guy Shrubsole, *Who Owns England? How We Lost Our Green and Pleasant Land, and How To Take It Back*, London: HarperCollins UK, 2019.
15 Torcuil Crichton, 'Scottish land owners accused of being country's greediest benefit claimants over £40m tax avoidance schemes', *The Daily Record,* 12 July 2013.
16 George Monbiot, 'The Meat of the Matter', www.monbiot.com, 6 October 2017; and George Monbiot et al, *Land for the Many,* Labour Party, 2019.
17 Simon Fairlie, 'Can Britain Feed Itself?' *The Land Magazine*, Issue 7, Summer 2009.
18 Charlie Clutterbuck, *Bittersweet Brexit: The Future of Food, Farming, Land and Labour,* Chicago: University of Chicago Press, 2017.
19 Jokubas Salyga, 'Why Migrant Farm Workers Are Living Four to a Caravan in a Time of Social Distancing' *Jacobin*, 5 May 2020.
20 Alex Veen, Tom Barratt, and Caleb Goods, 'Platform-capital's 'app-etite' for control: A labour process analysis of food-delivery work in Australia', *Work, Employment and Society*, 2019; Jamie Woodcock, 'The algorithmic Panopticon

at Deliveroo: Measurement, precarity, and the illusion of control', *Ephemera: Theory, Politics, Organization*, forthcoming.

21 Patrick Collinson, 'How do Deliveroo and Uber workers cope with precarious pay?' *The Guardian,* 20 October 2018.

22 Patrick Butler, 'Four million UK children too poor to have a healthy diet, study finds'. *The Guardian*, 5 September 2018.

23 Filip Sosenko, Mandy Littlewood, Glen Bramley, Suzanne Fitzpatrick, Janice Blenkinsopp, and Jenny Wood, 'State of Hunger: A study of poverty and food insecurity in the UK', 2019, p. 9.

24 Jane Dixon, 'From the imperial to the empty calorie: how nutrition relations underpin food regime transitions', *Agriculture and Human Values* 26(4), 2009, p. 326.

25 Amelia Hill, 'Coronavirus: 4.5m people in UK forced to become unpaid carers', *The Guardian*, 19 June 2020.

26 Angus Calder, *The People's War: Britain 1939-1945*, London: Jonathan Cape, 1969.

27 Alexandra Genova, 'It's Falling to Community Food Groups to Feed the Country During the Covid-19 Crisis', *Novara Media*, 19 April 2020.

28 The National Food Service, www.nationalfoodservice.uk

29 As I write, Prime Minister Johnson has just given in to popular demands to maintain a £120 million 'Covid summer food fund' providing free school meals for the poorest families over the summer holidays. Whilst a victory for campaigners the funds are mean – equating to just £15 per week, per child. See Andrew Woodcock, 'Boris Johnson to provide free school meal vouchers in major U-turn after Marcus Rashford campaign', *Independent*, 16 June 2020.

30 Larry Elliot, 'Wealth tax rise could raise £174bn to tackle Covid-19, expert says', *The Guardian,* 22 April 2020.

31 Jonathan Portes, Howard Reed and Andrew Percy, 'Social prosperity for the future: A proposal for Universal Basic Services', London. Institute for Global Prosperity, 2017, p. 45.

32 Callum Cant, *Riding for Deliveroo: Resistance in the New Economy*, Cambridge: Wiley, 2019, p. 153.

START EARLY, STAY LATE: PLANNING FOR CARE IN OLD AGE

PAT ARMSTRONG AND HUGH ARMSTRONG

Covid-19 has exposed too many weaknesses in the neoliberal capitalism system to count, especially when it comes to the most vulnerable. In the words of the World Health Organization's Regional Director for Europe, 'this pandemic has shone a spotlight on the overlooked and undervalued corners of our society'.[1] He was speaking of long-term care facilities, where the weaknesses have been particularly obvious. The infection and death rates have been depressingly high in places that provide primarily for older people who need 24-hour care. While there is no question that illness and age make this population vulnerable to infections, the extraordinary variation in proportion of Covid-19 deaths occurring in these homes[2] tells us that much more than age and illness is at work. For ten years our international, interdisciplinary research team has been documenting the profound weaknesses in nursing home care within Canada, Germany, Norway, Sweden, the UK, and the US.[3] Many of the current deficits in resident care can be attributed to various forms of privatization at the centre of neoliberalism.[4] Especially in Canada, the UK, and the US, nursing homes that are heavily funded by the public purse have been handed over to corporations, providing them with guaranteed pay and, in Canada at least, guaranteed full houses.

The lines between for-profit and not have become increasingly blurred by various neoliberal strategies. One of these involves non-profit and state-owned homes contracting out services to for-profit firms as – in denial of the literature on the determinants of health – services such as food, housekeeping, and laundry have been defined out of care and dismissed as ancillary. This contracting out has not only undermined teamwork, but has also resulted in poor food, inadequate cleaning, and limited laundry – all of which threaten health. At the same time, fewer and fewer spaces are available in these homes with government funding. The result is twofold. All those who manage to get into these homes have high care needs, and those who cannot are either forced into the for-profit sector or rely more on unpaid care, most of which is provided by women. For too many, neither of these is an option.

Another strategy blurring the lines is the promotion of for-profit managerial strategies within the non-profit and public nursing homes that remain. This means the lowest possible staffing levels, the shifting of as much work as possible to those with the least formal training, limiting workers' autonomy, pay, hours, and benefits, and relying on a labour force already made vulnerable by gender, racialization, and immigration status. Canada offers a case in point: over a third of those working as nurse aides, orderlies and patient service associates are immigrants, among whom some three in ten are Black, and another three in ten are Filipino.[5] Indeed, the various forms of privatization build on and reinforce existing divisions along gender, race, class, and other lines of inequities across high-income countries. A 2019 OECD report documents how this highly gendered care work that increasingly relies on immigrant labour is characterized by low pay, precarious employment, and exposure to a wide range of risks.[6] There has also been a privatization of costs. Reductions in state funding, combined with the need to squeeze out profits, mean more costs are shifted to residents, most of whom are women, and to their relatives. This is particularly obvious when families privately pay even more precarious women to help fill the resulting gaps in care,[7] or when families themselves provide basic care in the nursing home. Barely enough of everything, including supplies and safety equipment, were provided.

Barely enough pre-pandemic proved simply *not enough* during the pandemic – which exposed the disastrous consequences of all these developments. Workers moving from home to home in their struggle to get enough pay carried the virus with them. Low staffing levels, especially with family members and private companions no longer available to fill gaps, created such a crisis that the Canadian provinces of Ontario and Quebec had to call in the military to provide care. The military took the unprecedented step of reporting publicly on the inadequate nursing care, incorrect documentation, and on poor and unavailable food along with a lack of supplies, equipment, laundry, and cleaning.[8]

WILL DIGITAL TECHNOLOGY HELP?

The revelations of terrible conditions in many care homes are not new. There have been two major responses to such exposure in the past. One of them is the addition of more regulations, especially after scandals publicized in the media.[9] The scandals were most common in the countries with the highest proportion of for-profit homes. Although Sweden and Norway have few such homes and mainly responded to scandals within them by cancelling contracts, Canada, the UK, and the US, where there are many corporate homes, responded by adding regulations. Some of these were necessary but for the most part these regulations put the onus on the workers, paying little attention to working conditions and virtually none to home ownership or other structural issues.[10]

The other commonly proposed means of addressing poor care is the adoption of new technology in nursing homes – especially digital technologies as a subset of technology more generally, which can be thought of as 'the way we do things around here'. The most common direct care technology we have seen in place is alarm systems and movement detection devices. Although they can indicate a resident has a need for care, they can also be used to reduce the time workers need to spend in a resident's room, thus reducing resident's human contact. In our experience, the alarms are constantly going off, creating annoying noises while ruining any notion of these places as homes. And they can be a form of control over workers. With some of these technologies, the worker must turn the alarm off manually and the system automatically records how long it took for the worker to respond. Since the measure of the lack of a quick response ignores all the other tasks workers have to fulfill, workers learn work-arounds that allow them to trick the system.

Information technology is the most widely used technology in health services. As we have previously explained,[11] there are four basic kinds of information technology in the sector. One sort is the data on resources such as numbers of hospital beds, employees and patients. A second form produces and uses data on how work should be done: the protocols, guidelines, task definitions, and care pathways. A third kind measures and uses data to determine how many employees work for how long, at what speeds, and with whom. Finally, there are the technologies that record the consequences of healthcare management and practices; these include the data on such items as resident falls and outcomes.

All these forms are presented as science-based and objective while hiding the critical assumptions, purposes, and values embedded within them. The model is a medical one, resulting in a clinical focus that fails to document appropriately, and thus provide for, the social care that is so central to health in these places. What counts is what can be counted, and care defined as a relationship is not possible to capture with numbers. Presented as being evidence-based and thus about 'best practices', the implicit intent is to standardize care in ways that make it difficult either to take individual resident characteristics into account or to allow care workers to make choices based on their knowledge.

The information is designed to reduce costs and time as well to increase control over the work and the worker, just as Braverman showed for the manufacturing sector.[12] When information technologies were being introduced into health care, we found nurses who were initially enthusiastic about how new patient classification systems could document their skills and overwork, leading to more staff.[13] However, when the numbers showed such overwork, there was a reclassification of the data and the numbers were changed to show the reverse. Cleaners were less enthusiastic from the start, arguing that the detailed recording of every aspect of a room ignored the variability not only across the rooms but also those created by human behaviour. 'For instance, there is a long-term care patient who has a bed that would be gross, let's put it that way'. 'Sometimes there are accidents … some people pee down on the floor … they throw food out on the floor or whatever. I have to go back to clean the floor. This time is not counted'.[14]

Providing the data that ultimately result in care plans is usually done by the staff who undertake most of the direct care but who have the least formal qualifications. They report the numbers to the registered nursing staff who fill in the final forms. Compiling the data for later insertion into the forms takes time away from care: this was symbolized for us when we saw staff sitting at a dinner table tapping on the tablet recording how much a resident was eating while also trying to help that person eat. Staff often resist, both because they have no time and because they resent the control, by ticking off whatever will meet the care plan. Meanwhile this form of technology reinforces hierarchy and provokes resentment that undermines collaborative teamwork and decision-making. Digital information is also presented as the basis for funding and as a means of ensuring top-down accountability. Yet, as British Columbia's designated advocate for seniors suggests, the numbers provided by management are not verified.[15] Some are also kept unavailable because of the right to keep business secrets.[16] Moreover, the focus is on outcome measures, rather than also on structural and process ones, making democratic accountability limited at best.[17]

At the same time, it is the worker who provides the information that provides the basis for this control. A Canadian Nurse Practitioner's description of one common information system now used in care homes tells it all:

> [I]t's weird. It almost is robotic, mechanical. Yeah, that's really how I want to describe it. It's robotic mechanical nursing care. If this happens

> then you do this. If this happens then you do this. The computer is thinking for you and the humanity is lost in it … [T]he thing is people are feeling incapacitated to make their own clinical judgments without having the 'I don't know everything about it but the indicator came up'. You shouldn't need to have the computer tell you what the problems are with your person. It just seems ridiculous to me because you're the one telling the computer so then the computer can then tell you.[18]

Indeed, some new technology designed to address staff shortages actually deploys robots which are designed to 'fulfil tasks such as helping an elderly person up after a fall and raising the alarm, delivering food to an older person at mealtimes, and even ensuring they take crucial medication at the correct time'.[19] While such robots are not yet in widespread use in the countries we studied, small robotic toys are now common. What is already clear is that when robots are designed to work autonomously, they can pose a considerable risk when they fail. Think about how often our technology does not work or destroys our work. We have visions of robots putting diapers on our head and then telling us it is our fault.

More fundamentally, the adoption of robotic technologies that involve replacing workers with machines denies what is central to human relationships. Robots cannot be empathetic, have emotions, or make moral decisions.[20] Think of ensuring medications are swallowed rather than stored at the back of the mouth. Think of the fear when you fall and you only have a machine for comfort. Think of the missing conversation that is part of making the meal enjoyable, not to mention the importance of convincing people to eat. While the new communications technologies in nursing homes which assumed increasing attention during this pandemic have helped in linking isolated residents with the families prohibited from entering the nursing homes, they cannot replace a hug. Moreover, residents often require assistance to operate the devices, and staff have little time to spare to provide such help. Meanwhile, Canadian media have been inundated by families complaining about poor communications from management.

Our critique of digital technologies grows out of the feminist understanding of care as a relationship that involves empathy, human contact, emotional connection, and response to individuals, as well as attention to power inequities. For care workers, this means having the appropriate skills, enough time, and sufficient autonomy to support the relationship. And it means having the other working conditions and protections that allow for supportive care relationships, including culturally sensitive practices.

DARING TO DREAM: SOCIALIST PLANNING FOR ELDERCARE

'In most commentaries on the elderly, it has usually been assumed that the types of problem associated with old age can be easily resolved within the framework of capitalist society.'[21] And, we would add, it is often assumed both that the problems are mainly biological and that they begin after age sixty-five. To dare to dream about care in old age means thinking about an alternative framework.

Planning for care in old age must be about planning for socialism. Socialist approaches have often been criticized for their uniformity, for singular approaches that assume equity means sameness and that choice is to be rejected because it is necessarily about the right to buy. Instead of starting with a model that sets out one right way, we start with a set of principles that allow for diversity and for choice based on the equitable opportunity to follow different strategies. Indeed, this is our first principle.

Principle 1: There is no single right way to provide care for the older population. There is no perfect model, no blueprint for care that responds to both collective and individual needs. Instead we have to start designing care through democratic processes that take contexts and populations into account. We have no reason to assume that what works well for an Indigenous community on Hudson Bay will work well in the centre of Toronto, or what works well in various parts of Toronto would work well in London, England.

In developing and organizing these various forms, decision-making must be open and accessible. Although there is no single, perfect model, we can set out standards for democratic decision-making in establishing and operating care for older people; standards that ensure that all voices are heard and that these voices have an impact on a continuing basis. Providing people with the means to participate in meaningful decisions about small and large issues is critical not only to democracy but also to health.

Principle 2: To equitably participate in determining forms, we have to ensure equitable conditions throughout life. Most of the ingredients – often called the determinants of health – are familiar. Equitable participation means providing parents with the conditions that make having children a safe and supported option. It means universal, accessible, equitable childcare and education at all levels. It means full employment in meaningful work accessible to those with a range of capacities, without compulsory retirement. It means food security and decent housing for all. And it means income security for those old and the young. All of this would be designed to prevent systemic racism, and harassment of any kind while supporting social engagement.

Equitable participation also means ensuring universal access to appropriate, culturally sensitive, comprehensive health services. Health care is only one component in a healthy life but an essential one that needs to be transformed both in how healthcare workers are prepared and in how care is organized. It also means recognizing that the conditions of work are the conditions of care, that care is skilled work, and that care is a relationship.

These conditions are necessary elements in thinking about alternatives for care in old age because food, shelter, jobs and joy are essential to health and to the possibility of growing old well. They are also essential to balancing the pressures on each generation, allowing for a more equitable distribution of possibilities and pressures. Moving to greater equity in these material terms can help us move towards greater support for care in old age and for those who are old. It may help those who are now young think about becoming older adults.

Principle 3: We have to plan for and create supportive communities, in various forms. This can mean preventing box stores and requiring every neighbourhood to have such services as a bank, a pharmacy, a grocery store, a pub, a library, a coffee shop, a shared workspace, a theatre, and a hair salon. Within communities, we need to construct flexible housing that can accommodate households of different sizes and different approaches to living. This would provide support for congregate living as well as for individual households in various forms. This must include desegregation in housing and services, mixing ages, capacities and interests, along the lines of what has been termed 'universal design':

> Universal Design is the design and composition of an environment so that it can be accessed, understood and used to the greatest extent possible by all people, regardless of their age, size or disability. This includes public places in the built environment such as buildings, streets or spaces that the public have access to; products and services provided in those places; and systems that are available including information and communications technology.[22]

This means thinking through all aspects of design from the shape of door handles and lighting to clearing sidewalks and organizing transit, doing so in ways that involve the community. Within households, we need to provide supports for those who need them. This would include housekeeping, laundry, and food preparation assistance, as well as some clinical and social support. In doing so, we need to recognize that this is skilled work which requires decent pay and conditions and that the support must be structured to prevent reliance on unpaid work, especially the unpaid work of women.

APPLYING SOCIALIST PRINCIPLES TO NURSING HOMES

Care in old age means applying all these principles within nursing homes. Even with all these other measures, there will be people who need 24-hour nursing and other care that can be most effectively and equitably provided in congregate spaces. Indeed, this will be a choice for a significant number if care homes are an attractive, supportive option. To get there, we need to collectively provide multiple options to accommodate different populations, locations, and ways of living, as well as different social and clinical needs.

In fact, the determinants of health are at least as important within nursing homes as they are outside it. Food does not simply provide nutrition; it provides an opportunity for pleasure and social connections if it is provided in ways that tempt and respond to individual preferences in both food and companions. Clothes are integral to identity, which also means that laundry services and physical structures need to allow for clothing options. Supports for challenging activities and for both self-care and social connections are also critical to health. This means making joy as important a goal as safety; it means focusing on putting life into years rather than simply years into life. It also means making the entire range of workers within a nursing home part of the healthcare team.

The structure and organization of nursing homes should be democratically determined, in terms of both developing homes and operating them on a daily basis. This means ensuring that decision-making is open and accessible. Although there is no single, perfect model, we can set out democratic standards for care for older people and for those providing direct care for them, including family members and volunteers. These must be standards that ensure that all voices are heard and that they have impact on a continuing basis. This means that residents, workers, families, volunteers, and community organizations should have effective means for shaping care. The funders and managers of long-term care must be made accountable to those receiving and providing care. Collective and individual voices should play a continuing part in monitoring care, supported by surprise inspections that lead to education on improvements, backed up by effective enforcement mechanisms. All data on care should be publicly available and readily understandable, facilitating participation in meaningful, democratic decision-making.

Nursing homes must be part of a universal healthcare system, with enough spaces to make this care accessible to all those who need and want this care. Class would not influence admission, nor would gender, sexual orientation, race, or culture. Nursing homes require staff educated to care for the older population and staff provided with the time and right to provide the care they are educated to provide. This care education would no longer focus primarily on clinical needs but rather include the importance of social care and care as a relationship. Understanding care as a relationship means ensuring continuity in staff by providing the opportunity for full-time employment in the same home with decent pay and benefits, sufficient supplies and safety protections including protection from racism and sexual harassment as well as other forms of violence, and collective representation through unions. Staff would also have sufficient autonomy to apply their skills and the support for teamwork. Paid staff need enough time to provide for all resident needs without having to rely on the unpaid work of mainly female relatives and volunteers. There would still be space for participation of relatives and volunteers, but it would be an option rather than an obligation to fill the gaps in care that now exist.

The physical environment also needs to be transformed. This begins by locating nursing homes where people live and work now, so that friends and relatives can visit and workers can easily travel to their workplaces. The design would not only attend to the components central to universal design but would also build for flexibility. Rooms could be converted from single to double to congregate, which would allow individual residents options while also allowing for reorganization in the case of pandemics. Similarly, there would be multiple dining options, large closets to allow for varied clothes and kitchens as well as laundry rooms in every section that would support resident self-care. These sections would house no more than a dozen or so people within an overall structure that could accommodate many more. There would be direct access to the outside in protected spaces. Staff would have their own spaces for changing their clothes, eating, relaxing, and grieving.

There would be multiple services available within the nursing homes. This would not only include those services such as dentists, hairdressers, and gyms but also other services such as shops and pubs. We were in a nursing home in Norway, with a church and a small shopping mall just across the square, which was itself physically part of a huge complex that held the town swimming pool, the theatre, a cafeteria, a spa, a rock-climbing wall, and a day care centre. Each resident had their own room and bathroom, as well as direct access to the outdoors from their room through patio doors. Each room had a 'pantry', a small kitchen that allowed for some food and beverage preparation. At the same time, the nursing home section could be isolated from the rest if required. Integrating services in one building that brings the community in is one way of moving towards desegregation. Another is to invite other kinds of residents into the facility. For example, in a Swedish home the nursing home is combined with a student residence in ways that support mixing the generations.

Death is part of living in a nursing home. We need to plan for death in culturally sensitive and respectful ways, providing staff and families with the space and time to support the dying and to grieve. It also means providing for medically assisted dignified death and for palliative care alternatives.

Of course, all of this means no profit in care.

The pandemic has made it obvious that we do need to transform care for the elderly. There well may be some progress in the immediate post-pandemic context. But fundamental transformation means creating a different system from birth. Socializing health services can help demonstrate the benefits of collectively providing for care but we also need to develop strategies to achieve a democratic socialist transition that will allow for the kinds of democratic planning needed to overcome class, gender and racial inequalities, and not least to create the intergenerational equity that is the fundamental requirement for appropriate care in old age.

NOTES

1 H.H.P. Kluge, 'Statement-Invest in the overlooked and unsung: Build sustainable people-centred long-term care in the wake of COVID-19', Geneva: World Health Organization, 2020, available at: www.euro.who.int.

2 Canadian Institutes for Health Information, 'Pandemic Experiences in the Long-Term care Sector. How Does Canada Compare with Other Countries?' Ottawa: CIHI, 2020, available at: www.cihi.ca.

3 Pat Armstrong and Ruth Lowndes, eds, *Creative Teamwork: Developing Rapid, Site-Switching Ethnography*. New York: Oxford University Press, 2018. Our project, 'Reimagining Long-Term Residential Care: An International Study of Promising Practices' (Pat Armstrong, Principal Investigator) received funding from the Social Sciences and Humanities Research Council of Canada under grant # 412-2010-1004.

4 Pat Armstrong and Hugh Armstrong, eds, *The Privatization of Care: The Case of Nursing Homes*, New York: Routledge, 2020.

5 Statistics Canada, 'Study: The contribution of immigrant and population groups designated as visible minorities to nurse aide, orderly and patient services associate occupations', *The Daily*, 22 June 2020, available at: www150.statcan.gc.ca.

6 Organization for Economic Cooperation and Development and the International Labour Organization, 'New Job Opportunities for an Aging Society', 2019, available at: www.oecd.org.

7 Tamara Daly, Pat Armstrong, and Ruth Lowndes, 'Liminality in Ontario's long-term care facilities: Private companions' care work in the space "betwixt and between"', *Competition & Change* 19(3), 2015, pp. 246–263.

8 4th Canadian Division Joint Task Force, Op Laser – Jtfc Observations in Ltcf Ontario Long Term Care Homes, 20 May 2020, available at: www.scribd.com/document/463110038/Op-Laser-Jtfc-Observations-in-Ltcf-Ontario-Long-Term-Care-Homes.

9 Liz Lloyd, Albert Banerjee, Charlene Harrington, Frode F. Jacobsen, and Marta Szebehely, '"It is a scandal!": Comparing the causes and consequences of nursing home media scandals in five countries', *International Journal of Sociology and Social Policy* 34(1/2), 2014, pp. 2-18.

10 Albert Banerjee and Pat Armstrong, 'Centring Care: Explaining Regulatory Tensions in Residential Care for Older Persons', *Studies in Political Economy* 95, 2015, pp. 7-28.

11 Pat Armstrong, Hugh Armstrong and Karen Messing, 'Gendering Work? Women and Technologies in Health Care', in Ellen Balka, Eileen Green and Flis Henwood, eds., *Gender, Health and Information Technology in Context*, Basingstoke UK: Palgrave Macmillan, 2009, pp. 122-37.

12 Harry Braverman, *Labor and Monopoly Capital: The Degradation of Work in the Twentieth Century*, New York: Monthly Review Press, 1974.

13 Jacqueline Choiniere, 'A Case Study. An examination of nurses and patient information technology', in Pat Armstrong, Jacqueline Choiniere and Elaine Day, eds, *Vital Signs. Nursing in Transition*, Toronto: Garamond Press, 1993, pp. 59-88.

14 Pat Armstrong, Hugh Armstrong, Jacqueline Choiniere, Eric Mykhalovskiy and Jerry P. White, 'The Promise and the Price', in Pat Armstrong et al., eds, *Medical Alert. New Work Organization in Health Care*, Toronto: Garamond Press, 1997, pp. 46-7.

15 BC Office of the Seniors Advocate, *A Billion Reasons to Care: A Funding Review of Contracted Long-Term care in BC,* Vancouver: Office of the Seniors' Advocate, 2020, available at: www.seniorsadvocatebc.ca.

16 Gudmund Ågotnes, Frode F. Jacobsen and Marta Szebehely, 'The Growth of the For-Profit Nursing Home Sector in Norway and Sweden: Driving Forces and Resistance', in Pat Armstrong and Hugh Armstrong, eds, *The Privatization of Care: The Case of Nursing Homes,* New York: Routledge, 2020, pp. 38-50.

17 Tamara Daly, 'Public Funds, Private Data: A Canadian Example', in Pat Armstrong and Hugh Armstrong, eds, *The Privatization of Care: The Case of Nursing Homes,* New York: Routledge, 2020, pp. 125-40.

18 Pat Armstrong and Tamara Daly, 'Introduction' in Pat Armstrong and Tamara Daly, eds, *Exercising Choice in Long-Term Care*, Ottawa: Canadian Centre for Policy Alternatives, 2017, p. 20.

19 UK Department of Business, Engineering and Industrial Strategy, UK Research and Innovation, 'Care robots could revolutionise UK care system and provide staff extra support', October 2019, available at: www.gov.uk.

20 Bernd Carsten, Bernd & Mark Coeckelbergh, 'Ethics of healthcare robotics: Towards responsible research and innovation', *Robotics and Autonomous Systems* 86, December 2016, pp. 152-16.

21 Chris Phillipson, *Capitalism and the Construction of Old Age*, London: Palgrave, 1982.

22 Disability Act 2005. Ireland. Quoted in Centre of Excellence for Universal Design, at universaldesign.ie/About-Us.

HEALTH CARE, TECHNOLOGY, AND SOCIALIZED MEDICINE

PRITHA CHANDRA AND PRATYUSH CHANDRA

'… consumption and the other pulmonary diseases of the workers are conditions necessary to the existence of capital.'
Karl Marx[1]

At the time of public health crises like the current Covid-19 pandemic, the metaphors of war are used to unite the public with the state, to construct a social consensus behind the state's actions. The heads of states throughout the globe pose as chieftains in this quixotic war against an enemy who no one understands. War rooms are set up to manage data, propaganda, public reactions, and to control supplies, while the foot soldiers – doctors, nurses, other medical and supporting staff toil to deal with the actual and potential carriers of the enemy, including themselves. Of course, along with them are the baton-wielding workers of the agencies of surveillance – the police, security guards, etc. who are made to assist drones and other AIs to manage the panic and the *surplus-ed* population (migrants, homeless and poor) on the streets.

A disease is not an epidemic or a pandemic unless it is recognized as such, and this recognition is only partially determined by its biology. Of course, the suddenness and extent of death, and the engendering of fear are its necessary aspects. However, the trajectory of its spread, the nature of public reaction, and the way it is interpreted are mainly determined by non-biological factors such as the physical environment, socio-economic relationships, political structures, social attitudes, and intellectual-cultural atmosphere. An American historian of medicine Charles Rosenberg, based on his reading of Albert Camus' *The Plague*, underlined the episodic nature of epidemics eliciting a spectacular response. He considered an epidemic to be a social phenomenon which unfolds in a *dramaturgic form*, with progressive revelations, engendering individual and collective crises, and then drifting toward closure.[2]

Unlike earlier experiences, with Covid-19 we see an emergence of the whole world as a stage where the drama unfolds. This is, of course, due to the technological shrinkage of time and space in our age – now, microbes take flight. But the spectacular similitude of crises and responses at this level demonstrates how social structures, ideologies, and social values have converged globally. The rhetoric of war and the institution of quarantine, where everyone is a warrior, a victim, and a suspect at the same time, have mobilized individuals and communities to act out rituals that affirm *bellum omnium contra omnes* (the war of all against all), the foundation of capitalism.

Today, agencies the world over are paying tribute to the medical warriors who are fighting at the frontlines of the war against Covid-19. Financial incentives and benefits (sometimes to be accorded posthumously) are announced for these soldiers, world leaders fill their speeches with plaudits for them, and local citizens applaud them with the rhythmic chimes of bells and claps. Sometime in the future, the war will be over. The warriors will be back at their old posts in a 'new normal' world. This 'new normal' to which we will return will be the 'normal' tenfold more severe in alienation and individualism. This is the world that we have prepared ourselves for in the last few months through corporeal and mental self-isolation, and by the technologically-secured globalized institution of quarantine.

Some voices today are celebrating the possibility of a return to state socialism and welfarism, but the stronger tendency is toward a congealment of a technologically sophisticated global-surveillance capitalism, overseen by the state, based on real and manufactured panic of self-obsessed alienated individuals and their competitive survivalism. This is, of course, not an atmosphere conducive for a strong public health system but, rather, for reckless private appropriation of health resources – which will be the ground for further corporatization of medicine and health industries. Even the benign endeavour to understand the behaviour of emerging viruses and search for vaccination against Covid-19 by researchers in microbiology and medicine are caught up in the trade wars characterizing the capitalist crisis today. This is part and parcel of the global health industry's 'growing centrality as arena of capitalist accumulation'.[3] Today's new technological innovations in medicine, the integration of information technology and new managerial techniques have corporatized the field of medicine into a 'Medical-Industrial Complex' with its specific forms of industrial conflicts.

While the immediate task of controlling the current pandemic determines the actions of states, medical institutions, and research laboratories, several critical microbiologists, virologists, and political economists have done well to ask the structural question about the metabolic and ecological rifts that have unleashed new dangers for humanity. By looking at how 'microbes thrive in [the] "undercurrents of opportunity" that arise through social and economic changes, changes in human behaviour, and catastrophic events such as war and famine',[4] they have shown how capital in its pursuit to accumulate has eroded species barriers, allowing viruses endemic to particular species to come into contact with humans and domestic animals, leading to antigenic drift and shift.

To quote Marx, 'all progress in capitalist agriculture is a progress in the art, not only of robbing the worker, but of robbing the soil'.[5] It is still this kind of robbery of nature that perpetuates ecological crises. But, for the ecological crisis to become a ground to rethink structural transformation, it is not enough to locate it in the wreckage that capitalism accumulates. It must be understood as constitutive to capitalist social relations, having an intimate connection to the robbery of labour. It is in this sense that the particularization of these crises in the form of pathogens and impending diseases becomes crucial. This helps us to understand the ecological rift as central to everyday life and struggle in capitalism, and also to imagine a transformatory class politics.

To understand the reality behind and beyond today's spectacular rituals of salutations for public hospital workers and those in so-called essential services as 'warriors', we need to pay heed to what Norman Bethune meant when he exhorted his medical colleagues to 'organize ourselves so that we can no longer be exploited as we are being exploited by our politicians'.[6] He too called upon them to engage in a collectivized attack:

> Medicine must be entirely reorganized and unified, welded into a great army of doctors, dentists, nurses, technicians and social service workers, to make a collectivized attack on disease and utilizing all the present scientific knowledge of its members to that end. Let us say to the people – not 'How much have you got?' – but, 'How best can we serve you?'[7]

DISEASE IN THE HISTORY OF CAPITALISM: REVIVING BETHUNE

Norman Bethune (1890–1939) was a Canadian surgeon, and a pioneer in the field of thoracic surgery. He was a Communist and an anti-fascist who steeled himself in the Spanish Civil War, fought tuberculosis not just as a doctor but as a patient too, and died in 1939 in the Chinese liberation movement against the Japanese, after getting infected while treating patients without the necessary medical equipment. Norman Bethune was a product of an era that saw the beginning of an intensified industrialization of medicine and medical practices. He made his medical practice a ground for critiquing capitalism and the political economy of modern medicine. Bethune's ideas gain new meanings in the light of the medical crisis that we face today. He understood that the development in medicine – of its theory and practice – is not about a linear progress in medical sciences and technology. Being embedded in the socio-economic formation, it is a result of social contradictions and also constitutive of them.

Diseases are part of the necessary conditions of capital's existence not only in the sense that they are necessary corollaries of capitalist accumulation but also because they prepare labour for its subsumption by capital, for its commodification. During the current age of pandemics, we suddenly realize that we are part of the same humanity, despite all kinds of exclusion that surround us and our lives. Instead of accepting this togetherness as a necessary characteristic of our *species existence*, and thus acting according to our nature, we struggle hard to shield ourselves against it – thrusting toward extreme self-alienation. Capitalism is founded on individualism and competition, leading to an unquenchable thirst for *private appropriation*, which is actually a shield that makes us appear exclusive, beyond the reach of other beings – humans or non-humans. But this shielding is possible only by evermore *socialization of production* (mass production, through human cooperation), which is the basis of technologically advanced and sophisticated commodity production. The continuous contradiction between social production and private appropriation, which is the defining contradiction of capitalism, creates frequent glitches in the form of overproduction, underconsumption, and overaccumulation, leading to full scale, severe economic crises. These crises in themselves constitute, as Norman Bethune puts it, 'a deadly disease', requiring 'systematic treatment', not palliative measures from 'our political quacks', which are like 'aspirin tablets for syphilitic headache'.[8]

History is witness to the role of the second plague pandemic – starting with Black Death of 1348 – in begetting early European capitalism by creating labour shortages leading to technological innovations and the development of the labour market and regulation. Over the centuries, this led to the industrialization of disease management that shaped the theory and practice of medicine and pharmacy. In the nineteenth century, when politically coherent challenges to capitalism began to emerge in the labour movement, thinking about the sociological aspects of diseases and their management became crucial to labour. The question of public health became a potent ground for political conflicts. The development of vaccines and medicines, their production and distribution, and the approach and regulation of medical practice were some of the major issues in this regard. Frequent recurrence of epidemics and pandemics, along with colonization and wars, and the emergence of strong anti-capitalist revolutionary movements in the twentieth century led to the emergence of radical approaches in every field of knowledge, including medicine. Norman Bethune was a product of this era.

According to Bethune, after the industrial transformations of the nineteenth century, private health ceases to exist, since maladies and maladjustments of one section of the population affect other sections as well. In this sense, all health is public health. It is in this regard that Bethune talks about the problems of medical economics – of millions being sick, in pain, and hundreds of thousands dying prematurely due to inaccessibility to adequate and timely medical care, while practicing medicine as a 'luxury trade'.[9] Because of its inseparability from and embeddedness in the social fabric, medicine in capitalist societies 'is a typical, loosely organized, basically individualistic industry in this "catch as catch can" capitalistic system, operating as a monopoly on a private profit basis'.[10] Consequently, the pecuniary logic ('fee-for-service') is instilled into the very work process of medical practice in capitalism, which Bethune found so morally disturbing.[11] This embeddedness in the capitalistic industrial processes explains the chief contradiction of medical practice. On the one hand, medical knowledge (and scientific knowledge) has become so enormous that individualistic medical practice has become an impossibility. On the other hand, this same fact leads to specialization, which, in the context of industrialization and commodification of medical education, is kept out of reach for the majority of medical aspirants.

The way medicine was organized as a discipline and practice affected the approaches to diseases too, thus raising important epistemological issues. Bethune was dissatisfied with the prevalent approaches to pulmonary tuberculosis because they took an attenuated viewpoint of the disease, focusing on nothing but the local pulmonary lesion. Curing this disease required a holistic approach toward the infected individual – as a product of his social and physical environment – and, with the *tubercle bacillus* as just another factor in the environment of man, causing bodily and behavioral changes. According to Bethune:

> Any scheme to cure this disease which does not consider man as a whole, as the resultant of environmental strain and stress, is bound to fail. Tuberculosis is not merely a disease of the lungs; it is a profound change of the entire body which occurs when man, regarded as an organism acting under the dictation of, and the product of, his environment, fails

> to circumnavigate or subjugate certain injurious forces acting on his body and mind. Let him persist in continuing in such an environment and he will die. Change these factors, both external and internal, readjust the scene, if not the stage, and he, in the majority of instances, will recover.[12]

It was this recognition of the mutual embeddedness of economics and pathology that defined Bethune's unconventional life and work as a surgeon, and transformed him into a revolutionary. The practice of *socialized medicine*, as he conceptualized it, was not simply a demand on the state and doctors, but was, rather, a dimension of transformatory politics translated in the field of health care.

BETHUNE'S CONCEPT OF SOCIALIZED MEDICINE

It was through a critical (self) inquiry into the theory and practice of medicine that Bethune developed his conception of socialized medicine. For Bethune, there is a continuous ideological class struggle going on within the field of medicine. On the one hand are those with allegiance to individualism – reactionaries represented in medicine by those who uphold private property and monopoly of health distribution. On the other hand, we have those who envisage and engage in cooperative efforts for the betterment of one and all. Changing the economic system that breeds ill health, ignorance, poverty and unemployment is thus the only guarantee for providing universal health protection. Bethune considered socialized medicine as a negation of this system in medicine.

This concept, however, cannot be reduced to medical reforms like health insurance schemes, which are essentially based on the commodification of medicine and the establishment of an entire industry around it. Bethune considered these reforms to be 'bastard forms of socialism produced by belated humanitarianism out of necessity'.[13] In fact, for him, philanthropy and charity have kept the outmoded and wasteful private practice in medicine alive. They must be abolished, since 'charity debases the donor and debauches the recipient'.[14] They rob the public of their right to health protection. If there is no private disease, there cannot be private health protection. Bethune called for the abolition of individual selling and purchasing of medical care. His conception of socialized medicine envisaged an overhauling of the foundation of bourgeois medicine by considering health protection a public property that must be supported by public funds. The administration of health services must be 'to each according to his needs'. It calls for a revolutionary transformation by calling for a bottom-up transformation of health care based on its 'democratic self-government by the health workers themselves'.[15]

Bethune's scathing attacks on those who defended private practice and opposed socialized medicine in the name of individualism, incentive, choice, and bureaucracy were accompanied by his call for redefining 'medical ethics – not as a code of professional etiquette between doctors, but as a code of fundamental morality and justice between medicine and the people'.[16] Medicine and public health care need a holistic approach toward diseases, taking patients to be products of their social and physical environments. Hence, more than 'leading physicians', health care requires 'far-sighted, socially imaginative' leaders and statesmen in medicine[17] who are not just looking for interesting cases but seek to provide a collectivized attack on diseases, for which an understanding of the relationship of medicine with the larger society, state, and economy is necessary. Socialized medicine is a collective practice of delivering socially comprehensive and lasting results, rather than providing private service to people who can afford it. It is a challenge to the subsumption of medical labour by capital and a reclaiming of knowledge by humanity at large.

COVID-19 AND THE CONTRADICTIONS OF THE PUBLIC HEALTH SYSTEM

Evidently, the Covid-19 pandemic exposed the fragility of the public health systems of even those countries that boasted of well-organized national health services and health care to all. The top-down public health bureaucracies were unable to handle community specific needs (of the more vulnerable sections of the societies, like the poor, the elderly, immigrants, and people with medical conditions). Even general administrative measures like quarantine, shelter-in-place and lockdown could not be intelligently utilized in many places because of the lack of basic emergency facilities to deal with public disease threats like Covid-19. This crisis revealed that public health systems are not really grounded in the everydayness of community lives; therefore, they are unable to deal with the dynamic public health needs and emergencies. As is clear from an age-wise breakdown of Covid-19 cases, fatality is immensely higher among the elderly. Since the richer nations are rapidly aging societies, the public health focus should have been on this segment of population, but for the logic of capital they constitute a section of superfluous population (except, obviously, the rich consumers among them). They, along with the majority poor and immigrants, are constituents of the relative surplus population which is necessary as a reserve pool of workers and to control the price of labour power, not despite but because of their dispensability.

A public health system, however progressive and democratic it may be, in the wider environment of capitalism, can do nothing more than to police larger market processes. It tends to become bureaucratic without any sensitivity towards the vulnerable of the society, as it is focused only on the administrative aspects of the delivery of medical goods and services. The commodity nature of these deliverables is taken for granted. Thus, a public health system can provide at most an assurance of a level-playing market where the supply meets the demand. It does not affect the structure of the supply side of health care in any drastic sense. The dominance of supply-side economics and the dogma of Say's law ('directed demands') in medicine means a focus on specialized individuated medical services and goods and on personal illnesses that are rare and/or acute, rather than the diseases which are chronic and widespread, requiring not just a strong infrastructure for primary health care, but an overhauling of the social environment based on the capitalist organization and control of health resources, production, and distribution.

It is true that 'the development of the welfare state and one of its main components, a universal and comprehensive government health program, is directly related to the strength of the working class and its political and economic instruments'. This can help us understand 'why some countries have national health insurance, others have national health services, and the U.S. [along with many other countries, mainly in the South] has neither'.[18] In other words, strong public health systems prevalent in some western countries were definitely achievements of the social democratic and labour movements' pressure in the age of embedded liberalism and state-driven economies. But they were also a proof of capital's pliability to mould itself according to the posed circumstances, and turn them into an opportunity to accumulate. A public health system integrates the health market, and provides 'the rich pools of public revenue' for medical industries.[19] Furthermore, a public health system subsidizes the price of labour power by taking away the burden of financing the health care of the present and future of the workforce from various industries. Therefore, such systems are invested in bolstering corporate control of medical services. In the age of neoliberalism, with strong austerity measures on the part of the states, public health systems have increasingly been sucked into the process of intensive and extensive financialization of various facets of social life, giving new leverage to the insurance industry and its merger with capitalist interests in the healthcare industries. Much of the primary and general health care, along with mass vaccination campaigns throughout the world, especially in the Global South, has been left to the NGOs, funded by international agencies of philanthro-capitalism.

THE CASE OF INDIA

The case of India is interesting with regard to the extent of marketization in the health sector. Government spending on health care in 2020 is a measly 1.6 per cent of GDP. It has a pathetic public health system, where primary care is left totally at the mercy of the unorganized sector of an eclectic market of quackery, registered and unregistered private medical practitioners of diverse traditions of medicine and placebo provision, along with the NGOs. Yet, health care is one of the fastest growing industries in India, which boasts of being a medical hub with a formidable infrastructure for medical tourism in place.[20] It has become a part of the burgeoning 'wellness industry' that has emerged in conjunction with the pseudoscientific commercial globalization of India's traditional medical practices of Ayurveda, the physio-spiritual techniques of yoga and tantric hedonism – corollaries of the rise of the Hindu right wing.

Countries like India did not even bother to prepare themselves for Covid-19, while the WHO and other medical institutions were repeatedly advising them to increase testing and prepare the health system while still under lockdown. The leadership locked themselves in and just exhorted the public to be self-reliant, fending for themselves and working from home. Health workers of public hospitals and sanitation workers among others were applauded and encouraged to sacrifice themselves. While the rituals of quarantine and curfew were observed with much fanfare, nothing was done in terms of consolidating the health services to face the pandemic. In these countries that rely on cheap labour and an immense relative surplus population at all skill-levels, there is an absence of any meaningful system for public health. This is a reflection of the Malthusian commonsense immanent in capitalist state policies in labour surplus economies. The duality in markets in general and health markets in particular is reinforced by the state measures in these economies. Insofar as they could boast of an overall lower mortality rate among Covid-19 patients in comparison to the West, the main reason for this is their being countries of youth – the median age of these countries is lower. However, this is an indication of the deeper malaise of lower life expectancy. In countries that harbour this amount of 'superfluous population', Malthusianism is not an outmoded ideology – it becomes a strategy to sustain capitalist accumulation.[21]

Thus, the crisis of the various public health systems evident in the wake of the Covid-19 pandemic is grounded in the overall dynamics of capitalist production and social relations. The genesis of these systems lies in the general realization of the public character of the diseases and health. But capital does not waste any opportunity to instrumentalize the institutions that emerge out of the struggles of the people for a system of health care based on equity and universality. This only re-substantiates the basic fact that capital transforms every crisis to an opportunity. Any piecemeal reform within capitalism is bound to be subsumed in capitalist designs. It does not mean that nothing is achieved through these reforms – it just means that they are not enough to transcend capital relations. Hence, the root of the public health crisis today must be traced to the processes of the commodification of health and the industrialization of health care.

THE QUESTION OF HEALTH WORK

The current pandemic has brought out the class nature of the distribution of health care in capitalism and how this aspect of distribution is institutionalized in the very organization of the public health system. However, this is linked with the mode of production in healthcare industries, not only in the sense that it is overall controlled by the network of corporate and private capital. This control goes deeper into the internal structuring of the health industries. In fact, the way healthcare work has been militarized not just rhetorically but also actually through various legal and organizational mechanisms in different countries during this pandemic – and the way doctors, nurses, other health and sanitation workers have acted and reacted – is indicative of what has happened to the healthcare industries in recent decades.

Bethune's conceptualization of medical practice grasped the essential processes by which it is subsumed in capitalism. Commercialization reduced health (or medical labour) to a commodity, which had a use value, but only as the material bearer of exchange value or price. For the consumer, who is a patient and his family members, it serves as a use value; but for the provider, a medical practitioner, his art and knowledge are reduced to fees. In Bethune's time, however, health care was still 'a loosely organized, basically individualistic industry', as Bethune himself put. It was still a set-up organized around the private contract between a doctor and his patient – the process of medical labour was only formally subsumed by capital, and many times not even that. But with the growth and sophistication of medical knowledge and practice, cooperation and coordination between medical researchers and practitioners became imperative or inevitable.

The capitalist industrialization of medicine heightens commercialization by organizing health care in such a manner that it integrates the industrial organization and technology of mass production in the field of medicine. Thus, it reconstitutes the labour processes of health workers accordingly, along the lines of what Marx termed as 'the real subsumption of labour by capital', so their labour becomes more and more geared towards the extraction of surplus value. This transformation drastically affects the very epistemological approach in medicine and health care – towards diseases and patients, and towards the nature of medical research too, which must now be directed towards the purpose of sustaining the commercial and industrial efficacies of health care. This leads to capital accumulation in the health-related industries. Over the years, these processes of commercialization and industrialization have led to the growth in health-related industries – hospital and pharmaceutical industries, medical technology, laboratories, blood and organ banks, medical insurance etc. As Vicente Navarro has put it: 'Petty cottage medicine has been transformed into capitalist or corporate medicine in the same way that the dynamics of capitalism led to the change from petty commodity production to capitalist manufacture.'[22] The crisis of various national public health systems and the way states, industries and health workers have responded should be understood in the light of the dynamism of these processes.

When labour movements in different countries were forcing governments to enact reforms leading to the universalization of state-funded health care, medical professionals reacted negatively as they saw in these reforms a mortal threat to their autonomy.[23] They were reactionaries, as Bethune called them, trying to protect their individualistic and monopolistic control over medical knowledge and practice. To some extent the national lobbies of 'leading doctors' could delay or get their interests incorporated in the health policies. However, the real threat to health professionals came from the technological and managerial innovations recomposing every profession and industry. This process of re-composition tremendously intensified in the coming decades, especially since the 1960s with the crisis of Keynesianism and the rise of information technology. Most of the time the application of these innovations in medicine and health provision was initiated with the active participation of health professionals, as they tended to help in controlling subordinate health workers and even junior medical professionals.

Much of the new medical technology is embedded in the precision machines that informationalize medical work and data which, in turn, makes the occupations of medicine more intensive, discrete, and deskilled. The craftsmanship or art of a medical professional attending to patients becomes increasingly limited to collation of data produced by these machines and techniques. As a consequence, her work becomes quantifiable and manageable by the non-medical administration of hospitals and nursing homes. Hence, medical practice now is increasingly composed of the round-the-clock, perfectly discretized and synchronized practices, rather like the shop floor of a factory. But in this case it is a hospital where white-collared medical professionals mechanically perform their tasks, fix a problem, prescribe a medicine, without worrying about the overall health of the patient – the final human product of their assembly lines. The specialization that Bethune critiqued has become more and more a discrete set of tasks around specific machines. What was considered a pecuniary boon in his times has been reduced to drudgery today.

MEDICAL TECHNOLOGY AND CLASS STRUGGLE

The deployment of new technology in medicine is a means to degrade medical labour to feed into the profit-making 'medical-industrial complex'. It reduces the meaning of quality in health care to a set of 'numeric quality metrics', helping the management to impose techniques of lean production and problematic kinds of incentives that don't just degrade and alienate medical labour, but harm patients too. In the process of Taylorization in health care, what is considered wastage could be essential for 'healthier work rhythms' that 'include adequate time with patients, beneficial time for breaks or rest, and avoidance of stress'. Despite the rhetoric of teamwork, this process tends to encourage hyper-individuation through performance ratings and their incentivization. 'In health care an industrial approach imposes ever more external production pressures on clinicians' work processes.'[24] There is a paradigm shift in the function of Health Information Technology (HIT) tools from easing work to 'systems designed to control and standardize work'. The use of these tools diverts physicians' focus away from patients to fulfil the tasks commanded by HIT, and to various irrelevant data in the standardized format of Electronic Medical Records (EMRs), which do not really provide any insight into the patient's health. The administrative standardization of metrics for treating particular kinds of ailments leads to the standardization of treatments too, 'without considering the whole patient and the broader social context of care'.[25] Mike Cooley has rightly noted that 'IT systems frequently come between the professional and the primary task as the real world of touch, shape, size, form (and smell) is replaced by an image on a screen or a stream of data or calculation outputs. This can lead to high levels of abstraction where the ability to judge is diminished.'[26]

Today, alongside over-specialized doctors, there is also an emergence of super-specialty and single super-specialty hospitals that are exclusively engaged in the care of patients with specific ailments. The shift from general hospitals, catering to different ailments and a large number and variety of patients, to super-specialty hospitals catering to only a handful of them, is largely driven by the need to ease management issues, and create nimbleness in decision making with regards to both labour and technology. Their unparalleled infrastructure with state of the art medical technology brings in a fundamental shift in the organization of production in the health industry. With new technology such as non-invasive laparoscopy, or robotic surgical techniques, FMRI scanners, computers, health professionals are reduced to mere accompaniments from being the primary agents. In fact, 'as new treatments and new technologies are introduced, more health care is delivered by physician extenders (assistants, associates, paraprofessionals, and nurse practitioners)'.[27] Unsurprisingly, it was the nurses who first realized the functionalization of professionalism in this mode of production:

> We have come to the conclusion that professionalism in nursing is being used as both a carrot and a stick. As we try to become more 'professional' our eyes are glued on the 'carrot' of increased respect, rewards, and supposed improvement – and we do not see that behind our backs, professionalism is providing a 'stick' that is used to control and manipulate us.[28]

In fact, this critique of medical work was part of the churning among scientists and skilled service professionals from the late 1960s who were witnessing the Taylorization of their work processes and, for the first time, these intellectual workers were beginning to integrate with the labour movement not just as sympathizers, but as active participants. This is the context when the famous Lucas Corporate Plan was envisaged, where manual and mental workers combined to envisage a eudaimonic plan that could challenge capital as social relations and power, and reduce it to what it is – mere dead labour under the control of living labour, not vice versa.

CONCLUSION

Capital develops technology, sapping the labourer (in this case, medical labour). It seeks to reduce the productive forces – human and machine – to mere means. But it is still the human as living labour that innovates, and there lies its subversive potential. Technology is definitely not class neutral. In fact, it is shaped by the continuous open and hidden class struggle over work. As Marx already observed: 'It would be possible to write a whole history of the inventions made since 1830 for the sole purpose of providing capital with weapons against working-class revolt. We would mention, above all, the self-acting mule, because it opened up a new epoch in the automatic system.'[29] From the time of that self-acting mule to our times of artificial intelligence, this history of inventions is mainly about ever more sophistication of the automatic system.

To the extent that these inventions are made under the command of capital, the contradictions of capital are visible. All its contradictions ensue from the subversive autonomy of living labour, Marx argues, as its creativity must be harnessed for production and accumulation. By appropriating those inventions or machines – 'organs of the human mind which are created by the human hand, the objectified power of knowledge' – capital seeks to control the human mind and hand. It treats productive forces and social relations as 'two different aspects of the development of the social individual' as 'merely the means, for it to carry on production on its restricted basis'.[30] In fact, they are the material conditions for exploding that basis. What is for capital command over surplus labour time is actually disposable time for individuals and the whole society. The revolutionary subversion of capitalist technology is integration of the human mind with its 'organs'. The neo-luddite romantic aversion towards technological advancement is an externalized critique of capital which does not understand the implosive nature of the contradictions of capital and the liberatory possibility of such implosion for the human potential.

Socialized medicine, as Bethune understood it, is about the reappropriation of *the general intellect* (knowledge, and its objectification in machines and techniques) by society, for society. Its liberation from the 'restricted basis' of capital will allow it to realize its full potential. It is a resolution of the primary contradiction of capital, between socialized production and private appropriation – not in the purity of craft production in medicine, private production and private appropriation, but a more advanced stage of the socialization of both production and appropriation. It sees this potential in medical knowledge and technology that could be unleashed only with democratic self-government by the health workers themselves.

The contradiction that technology presents is sharpened in the daily class struggle around work. The labourer seeks to retain the power of judgement aligning it with the calculative capacity of machines, and capital attempts to sap it away. From individual frustration to full-scale revolts, all demonstrate the labourer's resistance. In recent years, as healthcare industries are increasingly becoming central to capital accumulation, medical workers have been vocalizing and organizing their anger against the pressure on the relative autonomy of their work, and their proletarianization. The pandemic and the way it is being handled globally has, on the one hand, tightened capital's grip on medical work; but on the other hand, it has exposed its vulnerability too – its necessary reliance on medical workers.

Marx once famously said that the conditions for cooperation among workers emerge in the very process of individualization and competition that capital enforces. With the sameness of experience 'broken up by their mutual competition', these workers cooperate initially not because of their own unity, but because of the oneness of the enemy. But as 'the various interests and conditions of life' become ever more equalized 'in proportion as machinery obliterates all distinctions in labour', mutual understanding and active cooperation start developing.[31] Hence, the *conditions* of cooperation and liberation must be found in the contradictions of capitalist technology that discretizes and deskills human labour, while positioning machines and computers in the mediational controlling role to reintegrate discrete labour units. These contradictions make the production process more vulnerable to industrial action – as a slight disturbance and sabotage in the highly synchronized work processes can lead to a complete shutdown, and incur an immense cost.[32] The speeding up of the economy through finance and technology makes it more prone to regular and devastating crashes.

Without going into the pedantic sociological debate *over identifying* physicians as workers or proletarians, it should be stressed that the focus on the process of deskilling and Taylorization of medical labour in general (what else is anyway the tendency of proletarianization?) can provide a ground for envisaging new labour politics around the reorganization of healthcare work. As mentioned, in the 1940s and 1950s, when the issue of public health care was raised, the labour movement saw in it the possibility of an increase in social wages, while capital found in it a freedom from expenses on workers' health. But independent health professionals at that time were anxious about losing their professional privileges. It is not that the intensification of industrialization and Taylorization of health work have completely done away with such anxieties. They are found even among various typical segments of the working class who are divided on the basis of skill-levels, wage differentials, designations, and identities. But the automation, algorithmization, and digital networking of work processes that define technology today are increasingly, to paraphrase Marx, equalizing and reducing every kind of work to an identical level, thus making the hierarchy of specialized work and exclusive appropriation merely an administrative control over workers and a burden on the productive forces. Generating scarcity and exclusivity through formal or institutional mechanisms to reproduce property relations has clearly aggravated the crisis in the health sector. However, the 'common experience of technological heteronomy'[33] and interdependence across industries provide the basis for re-envisaging collectivity in and beyond the health sector, too.

After the Great Depression, when liberal capitalism was on the verge of collapse, the adoption of policies of state-run or state-funded health care was part of the national consolidation of labour and resources, which was sought everywhere. But the fundamental aspects of Bethune's concept of socialized medicine could never be exhausted in the instrumentality of policy measures and temporal demands. Its epistemology, the critique of capitalism and the notion of medicine as social practice geared toward a radical restructuring of the society, where knowledge is the power of – not over – the human, are the insights that need to be mobilized today to challenge the global consolidation of state and capital in the age of emerging viruses. For Bethune, medicine was a critical social practice that was subsumed and instrumentalized under capitalism only by blunting its criticality that exposed the unhealthiness of capitalist social relations. Commodification and specialization led to the internalization of these relations in the health profession – its subsumption in the circuit of capital. However, since it was still mainly an individual profession, he could raise the issue of socialization of medicine as a moral and disciplinary commitment, of which he was himself a personification. But he was deeply aware of the trajectory of the profession, which led him to talk in terms of the collectivity of health workers and their self-government. In the wake of the Covid-19 pandemic, the need for such an empowered collective has become urgent, and the existential pressures on health workers and the community at large have led to its possibility, too.

NOTES

A shorter version of this paper was published in Socialist Project's online publication *The Bullet* (May 25, 2020).

1 Karl Marx, *Capital*, Volume 1, Translated by Ben Fowkes, London: Pelican Books, 1976, p. 612.
2 Charles Rosenberg, 'What Is an Epidemic? AIDS in Historical Perspective', *Daedalus*, 118(2), 1989, pp. 1-17.
3 Leo Panitch and Colin Leys, 'Preface', in Leo Panitch and Colin Leys, eds, *Socialist Register 2010: Morbid Symptoms*, London: Merlin Press, 2009, p. 1.
4 Richard M. Krause, *Foreword*, in Stephen S. Morse, ed., *Emerging Viruses*, Oxford: Oxford University Press, 1993, p. xvii.
5 Karl Marx, *Capital*, Volume 1, p. 638.
6 Norman Bethune's 1936 speech at a panel discussion on economic problems of medicine organized by the Montreal Medico-Chirurgical Society, reproduced in Sydney Gordon and Ted Allan, *The Scalpel, The Sword: The Story of Norman Bethune*, New York: Monthly Review Press, 1952, pp. 92-8.
7 Bethune in Gordon and Allan, *The Scalpel, The Sword*, p. 96.
8 Ibid. p. 93.
9 Ibid. pp. 93-4.
10 Ibid. p. 93.

11 Ibid. pp. 94-5

12 Norman Bethune, 'A plea for early compression in Pulmonary Tuberculosis', *The Canadian Medical Association Journal*, 27(1), 1932, p. 37.

13 Bethune in Gordon and Allan, *The Scalpel, The Sword*, p. 97.

14 Ibid. p. 96.

15 Ibid. p. 96.

16 Ibid. p. 95.

17 Ibid. p. 96.

18 Vicente Navarro, 'Why some countries have national health insurance, others have national health services, and the U.S. has neither', *Social Science & Medicine*, 28(9), 1989, pp. 887-98.

19 Leo Panitch and Colin Leys, 'Preface', p. 2.

20 Government of India's website for the promotion of investment in various industries, www.investindia.gov.in/sector/healthcare.

21 Mohan Rao, 'Abiding Appeal of Neo-Malthusianism: Explaining the Inexplicable', *Economic and Political Weekly* 39(32), 2004, pp. 3599-604.

22 Vicente Navarro, 'Professional Dominance or Proletarianization? Neither', *The Milbank Quarterly* Vol. 66, Supplement 2: The Changing Character of the Medical Profession, 1988, p. 66.

23 Pat Armstrong and Hugh Armstrong, 'Contradictions at work: struggles for control in Canadian health care', in Leo Panitch and Colin Leys, *Socialist Register 2010: Morbid Symptoms*, London: Merlin, 2009, pp. 145-67.

24 Gordon D. Schiff and Sarah Winch, 'The Degradation of Medical Labor and the Meaning of Quality in Health Care', Howard Waitzkin & The Working Group on Health Beyond Capitalism, eds, *Health Care Under the Knife: Moving Beyond Capitalism for Our Health*, New York: Monthly Review Press, 2018, p. 48.

25 Schiff and Winch, 'The Degradation of Medical Labor and the Meaning of Quality in Health Care', p. 54.

26 Mike Cooley, 'From judgment to calculation', *AI & Society* 21(4), 2007, p. 395.

27 Leonard Rodberg and Gelvin Stevenson, 'The Health Care Industry in Advanced Capitalism', *Review of Radical Political Economics* 9(1), 1977, p. 111.

28 Boston Nurses Group, 'The False Promise: Professionalism in Nursing', *Science for the People* 10(3), 1978, p. 20.

29 Karl Marx, *Capital*, Volume 1, p. 563.

30 Karl Marx, 'Outlines of the Critique of Political Economy (Rough Draft of 1857-58)', *Collected Works*, Volume 29, Progress Publishers, 1987, p. 92.

31 Karl Marx and Friedrich Engels, *The Manifesto of Communist Party*, London: Pluto Press, 2008, pp. 45-6.

32 Mike Cooley, 'Contradiction of Science and Technology in the Productive Process', in Hilary Rose and Steven Rose, eds, *The Political Economy of Science: Ideology of/in the Natural Sciences*, London: Macmillan, 1976, pp. 72-95.

33 Adrian Mengay, 'Digitalization of Work and Heteronomy', *Capital & Class*, 44(2), 2020, p. 283.

LIFE AFTER THE PANDEMIC: FROM PRODUCTION FOR PROFIT TO PROVISION FOR NEED

CHRISTOPH HERMANN

The global pandemic caused by the Covid-19 virus, more than any previous crisis, has demonstrated the difference between production for profit and provision for need. Privatized and marketized healthcare systems, with their focus on increasing efficiency, were not prepared to deal with the coronavirus. Years of cuts in healthcare expenses have largely eliminated reserve capacity necessary to cope with a sudden increase in need.[1] Within a few weeks, hospitals in areas that were particularly strongly affected by the virus reached maximum capacity and healthcare workers put in fourteen-hour shifts to deal with the inflow of patients. Perhaps the biggest scandal was that many of them were exposed to unnecessary risks, because hospitals lacked protective equipment such as masks and gowns which in normal times present unnecessary expenses and were subsequently eliminated by hospital administrators eager to cut costs.[2]

While cuts took place in all healthcare systems, privatized systems proved particularly ill-equipped to deal with the pandemic. It is not by accident that for-profit-nursing homes not only in the US but also in Canada and the UK were at the center of the spread of the virus. In order to make a profit, these homes are notoriously understaffed, while poorly paid workers lack appropriate training and equipment.[3] Of course, the situation in the US was made much worse by the dominance of the private sector in the health system overall: about 20 million Americans lacked healthcare coverage at the start of the crisis. Millions more lost their insurance with the termination of their employment. In at least one case, a person with Covid-19 symptoms but without insurance died because he was turned away by a private for-profit healthcare facility (even when people have health insurance, they are afraid to go to a hospital because of potentially hefty co-payments).[4] Perhaps the greatest absurdity was that some US hospitals temporarily closed during the crisis and/or laid-off staff, because the pausing of non-essential medical procedures minimized revenues.[5] Hospital closures, of course, are linked to a lack of oversight and coordination, which is unavoidable in a market-based system. Because of the lack of coordination, US hospitals, cities, and states struggled to buy medical equipment in China, outbidding each other and driving up prices.[6]

The response to the pandemic also showed that the market is of little help when it comes to a rapid provision of urgently needed goods and services. Traditional champions of market liberalism begged the US president to use the Defense Production Act to produce much-needed ventilators and governments assigned essential status to certain categories of workers who were required to continue to do their job in the midst of the lockdown. Essential workers, some of them poorly paid, subsequently risked their lives, while Wall Street bankers sheltered in their second homes in the Hamptons. And while the crisis showed which workers are really important for the reproduction of societies and which are not, there remains a massive pay gap between essential workers and those who make their money on Wall Street or perform other dispensable but profitable tasks (the fact that many of the essential workers are African-American, Latinos, and other minorities also contributed to the fact that these groups showed much higher infection and death rates for working-age people than the rest of the population).[7]

Perhaps the greatest flaw revealed by the crisis is capitalism's addiction to profit. The main goal of capitalist production is the maximization of profit; the satisfaction of needs is only a by-product in the endless process of accumulation. This means that the economy cannot simply pause during a lockdown and continue when the pandemic is under control. The insecurity of future profits instantly pushed the economy into an existential crisis. As a result, the crisis was not characterized by a lack of urgently needed supply, as one may expect during a period of large-scale economic inactivity. After a wave of panic buying most products reappeared on supermarket shelves. Obviously, there is enough output stocked up in rich countries to allow people to survive without working for a couple of months. Of course, they need money to do so. And while some countries granted payroll subsidies to companies holding on to their staff, unemployment quickly increased in the US, reaching record levels within a few weeks.[8]

Some people, subsequently, protested against the lockdown and the economic hardship caused by it. Many more did not protest but violated the shelter-in-place orders by leaving the house for non-essential work, including undocumented workers who neither qualified for stimulus money nor for unemployment benefit. The ensuing debate about opening-up the economy centered on the question of whether the saving of a few thousand lives was worth paying the price of a prolonged economic recession. But the real question should have been something else: was there an economic collapse even though we have enough food and other essential goods? The decision, then, should not have been between saving human lives and protecting the economy; the two are, in fact, interdependent. The real decision was between protecting human lives and maintaining capitalist profits. The priority of profits could be seen clearly in the massive rescue packages adopted by governments and central banks around the world. In the US, taxpayers received a $1,200 stimulus cheque plus a smaller amount for each child, but the total amount of money spent to support individuals and families pales in comparison to the trillions of dollars granted to businesses and injected into financial markets.[9]

While the coronavirus challenged the very foundations of the profit-driven economy, the lockdown provided the environment with a much-needed break. The pausing of industrial production together with the restriction of transportation, including international air travel, significantly reduced carbon dioxide emissions and other pollution.[10] As a result, residents of smog-plagued cities such as New Delhi could suddenly see the sky. The crisis has shown that a focus on essential needs can provide breathing space for the global ecosystem. However, at the same time the crisis also sounded the death knell to all attempts to solve the ecological crisis through profit-based incentives. The dramatic fall in oil prices caused by the decline in economic activities will undermine the shift to less damaging energy sources. The restriction of industrial output and travel means that, if no counter-measures are adopted, the price for carbon dioxide and other pollution credits will decline again, shortly after they have recovered from the 2008-09 crisis.

In sum, what in a needs-based economy would be a formidable healthcare challenge and, perhaps, a major disruption of social life, but not a crisis of social reproduction, at least not as long as there is sufficient supply, turned in the profit-driven economy of capitalism into an existential threat. The anxiety about falling profits could only be calmed by flooding investors, businesses, and credit institutions with massive amounts of money. As a result, the US government will record the highest debt in its history. While some people warn of debt becoming unsustainable, it is worth remembering that debt is nothing else than a claim on future social output. But who will need this future social output? Certainly not the banks and investors who finance the debt. And while the federal government accumulates debt, the states which bear the brunt of the health and social costs caused by the pandemic have already announced drastic budget cuts, affecting education and other services which people desperately need.[11]

Debt is, in one way, the flipside of profit. The fact that somebody can get more of the social product than she/he needs implies that somebody else doesn't get enough and subsequently has to ask for credit to make ends meet (unless there is more output than needed, which in a profit-driven economy results in an overproduction crisis). However, while debt is essential in a profit-driven economy, it is pointless in a needs-based economy (this does not mean that needs-based economies must not have stocks of goods and reserve capacities for unforeseen developments such as a pandemic or to help other countries that face a shortage in supply). When the goal is that everybody receives what she/he needs, there is no need to go into debt. Seen in reverse, when people only get what they need there is no basis for profit. In the remainder of the essay I will present some ideas for a needs-based economy.

TOWARDS A NEEDS-BASED ECONOMY

The idea that the main purpose of an economy is to satisfy human needs is far from new. In fact, we had needs-based economies for most of human history. The profit motive is a fairly new invention, closely linked to the emergence of capitalism. However, in pre-capitalist societies producers primarily focused on the satisfaction of their own needs, resulting in what Marx describes as production for self-use (even though parts of the output were claimed by a landlord or another authority).[12] Self-use typically means small volumes of output, which, in turn, limits the division of labor and discourages the development of labor-saving technology. The result is low productivity and economic stagnation. Given the ecological destruction caused by both industrial capitalism and industrial communism, some eco-socialists advocate a return to a more subsistence-oriented form of economic organization.[13] However, for many, and perhaps the majority, a subsistence economy is not an attractive alternative to the status quo. In addition to lacking many of the amenities of modern life, including art, education, and an advanced health care system, the lack of surplus makes subsistence economies particular vulnerable to disruptions of the production process caused, for example, by natural disasters or epidemics. While subsistence economies are usually centered on familial forms of reproduction, it is precisely collectivized capacities that allow human beings to tackle almost any challenge on earth, including the Covid-19 outbreak and the looming ecological crisis.

While production in subsistence economies focuses on self-use, capitalist production is geared towards the use of others.[14] Yet because these needs are mediated through markets and money, only those needs count that are backed by sufficient purchasing power. Hence the pharmaceutical industry tries to convince people in affluent countries to buy more drugs, some of them for imagined diseases, while at the same time ignoring millions in poor countries suffering from so-called tropical diseases.[15] Even in affluent countries, supermarkets throw away food before they give it to the hungry.[16] And developers build shiny condominium towers for professionals, while families are in desperate need of affordable and sustainable housing.[17]

Yet profit-orientation not only means the neglect of unprofitable needs, it also means that products are designed to maximize profit rather than usefulness. This, in turn, has major consequences for how needs are satisfied. To give an example that emerges in everyday life. The need for transport can be met on an individual base through auto-mobility, or it can be met by collective forms of transport such as buses and trains. While both meet the same need – to get from point A to point B – the car is widely prioritized in a profit-oriented transport system. The repeated sale of millions of cars promises much greater profits – for car producers, sales outlets, insurances, repair shops, lawyers, and in for-profit healthcare systems, even hospitals treating patients from traffic accidents – than the operation of a subway or another form of public transport. It is no accident that investors throw billions of dollars at the development of self-driving cars while public transport systems such as BART in San Francisco or the New York subway are crumbling. Yet, while auto-mobility promises greater profits, its usefulness is severely compromised by its negative impact on the environment, including nature, communities, and other road users.

In other cases, too, profits are maximized at the cost of usefulness. Industrialized agriculture, for example, increases output through the use of pesticides, fertilizers, and genetically modified crops, even though they can be harmful for the human organism – not to speak of massive harm inflicted on surrounding ecosystems.[18] In the same way, the food industry produces ultra-processed food that achieves remarkable profits, while lacking nutritional value and if eaten in large amounts can cause severe illnesses.[19] Especially in labour-intensive services profits are often increased at the cost of service quality.[20] The private care homes mentioned at the beginning of this essay are a prime example. But care homes are not alone. Private for-profit colleges in the US spend more on advertising, recruiting, and admission than on instruction. In fact, their pre-tax profits are as high as their teaching budget. Not surprisingly, for-profit colleges are among the worst institutions when it comes to teaching quality.[21] But even in the public sector the quality of services has suffered from decades of neoliberal cost cutting.

Obviously, a needs-based economy requires an alternative mode of articulating needs, one that does not depend on money and markets. The most obvious way is inviting people to articulate their needs in some form of democratic decision-making process. Rather than choosing from a variety of given products that, perhaps, are equally unsatisfying, users would have a say in what is produced and how it is produced. There are several models of how such a process can be organized and how technology could play an important role in facilitating decision-making processes with a large number of participants.[22] The same technology could also help to improve the planning processes. The platform economy, after all, is based on the rapid collection and distribution of information. Rather than selling commodities, the same information channels could be used to gather inputs for the development and distribution of products.

The main argument against democratic planning is that the extent of the participatory processes involved makes it inefficient. And most people can think of better ways to spend their time than sitting in endless meetings. Conventionally, efficiency is understood as the amount of output created by a given input. The more output, the greater the efficiency. Output is usually measured as the monetary value of what has been produced.[23] As a result, fast-food chains are more efficient than traditional restaurants even though the food has little nutritional value and even endangers the health of consumers.[24] Hospitals which limit patient stays to little more than the duration of an operation are highly efficient even though a significant number of patients have to come back for further treatment because they have been released too early.[25] Online universities are more efficient as one instructor can teach thousands of students, but students tend to learn less than in traditional classroom settings.[26] In contrast, fire brigades are inefficient if there are no fires to put out; prisons are inefficient if there are no prisoners to lock up; and doctors are inefficient if there are no patients to be treated. However, most people prefer the absence of fires, crimes, and epidemics to a more efficient public service. Hence while a profit-driven understanding of efficiency focuses on output, i.e. the goods and services that are sold to consumers, what really counts is outcome, i.e. the state of living and of the environment. Accordingly, participatory processes should be judged with respect to their contribution to desirable social and environmental outcomes. Taking time to find the right solution may very well pay off in the long run.

In addition, the discourse on efficiency hides a major shortcoming of the market-mediated form of distributing goods and services. The market model implies that needs are autonomous and only exist in individualized form – each consumer can freely choose between different products whereas in reality many needs are of collective nature – many consumers have the same need and their consumption decisions affect each other. To come back to the example of auto-mobility: an increasing number of consumers in the US and other countries decide to buy Sports Utility Vehicles, even though SUVs emit more carbon-dioxide, a major driver of climate change. The increase in SUV sales has in fact more than made up for recent improvements in fuel efficiency and the sale of electric cars.[27] However, SUVs are not only bad for the environment; because they are heavier and have higher bumpers than regular cars, they are also more dangerous for other drivers, bikers, and pedestrians. Growing safety concerns, in turn, encourage other people, especially those with small children, to buy SUVs, further undermining road safety and fuelling climate change. In contrast, a collective decision-making process could come to the conclusion that SUVs are a destructive way to satisfy the need for mobility and instead plan the production of lighter cars, which in absence of heavier automobiles provide the same safety as SUVs, while being less damaging for the environment, bikers, and pedestrians. Or, even better, they decide to promote public transport as an alternative to auto-mobility.

While people in a democratic economy are free to commonly decide what is produced and how it is produced, they need to take into account the consequences of specific forms of production and consumption for the environment and for future generations who want to live on this planet. In order to preserve existing ecological resources and biodiversity, production and consumption must be sustainable. The concept of sustainability goes back to the management of renewable resources such as forests and fisheries. Essentially it means limiting the use of a specific resource to the ability of the resource to renew itself – i.e. to cut only as many trees as can grow back over a certain period of time. Sustainability has partly been discredited by its use by the World Commission on Environment and Development: the authors of the Brundtland Report proposed sustainability as a possibility to allow for more growth while at the same time protecting the environment.[28] A number of critics have, subsequently, pointed out that the use of more energy-efficient technology will not be sufficient to stop ecological degradation. Growth may be less resource-consuming, but still demand more resources.[29] Proponents of the degrowth movement have subsequently argued that in order to protect the environment the economy in the developed world needs to shrink. The Western standard of living is too destructive and can only be maintained through widespread deprivation in the Global South.[30] However, while critics suggest that people in the Global North live beyond their ecological means, the problem is not reckless consumer behaviour. The problem is that profit-maximization demands more and more output, and, subsequently, growing consumption, regardless of whether there is a need for it.[31]

Tellingly, among the first Corona-related concerns voiced in the US was the fear that the outbreak of the virus in China would disrupt the supply-chain of such 'important' products as miniature superhero and other toys, a multi-million dollar-industry.[32] Yet, while American families are flooded with plastic toys and other products that can be produced cheaply in China (through super-exploitation of Chinese labour and the unmitigated pollution of the environment), millions lack access to adequate health care and other essential services. Ursula Huws has argued that commodification entails a process in which services are replaced by tangible output because of the much greater potential to increase profits through the use of economies of scale.[33] To give an example: it is much more profitable to develop a pill and sell it millions of times than to operate a hospital, no matter how much the hospital charges for an operation.[34] And given the private nature of its healthcare system it should not surprise that the US has one of the highest amounts of prescription drugs taken per head of population while at the same time also having the largest number of people skipping prescriptions because they cannot afford them.[35]

Temporarily profits can also be increased through speculation. Rather than producing more output, investors manipulate supply and demand, either by fuelling demand or withholding supply, and thereby drive up prices. The result is speculative bubbles. Investors who leave the market before the bubble bursts can make spectacular gains. The housing market is prone to speculative bubbles. [36] Yet while rising house prices offer the possibility to make money without producing anything, let alone something that is useful, the same house prices make it difficult if not impossible for low- and middle-income families to find a home. As a result, many households spend more than a third of their income just to have a roof over their head.[37]

Hence what may look like an excessive mode of consumption and what some have described as an imperial mode of living is in reality an undersupply of urgently needed (public) goods and services.[38] A production system that focuses on needs rather than profits could solve both problems at once: it could make sure that all essential needs are met – including, not least, adequate care homes for the elderly – while at the same time limiting resource consumption to a sustainable level. Contrary to what neoclassical economists want us to believe, human needs are not limitless; what is limitless is the accumulation of profit.[39] Even if he buys the most expensive commodities that money can buy, Jeff Bezos, the richest man on earth, still only spends a tiny fraction of his wealth on consumption.

Profit-orientation goes hand in hand with self-centeredness. Profit is increased by putting personal gains or the gains of a corporate organization before the benefits of another person/entity, the community, or the environment. In conventional economics the exclusive focus on personal interest is celebrated as the rational behaviour of *homo economicus*. Understood in this way, the thousands of healthcare workers who risked their lives and the lives of other family members during the pandemic acted irrationally – they should have quit, taken unemployment benefits, and returned to work when the virus was under control.[40] If people would really act only in their self-interest, capitalism would have collapsed a long time ago. It is precisely the concern for others that keeps capitalism going. However, the concern for others and the resulting mutual support is constantly challenged by capitalist competition. Competition not only forces capitalists to fight for profits, thereby enlarging the total amount of surplus; it also positions workers against each other when they compete for a job on the labour market or for their existing jobs when their employers threaten to relocate production to a low-wage country.

Competition implies that there are winners and losers. The goal of a needs-based economy is that everybody wins. The fact that another person, company, or country is successful is not a threat. To the contrary: success puts them into a position to provide support if needed. Hence while a profit-oriented economy thrives through competition, a needs-based economy prospers through cooperation and solidarity. After decades of neoliberal denial, the Covid-19 crisis has left little doubt about the merit of solidarity. A society in which people only look after themselves is doomed in a pandemic. While investors panicked and sold off stocks, employers laid off staff at record speed, and some in a show of unrestrained egoism refused to wear masks to protect the people around them, essential workers continued to do their job and risked their health for the community and society. It is only when people work together and put aside individual interests for the public good that societies can cope with challenges such as a pandemic. What works for containing the coronavirus, also works for a number of other challenges including poverty, homelessness, the lack of health care, education, and, most importantly, climate change. It is through solidarity, not monetary incentives, that global warming can be stopped, including solidarity between current and future generations.[41] Of course, the fact that people would have a say in collective decision-making processes, with participation not limited to the election of party representatives every other year, would make it a lot easier to show solidarity.

Solidarity promotes equality. The fact that people with plenty would help those in need reduces the gap between the rich and the poor. But a needs-based economy goes beyond redistribution. The coronavirus crisis has shown that poor people not only have less money; they suffer from inferior living and working conditions such as a lack of protective equipment, adequate housing, and access to health care and other essential services. In a needs-based economy all needs are equal, regardless of the purchasing power behind them. In fact, many of the extravagant wishes, including driving a car that can run 200 miles an hour or living in a house with 20 rooms, will become obsolete. Instead everybody will have a reasonable eco-friendly home, and a reliable and ecologically acceptable form of transport, along with effective health care and stimulating education. Of course, this will demand discussion about what needs are essential, and what constitutes a 'good life'. But the fact that people will have a say in democratic decision-making processes will make this procedure much easier.

TOWARDS A USE-VALUE SOCIETY

Marx noted that commodities have use-values and exchange-values. While use-value represents the usefulness of a good or service, exchange-value depicts the amount of other goods or money that can be gained in exchange for it.[42] Exchange-value is the basis for profit. Accordingly, commodity production is geared towards the maximization of exchange-value and this process involves the marginalization of use-value. An alternative to commodification should reverse this process and focus on the maximization of use-value. The result is what I like to call a 'use-value society'. The goal of a use-value society is not just to satisfy needs, but to satisfy them in an optimal and constantly improving manner. This implies not only that a use-value society would provide for more than the mere necessities of life; it also means that a use-value society could not be stagnant. Yet rather than changing for the sake of profit, as capitalist economies do, it would change to improve living conditions. And because of the focus on needs rather than money it could change without necessarily growing and destroying the environment.

While exchange values can be measured in units of money, the nature of use value is precisely that it cannot be expressed in quantitative terms.[43] Yet while we cannot measure usefulness, we can determine it in the same democratic decision-making processes that allow us to articulate our needs. Hence in a use-value society democratic planning not only serves to match supply and demand; it also serves as an instrument to judge improvements of goods and services or alternative ways to satisfy needs. However, in order to do so, the rather complex process of adjusting supply and demand must leave room for innovation. In order to promote innovation, democratic planning could be supplemented by the institutionalization of a process of use-value maximization that includes a specially trained group of use-value promoters (replacing today's managers), as well as an ongoing exchange between developers and potential users (substituting for what is currently known as market research). While production decisions should be made in a democratic fashion, there can still be some leeway for experimentation, adaptation, and occasional failure.

Maximizing use-value also demands a new understanding of economic efficiency. Rather than producing the greatest possible output with the smallest possible input, the goal is to create the most favourable outcome. In the case of health care, for example, the goal is not to treat as many patients as possible in a day or month; the goal is to prevent illnesses, including illnesses caused by anxieties about the future and poor working conditions. In the case of higher education, the goal is not to push as many students through the system as possible; the goal is that students learn essential bodies of knowledge and are trained in critical thinking while they attend college or university. In the case of transport, the goal is not to produce more automobiles, including electronically powered luxury cars.[44] The goal is to move people and goods around efficiently with the least possible impact on the environment. And in the case of agriculture the goal is not to produce as much corn, poultry, and other agricultural output as possible; the goal is to produce healthy and tasty food without destroying the environment.[45]

While the maximization of use-value depends on democratic decision-making processes, not all production needs to be planned. Markets are acceptable as long as producers primarily care about the use-value of their products. It makes little sense to democratically plan decentralized agricultural production. A local farmer's market is a perfectly fine instrument to distribute local fruits and vegetables. The same holds for local shops, restaurants, and other community-based service providers. Even labour can be allocated through markets, most likely through some form of internet platform, when workers' existence does not depend on the sale of their labour power. However, as in capitalist societies, the development of skills, knowledge, and experience, i.e. the formation of the use-value of labour, demands long-term planning and creation of public institutions that provide education and training.

The maximization of use-value also applies to the use-value of labor. In a use-value society there is no place for the deskilling and disempowerment of workers. Instead workers are encouraged to nurture their talents, develop their skills, and apply their knowledge. The promotion of use-value also implies an acknowledgment of the usefulness of work, resulting in an upgrading of socially useful jobs such as nurses and a downgrading of rather useless jobs such as stock traders. This, in turn, will fundamentally reshape current labour markets where individuals who perform socially questionable tasks such as betting on increasing or decreasing prices are awarded with top salaries, while others who do socially extremely useful work such as taking care of children and the elderly struggle to make ends meet.[46]

Nature also provides use-values. There is no human life without nature. Natural products and resources are used by human beings either directly for consumption or as inputs in the production of other useful goods and services. And while some use-values are lost for the foreseeable future in the consumption process, nature has the ability to renew many of its use values over time. Reproduction also involves adaptation and mutation, resulting in nature's stunning biodiversity. The maximization of the use-value of nature means limiting the destruction of nature to the smallest possible amount, while still providing an acceptable standard of living in both the Global North and Global South. This implies a focus on essential needs – what André Gorz has called sufficiency – and the consideration of the ecological effects of different ways of satisfying them.[47] As a result, a use-value society not only avoids waste; a use-value society also promotes a transition to more sustainable forms of living, including spatially adequate and energy-efficient homes, public transport, local food from local farms, using sustainable forms of agriculture, as well as various social services.

Contrary to other alternatives such as the one promoted by the degrowth movement, a use-value society does not imply sacrifices; instead it implies a qualitatively different mode of living which in fact can be superior to current living conditions in the US where poor-quality houses can cost up to a million dollars, people are stuck in traffic in their journeys to and from work, many eat industrialized food, cannot afford college, and have no or only limited access to health care.[48] Measured as GDP per capita, the US has one of the highest living standards in the world. This is higher than Germany, but this measure shields a great deal of the variations in the quality of life. On average, German workers work ten weeks less per year than Americans.[49] In a use-value society, people will have even more free time to pursue personal interests and to do useful things out of joy rather than coercion. In short, the mode of living will change, but for much of the population in the US and other countries, living conditions will improve rather than deteriorate.

Because it focuses on the satisfaction of needs rather than the expansion of profits, a use-value society will at some point have to break with capitalism.

Needs have no relevance in capitalism if they cannot be satisfied in a profitable manner through market exchanges. Profitability, in contrast, has no significance in a use-value society where needs are evaluated according to social relevance and decisions are made in a democratic manner, taking into account the effects of different options on the environment. Marxists usually refer to socialism as alternative to capitalism. Socialism is a contested concept, but the recent visions of a twenty-first century socialism that came out of Latin America had much in common with what I perceive as use-value society.[50] However, the concept of a use-value society is more modest and pragmatic. Use-value orientation is only one, albeit important, aspect of a socialist alternative. And while sharing the goal of a democratically controlled economy, the use-value society leaves room for local markets and small producers as long as they do not endanger use-value orientation. The prospect of a use-value society, consequently, is not only attractive for workers, but, potentially, for many social groups, including small farmers and small business-owners.

Most importantly, while socialism demands nothing short of a revolution, the transition towards a use-value society can start with small steps – and it can begin right away. The many cooperatives, not-for-profit organizations, and small firms that produce for local markets and make little or no profit already promote use-value, as do most small, family-owned farms. People who are engaged in production for self-use or the use by family members, friends, or the community also promote use-value, including through communal gardens, collective repair shops, public art projects, and various forms of voluntary work (arguably capitalism could not function without these activities meeting needs).[51] People who re-use and repair things rather than throwing them away also promote use-value by prolonging the usefulness of the respective goods. Public services and infrastructures have been undermined by decades of neoliberal austerity and restructuring; they can be re-built to become examples of use value-orientation, including health, child and senior care, education and transit. Yet in order to do so, services need adequate funding and students, users and patients, along with the workers who deliver these services must have a real say in their provisioning. This means genuine opportunities for active participation and administration – not just by taking surveys or forming committees that can voice concerns but have no power in decision-making processes. Positive experience with growing islands of use-value orientation in the sea of profit-maximization can, hopefully, pave the way for a systematic change, ending capitalism and tackling the ecological crisis.

NOTES

1 For an account of various health care 'reforms', see Leo Panitch and Colin Leys, eds, *Morbid Symptoms. Health under Capitalism*, Socialist Register 2010, London: Merlin Press, 2009.
2 Weeks after the outbreak, a survey commissioned by Nurses United in California showed that 88 per cent of nurses were still reusing single-use disposable respirators or masks. California Nurses Association, Press Release May 21 2020, available at: www.nationalnursesunited.org.
3 About a third of all Covid-19 deaths in the US affected nursing home residents; in California the proportion was 50 per cent. In Canada, the proportion of Covid-19 deaths has been around 80 per cent. Karen Yourish et al 'One-Third of All U.S. Coronavirus Deaths Are Nursing Home Residents or Workers', *New York Times*, 11 May 2020; for an analysis of the quality of care in US nursing homes see: Charlene Harrington et. al., 'Does Investor Ownership of Nursing Homes Compromise the Quality of Care?', *American Journal of Public Health*, 91(9), 2001, pp. 1452-55.
4 Jenny Gross and Tim Arango, 'Teenager's Death in California Is Linked to Coronavirus', *New York Times*, 24 March 2020.
5 Todd C. Frankel and Tony Romm, 'Historic financial decline hits doctors, dentists and hospitals – despite covid-19 – threatening overall economy', *Washington Post*, 4 May 2020.
6 Sarah Mervosh and Katie Rogers, 'Governors Fight Back Against Coronavirus Chaos: It's Like Being on eBay With 50 Other States', *New York Times*, 31 March 2020.
7 According to data published by the *Los Angeles Times*, almost 75 per cent of the 35-49 years old who died in California of Covid-19 were Latinos. The data is available at: www.latimes.com.
8 In the US, the Paycheck Protection Program was supposed to provide an incentive for companies to keep their workers on their payroll, but support was designed as a loan that could be forgiven under certain circumstances. Obviously, the program did not convince many employers to keep their staff and/or they could not get the support they needed. Paul Waldman, 'The Paycheck Protection Program Has Been a Disaster. Here's How We Can Replace It', *Washington Post*, 8 May 2020.
9 The 'stimulus checks' sent out to households accounted for 290 billion of the six trillion dollars rescue spending. Tim Logan, 'As Federal Stimulus Checks Arrive, How Are People Spending the Money?', *Boston Globe*, 21 April 2020.
10 At the height of the crisis, global carbon-dioxide emissions fell by 17 per cent; Fiona Harvey, 'Lockdowns Trigger Dramatic Fall in Global Carbon Emissions', *The Guardian*, 19 May 2020.
11 California has announced major budgets as a result of Coronavirus related expenses. As a result, University of California campuses have imposed a hiring freeze and laid-off non-tenure track staff.
12 Karl Marx, *A Contribution to the Critique of Political Economy*, New York: International Publishers, 1970, p. 5.
13 Maria Mies, *Patriarchy and Accumulation on a World Scale. Women in the International Division of Labour*, London: Zed Books, 1986.
14 Marx, *A Contribution*, p. 42.

15 Researchers have revealed that of 1,393 new chemical entities marketed to the pharmaceutical industry between 1975 and 1999, only 16 were for tropical diseases and tuberculosis; Patrice Trouiller et. al., 'Drug development for neglected diseases: a deficient market and a public-health policy failure', *Lancet* 359, 2002, pp. 2188-94.

16 Between 30 to 40 per cent of food in the US is not eaten. Retailers usually dump food that has not been sold rather than giving it away for free. According to one estimate, about ten per cent of the food supply on the retail level in the US ends up in the garbage where it creates additional costs for waste disposal. Dana Gunters et al., 'Wasted: How America Is Losing Up to 40 Percent of Its Food from Farm to Fork to Landfill', Natural Resources Defense Council, 2017, available at: www.nrdc.org.

17 For 'condo-fication' in Toronto, see Ute Lehrer and Thorben Widietz, 'Condominium Development and Gentrification: The Relationship Between Policies, Building Activities and Socio-economic Development in Toronto', *Canadian Journal of Urban Research* 18(1), pp. 140-61.

18 Eric Holt-Gimenez, *A Foodie's Guide to Capitalism*, New York: Monthly Review Press, 2017.

19 Robert Albritton, 'Between Obesity and Hunger: The Capitalist Food Industry', in Leo Panitch and Colin Leys, eds., *Morbid Symptoms. Health under Capitalism*, Socialist Register 2010, London: Merlin Press, 2009, pp. 184-97.

20 This was one of the main findings of a European research project on the impact of privatization on public services. See: Christoph Hermann and Jörg Flecker, eds, *Privatization of Public Services. Impacts for Employment, Working Conditions and Service Quality in Europe*, New York: Routledge, 2012.

21 US Senate Committee on Health Education Labor and Pensions, 'For Profit Higher Education: The Failure to Safeguard the Federal Investment and Ensure Student Success', Excecutive Summary, Washington, DC, 2012

22 See, for example: Michael Albert, *Parecon: Life After Capitalism,* London: Verso, 2013; Sam Gindin, 'Socialism for Realists', *Catalyst*, 2(3), 2017.

23 Because public goods and services are freely available or accessible at reduced costs, it is difficult if not impossible to determine public sector productivity. See: Christoph Hermann, 'The Public Sector and Equality', *Global Social Policy* 16(1), 2016, p. 16.

24 Mark A Pereira et al., 'Fast-food Habits, Weight Gain, and Insulin Resistance (the CARDIA Study): 15-year prospective analysis', *Lancet* 365, 2005, pp. 36-42.

25 Among patients with the most common procedures in U.S. hospitals, as many as one in five were readmitted within 30 days in 2010. Audrey J. Weiss, Anne Elixhauser and Claudia Steiner, 'Readmissions to US Hospitals by Procedure, 2010', Health Care Cost and Utilization Project, Statistical Brief 154, April 2013, available at: www.hcup-us.ahrq.gov.

26 Eric Bettinger and Susanna Loeb, 'Promises and Pitfalls of Online Education', *Evidence Speaks Reports* (2)15, Brookings Institute, 9 June 2017, available at: www.brookings.edu.

27 Laura Cozzi and Apostolos Petropoulos, 'Growing Preference for SUVs Challenges Emissions Reductions in Passenger Car Market', International Energy Agency, 15 October 2019, available at: www.iea.org.

28 World Commission on Environment and Development: *Our Common Future*, Oxford: Oxford University Press, 1987.

29 Wolfgang Sachs, *Planet Dialectics. Explorations in Environment and Development*, London: Zed Books, 1999, ch. 5.

30 Juan Martinez-Alier et al., 'Sustainable De-Growth: Mapping the Context, Criticisms and Future Prospects of an Emergent Paradigm', *Ecological Economics* 69, 2010, pp. 1741–47

31 While capitalism depends on growing output, individual capitalists increase profits by trying to pay their workers as little as possible, resulting in periodic overproduction/underconsumption crises.

32 Alistair Gray, 'MGA Boss Warns Coronavirus Could Lead to Toy Shortage', *Financial Times*, 23 February 2020.

33 Ursula Huws, *The Making of the Cybertariat. Virtual Work in a Real World*, New York: Monthly Review Press, 2003, pp. 66–7.

34 According to data compiled by NYU professor Aswath Damodaran the profit (before interest and tax) margin achieved by US pharmaceutical corporations is more than three times as high as the one attained by hospitals and other health care facilities (59 compared to 18 per cent); for the profitability of the pharmaceutical industry, see also: Marica Angell, *The Truth About the Drug Companies*, New York: Random House, 2005.

35 Dana O. Sarnak et al., 'Paying for Prescription Drugs Around the World: Why Is the U.S. an Outlier?', *Issue Brief*, Commonwealth Fund, October 2017.

36 David Harvey lists four property crashes in the US in the past hundred years: 1928, 1973, 1987, and 2008. David Harvey, *Seventeen Contradictions of Capitalism*, London: Profile Books, 2014, pp. 20–21.

37 National Low-Income Housing Coalition, 'The Gap: A Shortage of Affordable Homes', March 2017.

38 Ulrich Brand and Markus Wissen, *Imperiale Lebensweise. Zur Ausbeutung von Mensch und Natur im globalen Kapitalismus*, Munich: Oekom, 2017.

39 Elmar Altvater, 'The Foundations of Life (Nature) and the Maintenance of Life (Work)', *International Journal of Political Economy* 20(1), 1990, p. 23.

40 In the US, thousands of health care workers were infected with Covid-19 and hundreds died because of the coronavirus. Ariana Eunjung Cha, 'More Than 9,000 U.S. Health-care Workers Have Been Infected with the Coronavirus', *Washington Post*, 14 April 2020.

41 Paul Hampton, *Workers and Trade Unions for Climate Solidarity. Tackling Climate Change in a Neoliberal World*, New York: Routledge, 2005.

42 Karl Marx, *Capital* Volume I, London: Penguin Books, 1990, pp. 126–8

43 Marx, *Capital*.

44 The electric car pioneer Tesla, for example, exclusively focuses on upper-segment cars. 2019 prices range from $32,815 to $97,815. Tesla also produces high-priced electronic SUVs.

45 Holt-Gimenez, *A Foodie's Guide*, Conclusion.

46 For the low wages paid to care worker, see Sarah Thomason et al., 'At the Wage Floor: Covering Home Care and Early Education Workers in the New Generation of Minimum Wage Laws', UC Berkeley, Center for the Study of Child Care Employment, 2018, available at: cscce.berkeley.edu.

47 André Gorz, *Capitalism, Socialism, Ecology*, London: Verso, 1994, ch. 9.

48 In the Bay Area (where I live) family homes can easily cost one million dollars and still lack proper insulation. During rush hour, it can take an hour to cross the Bay Bridge

from Oakland to San Francisco. Without traffic it takes less than 15 minutes.

49 Christoph Hermann, *Capitalism and the Political Economy of Work Time*, New York: Routledge, 2015, pp. 175-66.

50 See, for example: Michael A. Lebowitz, *Build it Now. Socialism for the 21st Century*, New York: Monthly Review Press, 2006; Atilo Boron, *Den Sozialismus neu denken. Gibt es ein Leben nach dem Neoliberalismus*, Hamburg: VSA Verlag, 2010; Francois Houtart, 'From 'Common Goods' to the 'Common Good of Humanity', *Historia Actuel Online* 26 (Fall 2011), pp. 87-102.

51 One effect of the lockdown was that people started to home-make stuff, including making their own bread. As a result, flour was among the goods that disappeared from the grocery shelves.

DEMOCRATIC SOCIALIST PLANNING: BACK TO THE FUTURE

ROBIN HAHNEL

Early socialists were driven by a *conviction* and a *vision*.

Our predecessors were convinced that nineteenth and early twentieth century capitalism had proven to be an unmitigated disaster. While capitalism had generated the most dramatic increases in economic productivity humanity had ever experienced, it was squandering this productive bounty by unleashing terrible economic insecurity in the form of financial crises and recessions beyond anyone's control, and by widening the gap between 'haves' and 'have-nots' even in good times. Moreover, while capitalism gave the appearance of freeing everyone to consume, work, and invest as they pleased, in truth, ever more people ceased to have control over their economic destinies.

Our socialist predecessors were also guided by a vision of what to replace capitalism with. They wanted workers to not only manage themselves, they wanted councils of workers and consumers to plan and coordinate their various economic activities – democratically, equitably, and efficiently.

In the last hundred years we socialists have learned that capitalism is more resilient and adaptive than early socialists anticipated. In the twentieth century financial regulations and Keynesian stabilization policies were developed to ameliorate crises that went entirely unchecked in early capitalism. We socialists have learned that building a coalition capable of replacing the capitalist yoke with a more democratic, equitable, and efficient economic system is more difficult than early socialists imagined. History has taught us that if we are to succeed we must learn from our mistakes, deepen our understanding of social dynamics, create larger and more powerful movements, learn to work productively with those seeking to overcome other equally powerful forms of oppression, and become far more strategically and tactically flexible and nimble. And understandably, most discussion and disagreement among leftists over the past hundred years has been concerned with all these important matters.

But socialists have also learned through bitter experience that precisely how workers and consumers can manage and plan among themselves democratically, equitably, and efficiently is not as obvious as our predecessors assumed. And while discussion among leftists about how a socialist economy can best be organized and function has taken up less of our time and energy than debates over political strategy and program, nonetheless, over the years different competing schools of thought about what socialists should propose in place of capitalism have evolved.

Some socialists have continued to argue that there is nothing wrong – indeed, that there is everything right – about early socialist visions of an economic system in which workers manage themselves, and worker and consumer councils plan and coordinate their activities together. And it has been thirty years since Michael Albert and I first proposed a model of participatory economic planning for the twenty-first century to show that deviating from this vision, to instead champion a model of worker-owned enterprises coordinated by markets as a way of escaping the dying Soviet system of state enterprises coordinated by a central plan, was both unnecessary and a mistake.[1] The participatory economics 'model' has since been refined a number of times because it behooves those like myself, who continue to propose that councils of workers and consumers plan and manage their interrelated activities themselves, to explain concretely how they can do this, because it turns out it is neither obvious nor simple.[2]

The point of making a libertarian socialist vision more concrete is not to dictate to those who will live in some future economy what they must do – which is both absurd and impossible in any case. Instead, the point is to explain concretely how all the different kinds of decisions which must be made might be made without resort to either markets or authoritarian directives. The point is to show by counter example why workers and consumers need not expose themselves to the anti-social forces inherent in markets nor to the authoritarian dynamics inherent in central planning *because they can plan their interrelated activities perfectly well themselves*.

However, to do this we need to think carefully about what information workers and consumers will need to make sensible choices, and how that information can be generated. We need to design decision making procedures not only so people have decision making input in proportion to the degree they are affected, but also to eliminate perverse incentives for decision makers to behave contrary to the social interest. We need to explain how socialists can reconcile our conviction that fairness requires compensating workers according to their efforts and sacrifices, with the need for efficiency in allocating different categories of labor according to their opportunity costs. We need to explain how various kinds of long-term development plans, medium-term investment plans, and annual plans can be created democratically, and integrated in ways to take advantage of new information as it becomes available to update plans accordingly. And finally, we need to design procedures so that democratic economic decision making does not become so cumbersome and time consuming that it devolves into what socialist-feminist economist Nancy Folbre once warned might become a 'dictatorship of the sociable', as sensible people cease to devote inordinate amounts of time to meetings.

This essay reviews what the participatory economics model contributes to making the vision of early socialists more concrete, comprehensive, and convincing. While showing how and why new information technologies and capabilities are relevant to democratic socialist planning, it argues that whatever has prevented participatory planning from already being tried, it is *not* because it required some advance in mathematical theory, computational capacities, or information technologies yet to come. Participatory planning did not become possible only after mathematical theory evolved sufficiently to solve large, constrained optimization problems, only after computer capabilities evolved sufficiently to store and process large quantities of information quickly, and only after vast quantities of information could be accessed and communicated virtually instantaneously by anyone with a laptop computer.

RECONCILING DEMOCRATIC PLANNING AND AUTONOMY

The socialist calculation debate was launched in the early twentieth century when anti-socialists argued, first, that the amount of information *a decider* would need in order to allocate resources efficiently made the problem so large that it could not be solved even in theory; and second, that because of what came to be known as the 'tacit knowledge problem', *a decider* could not solve the problem in practice even if it were solvable in theory. By the 1970s advances in mathematical programming theory and computational capacity seemed to render the first objection moot, while advances in a creative literature on iterative planning procedures provided promising 'mechanisms' *a decider* might deploy to gather the tacit knowledge located in production units needed to make efficient decisions.[3] However, the key point is this: while early socialists championed conscious decision making over impersonal coordination by markets, they did not propose that one central *decider* coordinate the interrelated activities of different groups of workers and consumers. Instead they proposed that *the associated producers decide for and among themselves*. And these are not the same thing at all.

In both cases conscious decision-making is proposed to replace impersonal coordination by markets. And in both cases the product of conscious decision-making is a comprehensive plan for the entire economy. But participants on both sides of the socialist calculation debate assumed that a comprehensive economic plan in which the activities of large numbers of workplaces are coordinated with each other and with consumers requires a central planning authority of some kind. However, in truth it does *not*. With the benefit of hindsight we can now see that when early thinking about democratic planning by 'associated producers' was fleshed out in the twentieth century – both in theory by participants in the socialist calculation debate, and in practice in the Soviet Union – there was a fateful leap in thinking. It was assumed that a central planning authority is required to create a comprehensive economic plan. To borrow an analogy from Michael Lebowitz, it was assumed that such a large orchestra required a *conductor*.[4] This was the Achilles heel of real world, twentieth-century, centrally planned socialism.[5] The model of a participatory economy was designed to show how the musicians could perform perfectly well without a conductor. What should have always been the object of discussion and debate is this:

Concretely, how might worker and consumer councils and federations go about creating and coordinating long-term development plans, investment plans, and annual plans which are efficient, equitable, and sustainable in ways which give participants decision making power in proportion to the degree they are affected?

Answering this question requires us to go beyond wishful thinking and rosy rhetoric to explain in a matter-of-fact way how this can be done – how we might reconcile comprehensive planning with worker and consumer autonomy. This is what our participatory planning procedure, as refined over time, is designed to do.

Conceptually, the procedure is quite simple:

- The participants in the participatory planning procedure are worker councils and federations, consumer councils and federations, and an Iteration Facilitation Board (IFB) which plays a perfunctory role.
- At the beginning of each round of planning the IFB announces current estimates of the opportunity costs of using all natural resources, categories of labour, and capital goods available, as well as current estimates of the social cost of producing different capital goods, intermediate goods, and consumption goods and services. These estimates can be thought of as 'indicative prices' since they provide useful 'indications' of what it costs society when we use

different primary inputs from nature and different kinds of labour, and what it costs society to produce different goods and services.

- Neighbourhood consumer councils respond by making consumption proposals. That is, they propose what goods and services their households want to consume. Worker councils respond by making production proposals. That is, they propose what 'outputs' they want to produce and the 'inputs' they want permission to use to accomplish this – including not only intermediate goods they need from other worker councils and capital goods they want to use, but natural resources and different kinds of labour they would need as well.
- The IFB adds up all the demands and supplies for each final good, intermediate good, capital good, natural resource, and category of labour, and adjusts its estimate of the opportunity or social cost of the good – its 'indicative price' – up or down in proportion to the degree of excess demand or supply for the good in the latest round of proposals.
- These steps are repeated in subsequent rounds, or 'iterations', until there is no longer any excess demand for any final or intermediate good, capital stock, natural resource, or category of labour.

While the basic procedure is simple enough to describe, explaining how to make it easy for councils to decide whether to approve or disapprove one another's proposals, demonstrating why, under standard assumptions, the procedure will yield a feasible plan, and proving that the plan reached will be far more efficient than what any market system can hope to achieve is not always easy – sometimes because it requires some economic and mathematical training, and sometimes because there is a great deal of devil in the details. For example, it is important to show how the above procedures can handle externalities, public goods, and non-competitive industry structures in incentive compatible ways. It is also important to demonstrate why there is good reason to believe the number of 'iterations' required to reach a feasible plan will not be impractical. And it is important to explain concretely how investment and long-term development planning can also be done democratically and efficiently, and how to use information revealed by subsequent annual plans to correct and update longer term plans to mitigate welfare losses.

MAKING PARTICIPATORY PLANNING BETTER

This section briefly explains five areas where we have now advanced the cause of fleshing out a more compelling and convincing vision for twenty-first century socialism with concrete proposals to solve problems that will inevitably arise.[6]

1. Opportunity Costs, Social Costs, and Social Rates of Return

A key problem is how to generate reasonably accurate estimates of the opportunity costs of using scarce productive inputs – be they different categories of labour, different 'services' from the natural environment, or different capital goods. The 'stocks' of these at any point in time are scarce, and should therefore be allocated to wherever they are most productive and generate the greatest increase in social wellbeing. While some claim only markets can generate this needed information, our participatory planning procedure not only yields a feasible and efficient plan, but in the process of doing so it also generates accurate estimates of the social costs of producing goods and services. As iterations progress, unlike market prices, our 'indicative' prices account for externalities in production and consumption as well as small numbers of producers in industries characterized by increasing returns to scale. And our participatory investment and development planning procedures generate reasonably accurate estimates of the social rate of return on investment in capital goods, education, infrastructure, and environmental protection and enhancement.

All this is important for two reasons: without accurate estimates of opportunity costs, social costs, and social rates of return on investments, it is impossible to know how to allocate scarce productive resources efficiently – which most economists readily acknowledge. But what may be even more important for socialists is that without such estimates it is impossible for worker councils, consumer councils, and federations to participate sensibly and without undue imposition on their time in economic decision-making. Unless they are provided with reasonably accurate estimates of opportunity costs, social costs, and social rates of return, worker and consumer councils cannot know if their own proposals are socially responsible, nor can they know whether they should vote to approve or disapprove proposals made by other councils. However, with reasonably accurate estimates of opportunity and social costs and social rates of return, worker and consumer councils can engage in socially responsible self-management without a central authority and without excessive burdens on their time.

2. A Level Playing Field for Public and Private Consumption

For as long as we have lived in market economies, the playing field for public and private consumption has been severely tilted in favour of private consumption. In many countries this has been going on for more than twenty generations, and has therefore taken a significant cumulative toll on people's attitudes, expectations, and the kinds of preferences it was 'rational' for people living under these biased conditions to develop. The participatory planning procedure levels the playing field by having consumer federations propose the amounts of different kinds of public goods their members want just as consumer councils propose what private goods their members want, thereby making it as easy for people to express their desires for collective consumption as private consumption. And since the cumulative effects of the historic bias against collective consumption in favor of private consumption in market economies has penetrated deeply, at least initially we suggest requiring representatives sent to consumer federations to formulate their proposals for public good consumption first, so individuals will know how much of their income remains when they formulate their requests for private goods during the different rounds of the annual planning procedure.

3. Externalities Extinguished

It has also become abundantly clear that private enterprise and markets have long exerted a bias in favour of production and consumption activities with negative external effects, and against activities which generate positive external effects. The most clear example of this failure, which now threatens civilization as we know it, is that activities which emit greenhouse gases are favoured because their negative external effects go unaccounted for in market prices; while activities which reduce emissions or sequester greenhouse gases are discouraged because their positive external effects go unaccounted for.

Therefore we have incorporated a Pollution Demand Revealing Mechanism (PDRM) into the annual participatory planning procedure which will: (a) generate reasonably accurate quantitative estimates of the damage from pollution, (b) reduce pollution to reasonably 'efficient' levels, (c) satisfy the 'polluter pays principle', (d) compensate the victims of pollution for damages suffered, and most importantly (e) induce pollution victims to truthfully reveal what they believe to be their damages from pollution. The PDRM is most useful for local pollutants, pollutants whose effects are not lethal, pollutants whose effects are relatively well understood by victims, and pollutants whose effects do not extend far into the future. Yet coming up with an 'incentive compatible' procedure that induces victims to reveal the damage pollution causes is not a trivial accomplishment. Combined with our long-run environmental planning procedure it goes a long way to addressing a glaring historic weakness that socialists, collectively, must answer for: an inexcusable failure to come to environmental awareness sooner.

4. Income Distribution and Incentives

The debate over how to distribute the burdens and benefits of economic activity equitably has long been hotly contested. The first question is: what *is* a fair distribution of the burdens and benefits of economic activity? The second question is: how can this distribution best be achieved? And a third question is: are there trade-offs between distributing income fairly, inducing effort, and allocating labour to different workplaces efficiently? We propose clear answers to all three questions: (1) what is fair is to each according to his or her efforts and sacrifices; (2) co-workers are best suited to estimate differences in effort and sacrifice among them; and (3) there *need be no conflict* between fairness and efficiency. Rather than repeat our arguments for coming to the first two conclusions and defending them against criticism here,[7] we comment briefly on the third question.

We have argued that if different kinds of labour are to be allocated efficiently users must be *charged* according to their different opportunity costs. We have also argued that if workers are to be compensated fairly they must be rewarded or *paid* according to their efforts and sacrifices. *And, we have not only admitted, but insisted on the fact that the two are often not the same.* We have proposed a solution to this dilemma, which we believe advocates for models of market socialism have ignored because they have no solution. Our solution is this: When calculating the social cost of inputs requested by worker councils, to be compared with the social benefits of the outputs they propose to make, *worker councils should be charged* for scarce labour services of their members which they want to use *according to their opportunity costs*. This will ensure that labour is allocated efficiently among different workplaces. However, *workers should be paid according to their effort and sacrifice*, as determined by an effort rating committee of their co-workers. This will ensure that workers are compensated as fairly as is possible.

5. Integrating Long-Run and Short-Run Plans

Investment and development planning also need be done in ways which are democratic, efficient, and participatory. What is obvious as soon as we recognize the practical necessity of creating both short-run and long-run plans is that results from long-term plans are needed by those creating annual plans. Before we do annual planning we need to know how much of each capital good must be produced – which must be decided by the investment plan. We need to know what resources must be allocated to the educational system to train and teach various skills to the present and future workforce – which must be decided by the long-run education plan. We need to know what resources must be allocated to environmental protection and enhancement – which must be decided by the long-run environmental plan. And we need to know in what industries an economy should try to develop comparative advantages for international trade – which must be decided by the long-run, strategic international economic plan. In these ways the results from longer-term plans commit those who engage in annual planning to certain things they *must* accomplish during the year.

What is less obvious is how the results from annual planning can be used to identify mistakes in assumptions made when longer-term plans are first created, so longer-term plans can be modified to reduce losses in well-being. When investment and development plans are made there is no alternative to formulating *estimates* of what future labour supplies will be, what consumer preferences will be in the future, and what technologies will become available in the future. However, if these estimates prove to be inaccurate, as they inevitably will to some extent, then investment and development plans will fail to maximize social well-being because they will call for either too little or too much investment of different kinds.

Once it is conceded that as a practical matter economic planning cannot be done in one single operation over many, many years, but must instead be done as separate procedures – i.e. there must be an annual planning procedure, an investment planning procedure, and various long-term, development planning procedures – one must deal with the question of how to integrate these different planning procedures with one another. If one cannot explain how this can be done to minimize inevitable efficiency losses due to inaccurate estimates of future parameters in longer-term plans, the argument against comprehensive economic planning is strengthened.

It is crucial to integrate these planning efforts with annual planning efforts to identify errors in assumptions made when longer-term plans are drawn up, and revise those plans in light of better information when it becomes available to mitigate welfare losses. But as we have recently shown, results from subsequent annual plans can be used to reveal where errors were made when investment and development plans were initially created.[8] At which point investment and development plans can be revised in light of the new, more accurate information to mitigate welfare losses. The revised investment or development plan cannot perform as well as an initial plan based on accurate estimates because it cannot undo the damage done by inaccurate estimates before they were caught. But a revised plan can nonetheless perform better than permitting the initial plan to proceed uncorrected.

WHERE NEW TECHNOLOGIES CAN BE HELPFUL

In 2021 market systems do not have to prove they are a practical possibility.

Nor do centrally planned economies have to prove they are 'viable'. A number of centrally planned economies functioned for many decades in the twentieth century. And while I have never recommended central planning, and do not mourn its demise, it cannot be denied that in some respects centrally planned economies were not only viable, sometimes they were 'real world' success stories. No country had ever overcome underdevelopment and industrialized as rapidly as the centrally planned Soviet economy did during the 1930s. Had the Soviet Union not industrialized at an unprecedented rate, it is hard to imagine it would have been able to break the back of the Nazi war machine during the Second World War, in which case the remainder of the twentieth century might have looked very different for everyone.

Unfortunately however, as the twenty-first century is poised to enter its second quarter, we cannot point to any example where something resembling the kind of participatory planning we have proposed has ever had a chance to prove its viability in a real world setting. This is not to say that libertarian socialism has never risen beyond the status of a protest movement and vision. Nonetheless, it is not possible to point to any example where something like the participatory planning procedures we propose ever functioned long enough so that its 'practicality' cannot be questioned.

So we cannot 'prove' that participatory planning is a practical possibility by pointing to some real world example, as one can in the case of market and centrally planned economies. Nor has any government yet been willing to test its practicality by simulating the participatory planning procedure as a real world laboratory experiment to see what would happen. Until such time as the practicality of annual participatory planning can be tested in one of these ways, what we are left with are computer simulation experiments.[9]

There are limitations to what computer simulations of worker and consumer councils can tell us, and there is more simulation work to be done, so any conclusions at this point are provisional. Nonetheless, early results suggest that annual participatory planning is more 'practical' than sceptics warned. Based on hundreds of different simulation 'experiments' where we began with the opportunity and social costs from the previous year, made changes in the utility functions of thousands of consumer councils, and in the production functions of thousands of worker councils which corresponded to the kinds of changes that typically occur from year to year, it never took more than 7 iterations, and on average took only 5.2 iterations to arrive at a plan for the following year. If computer simulations are indicative, and if these results hold up after more testing, fears that the kind of participatory planning we espouse would prove to be too time consuming, and therefore impractical, appear to be unfounded.

None of this simulation research would have been possible with technologies available even fifteen years ago. Nor could central planning even stake a claim to being efficient prior to advances in mathematical theory, computational capacity, and 'iterative mechanisms' central planners might use to gather 'tacit knowledge' from production units. Yet efficient participatory planning was always possible. So discussion of information processing capabilities is at best tangential, and at worst misleading regarding whether or not what early socialist visionaries imagined and wanted was indeed, possible. The procedures we propose do not require advanced mathematical methods and computer power sufficient to solve a large constrained optimization problem, nor do they require any of the new technologies which now provide anyone access at negligible cost to vast quantities of information beyond our wildest dreams only a few years ago.

To be clear, we have sometimes used these mathematical tools to explain the logic of the planning procedures we propose; and without advances in computer capacity and software over the past twenty years, we could never have carried out the computer simulations of our participatory planning procedure we have now completed. But this should not be confused with mathematical calculations required of any participant in order to engage in participatory planning. As all economists who teach microeconomic theory know, theoretical analysis of 'the logic' of consumer behaviour under capitalism requires having a theoretical consumer solve a constrained optimization problem. But few if any real consumers formulate and solve a Lagrangian maximization problem before they go shopping. Which means, we must search for different reasons other than these for why libertarian socialism has yet to have an opportunity to prove its merits. We must search among a host of historical, political, and ideological obstacles which, unfortunately, still remain to be overcome.

This is not to say that new developments in information processing technologies have not made participatory planning easier to implement and more efficient. Recent advances in information processing make it easier and faster to (1) make and revise proposals during planning, (2) approve or disapprove proposals by others during planning, (3) individualize adjustment of opportunity and social costs for different goods during planning, and (4) do more planning virtually, without need for people to take the time to meet in person. But even more importantly, advances in information processing capabilities make it easier to (a) translate planned production in a smaller number of 'coarse' categories into a much larger number of more 'refined' categories, (b) turn a comprehensive production/consumption plan into a delivery plan which links particular suppliers with particular users, and

(c) adjust production and distribution *after* plans have been approved when unforeseen circumstances arise, as they inevitably do.

A number of critics have rejected participatory planning on these grounds. David Schweickart ridiculed consumption planning as 'nonsense on stilts' since 'unless requests are made in excruciating detail producers won't know what to produce'. Seth Ackerman has dismissed participatory economics for this reason as well, pointing out that 'there are more than two million products in Amazon.com's "kitchen and dining" category alone'.[10] Erik Olin Wright put it this way:

> The problem is that the gross categories provide virtually no useful information for the actual producers of the things I will consume. It does not help shirt-makers very much to know, based on the aggregation of individual household consumption proposals, that consumers plan to spend a certain per cent of their budget on clothing; they need to have some idea of how many shirts of what style and quality to produce since these have very … different opportunity costs.[11]

Since this concern became widespread we decided to give it a name and call it the 'size 6 purple women's high-heeled shoe with a yellow toe problem'. Quite simply the problem is this: a shoe producer must know to produce a size 6 purple women's high-heeled shoe with a yellow toe. The producer must know that size 5 will not do, a red toe will not do, a low heel will not do. However, it is unreasonable to expect the consumer who will eventually discover she wants a size 6 purple women's high-heeled shoe with a yellow toe to specify this at the beginning of the year as part of her annual consumption request.

How does a shoe producer in *any* economy know to produce a size 6 purple women's high-heeled shoe with a yellow toe, rather than a slightly different shoe? In a market economy shoe producers guess what shoe consumers will want when they decide to go shoe shopping. Producers guess based on past sales, on any consumer research they engage in, and on government projections of changes in relevant economic variables such as the distribution of income among households. And recently, many large companies have started to use newly available data gathering and processing capabilities to predict what products particular customers will want in the future. When I go to the Amazon website to inquire about some book, Amazon now tells me what other books I might be interested in buying. In other words, in market economies producers guess what to produce – because most sales are not arranged through pre-orders – and producers use advertising to try to influence consumers to buy what they have produced. New technologies of automated inventory supply management, 'on time' production, and consumer data base mining have made their guess work more accurate, but *in the end producers in market economies are still guessing.*

However, there is often a great deal of inefficiency that results from this guessing game that is an intrinsic feature of market economies. Unlike planned economies, in market economies there is no attempt to coordinate all the production and consumption decisions actors make before those decisions are translated into actions. As a result a great deal of what economists call 'false trading' occurs. False trades are trades individual parties make at prices that fail to equate supply and demand – which actually occurs more often than not. While seldom emphasized, competent economic theorists know that all false trading generates inefficiency to some extent, and dis-equilibrating forces operate in market systems alongside equilibrating forces when quantities adjust as well as prices. The notion that in market economies the convenience consumers enjoy of not having to pre-plan their consumption with producers comes at no price is based on the grossly unrealistic assumption that market economies are always in general equilibrium. For all their faults, twentieth century planned economies did not experience major depressions, or even significant recessions caused by mutually reinforcing dis-equilibrating forces in markets that all too often go unchecked by well-timed countervailing fiscal and monetary policies in market economies. But how will all this work in a participatory economy where there *is* a self-conscious attempt to coordinate production and consumption decisions *before* production begins?

Let's begin with information consumers will have about what is available. Ironically, the two million products in the Amazon.com 'kitchen and dining' section is not an insurmountable problem rendering comprehensive economic planning of any kind impossible. Instead it is a wonderful example of how consumers today can easily be made aware of the tremendous variety of products that will be available in a participatory economy. Just as Amazon.com can list millions of products – providing pictures and details about their characteristics – consumer federations can provide this service to consumers in a participatory economy for any who wishes to shop online. And for those who prefer what some of my students once told me were 'the pleasures of malling it', consumer federations can host shopping malls where anyone who wishes can go to see and be seen, and walk away with information on whatever strikes their fancy. Information about product improvements can be provided by consumer federations as well. The fact that it will be consumer federations providing information about products, rather than producers singing their own praises as is the case in market economies, should be a significant change for the better.

But, how, critics ask, will consumers pre-order? It is important to distinguish what we need from what we do *not* need to accomplish in the annual participatory planning process. When the year starts any shoemaking worker council with an approved proposal knows it should start making shoes. It also knows how much cloth, leather, rubber, etc. it has been pre-authorized for during the year, and how many shoes it has said it can make. It also knows that X per cent of the shoes it made last year were women's shoes, and Y per cent of the women's shoes it made last year were size 6. How does it know whether to start making size 6 purple women's high-heeled shoes with a yellow toe, or size 6 purple women's high-heeled shoe with a red toe? It does just what a shoemaking company in a market economy does: *It makes an educated guess.*

Then, as soon as actual consumption begins new information becomes available. Suppose purchases of size 6 purple women's high-heeled shoes with a yellow toe are lower than producers expected while the red toed shoes are disappearing like hot cakes. This kind of new information is what helps worker councils answer the question of exactly what kind of shoe it should be producing. The answer is basically the same as in a market system in regards to moving from a 'coarse' decision about shoe production to a 'detailed' decision about size 6 purple women's high-heeled shoes with a yellow toe production as the year progresses.

All of these new information technology capabilities, which help producers discover what consumers want in greater detail, and discover changes in consumer preferences faster, can make socialist economies more efficient as well as capitalist firms more profitable. And whereas in market economies producers will try to influence what I want to buy through advertising, since worker councils and individual workers are guaranteed compensation commensurate with their efforts and sacrifices, *and* will find it difficult to achieve greater compensation than they deserve in a participatory economy, there is far less temptation for them to engage in this kind of manipulative behaviour than there is for capitalist firms owned by absentee owners.

In any case, this first kind of new information fills in the details producers need to know about exactly what kinds of shoes people want, which is why consumers do *not* need to specify these details when submitting their personal consumption requests during the planning procedure. Submitting personal consumption requests during planning is not impossibly burdensome because the form would only need to have an entry called 'shoes' for one to put a number after, not an entry called 'size 6 purple women's high-heeled shoes with a yellow toe'! Those kinds of details are revealed by actual purchases as the year proceeds.

It is also important to distinguish between a worker council production plan that was approved as 'socially responsible' before the year began, and what a worker council is credited for at the end of the year. Work plan approvals are based on *projected* social benefit (SB) to cost (SC) ratios. However, worker councils are credited for the social benefit to cost ratio of *actual* outputs delivered and accepted, and *actual* inputs used during the year. Similarly, consumers, and consumer councils and federations are charged for what they actually consume during the year, not what was approved for them in the plan. Any differences are recorded as increases or decreases in the debt or savings of individual consumers, neighbourhood councils, and consumer federations. It is last year's *actual* social benefit to cost ratio that serves as a cap on average effort ratings worker councils can award members. So if their approved production plan had a SB/SC ratio of 1.09, but their actual ratio at year's end turns out to be 1.03, the cap on average effort ratings for workers in the council next year is 103 not 109. Therefore, a worker council which failed to respond to signals that become available during the year about what consumers truly like would in all likelihood end up with a lower actual social benefit to cost ratio, and consequently a lower average effort rating, and lower average incomes for the following year. So contrary to Schweickart's accusation, worker councils in a participatory economy have every incentive to find out what people want.

Ironically, perhaps the most common objection people have raised to our model of a participatory economy arises from a simple confusion over what a comprehensive economic plan is, and is not. A comprehensive economic plan is *not* a detailed plan of the kind that Wright once incorrectly assumed, and Schweickart ridiculed as 'nonsense on stilts'. Once that misunderstanding about comprehensive plans is laid to rest, the question is simply if it is possible to (a) fill in the necessary details from consumers orders which producers need, and (b) respond to changes which were not foreseen when the plan was agreed to. Necessary details producers need *can* be added to comprehensive economic plans, and adjustments *can* be made during implementation in perfectly satisfactory ways, which are considerably enhanced by new information technologies and capabilities.

But what about making post-plan adjustments, which will always be necessary? Actual purchase patterns during the year reveal more than needed details about consumer desires. They also signal when consumers have changed their minds. How to increase or decrease production of shoes because consumers have changed their minds must be negotiated between the shoe industry federation and the national consumer federation. Again, there are different ways these adjustments might be handled, each with its pros and cons. But the crucial questions are: to what extent will the shoe industry or consumers bear the burden of adjustments? And will shoe customers who change their demand for shoes be treated any differently from shoe customers who do not?

In the case of excess supply the issue reduces to whether or not producers will be credited for shoes that are added to inventories, and if so how much. The case of excess demand is more complicated. To raise shoe production more resources will have to be drawn away from industries experiencing excess supply. Beyond crediting shoe workers for working longer hours, will the indicative prices of shoes and the resources used to produce them be increased above their levels in the plan, or not? If shoe production is not raised sufficiently to satisfy all who now want shoes, will those who did not increase their demand above what they ordered be given preference? Those living in a participatory economy will have to debate the pros and cons of different answers to these questions. But, our point is simply that these questions can all be answered, and new information processing capabilities make the answers easier and more efficient to implement.

The difference between a planned economy and an unplanned, market economy is that to the extent that consumers submit proposals that reflect changes they anticipate in their tastes, and to the extent that worker councils submit proposals that reflect anticipated changes in their technologies and work preferences, the approved plan is our best guess of what should be done, and therefore reduces the number and size of adjustments necessary. All mechanisms for making adjustments in a market economy are available if wanted in a planned economy as well, although presumably a participatory economy would put a higher priority on mechanisms which distribute the costs of adjustments more fairly.

To summarize: from year to year consumers' incomes change, and consumers' desires change. Signalling producers about how these changes are likely to affect their demands for different goods and services is what planning and pre-ordering is for, and why it is quite useful for producers. Necessary details can be filled in from consumer profiles and actual purchases during the year, and adjustments can be negotiated with the aid of instantaneous inventory supply line prompts which new information technologies now make possible for worker councils and federations to use. But just because pre-ordering lacks detail and people change their minds does not mean the planning process is pointless. If we want consumers to influence what is produced in the economy, and if we are going to decide what is produced in large part through a planning procedure, then we need consumers to provide their best guesses about what they will want. We don't need them to agonize over their proposals, we don't need unnecessary details, and we certainly can accommodate them when they change their minds.

CONCLUSION

Is the adjustment process described above really just a market after all? Clearly, approved consumption plans are not treated as binding contracts since individuals are free to change their minds as the year proceeds. Moreover, one possible option for making adjustments would allow indicative prices to rise when excess demand for something appears during the year, and indicative prices to fall in the case of excess supply. In which case, if it looks like a market, and smells like a market, isn't it a market? The answer is an emphatic 'no!' for these reasons:

(1) In market economies there is no plan that has been agreed to at the beginning of the year. There is no plan where people had an opportunity to affect production and consumption decisions roughly in proportion to the degree they are affected. There is no plan that incorporates effects on 'external parties' which are ignored by buyers and sellers who make the decisions in market economies. There is no plan that would be efficient, fair, and environmentally sustainable if carried out.

(2) Even when adjustments are made during the year, in a participatory economy individual buyers and sellers do not negotiate adjustments between themselves however they see fit, including any adjustment in prices. Instead, adjustments are negotiated socially through industry and consumer federations. And whether or not to adjust indicative prices is also a social decision, so that fairness as well as efficiency can be taken into account.

(3) Markets are the aggregate sum of haggling between many self-selected pairs of buyer-sellers. Neither participatory planning nor the adjustment procedures we propose permit self-selected buyer-seller pairs to make whatever deals they want – because we have learned that the consequences of allowing this are unacceptable for a host of reasons.

Information processing capabilities which were beyond most people's dreams fifty years ago can improve outcomes considerably by making the planning procedure itself much faster and more efficient, by greatly facilitating the translation of requests from users expressed in coarse categories into more refined categories needed by producers, and finally, by making post-plan adjustments more easy and quicker. However, even when refining categories and making adjustments is done in similar ways to how this is done in market economies, there is a fundamental difference between economies which begin with a comprehensive plan, as we propose, and market economies, which do not.

So what are we to make of some new proposals which begin by pointing out that modern 'super' computers, or new information technologies, finally make it possible to create a detailed, comprehensive economic plan without resort to markets? Paul Cockshott and Allin Cottrell have argued that modern computers make their proposal for calculating an efficient comprehensive plan possible.[12] More recently, Dan Saros argues that new information and communication technologies now make his proposal for creating a detailed comprehensive economic production *and* delivery plan practical.[13] While there is much of interest in their proposals, I believe neither creates the kind of collaborative, participatory, decision making process giving worker councils considerable autonomy which our proposal for development, investment, and annual planning does. Nor do I believe either Cockshott and Cottrell or Saros' procedures would create plans which are efficient, whereas we have demonstrated how and why our procedures will.[14]

There are of course endless details and complexities one could pursue regarding exactly how a participatory economy would function. These will be coped with and decided by the people who live in a participatory economy. The issue before us is simply if there are perfectly straightforward possible solutions to these problems, and therefore if a participatory economy is, indeed, a practical possibility. We have shown it always was. The relevance of new information technologies is only that they make whatever straightforward solution to these problems people choose to implement faster and more efficient.

NOTES

1 Michael Albert and Robin Hahnel, *Looking Forward: Participatory Economics for the Twenty First Century*, Boston: South End Press, 1991; and *The Political Economy of Participatory Economics*, Princeton NJ: Princeton University Press 1991.

2 *Economic Justice and Democracy: From Competition to Cooperation,* New York: Routledge, 2005; *Of the People, By the People: The Case for a Participatory Economy,* Chico, CA: AK Press, 2012; with Erik Olin Wright, *Alternatives to Capitalism: Proposals for a Democratic Economy*, London: Verso, 2016; and most recently, *Democratic Economic Planning,* Cambridge UK: Cambridge University Press, 2021.

3 While this literature provided innovative ways for central authorities to elicit 'tacit knowledge' known only to those in production units, its procedures were not necessarily "incentive compatible." For an in depth discussion, see chapter 3 in *Democratic Economic Planning*.

4 See Michael Lebowitz, *The Contradictions of "Real Socialism": The Conductor and the Conducted*, New York NY: Monthly Review Press, 2012.

5 For an intriguing analysis of the political debates in Yugoslavia from 1945 to 1990 over plan versus market, worker self-management versus decision making by political bodies, and centralization versus decentralization see: Darko Suvin, *Splendour, Misery and Possibilities: An X-ray of Socialist Yugoslavia,* Brooklyn NY: Haymarket Books, 2015.

6 *Democratic Economic Planning,* Parts III, IV and V.

7 Interested readers should see Robin Hahnel 'Economic Justice', *Review of Radical Political Economics* (37)2, 2005, pp. 131-54; 'Exploitation: A Modern Approach', *Review of Radical Political Economics* (38)2, 2006, pp. 175-92; and "Economic Justice: Confronting Dilemmas," *Journal of Economic Issues* (54)1, 2020, pp. 19-37.

8 *Democratic Economic Planning,* Parts IV and V

9 A detailed explanation of exactly how the simulations were done, and a report on the results from all the different 'experiments' we conducted, is contained in chapter 8 of *Democratic Economic Planning.*

10 David Schweickart, 'Nonsense on Stilts,' *ZNet,* 2006, available at: zcomm.org. Seth Ackerman, 'The Red and the Black', *Jacobin* 20 December 2012.

11 Eric Olin Wright, *Alternatives to Capitalism: Proposals for a Democratic Economy,* London: Verso, 2016, p. 26.

12 See W.P. Cockshott and A. Cottrell, *Toward a New Socialism,* Nottingham UK: Spokesman Books, 1993.

13 See Dan Saros, *Information Technology and Socialist Construction: The end of capital and the transition to socialism,* New York NY: Routledge, 2014.

14 See the Appendix to *Democratic Economic Planning* where I present and evaluate not only the proposals of Cockshott, Cottrell, and Saros in depth, but proposals for how to do comprehensive economic planning by Pat Devine and David Laibman as well.

POSTCAPITALISM: ALTERNATIVES OR DETOURS?

GREG ALBO

More than a decade after the 'great financial crisis' erupted in the US and quickly swept across the world, the detritus of unmet financial claims and devalued labour still lay strewn across the economic landscape and central bank balance sheets. International economic authorities that were already cautious about the prospects for global capitalism in 2019 – a 'delicate moment' according to the IMF – turned even more circumspect as the global pandemic came to wreak havoc on economic growth and government fiscal positions.[1] Investors and states alike looked to hedge against mounting risks – unsustainable credit levels, asset bubbles, weaknesses in new investment spending and aggregate demand, and tensions over tariffs in the international trading system – but could envisage 'no simple mechanisms for reducing these sources of fragility that now exist'.[2]

For all the ideological discrediting of 'free and efficient markets' this entailed, the long recession barely loosened the grip of neoliberalism on economic policy. Austerity and the drive to monetize public assets retained primacy in fiscal policy settings; exceptional monetary policies continued to buttress credit and equity markets with the winding down of quantitative easing and low interest rates holding steady for the future; post-crisis banking regulations were loosely implemented and new credit instruments continued to emerge in the shadows of formal bank lending. Above all, finance capital maintained its hold over the accumulation process; and flexibilization remained the policy praxis in wage-setting and welfare policy alike, in a neoliberal policy regime which still set the parameters for 'feasible capitalism' and 'actually-existing liberal democracy'.[3]

The obstacles to finding an exit from neoliberalism – not to mention capitalism itself – became increasingly expressed in political frustration. The hard right often appeared as the most willing to challenge conventional economic policy and the hollow rituals of liberal democracy, and the most adept at mobilizing anger and anxieties into populist and racist movements across Europe and North America.[4] Those who expected the crisis to provide an opening for, or even compel, social democratic parties to break from their Third Way support for neoliberal globalization since the 1990s have been frustrated by the response. The strategic offerings, from both social democratic party leaders and policy intellectuals, have barely renewed its policy mix: state-supported competitiveness strategies centred on extending high-tech across all sectors; a recycling of training policies to match the skill algorithms of the 'digital economy'; infrastructure spending leveraged through public-private sector partnerships and designated capital funds; and a battery of technical reforms to remedy governance deficits in the practices of the new public management.

Joseph Stiglitz, as perhaps the most prominent example, has pitched an alternative agenda around an expanded 'public option' so threadbare in its egalitarian and policy ambitions as to actually reveal the resignation of social democracy to the mere renewal of 'competitive corporatism' – the search for a 'progressive capitalism based on a new social contract between voters and elected officials, between workers and corporations, between rich and poor, and between those with jobs and those who are un- or underemployed'.[5] And even as sharp an analyst as Wolfgang Streeck, once the forceful advocate of the skills and innovation strategy of 'diversified quality production' in the 1990s, has more recently showed that the only social democratic twist to an increasingly contradictory neoliberal economic policy regime amounts to little more than 'buying time'. He no longer offers anything remotely resembling an alternative socialist agenda, or even a conjunctural strategy for overturning what he calls the neoliberal 'consolidation state'. The political pessimism which accompanies the question he now poses in *How Will Capitalism End?* leaves Streeck, for all the biting indignation he levels at oligarchs and neoliberal policy-makers, in the post-democratic camp of progressives stumbling for a path back to national Keynesianisms.[6]

To be sure, the main political reference points in opposition to neoliberalism – the constituent organizations of the Party of the European Left, the platforms associated with the left coalitional Iberian governments, the policy proposals that emerged from the British Labour Party under the leadership of Jeremy Corbyn, and the Bernie Sanders candidacy in the Democratic Party presidential primaries – have, of course, disdained such pessimism as well as sought to go beyond advocating only a return to competitive corporatism.[7] Here, the characteristic programme has been along the lines of the annual Euro-Memorandum – itself something of a broad left consensus document: an anti-austerity reflationary fiscal policy;

an institutional re-design of the welfare state and collective bargaining; a more activist industrial and trade policy for the 'new economy'; state and employee 'social ownership' incursions into private corporations; a network of state development banks; and a renewal of democratic institutions (particularly targeted at the European Union level) to align administrative competencies with fiscal capacities across the scales of the state. In sum, an anti-austerity, 'Keynes-plus' reversal of the economic policy regime of neoliberalism, recalling the alternative economic strategies of the 1970s, but now set within a far less ambitious transitional policy matrix.[8]

There is, however, deep-seated scepticism toward any of these agendas amongst many of the most militant opponents of neoliberalism, who have insisted on the importance of advancing a 'postcapitalist' future.[9] For them, the necessary break from neoliberalism is too sharp, and the disintegration of the historical institutions of the left too severe, for a rehabilitation – at whatever scale of intervention – of a more egalitarian growth model that would recall the productivism and bureaucracy of postwar Fordism. Yet a more determined anti-capitalist seizure of power, occupation of the institutions of the state, and a programme of nationalization of the 'commanding heights' of the economy, is even less convincing for them. What is needed for renewing an emancipatory politic is thus quite different, and has been advanced in a variety of forms as projects for 'postcapitalism': in the construction of 'real utopias' offering new patterns of asset distribution and ownership 'over work'; in the extension of practices of 'commoning' autonomous from the capitalist state and 'apart from work' as value production; and in the 'acceleration' of the pace of technological change toward 'full automation' to open up a 'post-work' social horizon. Such postcapitalist projects, it is argued, prefigure a more direct, participatory democratic order as well as a more direct, less state-dependent means of transcending value production.

The question is, where exactly do these 'real utopias' of postcapitalism really take us? What openings do they suggest for the transformation of the economy and state necessary to sustain socialism as 'the *real* movement which abolishes the present state of things'?[10] That is, do they actually point beyond capitalism or rather offer a series of detours toward the renewal of a 'mixed economy' inside capitalism?

REAL UTOPIAS

The 'Real Utopias' book series associated with Erik Olin Wright began in the mid-1990s as an anti-capitalist critique of social inequalities, market failures, and the 'thin' democracy of capitalist society. Over the years, Wright himself used a variety of terms for the institutionalizations of his real utopias

– non-capitalism, economic democracy, democratic economy, democratic socialist economy, cooperative market economy, democratic egalitarian economy and, finally, *postcapitalist* democratic economy.[11] In his own capstone contribution to the series in 2010, *Envisioning Real Utopias*, Wright identified the purpose as 'rebuilding a sense of possibility for emancipatory social change by investigating the feasibility of radically different kinds of institutions and social relations that could potentially advance the democratic egalitarian goals historically associated with the idea of socialism'.[12] Yet while offering any number of social strategies and policy schemes for institutional reforms of 'dominant forms of social organization', these all amount to far less than anti-capitalist utopias, and much more as designs for inclusionary forms of ownership to bind workers more tightly to firms for productive efficiencies, and proposals for participatory modes of governance at the margins of the state.

One of the first volumes in the series, *Recasting Egalitarianism*, centred on a redistribution of capital assets within firms through incentive structures that would make for more cooperative and efficient workplaces. The key to this, as argued in the pivotal essay by David Gordon, was the recognition that 'productivity deserves paramount priority – especially among egalitarians; that market-based policies pursuing both egalitarian objectives and productivity-enhancement have greater promise than public interventions over-riding market outcomes; and there exists a set of specific market-based policies which could simultaneously reduce inequality and boost economic efficiency.'[13] To this end, 'productivity-enhancing governance structures' such as works councils, along with other measures such as productivity-sharing bonuses and employment security, would provide, Gordon concluded, the basis for a 'positive-sum' transition to more egalitarian relations made possible by cross-class collaboration between capitalists and workers.

Such positive class compromises – where capitalists give up resources and social power for productive efficiencies and competitiveness – became integral to Wright's version of paths to postcapitalism in his own *Envisioning Real Utopias* magnum opus. Wright contended here that capitalism is, in fact, an 'eco-system' encompassing three distinct sub-systems – the state, civil society, and the economy – with each having its own forms of power, institutional matrix and logic of reproduction. For Wright, Marx's economic-technological determinism subsumes and flattens these sub-systems making them all into instances of direct capitalist domination. This has unfortunately encouraged a socialist vision of breaking with capitalism in a 'decisive … victory of popular forces … resulting in the rapid transformation of the structures of the state and the foundations of economic structures'. Such 'ruptural strategies' necessarily rule out immediate material gains for subordinate classes and their allies, which are necessary to hold a progressive political bloc together, and make it 'unlikely that a ruptural transition to socialism would be sustainable under democratic conditions'.[14]

Instead, in Wright's sociology of egalitarian transition, 'interstitial' strategies are designed to avoid confrontational class struggles in favour of 'relatively small transformations [which] cumulatively generate a qualitative shift in the dynamics and logic of a social system'; while 'symbiotic' strategies are advanced to allow for class compromises which secure working-class material gains and social power by helping to 'solve certain real problems faced by capitalists and other elites'. The task, then, is not 'to propose blueprints' for socialism, but to offer a 'socialist compass' of viable institutional designs and democratic practices 'supporting the conditions for noncapitalist alternatives'.[15] Since capitalism is never 'pure' and economies are always 'hybrids' of different logics, institutions, and practices, 'capitalist societies always contain at least some socialist elements, through the ways collective actors in civil society influence the allocation of economic resources indirectly through their efforts to influence the state and capitalist corporations'.[16]

Wright's compass thus pointed to potential pathways already internal to capitalism that at the same time, as he sees it, potentially lead beyond it. After rejecting 'statist options' for their inevitable drawbacks demonstrated by historical experience, the five other options identified as both feasible and desirable – the social economy, cooperative production, social capitalism, participatory governance, and associative democracy – constitute Wright's map of 'real utopias'. The examples offered of each of these – open cyber-platforms (as with Wikipedia),[17] workers' coops (as in Mondragon),[18] employee stock ownership plans (ESOPs – as in the Quebec Solidarity Fund), participatory budgeting (as in Porto Alegre), and tripartite cooperation (as in labour market training partnerships)[19] – have little or no obvious commonalities or synergies. But, consistent with the Real Utopias project as a whole, they offer a plurality of 'micro-strategies' to democratize capitalism, however incrementally, by layering participatory governance forms over the 'asset mix' of ownership, relations of authority, and skills that underpin the organization of firms in the capitalist sector. These arrangements all still operate within existing value production and class relations of capitalist firms and markets, but they all involve establishing institutional frames and processes of social empowerment in civil society which, once 'scaled-up', would ensure that capitalist logic and institutions will be 'eroded' as egalitarian social power grows, and as cooperation with capitalists gives way to democratic empowerment.

Despite its elaborate theoretical architecture, Wright's 'real utopias' turn out to be surprisingly conventional and underwhelming in relation to his postcapitalist goals.[20] All the institutional schemes are not only intertwined with the stability and expansion of markets for their self-reproduction, they equally operate as mechanisms for social incorporation within capitalism in their own right. Wikipedia depends on market philanthropy and unpaid labour reflective of the inequalities of capitalism, and is far removed from the social provisioning of public libraries. The cooperative sector must sell its goods in markets where costs and competitive imperatives are set by the capitalist sector and the law of value. ESOPs extend legal ownership and give 'voice' to employees, but the dominant capitalist groups retain control of the allocation and disposition of assets while the authority relations of ownership condition the strategies of unions and workers in dealing with the corporations to take account of competitiveness. Participatory budgeting may redraw the allocative margins of municipal finances and facilitate participation in neighbourhood councils, but its decisions are limited by urban fiscal capacities and planning, which are in turn dependent upon capitalist development. Tripartite class compromises formally extend worker and community participation, while also building the ideological and institutional supports for maintaining firm and sectoral competitiveness and containing hostility to capitalist class power.[21]

It is hard to see how a 'scaling-up' any of these projects transforms them into noncapitalist logics that overwhelm their 'system-maintenance' role of providing institutional mechanisms for inclusion of workers and the marginalized in capitalist economies. Wright's strategic calculation rests entirely on the hybridity claim – that 'no actual living economy has been purely capitalist'.[22] The corollary is that capitalism will continue to reside in socialism and so we are just making assessments of 'sociological variables' and 'causal primacy' and not political alignments, class struggles, and socialist strategies to build working-class capacities.

Envisioning Real Utopias is wracked by hedges and qualifications – offering simply 'a menu of strategic logics and an indeterminate prognosis for the future'. Of course, no one knows how the future will unfold and where and under what conditions new possibilities will emerge. But Wright's pathways to utopia offer little more than routes to a quite familiar 'mixed economy', renamed as societal 'hybrids', far removed from a vision of collective ownership, workers' control, and radical democratization of the state. Indeed, socialism is recast as little more than the shuffling of the allocation of asset mixes – 'the greater the degree of social empowerment over the ownership, use, and control of economic resources activities, the more we can describe an economy as socialist'.[23] All Wright's pathways are indeed 'real' and 'feasible': capitalism has always incorporated varieties of institutional forms and ownership patterns without overturning value production, a market in labour, or disrupting the administrative logic of the capitalist state. In searching for postcapitalist exits, Wright's compass only points toward innumerable detours.

COMMONING

The road to postcapitalism by means of 'commoning' is often associated with the theoretical tendency of 'autonomous Marxism' (although analogous alternatives can be found in the many adherents to 'solidarity economies').[24] The history of capitalism is layered with scores of movements of quite varied political persuasions building spaces of social cooperation and voluntary communities apart from the market. Today, this is often raised in terms of reclaiming and extending the 'commons' as a space where resources, institutions, and social practices might escape the disciplines of value production – and hence apart from waged work – and the capitalist state. But there is far less agreement on the anti-capitalist exit routes to take.

For Michael Hardt and Antonio Negri, the revolutionary dynamic of the information and communication technologies (ICT) overthrows Fordist mass production, Taylorist labour processes, and managerialist knowledge and, in the process, dissolves the industrial working class, public provisioning, anD the 'vertical' hierarchies of the capitalist state and firms. In contrast, the 'biopolitical production' of intangible values and products of ICT pivots on information, immaterial labour, and 'cognitization', forming into 'horizontal' organizational networks. This knowledge is decentred, spread across the network and, moreover, is now 'a central productive force' beyond the command and control of states and firms. Thus, for Hardt and Negri, 'the production of knowledge itself is value creation … the more [capital] is forced to pursue valorization through knowledge production, the more knowledge escapes its control'.[25] As immaterial labour is constituted through the information flows of global networks outside traditional work relations, bio-political production infuses, in an unprecedented way, all of social life. In blurring the boundaries between production and social reproduction, the quantitative growth of immaterial labour breaks the quantitative linkage – hence the disciplining role – between abstract labour and capitalist value production.[26]

The space for new forms of democratic practices and commons apart from work is, for Hardt and Negri, enabled by the transformations in work itself. What capital now attempts to enclose and appropriate through bio-production is what the social relations of immaterial labour depends upon and produces in 'common' – 'our communication, collaboration, and cooperation'.[27] These modes of interconnection are central to the capitalist exploitation of immaterial and intangible labour. But in the process of production the 'excess' of these information flows cannot be captured by capital, and so Marx's 'collective worker' is reconstituted as a 'singularity' at key nodal points, which re-emerges in their plurality as a unified social subject – the 'multitude'.[28] 'Behind our backs', so to speak, the network of bio-political labour produces, outside of capitalist control, a 'common' space, a 'general intellect', even a 'common wealth'. In the 'changing composition of capital ... today the general intellect is becoming a protagonist of economic and social production'.[29]

The new communicative network is horizontalist in its mode of organization, providing the multitude a pivotal position in the social relations of the network outside traditional unions, parties, and states, and an advantage in their struggle against the vertical hierarchies of 'capitalist control'. The emergent democratic capacities of immaterial labour, however, have no clear institutional terrain or organizational agency in which they cohere apart from the 'common' as both the space of action and result. That is, the biopolitical reproduction of daily life now dominates production and all else. Indeed, with the transformation of the state set to the side, the seizure of the means of production within the firm is enabled by a logic of technological transformation creating a revolutionary process – a 'common' – of practices, spaces, habits of life. From here, the radical ambitions of Hardt and Negri dissipate into the most predictable and incremental of reforms 'demanded of existing governments': the 'basic means of life' (as in universal healthcare and a guaranteed income), 'equality against hierarchy' (as in basic education and knowledges for citizenship), 'open access to the commons' (as in government support for developing scientific knowledge as productive common wealth).[30] Thus, having started with the potentials of 'the common' forming in the bio-politics of the network, Hardt and Negri end with political 'demands to make on today's ruling powers' that merely take a detour back to the promises of the social democratic welfare state and regulatory controls on capital.

The thesis that a multitude forged in the digital networks of capitalism engaged in value production is, at the same time, the social force capable of establishing the commons of postcapitalism was found by many other proponents of postcapitalism to be far from convincing. Insofar as it was imperative that anti-value struggles also take up alternatives autonomous from the state, then these struggles rather need to be located in the social needs of everyday life. It is here that alienated labour might be vanquished, in the cracks in the system, through 'common' spaces and provisioning distant from the logic of endless accumulation and the fetishism of 'capturing' state power. John Holloway, for instance, contended that any organizational space opened up by the technologies of the network still failed to grapple with the obstacle of the state and the internalization of the capital relation – there is no outside. Indeed, autonomy from the state is fundamental for 'you cannot build a society of non-power relations by conquering power. Once the logic of power is adopted, the struggle against power is already lost.' The negation of the disciplines of abstract labour and the state's 'power-over' can only be countered by the 'anti-power' found in the 'relations we form all the time' – relations of cooperation and community, gardening, goofing-off at work, playing music, of resistance, and so on.[31]

These activities of daily life say 'NO!' to capital insofar as they are, in substance, anti-value expressions of freedom apart from dependency on the capitalist state. For Holloway, their 'concrete doing' in practice 'overflows' the logic of capital by evading transformation into abstract labour and it is this which opens space for the 'rebellion in everyday life' against the labour that produces capital, and for the validation of social relations of self-determination 'against and beyond value'. The negation of capital comes, then, from the outside, far from the illusory struggles of parties and unions for a claim on state power. Holloway's 'move against and beyond capital' is an unrelenting act of refusal of being enclosed in the capital relation, such that even the 'struggle of internet workers in Seattle, say, is not a positive common class composition but rather the community of their negative struggle against capitalism'. This struggle, Holloway insists, is also the 'coming together to form alternate projects for the organization of our doing' and to strive to create 'new articulations … beyond the particular cooperative project'. Notably, nothing is said here about how, and by what 'anti-power', are the means of production to be socialized, or about what exits from capitalism as a system of political economy can be found that entirely skirt the state. In the enormous void between the 'doing' – from community gardening to occupying factories to the revolutionary agenda of the 'creation of a new common', between the 'movements from below' and the politics of governance through the 'commune of communes'[32] – all roads to postcapitalism appear open, but without any maps, and with very few detours squarely posted.

Silvia Federici famously offered a more direct and programmatic postcapitalist strategy in the form of 'a refusal of alienated labour' taking shape

– in the struggles for needs (use) against value (exchange) in the reproductive work of daily life in ways that '"valorizes" us … [for] integration in the labor market but also against it'.[33] For her, like for Hardt and Negri, the appeal of the thesis of 'the multitude' is that 'a society built on the principle of "the common" is already evolving from the informatization of production'; indeed, is already 'immanent' in the organization of work and production that ceaselessly produce the symbols, commodities, and money-capital of the global flows of accumulation. Yet, the networks of digital capitalism are thoroughly integrated into global value chains, and are 'extremely destructive, socially and ecologically'. Moreover, the emphasis on information as knowledge production, with the internet making a new 'common space', evades the reproduction of everyday life fundamental to the experience of women, and this unleashes the 'potential to create forms of reproduction enabling us to resist dependence on wage labour and subordination to capitalist relations'.[34] For Federici, the 'commoning of the material means of reproduction is the primary mechanism by which a collective interest and mutual bonds are created'. A 'network of cooperatives' anchored within the activities of social reproduction, activities that 'cannot be robotized', could form 'outside' value relations and thus challenge the very conditions of existence of the capital relation.[35] Eldercare, childcare, mutual aid, food banks, housing co-ops could form an 'anti-capitalist commons … best conceived as autonomous spaces from which to reclaim control over our life and the conditions of our reproduction … to counter the processes of enclosure and increasingly disentangle our lives from the market and the state'.[36]

Yet it is hard to envision how mass provisioning could actually be realized, especially through decentralized community spaces, without any specification of the extra-market coordinative institutions for financing, facilitating access, ensuring mobility, equalizing caring capacities between public and cooperative providers, and so forth. Indeed, such 'solidarity economies' and 'communities of care' as Federici points to most often emerge as survival strategies when market incomes collapse or state policies of austerity erode social redistribution and public spaces.[37] It is not clear how such 'doing' negates the market dependence of working-class families on value production, as opposed to being totally consumed by the struggle to extract resources from the state and capital to sustain non-commodified social reproduction. Nor is it possible to separate autonomous cooperative social relations of the commons from the bureaucratic relations of the capitalist state in its constant reconfiguring of public spaces and administrative practices.

A 'post-capitalist transformation' depends, then, as Massimo DeAngelis suggests, on 'strengthening the commons and maximizing their autonomy from state and capital, while still interacting with the latter when necessary'. An 'accumulation of the commons' begins from understanding the 'two-fold character' of common goods as both use values satisfying 'socially determined needs' and as a 'use value for a plurality' who claim ownership as an element of a 'commons'. In other words, 'common goods are the elementary form of wealth of a postcapitalist world'. The pooled resources and claims of common ownership establish the practices of 'commoning' – as social labour 'doing in common'. The 'value practices' of commoning form a self-reproducing system, outside the logic of surplus value extraction and autonomous from the state, meeting common needs and 'generating communities of struggle and resistance', along the lines of the MST landless movement in Brazil or the localist self-management of public goods and services of Barcelona en Comú.[38]

But even this emergent 'commoning mode of production', as DeAngelis refers to these practices, appears less as a break from, than co-existence alongside, the system of capitalist production. As DeAngelis concedes, the recognition of the often-posed problem, in both political economy and state administration, of establishing boundaries between states, markets, and a 'third sector', radically shifts the project of postcapitalism and the claims of autonomy: 'So, for example, a pool of resource units of a cooperative of labourers involved in manufacturing and exposed to the pressure of competition, that is, cost minimization, puts pressure on them to externalise costs to the environment and wages as for any corporate sector. The strategic problem faced by postcapitalist commons is here how to extend the boundaries of their operations, through development … to include the ecological and capitalist systems with which they interrelate.'[39] A 'new commons deal' – aimed at establishing 'a collective effort, through the commoners' democratic management of constraints, costs and rewards, to increase all sorts of commoning across different social actors involved in the corporation or public service' – would have to engage in a 'strategic coupling' that makes 'capital and state complexity available for commons development'. In the bargain of such a 'new deal', 'the commons require a range of products of capitalist industry, capital depends on the resources created by peer-to-peer networks in cyberspace … for capitalist innovation; and the basic work of reproduction in households'.[40]

Yet it is hard to avoid seeing here certain parallels with the myriad of schemes for 'inclusionary ownership' and 'stakeholder capitalism' to offset the worst abuses of neoliberalism by revamping corporate governance. In this, the commons road to postcapitalism looks like a long way round to arrive at a destination which remains a sub-system of a conventional 'mixed economy' of private and public goods. Rather than an exit from capitalist value production, the practices of commoning, in all their variations, run straight into the capitalist state.

FULL AUTOMATION

In counterpoint to those who rooted their postcapitalism in commons *outside* value production, there has been a spate of recent attempts to locate postcapitalism in an 'acceleration' of technical change *within* value production. If the technical changes associated with digital capitalism are pushed to their limits, the advance of productivity could produce – and, to some degree, they claim, already have – a future that is 'post-scarcity' and even 'post-work'. The small-scale, horizontalist, autonomous politics of commoning that inspires much of the left today is simply not up to the task of taking this on, let alone overturning global neoliberalism. As Nick Srnicek and Alex Williams put it, in their provocative manifesto *Inventing the Future: Postcapitalism and a World Without Work*, 'arguments for withdrawal or exit too easily confuse the idea of a social logic separate from capitalism with a social logic that is antagonistic to capitalism ... Yet capitalism has been and will continue to be compatible with a wide range of different practices and autonomous spaces.'[41] Instead, what needs to be accounted for is the logic of the new technologies fundamentally transforming capitalism.

As also portrayed by Paul Mason, in his *Postcapitalism: A Guide to Our Future*, 'information technology expels labour from production, destroys pricing mechanisms and promotes non-market forms of exchange. Ultimately, it will erode the link between labour and value altogether.'[42] Trying to uncover a postcapitalist transition in industrial production, or even in the post-Fordist vision of high value-added manufacturing employing increasingly skilled workers favoured by social democracy, is just as backward-looking as envisioning a 'commons' as a substitute for collective service provisioning (including those provided by neoliberal administrations). For Mason, the blockage to a postcapitalist transition lies with the neoliberal faith in markets. Since the 'great financial crisis' the politics of austerity has further reinforced a low investment, low growth economic context that is steadily evolving into a protracted 'de-globalization crisis'. The neoliberal policy regime is fundamentally mismatched with the economic governance necessary for the organizational logic of 'info-capitalism'. Hence a potential 'long upsurge' of growth from an acceleration of investment in communication networks, AI, and robots is being choked-off rather than having already been realized (as Hardt and Negri imagine). For Mason, this is the pivotal policy and political challenge: 'information technology has robbed market forces of their ability to create dynamism. Instead it is creating the conditions for a postcapitalist economy.'[43]

For its proponents like Mason, info-capitalism opens the possibility – even demands – a postcapitalist future as 'the technologies we've created are not compatible with capitalism'. Digital labour working across networks produces new processes and products that escape traditional corporate hierarchies: open-source code (like Linux), cooperative production platforms (Wikipedia among others), generalization of the information economy (through the education sector and new logistics and tracking capacities), and by the unprecedented ability to produce additional units with marginal costs tending toward zero.[44] In an age of info-capitalism, the monopolization of production in giant corporation networks becomes impossible, except at great social cost. And with production processes and products so easily multiplied at zero marginal cost, infinite supply effaces the scarcities that are necessary to regulate capitalist markets via the pricing mechanism. In sum, 'the main contradiction of modern capitalism is between the possibility of free, abundant socially-produced goods, and a system of monopolies, banks and governments struggling to maintain control over power and information. That is, everything is pervaded by a fight between network and hierarchy.'[45]

Quite unlike previous technological revolutions in capitalism, the pivotal battle is now seen as taking place on the terrain of the labour market insofar as collaborative networks of knowledge workers engaged in production and design, unconstrained by managerial hierarchies, face a continual displacement of their direct labour by ever-smarter automation. The tendency of dead labour to replace living labour in capitalist labour processes is now, for Mason, at a crucial turning point: labour as the source of new value becomes insignificant to production since marginal cost (and thus also price in the context of market competition) is driven, 'over time, towards zero – eroding profits in the process'. In the already emerging new social relations of postcapitalism, information becomes the central input to the forces of production; goods are easily reproduced and no longer scarce, easily shared, and cooperatively owned thus transforming the relations of appropriation and exchange; and, crucially, 'work – the defining activity of capitalism – is losing its centrality both to exploitation and resistance'.[46] Indeed, insofar as the 'main faultline in the modern world is between networks and hierarchies', it is the 'networked individual' (the 'sublated' working class) that is 'kicking [postcapitalism] off everywhere', not least by connecting with the revolt against 'bullshit jobs' in a world without (decent) work. And since the global climate crisis requires a societal mobilization to unleash the disruption of the information technologies, the 'urgency of the postcapitalist project' is such that 'it's no longer the property of the left, but of a much wider movement'.[47]

With the link between labour and value thus snapped, class and class conflict in the traditional socialist sense fades away as the critical social division capable of staking a path to postcapitalism. By assimilating themes from across the economics of digital capitalism, Mason's own 'revolutionary reformism' relies on the revolutionary forces of production to dig capitalism's grave. The reform track is 'iterative, modular and gradual' in setting-out, more or less, to reverse neoliberalism and facilitate the market dynamics of zero marginal cost – dubbed 'Project Zero' – to transition to a post-scarcity society. Mason's programme of reforms, guided by 'maximizing the power of information' and 'decentralizing control', ranges widely. It pushes the boundaries of the mixed economy through economic modelling (as opposed to planning) and mixed ownership forms (but including the socialization of some of the big tech companies and the utilities); building out the collaborations of the information sectors in shareware, peer-to-peer computing, and non-profit agencies; a universal basic income and shorter work-hours to address a post-work economy; and socializing leading segments of finance and energy (to reduce carbon emissions). Yet, in the context of his central thesis, this is less a programme than an insistence that the force of info-technologies be released from all hindrances so that productive collaborations can transform firms and 'non-market production'.[48] Here, the proposal is simple in theory – but it would actually be extremely complex in practice: to eliminate the technical and legal obstacles that block the digital multiplication that deliver output and productivity advantages at zero marginal cost, what Mason points to as arriving at 'free machines'.

A capitalist economy based on digital information, Mason suggests, cannot exist. 'Once capitalism can no longer adapt to technological change, postcapitalism becomes necessary.'[49] This is a brittle thesis. There are clear 'network' gains for both users and purchasers of data on usage to favour a single provider of access to a platform; providers gain all kinds of advantages from first point of access that further compounds their monopoly position; ease of user access and digital replication of software and operating systems hardly eliminates the administrative costs for providers or the attendant hardware and infrastructure costs, as the number of users increases; development and fixed costs (and average rates of profit on capital invested) still need to be accounted for in the unit price of commodities (whether material or information). The list could be extended, as info-capitalism has had no shortage of success in turning its particular cost structures into new spaces for value production.[50] As for Mason's reform programme, it still allows the banks and the financial sector generally to allocate capital (and thus manage credit); and it also would retain an extensive non-financial capitalist sector to secure diversity and innovation. In this context, it is necessary to ask where his postcapitalism actually pushes past the 'mixed economy' and brings capitalism and exploitation to an end. Nor is it at all clear how Mason's 'wiki-state' emerges out of the actual state at the centre of the neoliberal project, let alone how it begins to 'wither away' as its starts 'to nurture the new economic forms' of postcapitalism. We are simply left to hang on Mason's claim that 'technology has created a new route out'.[51]

Many of the premises of Srnicek and Williams' *Inventing the Future* are shared with Mason, but their focus is far more distinct in politics and programme. For Mason, postcapitalism is already being made by info-capitalism and the left must find its place within the networks. But in Srnicek and Williams' imagined future of technological possibilities, freedom from wage-labour would have to be led by a 'hegemonic' left 'moving beyond defensive struggles'. This would require, as well, severing with the 'folk politics' of the 'horizontalist' and 'localist' left, with their nostalgia for a lost 'commons' without either programme or organizational capacity to achieve it. This is a politics which is too 'partial, temporary and insufficient' for a 'truly postcapitalist world'. Yet their own 'Accelerate Manifesto' still puts the greatest emphasis not on political strategy but an inevitable technological 'future' – 'an alternative modernity that neoliberalism is inherently unable to generate'. The task for the left is to re-appropriate digital technologies as 'these material platforms … can and will be repurposed and reformatted for post-capitalist ends'.[52] For these ends, it is not mainly the repurposing that makes an alternative future. It is the inherent socialization of science and technology in machines, whether robots or digital information, with their labour-saving bias, which makes possible an alternative post-work future no longer trapped in the necessities of wage-labour. Their 'first demand', therefore, 'is for a fully automated economy'. As a political project of the left, the task is to form strategies and policies to 'enthusiastically accelerate' all capitalist 'tendencies toward automation and the replacement of human labour … beyond the acceptable parameters of capitalist social relations'.[53] Capitalism, in other words, is now not so much blocking human liberation as it is 'constricting technological development' and, thus, the left is obligated to accelerate automation not merely as political vision but as a political commitment.

Since the war against neoliberalism has to pass through the digital technologies of automation, it is its realization in a counter-hegemony of 'post-work' that is the foundation for the rest of the programme – reduction of the work week, a universal basic income, and the dissolution of the work ethic. These are, Srnicek and Williams point out, minimal demands that recognize the growing surplus of labour from stagnation and automation, but they also potentially integrate a range of demands from anti-racists, feminists, and ecologists in a complete restructuring of all work and ecology. With full automation and post-work ensconced at the centre of a new hegemony – a new 'form of universal action ... supplanting neoliberal capitalism' – a full array of political options open up: new forms of 'additive' manufacturing to meet needs, global logistics moving goods without human labour, block-chain technology enabling a new money of the commons, a range of post-scarcity goods, new modes of public deliberation and planning, and more.[54]

But if these demands advance a detailed project of post-work in ways Mason neglects, many of the same dilemmas remain.[55] Robotization and automation arise out of the competitive imperatives internal to capital accumulation; capitalists have no need for a left to demand more of them, so as to lay the foundation for postcapitalism. And as with those on the left who once mistook the real meaning of the old Fordist productivity pacts between companies and unions, and then grasped for post-Fordist strategies, there appears even in Srnicek and Williams, as in Hardt and Negri, an expectation (since they are largely silent on this) that info-capitalism will undo, rather than reinforce, hierarchical organizational structures that are central to the bureaucratic and authoritarian relations of capitalist firms and states, let alone to reproducing the powers of finance capital. Moreover, it is never clear how the post-work 'transitional demand' to reduce the market dependence of workers on the purchasing power of the wage can be reconciled with the parallel demand for full automation, which is predicated upon surplus value production in its most technologically dynamic forms.

There is here a residual techno-economic determinism – that it is technology that establishes the terrain of struggle and what is possible, that breaks through and disrupts the barriers posed by the capitalist state and the organized capitalist class. This is, for socialists, always a flawed political mapping, a displacement of the primacy of politics that must be at the centre of socialist strategy and calculation. In the end, these proponents of full automation, replicating one of greatest limitations of traditional social democracy in the twentieth century, rely more on capital itself than on class struggles from below to get to beyond capitalism, and thus end up, as Rosa Luxemburg once cautioned, only with 'modifications of the old order'.[56] As with the Real Utopias project, and the various approaches to commoning, those advocating full automation in the name of postcapitalism offer detours rather than signposts to a democratic socialist future in the twenty-first century.

NOTES

1 The chief economist for the IMF, Gita Gopinath, summarizing a recent *World Economic Outlook* here: 'The Global Economy: A Delicate Moment', *IMF Blog*, 9 April 2019, at www.blogs.imf.org. In its June 2020 update, world economic growth was projected at an unprecedented -4.9 per cent – 'a crisis like no other, an uncertain recovery'. See: IMF, *World Economic Outlook Update, June 2020*, at www.imf.org.
2 'Why the World Economy Feels So Fragile', *Financial Times*, 9 January 2019. See also the running commentary on these issues at Michael Roberts' blog at www.thenextrecession.wordpress.com.
3 See: Leo Panitch and Greg Albo, eds, *Socialist Register 2019: A World Turned Upside Down?*, London: Merlin Press, 2018.
4 Leo Panitch and Greg Albo, eds, *Socialist Register 2016: The Politics of the Right*, London: Merlin Press, 2015.
5 See: Joseph Stiglitz, 'Progressive Capitalism Is Not an Oxymoron', *New York Times*, 19 April 2019; Joseph Stiglitz, *People, Power, and Profits: Progressive Capitalism for an Age of Discontent*, New York: WW Norton, 2019, Part II. One could also cite the recent writings of Will Hutton, Paul Krugman and Robert Reich, with the most elaborated attempt to find such a renewed social contract centred on skills and educational opportunities being Torben Iverson and David Soskice, *Democracy and Prosperity: Reinventing Capitalism through a Turbulent Century*, Princeton: Princeton University Press, 2019. For 'competitive corporatism' as a self-admitted variant of neoliberalism see: Colin Crouch, *Making Capitalism Fit for Society*, Cambridge: Polity 2014.
6 See: Wolfgang Streeck, *How Will Capitalism End*?, London: Verso: 2016; *Buying Time: The Delayed Crisis of Democratic Capitalism*, London: Verso, 2013; 'On the Institutional Preconditions of Diversified Quality Production,' in Egon Matzner and Wolfgang Streeck, eds., *Beyond Keynesianism: The Socio-Economics of Production and Full Employment*, Aldershot: Elgar, 1991.
7 Leo Panitch, Sam Gindin and Stephen Maher, *The Socialist Challenge Today: Syriza, Corbyn, Sanders*, Chicago: Haymarket Books, 2020.
8 See for example: EuroMemo Group, 'EuroMemorandum 2019,' at www.euromemo.eu.
9 Postcapitalism is a term that escapes easy definition with its many usages. The term is initially linked to Peter Drucker's *Post-Capitalist Society* (New York: HarperCollins, 1994), with its thesis of an organizational evolution of information production and knowledge workers internal to capitalism from new technologies replacing capital as social wealth. As such, it had a lineage going back to the many postwar theories of managerialism, technostructures, the end of ideology, and the like. The theme of knowledge production in the overall trajectory of capitalism remains important to most usages of the term; as such, postcapitalism is neither a defined project or end-state but a process of societal transformation. On the left, postcapitalism is mostly seen as set apart from historical attempts at a transition to socialism as a new mode of production; and it is also distinguished from anti-capitalist movements merely attempting to extract reforms from the state.

10 Karl Marx, *The German Ideology*, 1945, at www.marxists.org.

11 The last term was used in his final book, *How to Be an Anticapitalist in the 21st Century*, London: Verso, 2019, p. 72.

12 Erik Olin Wright, *Envisioning Real Utopias*, London: Verso, 2010, p. 1. There are a number of other examples of projects also focused on the accumulation of micro-strategies as alternatives: J.K. Gibson, *A Postcapitalist Politics*, Minneapolis: University of Minnesota Press, 2006; Boaventura de Sousa Santos, ed., *Another Production is Possible*, London: Verso, 2007; 'Special Issue: Gazing at Power in Community Economies,' *Rethinking Marxism*, 32(3), 2020; Luke Martell, 'The Democratic Economy: Beyond Globalization and Neoliberalism,' *Alternate Routes*, 31(1), 2020.

13 David Gordon, 'Conflict and Cooperation: An Empirical Glimpse of the Imperatives of Efficiency and Redistribution,' in Sam Bowles and Herbert Gintis, eds, *Recasting Egalitarianism: New Rules for Communities, States and Markets*, London: Verso, 1999, p. 181.

14 Wright, *Envisioning Real Utopias*, pp. 124, 303, 318.

15 Wright, *Envisioning Real Utopias*, pp. 321, 337, 128-9.

16 Wright, *Envisioning Real Utopias*, p. 125.

17 Similar to what we shall see with Hardt and Negri in the next section, Wright suggests that 'new technological platforms for facilitating network formation...will help dramatically spread the space for counter-system economic practices'. See: 'Reply to Comments on *Envisioning Real Utopias*,' *New Political Science*, 34(3), 2012.

18 There is a revival of sorts of workers' and other cooperatives as a strategy for postcapitalism 'in work'. These strategies build on traditional themes of alternative decision-making and management over workplaces (as commented on by Owenite socialists and Marx alike), but now are often tied to wider plans for 'community wealth-building', 'workers' enterprises', and complexes of cooperatives built from 'recuperated' industry. See: Gar Alperovitz, *America Beyond Capitalism*, Boston: Democracy Collaborative Press, 2011; Richard Wolff, *Democracy at Work*, Chicago: Haymarket, 2012; Peter Ranis, *Cooperatives Confront Capitalism*, London: Zed, 2016.

19 Wright invokes many other examples – basic income, co-management regulation of eco-systems, labour venture capital funds, wage-earner funds, the NGO third sector, and so on. But these are the most prominent ones in the text.

20 Of course, socialist parties historically adopted a range of practical tactics in the form of unions, cooperatives, and cultural clubs, as part of building working-class organizational strength. But as Vivek Chibber points out, Wright's pathways are distinct sub-strategies unclearly linked to a class project and assume a steady accumulation of noncapitalist practices without an 'organized pursuit of power'. This is, in a way, a blistering critique suggesting the goal is nothing and the movement is nothing too. See: 'A Blueprint for Socialism in the Twenty-First Century,' *Tribune*, August 2, 2020.

21 See the critical evaluations in: Leo Panitch, 'Erik Olin Wright's Optimism of the Intellect,' *New Political Science*, 42(1), 2020; 'Discussion Forum: Envisioning Real Utopias,' *Socio-Economic Review*, 12(2), 2012; Tom Mayer, 'Envisioning Real Utopias,' *Critical Sociology*, 4(6), 2015.

22 Wright, *Envisioning Real Utopias*, p. 123.

23 Wright, *Envisioning Real Utopias*, pp. 364, 128.

24 Luca Basso, *Marx and the Common*, Chicago: Haymarket, 2015.

25 Michael Hardt and Antonio Negri, *Commonwealth*, Cambridge: Harvard University Press, 2009, pp. 287, 267-8.

26 Colin Cremin and John Roberts, 'Postmodern Left-Liberalism: Hardt and Negri and the Disavowal of Critique,' *Critical Sociology*, 37(2), 2011; David Harvey, 'Commonwealth: An Exchange', *Artforum*, November 2009.

27 Michael Hardt and Antonio Negri, *Multitude*, New York: Penguin, 2004, p. xv. The 'fragment on the machine' section in Marx's *Grundrisse* is influential here and across many theorizations of postcapitalism. See: Frederick Pitts, 'Beyond the Fragment: Postoperaismo, Postcapitalism and Marx's "Notes on Machines", 45 Years On,' *Economy and Society*, 46(3-4), 2017.

28 For Hardt and Negri's recent brief restatement of their 'intention to develop a conception of class that refers not only to the working class but is itself a multiplicity, a political formation that makes good on the gains of the multitude', see their: 'Empire, Twenty Years On', *New Left Review* 120, Nov-Dec 2019, pp. 87ff.

29 Michael Hardt and Antonio Negri, *Assembly*, New York: Oxford University Press, 2017, p. 114. In this text, they extend the range of the commons to such things as socialization of the fixed capital infrastructure of the network and a claim that a guaranteed basic income might serve as money of the common. Both of these they see as critical to enabling the 'entrepreneurship of the multitude'. See: Christian Fuchs, 'Reflections on Hardt and Negri's Book "Assembly",' *TripleC*, 15(2), 2017.

30 Hardt and Negri, *Commonwealth*, pp. 380-82. See the critique by Jodi Dean: 'The Actuality of Revolution,' in Leo Panitch and Greg Albo, eds, *Socialist Register 2017: Rethinking Revolution*, London: Merlin, 2016, pp. 73-75.

31 John Holloway, *Change the World Without Taking Power*, London: Pluto, 2005, p. 17, Ch. 9; *Crack Capitalism*, London: Pluto 2010. For a critique of this conception, from grassroots struggles in Latin America, see: Manuel Larrabure, 'Post-Capitalist Struggles in 21st Century Latin America: Cooperation, Democracy and State Power,' York University, PhD Thesis, 2016.

32 Holloway, *Change the World Without Taking Power*, pp. 222-3, 164, 239, 240, 241.

33 Silvia Federici, *Revolution at Point Zero: Housework, Reproduction, and Feminist Struggle*, Oakland: PM Press, 2012, p. 2. As George Caffentzis puts it, in his *In Letters in Blood and Fire: Work, Machines, and the Crisis of Capitalism*, Oakland: PM Press, 2013, p. 249: 'For much of the history of the working class, this power to be able to refuse work has been rooted in the existence of common property resources or commons that people could access independent of their status as waged workers. Thus, in my view, "wage struggle" includes the power to preserve old commons and to create new ones.'

34 Federici, *Revolution at Point Zero*, p. 142.

35 Federici, *Revolution at Point Zero*, pp. 144, 146.

36 Federici and Caffentzis, 'Commons Against and Beyond Capitalism,' *Upping the Anti: A Journal of Theory and Action,* 15, 2013, esp. pp. 92, 144. See also Camille Barbagallo, Nicholas Beurst, and David Harvie, eds, *Commoning with George Caffentzis and Silvia Federici*, London: Pluto, 2019.

37 The usage of 'commons' in postcapitalist writing is often sweeping, encompassing all kinds of social and economic alternatives not undertaken by large capitalist firms. This includes solidarity economies, community localism, the new municipalism, and 'common-oriented enterprises'. At times, this also embraces the 'public goods' provided by the state (as conventionally defined), but at other times not. See: Manuel Castells, et

al., *Another Economy is Possible*, Cambridge: Polity, 2017; Lara Monticelli, 'Embodying Alternatives to Capitalism in the 21st Century,' *TripleC*, 16(2), 2018; William Tabb, 'What if? Politics and Post-Capitalism,' *Critical Sociology*, 40(4), 2014.

38 Massimo DeAngelis, *Omnia Sunt Communia: On the Commons and the Transition to Postcapitalism*, London: Zed Books, 2017, pp. 15, 18, 29-30, 119-23, 231.

39 DeAngelis, *Omnia Sunt Communia*, p. 128. On the limits of commons in their mutual dependence on capitalist markets: Vangelis Papadimitropoulos, 'Reflections on the Contradictions of the Commons,' *Review of Radical Political Economics*, 50(2), 2018.

40 DeAngelis, *Omnia Sunt Communia*, pp. 332, 334, 341. Along these lines, see the suggestions for platform cooperatives, P2P networking, and so on, all assisted by a Chamber of Commons or Commons-Oriented Entrepreneurial Associations, in: P2P Foundation, *Commons Transition and P2P: A Primer*, Amsterdam: Transnational Institute, 2017; *Commons Transition*, at commonstransition.org. Or Guy Standing's focus on governance over public lands, resources, and assets: *Plunder of the Commons: A Manifesto for Sharing Public Wealth*, London: Pelican, 2019.

41 Nick Srnicek and Alex Williams, *Inventing the Future: Postcapitalism and a World Without Work*, London: Verso, 2015, p. 48.

42 Paul Mason, *Postcapitalism: A Guide to Our Future*, New York: Farrar Strauss and Giroux, 2015, p. 179. See also his earlier *Why It's Kicking Off Everywhere*, London: Verso, 2012.

43 Mason, *Postcapitalism*, pp. 29-30; 'The End of Capitalism Has Begun,' *The Guardian*, 17 July 2015.

44 As conceptually developed and loosely popularized respectively: Paul Romer, 'Endogenous Technical Change,' *Journal of Political Economy*, 98(5, Part 2), 1990, p. 117; Jeremy Rifkin, *The Zero Marginal Cost Society*, Basingstoke: Palgrave, 2015.

45 Mason, *Postcapitalism*, pp. xiii, 144; see also Rob Lucas, 'The Free Machine,' *New Left Review*, 100, 2016.

46 Mason, *Postcapitalism*, pp. 120, 179.

47 Mason, *Postcapitalism*, pp. 212, xvi.

48 On the possibilities for redesigning the global economy and firms, including new forms and possibilities for planning, see Evegeny Morozov, 'Digital Socialism,' *New Left Review*, 116/117, 2019; Leigh Phillips and Michael Rozworski, *The People's Republic of Walmart*, London: 2019.

49 Mason, *Postcapitalism*, pp. 143, xiii.

50 Christian Fuchs, 'Henryk Grossman 2.0: A Critique of Paul Mason's Book "Postcapitalism",' *TripleC*, 14(1), 2016, pp. 234-6; Joseph Choonara, 'Brand New, You're Retro,' *International Socialism*, 148, 2015.

51 Mason, *Postcapitalism*, pp. 268-9, Ch. 10, 273, xiv.

52 Alex Williams and Nick Srnicek, '#Accelerate Manifesto for an Accelerationist Politics,' *Critical Legal Thinking*, May 2013, S.24, S.11, at criticallegalthinking.com. There are many social theory strands that precede and also develop the 'technological accelerationism' theme: Michael Laurence, 'Speed the Collapse?: Using Marx to Rethink the Politics of Accelerationism,' *Theory and Event*, 20(2), 2017; Mackenzie Wark, *Capital is Dead*, London: Verso, 2019.

53 Srnicek and Williams, *Inventing the Future*, pp. 1-2, 109, 181. Some of the underlying trends, as well as potentials for socialization of high-tech companies, are explored further in: Nick Srnicek, *Platform Capitalism*, Cambridge: Polity, 2017.

54 *Inventing the Future*, pp. 127, 136, 181-3. The optimism on the possibility of technological

accelerations reinventing communism and a response to climate change is developed further, even extremely so, in Aaron Bastani, *Fully Automated Luxury Communism: A Manifesto*, London: Verso 2019.

55 A wide-ranging assessment of these views and others on technological futures is valuably presented in Nick Dyer-Witheford, Atle Mikkola Kjosen, and James Steinhoff, *Inhuman Power: Artificial Intelligence and the Future of Capitalism*, London: Pluto, 2019. Also see: Ana Dinerstein and Frederick Pitts, 'From Post-Work to Post-Capitalism?,' *Journal of Labor and Society*, 21(4), 2018.

56 Rosa Luxemburg, 'Reform or Revolution,' *Rosa Luxemburg Speaks*, New York: Pathfinder, 1970, p.78.

Also Available

Socialist Register 2020: Beyond Market Dystopia – New Ways of Living
Edited by Leo Panitch and Greg Albo

How can we build a future with better health and homes, respecting people and the environment?
Connecting with and going beyond classical socialist themes, each essay in this volume combines analysis of how we are living now with plans and visions for new strategic, programmatic, manifesto-oriented directions for alternative ways of living.

Contents:

ISBN 978-0-85036-752-2 paperback
978-0-85036-753-9 hardback

Socialist Register 2019: A World Turned Upside Down?
Edited by Leo Panitch and Greg Albo

Since the Great Financial Crisis swept across the world in 2008, there have been few certainties regarding the trajectory of global capitalism, let alone the politics taking hold in individual states.
This has now given way to palpable confusion regarding what sense to make of this world in a political conjuncture marked by Donald Trump's 'Make America Great Again' presidency of the United States, on the one hand, and, on the other, Xi Jinping's ambitious agenda in consolidating his position as 'core leader' at the top of the Chinese state.

Contents:

ISBN 978-0-85036-735-5 paperback
978-0-85036-736-2 hardback

Socialist Register 2018: Rethinking Democracy
Edited by Leo Panitch and Greg Albo

This volume seeks a re-appraisal of actually-existing liberal democracy today, but its main goal is to help lay the foundations for new visions and practices in the development of socialist democracy. Amidst the contradictions of neoliberal capitalism today, the responsibility to sort out the relationship between socialism and democracy has never been greater. No revival of socialist politics in the 21st century can occur apart from founding new democratic institutions and practices.

Contents:

ISBN. 978-0-85036-733-1 paperback
978-0-85036-732-4 hardback